# *The Ultimate A-to-Z Bar Guide*

# The Ultimate

# A -to- Z

## Bar Guide

**Sharon Tyler Herbst
and Ron Herbst**

*Broadway Books* *New York*

**BROADWAY**

Broadway Books titles may be purchased for business or promotional use or for special sales. For information, please write to: Special Markets Department, Bantam Doubleday Dell Publishing Group, Inc., 1540 Broadway, New York, NY 10036.

BROADWAY BOOKS and its logo, a letter B bisected on the diagonal, are trademarks of Broadway Books, a division of Bantam Doubleday Dell Publishing Group, Inc.

*Library of Congress Cataloging-in-Publication Data*

Herbst, Sharon Tyler.
　The ultimate A-to-Z bar guide / Sharon Tyler Herbst and Ron Herbst.
　　p.　cm.
　Includes bibliographical references and indexes.
　ISBN 0-7679-0197-5 (pbk.)
　1. Bartending—Handbooks, manuals, etc.　2. Cocktails.
I. Herbst, Ron.　II. Title.
TX951.H545　1998
641.8′74—dc21

98-16073
CIP

FIRST EDITION

*Designed by Ralph Fowler*
*Illustrations by Jackie Aher*

00　01　02　10　9　8

# Contents

# Acknowledgments

Books are an amalgamation of experiences and knowledge, and no book is written in a vacuum, particularly one on such a convivial subject as cocktails. Friends and family were more than happy to contribute their palates and opinions to the cause, with nary a complaint from the lot. And so we send hugs and heartfelt thanks to everyone who gave their enthusiastic support for this project. A toast to Sharon's parents—Kay and Wayne Tyler—who've cheerfully converted from stirred to shaken Martinis; and to the memory of Ron's folks, Ruby and Ruben Herbst, who would be very proud; and to Sharon's bright and ebullient sister Tia Leslie, who's been known to enjoy a Margarita or two; and to our dear drinking buddies Lee and Susan Janvrin for all the good times in cities like San Francisco, New Orleans, and Las Vegas. And we lift our glasses with a hearty "Cheers!" to all the bartenders in all the cities who've made us a perfect cocktail and served it with a smile.

The skills of countless individuals go into the creation of a book this size. We're proud to be part of the Broadway Books family, whose dedicated professionals see to it that an actual "book" takes shape from a 750-page manuscript. The first person we want to thank is our editor Harriet Bell, who's wise and wickedly funny. She also must have incredibly good judgment—after all, she brought this book idea to us! And a huge debt of gratitude to Broadway Books president-publisher Bill Shinker, the driving force behind the concept for the Broadway bar guide. Then there's dear Alexis Levenson, Harriet's editorial assistant, who has the answers to all the questions, and who invariably is in a good mood. And the delightful and talented Sonia Greenbaum, copy editor extraordinaire, who *always* makes the words flow as they should. And of course this book would never have taken shape without production editor Janice Race, who we call our "shepherd" because she coaxes everything into the perfect form. The gorgeous cover is the creation of creative director Roberto de Vicq de Cumptich, also known as "the man with five names" and "emperor of design." And there would be nothing but plain typeset pages between the covers were it not for the genius of design manager Ralph Fowler. Of course, no book could become all it should be without the talents of publicity wizards Trigg Robinson and Caitlin Connelly. And there are dozens of behind-the-scenes people at Broadway Books who labored tirelessly without fanfare to make this book what it is, and for that we sincerely thank them. And last but never least is our agent, the urbane Fred Hill, a savvy negotiator.

# The New Cocktail Culture

*The trouble with the world is that everybody in it is three drinks behind.*

HUMPHREY BOGART, AMERICAN ACTOR AND COCKTAIL LOVER

Famed British satirist Samuel Butler once said, "The human intellect owes its superiority over that of the lower animals in great measure to the stimulus which alcohol has given to imagination." Of course these words were penned in the seventeenth century, which only goes to show that what goes around comes around . . . or everything old is new again. Yes, cocktails are definitely back in a major way. But with a twist, as a new generation passionately embraces the retro cocktail heyday of the 1940s and '50s and mixes it with twenty-first-century flair to create a hip new cocktail culture that's sexy, inventive, and exciting, with a generous jolt of *attitude*.

With *The Ultimate A-to-Z Bar Guide* as your "cocktail connection," you'll be right in the swing of things. We've compiled what we hope is an intoxicating blend of drink recipes and terms in an easy-to-use A-to-Z format, complete with liberal dashes of humor through jokes and quotes from the famous and infamous. And we've topped it all off with an ample spritz of cocktail techniques, tips, history, etymology, and phonetic pronunciations.

So, you ask, just what's in this tasty little tome? First of all, there are over 1,000 drink recipes—more than most people will need in a lifetime. You'll find everything from timeless classics like the Martini, Manhattan, and Mint Julep, to newer raves like Sex on the Beach, Liquid Cocaine, and Kamikaze. There are short drinks, tall drinks, even super-small drinks—hot, cold, flaming, frosty, creamy, boozy, and boozefree cocktails for any and every occasion. But recipes aren't *all* you'll find in *The Ultimate A-to-Z Bar Guide.* There are 600 definitions for cocktail- and drink-related terms for liquors, liqueurs, mixers, wine, and beer, as well as bartender lingo and general cocktail phraseology.

Good hosting starts with the basics, and this book is brimming with everything you'll need to prepare drinks that will establish your reputation as an accomplished barsmith. You'll learn dozens of insider's tricks of the cocktail trade including: How to choose the right glassware; what bar tools (from citrus strippers to cocktail shakers) can make life easier; how to stock a home bar with everything from spirits to mixers to garnishes; drink-mixing techniques, from stirring to shaking (and, no, you can't "bruise" gin or any other liquid); how to create fruit garnishes and make decorative punch-bowl ice rings and flavored ice cubes; how to make flaming and layered drinks; tips on opening champagne and wine bottles; and much, much more.

And because the measure of a good drink is *exact* measurements, you'll find accurate equivalents for everything from a dash to a gallon—no vague "1 part this, to 2 parts that" in this book. You'll also find equivalents for nonalcoholic ingredients (such as the amount of juice in a lemon), plus a chart on common sizes of wine and spirit bottles. Speaking of wine, there's also plenty of information for wine and beer lovers, from styles and brands to how to store, pour, and serve both libations.

But there's more, including step-by-step guidelines for how to order wine in a restaurant, plus a section on the art of toasting, complete with dozens of toasts for almost any occasion. There's also an important segment on responsible drinking. And if you tend to overindulge, there's information on how to avoid a hangover as well as charts on blood alcohol levels and current state laws on blood alcohol limits for driving while intoxicated. And for those who just *have* to know, there are calorie counts for beers, wines, liquors, liqueurs, and mixers. Last but not least, we've created four indexes (more than any other book of this kind) to enable you to find just the drink you want.

One thing that became abundantly clear while writing this book is that there are absolutely *no* absolutes in making drinks. While some declare the perfect Martini is stirred, not shaken, others insist it be shaken, not stirred. But that's part of what makes the cocktail culture infinitely intriguing and so much fun. Bottom line? It doesn't take special talent to create most drinks—anyone can do it with a little know-how. And you'll find a lot of know-how in this comprehensive, user-friendly bar companion. So, relax, have fun, and enjoy being the hit of the party, not only because you're mixing the drinks, but because you're doing it with confidence and flair. Cheers!

# How to Use This Book

This book was created to be exceedingly user-friendly. The body of it is arranged in an A-to-Z format in which everything from drink recipes to definitions of liquors, liqueurs, and cocktail terms is arranged alphabetically and extensively cross-referenced. Measurements are listed in ounces and—since many jiggers don't have measurement markings—also in common liquid units, such as tablespoon, ¼ cup, and so on. The following information should make using *The Ultimate A-to-Z Bar Guide* a snap:

**Entries Are Alphabetized** by letter, rather than by word, which means that multiple-word entries are treated as single words. For instance, the listing **applejack** is positioned between **apple-flavored spirits** and **Apple Juice Fizz**. Common-usage acronyms and abbreviations appear in their natural alphabetical order—**A.J.** follows **Airelle** and precedes **akvavit.**

Entries for cocktail recipes are capitalized; terms are in lower case unless capitals are required for the proper word form. For example, **Grand Marnier** is capitalized because it's a brand name, while terms like **infusion** and the generic **ouzo** are in lower case. Words that can be easily mispronounced have phonetic pronunciations (*see* Pronunciation Guide, page 3). A term with more than one meaning will have all the definitions shown in numerical order within the main listing.

**Cross-References** are indicated by SMALL CAPITALS and may appear in the body of a definition, at the end of a definition, or in lieu of a definition. In an effort to make using *The Ultimate A-to-Z Bar Guide* quick and easy, cross-referencing is particularly comprehensive. *Cross-references within a definition* are used either when the term may not be familiar to the reader, or to point out that there's additional information relevant to a term. A cross-referenced word will only appear in small caps once in each listing. *Cross-references at the end of a definition* refer to other entries related to the listing. For example, the recipe for **Gin Fizz** also refers readers to DANISH GIN FIZZ and RAMOS FIZZ. A *cross-reference instead of a definition* is listed when a word is fully defined elsewhere. For example, the listing for **Genever** states: *see* GIN. *Cross-references for different spellings* of a term are also included—**akvavit,** for instance, refers the reader to the more common spelling of **aquavit.**

# 2   How to Use This Book

**Italics** are used in this book for several reasons: One is to point out that the term being defined also goes by another name—**Peter Heering** is also called *cherry Heering*. Additionally, italics are used to indicate foreign words and publication titles, as well as to highlight cross-references at the end of a listing (the end of the **bourbon** entry states: *See also* TENNESSEE WHISKEY).

**Boldface** is used for recipe and entry headings as well as for subentries within a definition. This makes it easy for the reader to scan an entry quickly for information. For example, in the term **whiskey,** boldface lettering is used to highlight various types—**straight whiskey, blended whiskey, light whiskey**—each of which precedes a detailed explanation. Boldface print is also used to help the reader quickly find words that have been cross-referenced to, and defined within a definition. For example, in **distillation,** the words **pot still** and **continuous still** are in boldface, since they explain information essential to the distillation process.

**Icons** are used as follows:

   Y Glass icons (see page 9) for each recipe, indicating appropriate bar glass

   ➤ icon indicates a recipe variation

   ✳ icon indicates a nonalcoholic recipe.

# Pronunciation Guide

In the A-to-Z section, foreign words and those which might be easily mispronounced are accompanied by pronunciations, which are enclosed in brackets [- -]. We've always thought that the standard phonetic alphabet and diacritical marks such as a tilde (~), diaeresis (··), breve (˘), and circumflex (ˆ) slow readers down when they have to look up the symbol in a separate chart to see how it affects pronunciation. So we've used the "sounding out" form of phonetics, with the accented syllable indicated by capital letters. For example, the common dictionary-style phonetic for the word *Toreador* (a cocktail) would normally be phoneticized as tôr´e ə dôr. In this book, however, the word is simply sounded out as TOR-ee-uh-dor.

Following is a list of the basic sounds employed in this book's pronunciations:

| | | | |
|---|---|---|---|
| **a** | as in *can* or *add* | **j** | as in *gin* or *juicy* |
| **ah** | as in *father* or *balm* | **k** | as in *cool* or *crisp* |
| **ay** | as in *date* or *face* | **o** | as in *odd* or *bottle* |
| **ch** | as in *church* or *beach* | **oh** | as in *open* or *boat* |
| **ee** | as in *steam* or *beer* | **oo** | as in *food* or *boo* |
| **eh** | as in *set* or *check* | **ow** | as in *cow* or *flour* |
| **g** | as in *game* or *green* | **uh** | as in *love* or *cup* |
| **i** | as in *ice* or *pie* | **y** | as in *yellow* or *yes* |
| **ih** | as in *if* or *strip* | **zh** | as in *beige* or *vision* |

## FOREIGN SOUNDS

**eu** This sound is made with the lips rounded as if to say *oo* (as in *food*) while trying to say *a* (as in *able*).

*n* An italicized *n* indicates that the *n* is not pronounced, and the preceding vowel has a nasal sound.

*r* An italicized *r* indicates that the *r* sound should be diminished, with a sound more like *w*.

**rr** The appearance of *rr* indicates the sound of a rolling *r*.

# Bar Equipment

The right tools make mixing cocktails a snap. Here's a list of equipment and gadgets that will make life easier in your home bar.

**Barspoon** A long-handled spoon used for stirring drinks in a tall glass or in a mixing glass. An ice-tea spoon is a good substitute.

**Blender** Not obligatory, but good for making slushy drinks like FROZEN DAIQUIRIS and fresh-fruit concoctions like fruit smoothies.

**Bottle opener** *see* CAN/BOTTLE OPENER

**Can/bottle opener** Every bar should have at least one, the most common being a "church key"—a small metal tool with a pointed triangular end for piercing cans and a rounded end for popping off metal bottle caps.

**Champagne stopper** A special spring-loaded stopper with two metal wings that fold down and over the neck of a champagne (or other sparkling wine) bottle.

**Church key** *see* CAN/BOTTLE OPENER

**Citrus reamer** *see* JUICER/CITRUS REAMER

**Citrus spout** Also called a *lemon spout*, this gadget is great for when you only want a small amount of juice. It's screwed into the stem end of a lemon, lime, or orange, the juice is extracted (there's a built-in strainer), and then you can store the fruit (spout in place) in the refrigerator. *See also* JUICER/CITRUS REAMER.

**Citrus stripper** A special stainless-steel tool with a notched edge that cuts ¼-inch-wide strips from citrus rinds. *See also* VEGETABLE PEELER.

**Corkscrews; corkpullers** A typical corkscrew has a pointed metal spiral with a transverse handle at one end. There are many varieties of corkscrews, some of which are quite elaborate. The most important part of the corkscrew is the spiral screw (also called *worm*). It should be thin and tapered with a sharp point that's not centered but rather keeps in line with the rest of the spiral. Because fine wines generally have long corks, the screw should be about 2½ inches long so it can run the length of the cork to ensure that the bottom of an older and possibly fragile cork doesn't break off as it's removed. Look for a corkscrew that provides maximum leverage. Some of the most popular openers are: (**a**) The small, classic **waiter's friend** that folds up like a pocket knife; (**b**) The **wing opener,** which consists of a center screw with a handle on each side—the handles move up and down like wings; (**c**) A hand-held device called a **leverpull** that works by simply pulling the handle;

BARSPOON

BLENDER

CHAMPAGNE STOPPER

CAN / BOTTLE OPENER

CITRUS SPOUT

CITRUS STRIPPER

CUTTING BOARD

A. WAITER'S FRIEND

C. LEVERPULL

D. CORKPULLER

B. WING OPENER

CORKSCREWS / CORKPULLERS

FUNNEL

JIGGER

ICE BUCKET AND TONGS

JUICERS / CITRUS REAMER

KNIVES

MEASURING SPOONS

ICE CRUSHERS

MEASURING CUPS

MIXING GLASS

MUDDLER

PITCHER

BOSTON SHAKER

STANDARD SHAKER

STRAINER

VEGETABLE PEELER

(**d**) The popular **corkpuller,** also known as the **butler's friend,** which has two thin parallel prongs connected at the top by a transverse handle—you push the prongs down between the inside of the bottle neck and the sides of the cork, then pull and turn at the same time to slide the cork out. There are also mounted corkscrews that insert the spiral screw into the cork and then remove the cork by pulling the handle in a single direction. Some will recork the bottle by reversing the handle. *See also* Opening Wine and Champagne Bottles, page 25.

**Cutting board** Good for cutting lemon wedges and so on. A small board takes up less room in the bar.

**Funnel** Handy for transferring liquids back into a bottle.

**Hawthorne strainer** *see* STRAINER

**Ice bucket and tongs** A bucket keeps ice colder longer—tongs are a nice touch when adding ice cubes to drinks.

**Ice crusher** There are a wide variety of ice crushers, from manual crank styles to electric. *See also* Ingredients (Ice Tips), page 16.

**Jigger** These come in all sizes, the most common being the double-ended jigger with a 1-ounce measure on one end, $1\frac{1}{2}$ ounces on the other. But some jiggers go up to 3 ounces, so be sure you know how much a jigger holds before you use it.

**Juicer/citrus reamer** There are dozens of styles, ranging from small, hand-held reamers, to those that straddle a measuring cup and have a built-in strainer, to electric juicers. *See also* CITRUS SPOUT.

**Knives** Several sizes come in handy in the bar, including a sharp paring knife and a small serrated knife (great for slicing citrus fruit and soft fruit like peaches), some of which have forked tips. The sharper the knife, the easier it is to use, but *never* sharpen a serrated edge.

**Measuring cups** There are two different types of measuring cups. *Dry measuring cups* are used for ingredients like sugar and chopped fruit. They typically come in a nested set of 5 cups, ranging from $\frac{1}{8}$ cup to 1 cup. *Liquid measuring cups* are commonly made of glass and range in size from 1 to 8 cups; the latter is large enough to be used as a bowl.

**Measuring spoons** Important because many drinks call for $\frac{1}{2}$ ounce of an ingredient—jiggers rarely have a half-ounce marking, but 1 tablespoon equals $\frac{1}{2}$ ounce. A common set of 6 nested measuring spoons ranges from $\frac{1}{8}$ teaspoon to 1 tablespoon.

**Mixing glass** A large (at least 16 ounces) glass that sometimes has a pouring spout. It's used for stirring drinks with ice. Any large glass will do—many people simply use the glass half of a Boston shaker (*see* SHAKERS).

**Mixing spoon** *see* BARSPOON

**Muddler** A bar muddler (typically made of wood because it won't scratch glass) has a broad, rounded, or flattened end with which to crush ingredients like mint leaves. A ceramic mortar and pestle can also be used to crush ingredients, which are then transferred to the mixing or serving glass. A muddler is only useful if you make drinks like MINT JULEPS—even then, a long-handled spoon can be used to crush mint and other ingredients.

**Pitcher** A medium-size glass pitcher is good for everything from serving drinks to adding plain water for simple combinations like Scotch and water.

**Shakers** There are two basic styles of shaker. A standard "cocktail" shaker typically has three pieces—the container, a lid with a built-in strainer, and a cap for the lid. Buy a stainless-steel shaker—aluminum versions don't get drinks as cold. A Boston shaker has two halves (one stainless steel; the other glass) that fit together end to end. With a Boston shaker, a coil strainer is necessary to hold back the ice after a drink has been mixed. *See* Tricks of the Trade (Shaking and Stirring), page 26.

**Strainer** A Hawthorne bar strainer—flat and edged with a spring coil—fits inside mixing glasses and shakers and is essential for straining the drink mixture off the ice.

**Vegetable peeler** Good for making thin, wide citrus strips. *See also* CITRUS STRIPPER.

# Glassware
## ICONS AND DESCRIPTIONS

**Beer mug** 10 to 16 ounces; customarily made of glass and generally used for beer

**Brandy snifter** Ranges in size from mini (5 ounces) to jumbo (25 ounces); short-stemmed with a relatively large bowl, used for brandy and some liqueurs

**Champagne glass** 4 to 10 ounces; the preferred glass for champagne is the tall, graceful **flute** or the **tulip,** since each has a smaller surface from which bubbles can escape and will showcase more of the wine's bouquet. The **champagne saucer glass** allows both bubbles and bouquet to escape.

**Chimney glass** *see* COLLINS GLASS

**Cocktail glass** 3 to 10 ounces, the classic stemmed glass (sometimes referred to as a *martini glass*) for drinks without ice. Today's "martini glasses" often have long, thin stems and larger bowls than most cocktail glasses.

**Collins glass** 10 to 14 ounces, slightly slimmer than the HIGH-BALL; named for the drink. The **tall collins glass** (also called a *chimney glass*) holds about 16 ounces and is used for SINGAPORE SLINGS and ZOMBIES.

**Cordial glass** 1 to 2 ounces (the smaller of the two is also called a *pony*); a tiny stemmed glass used for brandies, liqueurs, and POUSSE-CAFÉS

**Delmonico glass** *see* SOUR GLASS

**Double old-fashioned glass** *see* OLD-FASHIONED GLASS

**Flute glass** *see* CHAMPAGNE GLASS

**Frappé glass** *see* PARFAIT GLASS

**Highball glass** 8 to 12 ounces; most common bar glass, used for everything from BLOODY MARYS to FIZZES to, of course, HIGHBALLS

**Hurricane glass** 12 to 16 ounces; shaped like a hurricane lamp, used for HURRICANES and other tropical drinks

**Irish coffee mug** 8 to 10 ounces; usually made of tempered glass and used for IRISH COFFEE and other hot drinks such as HOT BUTTERED RUM

**Jigger** *see* SHOT GLASS

**Margarita glass** 10 to 14 ounces; used for MARGARITAS and DAIQUIRIS

BEER MUG   BRANDY SNIFTER   CHAMPAGNE   COCKTAIL   COLLINS

CORDIAL   DOUBLE OLD-FASHIONED   HIGHBALL   HURRICANE   IRISH COFFEE

MARGARITA   OLD-FASHIONED   PARFAIT   PILSNER   POUSSE-CAFÉ

PUNCH CUP   SHERRY   SHOT   SOUR   RED WINE WHITE WINE

**Martini glass** *see* COCKTAIL GLASS

**Old-Fashioned glass** 4 to 8 ounces (also called a *rocks glass* and *whiskey glass*); dubbed for its namesake cocktail, but used for many on-the-rocks drinks. A **double old-fashioned glass** holds 12 to 16 ounces.

**Parfait glass** about 8 ounces; specialty glass used for fruit or frozen drinks; also called a *frappé glass.*

**Pilsner glass** 10 to 16 ounces; generally used for beer

**Pony glass** *see* CORDIAL GLASS

**Pousse-Café glass** 2 to 4 ounces; used for the layered drink after which it's named

**Punch cup** 6 to 8 ounces; used for punch

**Rocks glass** *see* OLD-FASHIONED GLASS

**Saucer glass** *see* CHAMPAGNE GLASS

**Sherry glass** 3 to 4 ounces; used for sherry, liqueurs, and apéritifs

**Shot glass** 1 to 3 ounces; used for measuring and serving and for some drinks like SHOOTERS

**Snifter** *see* BRANDY SNIFTER

**Sour glass** 5 to 6 ounces; also called a *whiskey sour glass* and *delmonico glass* and classically used for sours of all kinds

**Tulip glass** *see* CHAMPAGNE GLASS

**Whiskey glass** *see* OLD-FASHIONED GLASS

**Whiskey sour glass** *see* SOUR GLASS

**Wineglass** The white wineglass holds from 6 to 12 ounces, the slightly larger red wineglass (8 to 24 ounces) has a rounder, more balloonlike shape.

# Liquid Assets—Stocking a Home Bar

With the following ingredients on hand you ought to be able to prepare the cocktails most people request. Of course, your home bar should be tailored to suit your personal taste and those of your guests. For example, if only one of your friends drinks bourbon, there's no reason to invest in a 750-milliliter bottle (although it's a better buy and won't spoil). On the other hand, if most of them drink vodka, then it makes sense to buy the largest bottle available. Bottom line: Buy what you'll use most. And don't forget that your drinks will only be as good as the ingredients that go into them, so buy the best you can afford.

## SPIRITS*

Bourbon
Brandy
Cognac
Gin
Liqueurs (the basics: coffee-
    and orange-flavored, plus
    crème de cassis)

Rum, light and dark
Scotch
Tequila
Vermouth, sweet and dry
Vodka
Whisky (Canadian)
Wine, red and white (dry)

*Extras: port; your favorite liqueurs; sherry, dry

## MIXERS (generally should be cold)

Citrus juices,
    lemon, lime, and orange,
    (preferably fresh)
Club soda
Coconut milk
Cola
Cream, heavy and/or
    half & half

Ginger ale
Lemon-lime soda
Tomato juice or V-8 juice
Tonic water
Water, plain or mineral

### FLAVORINGS

Bitters
Grenadine
Orange flower water
Orgeat syrup
Passion-fruit syrup
Pepper
Rose's lime juice

Salt
Sugar, powdered and
    granulated
Sugar syrup
Tabasco sauce
Worcestershire sauce

### GARNISHES

Celery
Cinnamon, ground and sticks
Cucumbers
Lemons
Limes
Maraschino cherries
Mint sprigs

Nutmeg, grated
Olives, stuffed or pitted plain
Onions, cocktail
Oranges
Pineapple, slices or spears
Salt (preferably coarse)
Strawberries

# Ingredients

Every ingredient that goes into a cocktail affects its flavor, so the first rule of thumb is to use the best you can afford. Definitely use fresh juices (particularly lemon and lime) whenever possible, certainly fresh (not canned) fruit for garnishes and, of course, quality liquors. Room-temperature ingredients melt the ice faster, so mixers like fruit juice and club soda should be cold. The following ingredients are listed alphabetically. See also Liquid Assets, page 11; Tricks of the Trade, page 24.

**Butter** For drinks like HOT BUTTERED RUM, unsalted butter is preferable to the salted version. However, because salt acts as a preservative, unsalted butter doesn't stay fresh as long as its salted counterpart, so double-wrap leftovers and store in the freezer.

**Cream** Unless otherwise indicated, the word "cream" describes heavy (whipping) cream. If half & half is substituted for cream, the resulting drink will not be as thick or rich. Definitely *don't* substitute milk for cream—it's better to choose another drink than end up with a thin, wimpy version of the original. Make drinks that contain cream and lemon (or other citrus) juice just before serving because the juice's acid begins to clot and thicken the cream shortly after they're combined.

**Eggs** The recipes in this book use large grade AA eggs. To prevent pieces of eggshell from falling into a drink mixture, break the egg into a small bowl before adding it to the other ingredients. That way, it will be easier to remove any bits of shell that break off. Separating eggs is easier if they're cold. An inexpensive egg separator (available in kitchenware stores and some supermarkets) makes separating eggs easy. Or crack an egg into a funnel set over a bowl or cup—the white falls through, the yolk won't. The time-honored method of separating eggs by passing the yolk back and forth from one half of the shell to the other while the white slips into a bowl below is generally fine, but you should know that minute bacteria on the shell's surface might transfer to the raw egg.
  **Beating egg whites** You'll get more volume out of beaten egg whites if they're at room temperature. To warm cold egg whites quickly, set the bowl of whites in a larger bowl of warm water. Stir occasionally until whites have reached room temperature.

**How to divide egg whites in half** Certain drinks call for only ½ egg white (1 tablespoon). But trying to divide an egg white in half is like working with soft Jell-O—it wobbles all over the place and won't cooperate. That is, unless you know the trick, which is to first use a fork to beat the white in a small bowl until frothy. Once it becomes foamy, simply pour the beaten white into a tablespoon. Either discard the other ½ egg white or cover and refrigerate for up to 3 days.

**Are raw eggs safe?** Although relatively rare, there have been cases of salmonella-related food poisoning in some parts of the United States (primarily the northeastern and mid-Atlantic states). Most cases have been due to improper handling (such as letting raw-egg preparations stand too long at room temperatures) in commercial establishments. Nevertheless, if you have doubts about your egg supply or suffer from a weakened immune system, it's best to *avoid all raw-egg preparations entirely*. **Pasteurized liquid whole eggs** (available in cartons in a market's refrigerated section) may be used instead—just substitute ¼ cup liquid eggs for each large egg, ⅛ cup for each egg yolk. **Egg substitutes** are not made from whole eggs, but comprise about 80 percent egg whites plus other ingredients, including nonfat milk, tofu, vegetable oils, and emulsifiers.

**Flowers** Flowers add an exotic touch to tropical drinks, but you should know that not all flowers are edible, which means they shouldn't touch anything that is. Purchase flowers that have been specifically grown for use with food and drink—they're available at specialty produce markets and some supermarkets. Flowers that have been sprayed with pesticide must never be used. And before using flowers from your garden (assuming they're pesticide free), call your local poison control center to make sure they aren't inherently poisonous.

**Fruit** It should go without saying, always use fresh fruit rather than canned—frozen fruit is passable sometimes, although not for garnishing, as it quickly loses its firm texture.

**Cherries** The ubiquitous maraschino cherry is called for in many drink recipes. This ultrasweet fruit comes in two colors—red and green—and is bottled in sugar syrup (almond flavored for red, mint for green). Marachino cherries also come in stemmed and unstemmed versions—stemmed cherries being the better choice for drinks because they have a built-in handle with which to retrieve the fruit from a drink. If you actually like the flavor of maraschino cherries, but have given them up because you heard they contain harmful dyes, your worries are over. The U.S. government banned the use of such dyes several years ago. Unless otherwise indicated, red maraschino cherries are used in the drinks in this book.

**Garnishing with citrus twists** A "twist" is simply a slice of lemon (sometimes orange or lime) peel. Cut twists just before using so they're as fresh as possible. Before dropping a twist into a drink, hold it at both ends, colored part down, and give it a twist just above the drink's surface. If the lemon (or other citrus) is fresh, this twisting motion produces an infinitesimal spray of lemon oil into the drink. Some people like the rim of their glass rubbed with the peel before twisting.

**How to cut a twist** If you need a lot of twists, cut off both ends of a lemon. For nonprofessionals it's easier to cut the fruit in half lengthwise; pros can leave the lemon whole. Use a barspoon (a grapefruit spoon works great) to separate the fruit from the peel. Scoop out the fruit, taking as much of the white pith with it as possible. Then cut the rind lengthwise into 1/4-inch strips. Alternatively, a citrus stripper can be used to remove strips of peel. This tool (available in gourmet stores) only takes off the colored portion of the rind, leaving the bitter pith behind. Or you can use a sharp paring knife or vegetable peeler to slice off thin, 1/2-inch-wide strips of peel.

**Garnishing with fruit** In general, most fruit is peeled before being cut into slices or wedges for garnishes. The exception is citrus fruits (oranges, lemons, limes), whose peel should be thoroughly but gently washed (so as not to remove flavorful oils) before the fruit is cut. **To cut fruit slices** (oranges, lemons, limes, and bananas), use a sharp knife or one with a serrated edge to cut crosswise slices about 1/4 inch thick. Make one cut from the outer edge to the center of the slice to make a slot for the fruit to straddle the glass rim. **For half slices,** cut the fruit in half, put the flat side down, and cut crosswise into 1/4-inch slices. Make a cut from the center to the inside edge of the peel to hook the fruit over the glass rim. **For wedges,** slice the fruit lengthwise in half; cut each half lengthwise into quarters or eighths, depending on the size of the fruit. **To cut long spirals of peel** for drinks like coolers, begin at one end of a lemon (or other fruit) and use a citrus stripper (see the previous section on "How to cut a twist") or a sharp paring knife to cut around and down the fruit, creating a long, continuous spiral peel. **To keep fruits from darkening**

(like bananas, peaches, and apples), use a pastry brush to lightly coat the cut surface with lemon or lime juice; blot off excess. **Fruits with pits,** like cherries and apricots, should be pitted before garnishing a drink. Pit cherries using a cherry pitter or the tip of a vegetable peeler or a pointed knife. **Melon** can be either peeled and cut into small wedges, or into balls with a melon-baller, available at gourmet shops.

**Fruit Juices** Whenever possible, use fresh fruit juices—fresh lemon and lime juice are preferable to the bottled versions, which have an unnaturally acidic edge. Fresh orange juice is also preferable, although juice made from frozen concentrate is certainly acceptable. If you want to substitute fresh lime juice for ROSE'S LIME JUICE (which is sweetened), add 1 teaspoon confectioners' sugar for each tablespoon juice. **Tips on getting maximum juice from fruit:** 1. Buy lemons and other citrus fruits that are heavy for their size—they'll be much juicier than their lightweight counterparts. 2. Room temperature fruit yields more juice than refrigerated fruit. 3. Before juicing, soften the fruit by rolling it around on the countertop with your palm a few times. Or prick the skin in several places with a fork (don't go all the way through to the flesh); microwave on HIGH (100 percent power), uncovered, for 10 to 20 seconds, depending on the size of the fruit. Let stand 2 minutes before rolling the fruit between your palm and the countertop. 4. If you only need a little juice, soften the fruit as previously indicated, then insert a citrus spout—a nifty gadget that allows you to squeeze out small amounts of seedless juice (*see* Bar Equipment, page 4). 5. Leftover fresh-squeezed citrus juice can be covered and refrigerated for up to 5 days.

**Ice Tips** Ice that doesn't taste good can ruin a drink's flavor, and ice can only taste as good as the water from which it's made. Water that's highly chlorinated or otherwise off-flavored can spoil a drink. Likewise, ice made in a home freezing compartment can easily absorb odors from other foods. Taste the ice first—if it tastes bad, buy packaged ice. Ice cubes are the most versatile choice, as they can be used as is or crushed. Inexpensive manual or electric ice crushers are widely available (*see* Bar Equipment, page 6). If you don't have an ice crusher, simply place ice cubes in a heavy-duty plastic bag, seal, then wrap in a heavy towel; whack away with a mallet, rolling pin, or other heavy instrument until the ice is crushed as desired. Remember, crushed ice melts much faster than ice cubes and will dilute a drink more quickly.

**Punch Bowl Ice** When buying a block of ice for a punch bowl, make sure it will fit your bowl and still leave room for the punch. If you can't find a block small enough, and don't want to take the time to whittle a large block down, make your own block of ice. Simply fill a plastic or metal container of the appropriate size with water and freeze for at least 24 hours before you need it. Ring molds, like angel food cake or Bundt pans, make attractive ice "blocks." Don't use a glass container, which can crack as the water freezes. Punch bowl ice can be covered tightly and kept frozen for up to 2 weeks until ready to use. To unmold, dip the bottom of the container in cool to lukewarm water; turn out onto a piece of heavy-duty foil. Rewrap and place in the freezer until just before serving time. **For a decorative ice mold,** fill the container half full of water; freeze until solid. Place fruit (grape clusters, pineapple rings, orange or lemon slices, etc.) on the surface of the ice. Carefully pour cold water to cover the fruit; freeze until solid. If necessary, add more water to fill the container to the top and freeze.

**Flavored Ice Cubes** The flavor of any iced drink will be less diluted if the ice cubes themselves are flavored. The flavor you use depends on the drink to which they will be added: tomato-juice cubes for BLOODY MARYS or coffee cubes for iced coffee drinks. When using lemon or lime juice to flavor cubes, dilute it by at least half with water. And forget about trying to make booze cubes by freezing rum, gin, etc. Alcohol freezes at a much lower temperature than water or juice, so it'll never happen. The amount of liquid needed depends on the size of the ice-cube tray—most trays hold 10 to 14 regular-size cubes. You can also use the miniature ice-cube trays, but remember the smaller the cube, the faster it melts.

**MAKES ABOUT 12 REGULAR-SIZE ICE CUBES**

1¹/₂ to 2 cups liquid (fruit juice, coffee, tea, etc.)

Pour liquid into ice-cube tray. Freeze for about 6 hours, or until firm.

**Decorated Ice Cubes** Place a small piece of fruit (cherry, melon ball, pineapple chunk, raspberry, lemon, or orange twist) or an edible flower or flower petal (nonpoisonous and free of pesticide) in each section of an ice-cube tray. Cover with cold water that has been boiled and cooled (it will be clearer than water directly from the tap). Freeze until firm.

**Mixers** Just because mixers (tonic water, cola, ginger ale, and so on) are probably the least expensive ingredient in your cocktail-making repertoire doesn't mean they should be *cheap*. In many drinks a mixer comprises two-thirds of the mixture or more, which means that a second-rate mixer with an inferior flavor can ruin the blend. Store mixers in the refrigerator so they'll be nice and cold when added to a drink. Room-temperature liquids will cause the ice to melt faster and thereby dilute the drink. Reseal carbonated mixers, refrigerate and use within a day or two—after that, they lose their pizzazz.

**Nutmeg** Freshly grated nutmeg is called for in the recipes in this book, but commercially ground nutmeg can be substituted. However, freshly grated nutmeg has a lively, delicately warm and spicy flavor. Small jars of whole nutmeg (a hard, grayish-brown, egg-shaped seed about ¾ inch long) can be found in most supermarkets. Several styles of nutmeg graters and grinders are available in kitchenware shops. Most graters have a fine-rasp, slightly curved surface over which a whole nutmeg is rubbed. Many graters store the whole nutmegs in containers attached to the unit. Nutmeg grinders use a spring-mounted post to hold a whole nutmeg against a sharp blade that grates the nutmeg when a crank is rotated. A toothbrush is the perfect tool for cleaning nutmeg graters and grinders.

**Nuts** Whenever using nuts in a drink, toast them ahead of time to bring out their full flavor. Toast nuts in an ungreased skillet over medium heat, stirring frequently, until golden brown. Or oven-toast them at 350°F, stirring occasionally, for 10 to 15 minutes. Cool completely before using.

**Olives** There are myriad styles of olives in markets today—unstuffed, stuffed with everything from almonds to anchovies to garlic to bits of jalapeño pepper, and even some marinated in vermouth, rather than brine. Unless otherwise indicated, olives used to garnish drinks are green and pitted—whatever you choose first consider the flavor of a drink's ingredients. Olives are easier to handle if speared with a cocktail pick before being added to a drink.

**Onions, cocktail** The cocktail onions called for in some recipes (as in the GIBSON) are tiny (about the size of a regular marble) pearl onions that have been cooked and sometimes pickled. They're sold in small jars and are available in supermarkets and liquor stores.

Some cocktail onions are preserved in vermouth, a much nicer flavor element than salty brine. Check the label to see what you're buying. If all you can find is pickled onions, rinse them off and blot them dry before using them so that briny flavor doesn't permeate your drink.

**Pineapple** Pineapples are one of those fruits that don't ripen once picked, so make sure to buy them fully ripe. Choose a pineapple that is slightly soft to the touch with a full, strong color and no signs of greening. The stem end should smell sweet and aromatic. **To peel, core, and cut a pineapple,** by far the easiest method is to buy a relatively inexpensive gadget called a pineapple peeler/corer, which peels and cores the fruit in one motion. To peel a pineapple by hand, use a very sharp knife to cut off the base and the leaves. Stand the pineapple on one end and cut off strips of peel from top to bottom. To remove the "eyes," use the point of a paring knife to cut a wedge-shaped groove on either side of the eyes, following their diagonally spiraling pattern. Cut away as little of the pineapple flesh as possible. Alternatively, simply slice an unpeeled pineapple; lay the slices on a cutting board and cut the peel off. To core the fruit, cut the peeled pineapple in quarters, then stand the quarters on one end and cut downward to remove the core. Although the core is tough, strips of it make good swizzle sticks for drinks.

**Sugar Syrup** A cooked solution of sugar and water that can be made in several densities, depending on the ratio of sugar to water. The following recipe is suitable for most bar purposes. Also called *simple syrup* and *gomme syrup*.

MAKES ABOUT 1 1/2 CUPS

2 cups sugar
1 cup water

Stir ingredients together in a small saucepan; bring to a boil. Immediately reduce heat to simmer; cook without stirring for 10 minutes. Cool to room temperature. Seal tightly and refrigerate indefinitely.

**Sweet & Sour Mix** Many bartenders couldn't do without this short-cut commercial mix that combines the flavors of—you guessed it—sweet and sour. This distinctly acidic mix is used in place of sugar syrup and lemon juice. Unfortunately, its flavor in no way compares to the refreshing zing of freshly squeezed lemon juice. Sweet & sour mix is available in liquor stores. Following is a homemade version, which at least starts with fresh lemon juice.

**MAKES ABOUT 1 QUART**

1 egg white
1 cup sugar
16 oz. (1 pint; 2 cups) water
16 oz. (1 pint; 2 cups) fresh lemon juice

Whisk egg white until frothy. Mix in sugar, then water and lemon juice. Seal tightly and refrigerate for up to 5 days.

**Water** If your tap water doesn't taste good, neither will drinks mixed with it. Use bottled distilled or spring water for the best results.

# Measurements and Ingredient Equivalents

Taking the measure of things in life is important—particularly when making cocktails. Guessing amounts can ruin a drink, and it means you've wasted the ingredients. Following are common measurements you might need for "tending bar."

## BAR MEASUREMENTS

1 dash.............$1/16$ tsp.

2 dashes .........$1/8$ tsp.

4 dashes .........$1/4$ tsp.

1 tsp. ..............$1/6$ oz.; $1/3$ Tbsp.

$1/2$ Tbsp. ...........$1/4$ oz.; $1\frac{1}{2}$ tsp.

1 Tbsp. ...........$1/2$ oz.; 3 tsp.

$1/4$ cup.............2 oz.; 4 Tbsp.

$3/8$ cup.............3 oz.; 6 Tbsp.

$1/2$ cup.............4 oz.; 8 Tbsp.

$3/4$ cup.............6 oz.; 12 Tbsp.

1 cup .............8 oz.; 16 Tbsp.

$1/4$ oz...............$1/2$ Tbsp.; $1\frac{1}{2}$ tsp.

$1/2$ oz...............1 Tbsp.; 3 tsp.

$3/4$ oz...............$1\frac{1}{2}$ Tbsp.; $4\frac{1}{2}$ tsp.

1 oz. ..............$1/8$ cup; 2 Tbsp.

pony ..............1 oz.; 2 Tbsp.

$1\frac{1}{2}$ oz. ...........3 Tbsp.

jigger .............$1\frac{1}{2}$ to 3 oz.; 3 to 6 Tbsp.

$1\frac{3}{4}$ oz. ...........$3\frac{1}{2}$ Tbsp.

2 oz. ..............$1/4$ cup; 4 Tbsp.

$2\frac{1}{2}$ oz. ...........scant $1/3$ cup; 5 Tbsp.

3 oz. ..............$3/8$ cup; 6 Tbsp.

4 oz. ..............$1/2$ cup; 8 Tbsp.

6 oz. ..............$3/4$ cup; 12 Tbsp.

8 oz. ..............1 cup; 16 Tbsp.

12 oz. ...........$1\frac{1}{2}$ cups; $3/4$ pint

16 oz. ...........2 cups; 1 pint

24 oz. ...........3 cups; $1\frac{1}{2}$ pints

pint................2 cups; 16 oz.

quart..............2 pints; 4 cups; 32 oz.

gallon ............4 quarts; 8 pints; 16 cups; 128 oz.

## INGREDIENT EQUIVALENTS

banana...............................1 medium = $1/2$ cup puréed

butter .................................1 stick = $1/2$ cup; 8 Tbsp.

cream .................................8 oz. = $1/2$ pint; 1 cup; 2 cups whipped

egg......................................1 large = 3 Tbsp. (yolk = 1 Tbsp.; white = 2 Tbsp.)

lemon .................................1 medium = 3 Tbsp. juice plus 2 to 3 tsp. grated peel

lime.....................................1 medium = $1\frac{1}{2}$ Tbsp. juice plus 1 to $1\frac{1}{2}$ tsp. grated peel

orange................................1 medium = $1/3$ cup juice plus 2 Tbsp. grated peel

sugar, brown.......................1 pound = $2\frac{1}{4}$ cups packed

sugar, granulated ...............1 pound = $2\frac{1}{4}$ cups

sugar, powdered ................1 pound = 4 cups unsifted

# Sizes of Wine and Spirit Bottles

The United States has been using metric measurements since 1979 for wine bottles, and since 1980 for spirit bottles. The standard wine and spirit bottle size was set at 750 milliliters (ml) or approximately 25.4 ounces (oz.), which is almost exactly equivalent to an American fifth (⁴/₅ of a quart, or 25.6 oz.). In the U.S., other legal wine bottle sizes include 50 ml, 100 ml, 187 ml, 375 ml, 500 ml, 1 liter, 1.5 liters, and 3 liters. Wine may also be bottled in sizes larger than 3 liters if the capacity is in round numbers—4 liters, 5 liters, 6 liters, and so on. Other bottle-size terms (including French bottle nomenclature not legally defined in the United States) are sometimes still used in wine circles. Older spirit bottle terminology such as half-pint, pint, fifth, and half-gallon are no longer accurate descriptors for standard bottle sizes, although the term "fifth" is still widely used.

## WINE BOTTLE SIZES

| Common Bottle Terminology | Metric Measure | Fluid Ounces |
| --- | --- | --- |
| Miniature | 100 ml | 3.4 oz. |
| Split | 187 ml | 6.3 oz. |
| Half-bottle | 375 ml | 12.7 oz. |
| 500 millileter | 500 ml | 16.9 oz. |
| 750 millileter | 750 ml | 25.4 oz. |
| One liter | 1 liter | 33.8 oz. |
| Magnum | 1.5 liters | 50.7 oz. |
| Double Magnum; Jeroboam (in champagne) | 3 liters | 101.5 oz. |
| Rehoboam (in champagne) Jeroboam (in Bordeaux) | 4.5 liters | 152.2 oz. |
| Methuselah (in champagne) Imperial (in Bordeaux) | 6 liters | 202.9 oz. |
| Salmanazar | 9 liters | 304.4 oz. |
| Balthazar | 12 liters | 405.8 oz. |
| Nebuchadnezzar | 15 liters | 507.3 oz. |

# Tricks of the Trade
## BARTENDER'S SECRETS FOR HOME ENTERTAINING

A few tricks of the cocktail trade and you'll look like a real pro. The following techniques are listed in the order of use. For instance, the glasses have to be chilled, bottles opened, and ingredients measured *before* a drink is mixed. *See also* Ingredients, page 13. But, before we begin, here are the seven rules for making the perfect cocktail:

1. Use the best ingredients you can afford—cheap potables will show in the flavor of a drink.
2. Make sure mixers like fruit juice and club soda are fresh and cold.
3. Prechill the proper glass for the cocktail.
4. Measure carefully—free pouring can throw the balance of the drink completely off.
5. Use fresh, rock-solid ice to prevent drinks from becoming too watery.
6. Perfect the art of shaking and stirring ingredients with ice—proper dilution is part of a perfect cocktail.
7. Relax and enjoy your results!

## CHILLING GLASSES; FROSTING GLASSES

Cold glasses give your drink a nice icy jump start. To **chill glasses,** put them in the freezer for 10 minutes or in the refrigerator for 30 minutes. Or pack the glasses with crushed or cracked ice and let stand until cold—5 minutes should do it; discard the ice shaking out any water. **Frosted glasses** are used for beer or drinks like MARTINIS where the glass should be frosty cold. To achieve this effect, put glasses, beer mugs, and so on in the freezer for about an hour (depending on the freezer temperature). For ultrafrosty glasses, dip them in cold water, shake off any excess, and place in the freezer. If you use frosted glasses often and have enough freezer space, simply store some in the freezer to have ready when you want them. Always hold frosted glasses by their stems or handles so as not to ruin the frosted effect.

## FROSTING GLASS RIMS WITH SUGAR OR SALT

Some recipes call for coating the rim of a glass with sugar or salt. Just dip the rim in water, liquor, or fruit juice (such as lime juice for

## SPIRIT BOTTLE SIZES

| Metric Measures | Fluid Ounces | Metric Measures | Fluid Ounces |
|---|---|---|---|
| 100 ml | 3.4 oz. | 750 ml | 25.4 oz. |
| 200 ml | 6.8 oz. | 1 liter | 33.8 oz. |
| 500 ml | 16.9 oz. | 1.75 liters | 59.2 oz. |

MARGARITAS), then shake off the excess liquid before dipping the rim into a saucer of sugar (typically granulated) or salt (preferably coarse). The rim can also be dampened by simply dipping your fingertip into a liquid, then running it around the glass rim. Or run a lemon, lime, or orange wedge around the rim of a glass before dipping it in the sugar. Sugar- or salt-frosted glasses may be prepared in advance and stored in the freezer or refrigerator until needed.

### OPENING WINE AND CHAMPAGNE BOTTLES

**Still (Nonsparkling) Wine** Using a sharp knife or a special foil-cutter (available at wine or gourmet shops), cut through the capsule (the casing that covers the bottle lip and cork) about ¼ inch below the bottle lip; remove the capsule. Wipe the rim of the bottle and the top of the cork with a clean damp towel to remove any residue. There are several styles of corkpullers and corkscrews (*see Bar Equipment, pages 4–6, for detailed information*) available, and the removal technique depends on the opener. **To use a corkpuller,** which consists of two thin parallel metal prongs connected by a handle, push the prongs down between the inside of the bottle neck and the sides of the cork, then simultaneously pull and turn until the cork comes out. **To use a corkscrew,** position the screw (also called *worm*) in the cork's center and, gently pressing downward, twist the screw clockwise into the cork as far as it will go. This reduces the possibility of pieces of cork breaking off and falling into the wine and it helps keep the cork intact for reuse, if necessary. Once the screw is firmly seated, gently ease the cork out of the bottle. If a cork breaks off during this process, carefully try to reinsert the corkscrew. Or use the thin prongs of a corkpuller to capture the remnant of cork shell in the bottle. If the cork gets pushed into the bottle, try extracting it with a special cork-retrieval tool, available at wine and gourmet shops. Lacking such a tool, carefully DECANT the wine into a carafe. You can also buy a neat gadget that looks like a pouring spout with a built-in strainer. It fits right into the neck of a wine bottle, costs only a couple of dollars, and makes quick work out of decanting your wine. Or you can simply pour the wine (very carefully) with the cork still in the bottle—not aesthetically ideal, but okay in an emergency!

*She made the appropriate oos and ahhs, and pretended with him that opening the champagne bottle was a difficult and dangerous masculine task.*

LEN DEIGHTON, NOVELIST

**Champagne** Contrary to what movies portray, the opening of champagne should not be accompanied by a loud "POP," the cork catapulting across the room, the champagne gushing from the bottle. Here's how to do it properly: Remove the foil and the wire that cages the cork. Keeping your hand over the cork in case it ejects prematurely, hold the bottle at a 45-degree angle, making sure it's not pointed at anyone. With the fingers of one hand over the cork, gently rotate the bottle (not the cork) with your other hand. As you feel the cork begin to loosen and lift, use your thumb to ease it gently from the bottle. The cork should release with a gentle "poof" rather than a loud "POP." **Serve champagne** in the tall, slender glasses known as flutes, which are much better for retaining the wine's effervescence and showcasing its bouquet than the old-fashioned, shallow saucer glasses.

### MEASURING INGREDIENTS

Unless you're a pro, it's a good idea to use precise measurements when making drinks. Because jigger sizes vary (1½ ounces is the average), all recipes in this book give measurements in tablespoons as well as ounces. *See also* Bar Equipment (Jigger; Measuring cups; Measuring spoons), page 6.

### SHAKING AND STIRRING

Shaking and stirring are done both to chill a drink and mix the ingredients. Either technique will create a smooth texture in drinks like a MANHATTAN or a MARTINI as the melting ice emulsifies into the other ingredients—proper dilution is part of the art. As a general rule, clear drinks are stirred and those with hard-to-combine ingredients (like eggs, sugar, cream) are shaken (or processed in a blender). But rules are made to be broken—just ask James Bond, who insists on his shaken Martini. When a drink is shaken, minuscule ice shards and air bubbles form, creating a misty appearance—not exactly the end of the world. Besides, if you wait a minute or two, the haziness dissolves into crystal clarity. Oh, and in case you're wondering, gin—or any other kind of liquor, for that matter—cannot be "bruised" by shaking!

## BASIC GUIDELINES FOR SHAKING *OR* STIRRING

1. Whether using a Boston shaker or a cocktail shaker (*see* Bar Equipment (Shakers), page 7), start by filling it half to two-thirds full with ice, cubes or cracked, whichever the recipe calls for. The ice goes in first, so it cools the container as well as the ingredients as each is added.

2. The order in which the ingredients go into the shaker doesn't matter.

3. Don't make more than two drinks at a time in a shaker—some shakers can't accommodate more than one large, multi-ingredient drink.

4. The longer you shake or stir a drink, the more diluted it will become as the ice melts.

5. Immediately pour a shaken or stirred drink into a chilled glass. Letting it sit on the ice will only dilute it.

6. Don't add a sparkling beverage like club soda until after a drink is poured from the shaker; then stir it gently to retain its effervescence.

**Shaking** Don't fill the shaker to the brim—leave room for the ingredients to move around. *Tightly* attach the lid (or, for a Boston shaker, the steel shell over the glass). Holding the shaker with both hands (one on each end), shake it up and down; when the shaker's frosty cold, the drink is usually ready. If using a Boston shaker, turn the glass part upright and loosen the steel container by giving it a light whack with the heel of your hand. Then invert the shaker again, so the liquid flows into the steel container; remove the glass portion. Place a strainer over the top to retain the ice, and pour the drink into a chilled glass. **Shaking drinks made with eggs** requires extra-vigorous action to make sure the egg becomes well incorporated.

**Stirring** Stirring a drink with ice can be done in a cocktail shaker, a Boston shaker (either half), or sometimes right in the glass in which it's served. **Stirring in a shaker** Fill the shaker at least halfway full of ice cubes, then add the ingredients. With a barspoon or other long-handled spoon, stir vigorously for 10 to 20 seconds so the ice can thoroughly chill the ingredients. Strain into a serving glass. **Stirring in a glass** In general, put the ice in the glass first, add the ingredients, and stir.

*In mixing, the important thing is the rhythm. Always have rhythm in your shaking. Now a Manhattan, you shake to fox-trot time, a Bronx to two-step time. But a Martini you always shake to waltz time.*

NICK CHARLES (WILLIAM POWELL), IN THE FILM *THE THIN MAN*

### POURING

Pour drinks as soon as they're mixed—letting them sit on the ice will dilute them. If you've filled the glasses and have some mixture left over, strain it into a small pitcher or other container and refrigerate until you're ready to serve seconds. When making several drinks at once (like blender MARGARITAS), make sure everyone gets the same amount by lining up the glasses, filling each one halfway, then going back and filling each glass to the same level. Remember to leave room for garnishes.

**Pouring wine** Only fill each glass one-third to one-half full to allow plenty of room for the wine to be swirled in order to better develop its aroma. Just as you finish pouring the wine and are returning the bottle to the upright position, give the bottle a slight twist—a simple technique that eliminates dripping.

**Pouring beer** down the side of the glass minimizes foam, pouring it directly into the glass produces maximum foam. For the best of both worlds, begin pouring the beer down the side and then, when the glass is half full, pour it directly into the center.

### BLENDER TECHNIQUES

For drinks made in a blender always use crushed ice; to make your own crushed ice, *see* Ingredients (Ice Tips), page 16. Prepare the crushed ice in advance and store it in a plastic bag in the freezer. Put the drink ingredients in the blender jar first. If you're using pieces of fruit, process the liquid ingredients and the fruit until puréed before adding the ice. Whenever you use the blender, make sure the cover is securely attached before turning on the machine. Start at low speed and gradually increase to medium, blending until smooth, about 15 seconds. Pour into the chilled glass. For thick, slushy drinks, more crushed ice can be added—just remember, the more ice, the more diluted the flavor. Freezing the fruit for drinks like MELON MARGARITAS will also produce a frostier mixture.

### MUDDLING

The word "muddle" simply means to mash or crush ingredients together to release their flavors. This technique is traditionally done with a **muddler,** a special wooden rod with a broad, rounded, or flattened end (available in gourmet and bar-supply stores). Wooden muddlers are preferred because wood doesn't scratch glass. If you don't have a muddler, use the back side of a spoon (a long-handled one if the drink is tall). The most well-known drink that employs muddling is the MINT JULEP, in which mint leaves are crushed together with sugar.

### HOT DRINKS

Serve hot drinks only in heatproof (tempered) glasses, cups, or punch bowls. Caution is the byword when using metal cups or mugs—metal holds heat so well it can easily burn your lips. Preheat nonmetal glasses, cups, or bowls by filling them with very hot water and letting them stand for about 3 minutes. To help disseminate the heat and to keep the container from cracking, place a metal spoon in the cup or glass (or a metal ladle in a punch bowl) and slowly pour the hot drink onto it.

### FLAMING DRINKS

The first thing to remember with flaming drinks is that caution is the byword. The secret to getting alcohol to flame successfully is to heat it just until warm. Overheating the alcohol will burn it off before it can flame; heating the alcohol fast over a high flame can create a potentially dangerous situation. You can heat liquor in a saucepan over medium heat, warming it only until bubbles begin to form around the edge of the pan. Or you can also warm it in the microwave for 10 to 15 seconds. Use a long-handled match to ignite the liquor, then pour it flaming into a drink. Some spirits—such as brandy—can be flamed right in the glass. Be sure to preheat the glass (invert it under hot running water, then dry it off), then pour warmed brandy into the glass and ignite.

Liquor can also be heated with other ingredients in a chafing dish. In some cases, a small amount of liquor can be flamed without preheating, as when 151-PROOF rum is floated on top of a hot drink, and thereby warmed enough to be flamed. When working with fire, it's always a good idea to have a box of baking soda on hand to douse any accidents, such as if flames somehow jump to a tablecloth (which won't happen if you're careful). *See also* the previous section, Hot Drinks.

### FLOATING AND LAYERING TECHNIQUES

Some recipes call for floating a liqueur or other spirit on top of another ingredient (as in some SHOOTERS) or a mixed drink (as when topping a drink with 151-proof rum), the purpose being to keep it separate. One drink in particular—the POUSSE-CAFÉ—is all about layering one liqueur on top of another, creating an elaborate, multicolored spectacular of sometimes seven or more layers.

The layering effect in Pousse-Cafés and other drinks is possible because every liqueur has a specific gravity (weight). You pour the heaviest cordial into the glass first, then float liqueurs of decreasing weights on top of each other. In short, the liqueurs are poured in ascending order of lightness. They must be poured slowly and steadily over the back of a spoon to slow the liquid's fall and distribute it evenly over the layer below. Making a successful layered drink takes patience, practice, a steady hand, and a double shot of good luck. Pousse-Café (and layered SHOOTER) recipes in this book are: AN-GEL'S DELIGHT; ANGEL'S KISS; ANGEL'S TIT; B-52; CHOCOLATE-COVERED CHERRY; MEXICAN FLAG; OATMEAL COOKIE; PEPPER-MINT PATTY; RUSSIAN QUAALUDE; SAVOY HOTEL; STARS AND STRIPES; TERMINATOR.

### TIPS FOR MAKING SUCCESSFUL POUSSE-CAFÉS AND OTHER LAYERED DRINKS

1. Know each ingredient's specific gravity (relative weight); *see* charts on pages 32–33.
2. Consider both color and flavor of the liqueurs you plan to use before building a Pousse-Café or other layered drink.
3. Check the size of the glass you're using before beginning to build a layered drink to make sure it's big enough to accommodate the recipe. Pousse-Café glasses can measure from 2 to

4 ounces; shot glasses, from 1 to 3 ounces; and cordial glasses, 1 to 2 ounces. The smaller the glass, the fewer layers.

4. Carefully measure out each liqueur before pouring.

5. Pour the heaviest liqueur into the glass first. Invert a spoon so the rounded side is up; position it just above the first layer with the tip touching the inside of the glass. *Slowly and steadily* (hasty pouring produces immediate disaster), pour the second liqueur over the back of the spoon. Repeat with subsequent layers.

6. Keep the glass *very* still—any sudden motion and the layers will collapse.

7. Keep your fingers crossed (but not while pouring)!

# Specific Gravity (Weight) of Liqueurs

For easy reference, here are two specific gravity charts—one lists ingredients by their weight, the other lists them alphabetically. A word to the wise: Factors such as flavoring agents, as well as alcohol and sugar content, can vary from brand to brand of the same type of liqueur (the weight of Kahlúa varies slightly from that of Tia Maria).

## INGREDIENTS LISTED BY WEIGHT (HEAVY TO LIGHT)

| | Specific Gravity | | Specific Gravity |
|---|---|---|---|
| Crème de banane; Crème de banana | 1.18 | Cranberry-flavored liqueur | 1.09 |
| Crème de cassis | 1.18 | Strawberry-flavored liqueur | 1.09 |
| Anisette | 1.17 | Triple Sec | 1.09 |
| Grenadine | 1.17 | Amaretto | 1.08 |
| Crème de menthe, green and white | 1.16 | Cherry-flavored brandy | 1.08 |
| Crème de cacao, white and dark | 1.15 | Peach-flavored brandy | 1.08 |
| Goldwasser | 1.15 | Sambuca | 1.08 |
| Coffee-flavored liqueur | 1.14 | Apricot-flavored brandy | 1.07 |
| Maraschino liqueur | 1.14 | Blackberry-flavored brandy | 1.07 |
| Apricot-flavored liqueur | 1.13 | Ginger-flavored brandy | 1.07 |
| Parfait amour | 1.13 | Rock & Rye | 1.07 |
| Blue curaçao | 1.12 | Peppermint schnapps | 1.06 |
| Cherry-flavored liqueur | 1.12 | Kümmel | 1.05 |
| Crème de noyaux | 1.12 | Peach liqueur | 1.05 |
| Blackberry-flavored liqueur | 1.11 | Peach schnapps | 1.05 |
| Orange curaçao | 1.10 | B & B | 1.04 |
| | | Sloe gin | 1.04 |
| | | Kirsch | 0.94 |

## INGREDIENTS LISTED ALPHABETICALLY

| | Specific Gravity |
|---|---|
| Amaretto | 1.08 |
| Anisette | 1.17 |
| Apricot-flavored brandy | 1.07 |
| Apricot-flavored liqueur | 1.13 |
| B & B | 1.04 |
| Blackberry-flavored brandy | 1.07 |
| Blackberry-flavored liqueur | 1.11 |
| Blue curaçao | 1.12 |
| Cherry-flavored brandy | 1.08 |
| Cherry-flavored liqueur | 1.12 |
| Coffee-flavored liqueur | 1.14 |
| Cranberry-flavored liqueur | 1.09 |
| Crème de banane; Crème de banana | 1.18 |
| Crème de cacao, white and dark | 1.15 |
| Crème de cassis | 1.18 |
| Crème de menthe, green and white | 1.16 |

| | Specific Gravity |
|---|---|
| Crème de noyaux | 1.12 |
| Ginger-flavored brandy | 1.07 |
| Goldwasser | 1.15 |
| Grenadine | 1.17 |
| Kirsch | 0.94 |
| Kümmel | 1.05 |
| Maraschino liqueur | 1.14 |
| Orange curaçao | 1.10 |
| Parfait amour | 1.13 |
| Peach-flavored brandy | 1.08 |
| Peach liqueur | 1.05 |
| Peach schnapps | 1.05 |
| Peppermint schnapps | 1.06 |
| Rock & Rye | 1.07 |
| Sambuca | 1.08 |
| Sloe gin | 1.04 |
| Strawberry-flavored liqueur | 1.09 |
| Triple Sec | 1.09 |

# Ordering Wine in a Restaurant

If ordering wine in a restaurant is intimidating because you have an audience (dining companions and waitperson), here are some tips to make life easier.

- All but the most modest restaurants have a wine list, or at least a "blackboard" listing their wines. Some restaurants offer only "house wines" (one each, red and white), often by glass or carafe, which can be perfectly fine, but can also be *dreck*. Ask the server the brand name, vintage, and style (ZINFANDEL, CHARDONNAY, MERLOT, etc.) of the house wine and don't be shy about asking to taste it before ordering.

- Wine lists generally arrange wines by color (red or white) and/or country of origin (U.S., France, Italy, etc.). The best wine lists add the wine's name, vintage, region, and, sometimes, the vineyard, such as "1994 Chateau St. Jean Chardonnay, Robert Young Vineyard, Alexander Valley." Some lists number their wines—so if you can't pronounce a wine's name you can simply order "Number 102."

- The standard markup for wines in restaurants is 2 to 2½ times retail.

- Some restaurants have a *sommelier* (wine steward), who can answer questions or assist you in your wine choice. A good *sommelier* will make you feel comfortable, not intimidated. In the majority of restaurants, a waitperson performs *sommelier* duties.

- When the waitperson or *sommelier* brings the wine to the table and presents it to you, glance at the label to be sure it's the one you ordered. The server will then open the wine and present the cork. An educated nose will detect any odor that's not right, although sniffing the cork is considered pretentious by some and it certainly isn't necessary. It's a good idea, however, to check the cork bottom for moisture—a sign that the wine was stored properly on its side. A moldy or crumbly cork signals deterioration—order another bottle.

- The *sommelier* will then pour a small amount of wine into your glass. Gently swirl it to release the aroma, smell it, and take a sip—smell and taste are the best criteria of whether or not a wine is sound. If it doesn't have any rank flavors or odors (such as vinegar), it's most likely fine. Returning a wine simply because you don't like it as much as you thought you would isn't appropriate. Remember that a wine's flavor and aroma expand and develop as it aerates. Don't make the tasting process long and involved—the *sommelier* or server has other things to do.

- After tasting and approving the wine, simply say "thank you" to the server, a signal that the wine may be poured for your companion(s).

- In some states, such as California, it's perfectly acceptable to bring your own wine, particularly if it's a special or rare bottle. Before presuming that it's okay, however, call the restaurant first and inquire—also ask the amount of the corkage fee, a charge for opening and serving the wine you bring.

# The Art of Toasting

*A toast is all at once a poem, a public prayer, a proverb, a secret sentiment, a roast, a bit of wit, and a veritable verbal badge of social facility . . . a good toast is hard to find.*

DAVE FULMER, AMERICAN ACTOR, DIRECTOR, WRITER

Toasting, a verbal salute before quaffing a drink, was originally called "drinking healths." The practice is certainly nothing new. Legend has it that Nordic warriors sometimes drank their pledges from a fallen enemy's skull (*skalle*), from which comes today's customary Scandinavian toast *Skål,* meaning "bowl." Historians tell us that the practice of toasting began in Rome, where a piece of charred bread was placed in a goblet to mellow the wine's flavor. It was an elementary version of a winemaking technique used for centuries—charring the interior of barrels to add character to wine. By the seventeenth century, the English were flavoring wine with a float of spiced toast, which was consumed when glasses were raised to the occasion. If the glass was a communal goblet, the guest of honor was obliged to eat the soggy leavings. Those who like their bread products crisp and their wine without debris join us in celebrating the fact that toasting today is sans *toast.*

A good toast is hard to find, so here are some to give you a head start (or maybe inspiration to make up your own) for those times you have to stand up and say something romantic, pithy, eloquent, profound, or just plain irreverent.

## GENERAL

To a full moon on a dark night and a smooth road all the days of your life.

May you be poor in misfortune, rich in blessings, slow to make enemies, and quick to make friends.

Here's to God's first thought: Man. Here's to God's second thought: Woman. And since second thoughts are always the best, here's to women!

# 𝒯OASTING PROTOCOL

*Always let the host propose the first toast. If it doesn't look like it's going to happen, quietly ask if you can give a toast.*

*Before beginning a toast, make sure everyone's glass is filled.*

*Whether you toast standing or sitting is up to you—be comfortable. As a general rule of thumb, at small dinner parties the toast can be done sitting. At a formal dinner or in a large group, it's better to stand (although guests can remain sitting).*

*To make the toast, lift the glass out in front of you at shoulder level while looking at the one being toasted, state your toast (keep it short), then sip your drink and salute the toastee with your glass before setting it down.*

*Other guests join the one who is toasting by also taking a sip. If you don't drink alcohol, take a sip of water or other liquid.*

*If you're the object of the toast, don't drink, but acknowledge the honor with a nod.*

*Guests of honor may respond with their own toast, but it's not obligatory.*

May the road rise to meet you,
May the wind be always at your back,
The sun shine warm upon your face,
The rain fall soft upon your fields,
And until we meet again
May God hold you in the hollow of his hand.
—*Traditional Irish Toast*

Here's lookin' at you, kid.
—*Humphrey Bogart* (*in the film* Casablanca)

May all your troubles be little ones.

May we always be happy and our enemies know it.

Here's to you, as good as you are,
And here's to me, as bad as I am;

And as bad as I am, and as good as you are,
I'm as good as you are, as bad as I am.

Candy is dandy, but liquor is quicker.
—*Ogden Nash*

To long lives and short wars.
—*Colonel Potter, on TV's* M*A*S*H

Laugh and the world laughs with you; cry and it laughs anyway.

Here's to sirloin when you're hungry,
Whiskey when you're dry,
Greenbacks when you're busted,
And Heaven when you die!

Here's a toast to all who're here,
No matter where you're from;
May the best day you've ever seen
Be worse than your worst to come.

May the most you wish for be the least you get.

## BIRTHDAYS

May you live as long as you want,
and never want as long as you live.

It's never too late and you're never too old—Noah was 600 years old before he learned how to build an ark.

The good die young . . . the young die good . . . wouldn't you rather be old?

You're not as young as you used to be, but then you're not as old as you're going to be.

Don't think of it as another YEAR older—just think of it as one DAY older than yesterday.

To your birthday—no matter how old you are, you don't look it!

May you live to be a hundred, plus a year to repent.

The good die young, so here's to living to a ripe old age!

Here's hoping that you live forever and mine is the last voice you hear.
—*Willard Scott*

May you live all the days of your life.
—*Jonathan Swift*

## FRIENDS

Here's to good friends, who know you well and like you anyway.

Here's to cold nights, fine wine, and good friends to share them with.

Here's to Eternity—may we spend it in as good company as we have tonight.

Old friends are scarce,
New friends are few;
I'm glad to find
Both in you.

Here's to you, and here's to me,
Best of friends we'll always be.
And if by chance we disagree,
Then screw you and here's to me.

May your hand always reach out in friendship and never in want.

## LOVE

Here's to Cupid, the little squirt,
He's lost his pants, he's lost his shirt,
He lost it all except his aim,
Which proves that love's a losing game.

I've known many and liked a few,
But loved just one, so here's to you!

Love may not make the world go around but it sure makes the ride worthwhile.

Here's to kissing those we please and pleasing those we kiss.

To the men (gals) I've loved
To the men (gals) I've kissed
And sincere apologies
To the men (gals) I've missed.

Here's to the girls that call you "honey,"
They drink your wine and spend your money,
They put you to bed and hug you tight
And cross their legs and say "good night"!
—*George Ade*

To men (women): You can't live with 'em,
and you can't shoot 'em.

## WINE

To wine—God's next best gift to man.
—*Ambrose Bierce*

Here's to champagne, the drink divine,
It makes us forget our troubles.
It's made of four dollars worth of wine
And twelve dollars worth of bubbles!

God, in His goodness, sent the grapes
To cheer both great and small;
Little fools will drink too much,
Great fools none at all.

Wine improves with age—the older I get the more I like it.

## SUCCESS

Let us toast the fools—but for them, the rest of us could not succeed.
—*Mark Twain*

If you're not the lead dog, the view never changes—here's to success.

# ⑨oasts Around the World

*The following toasts are roughly equivalent in feeling to "To Your Health," "Cheers" and "Bottoms Up!"*

| | | | |
|---|---|---|---|
| Albania | Gezuar | Italy | Salute; Cin Cin |
| Armenia | Genatzt | Japan | Kampai; Banzai |
| Australia | Cheers | Korea | Deupstita |
| Austria | Prosit | Mexico | Salud |
| Belgium | Op uw gezonheid | Netherlands | Proost; Geluch |
| Brazil | Saude; Viva | Norway | Skål |
| China | Kan pei; Wen lie; Yam sing | Pakistan | Jama Sihap |
| | | Philippines | Mabuhay |
| Czechoslovakia | Na Zdravi; Nazdar | Poland | Na zdrowie; Vivat |
| | | Portugal | A sua saúde; Eviva |
| Denmark | Skål (Skoal) | Romania | Noroc |
| England | Cheers; Wassail | Russia | Na Zdorovia |
| Egypt | Fee Sihetak | Saudi Arabia | Bismillah |
| Finland | Kippis; Maljanne | Scotland | Hoot mon |
| France | Santé; A votre santé | Singapore | Yam seng |
| Germany | Prosit | Spain | Salud |
| Greece | Stin ygia sou; Eis Igian | Sweden | Skål |
| Greenland | Kasugta | Taiwan | Gun Bi |
| Hawaii | Kamau | Thailand | Chai yo |
| Holland | Proost; Geluch | Turkey | Serefe |
| Hungary | Egeszegedre | Ukraine | Boovatje zdorovi |
| Iceland | Santanka nu | United States | Cheers; Here's How; Bottoms Up; Here's Lookin' at You |
| India | Aap ki Shubh kai liyai | | |
| Indonesia | Selamat | | |
| Ireland | Sláinte | Yugoslavia | Zivio; Zivelli |
| Israel | L'chaim; Mazel tov | | |

# Calories Count!

The following chart will help you determine what some beverages might do to your waistline.

| Beverage | Approximate Calories per Ounce | Beverage | Approximate Calories per Ounce |
|---|---|---|---|
| Ale | 18 | Liquor, 86 proof | 70 |
| Beer, lager | 12 | Liquor, 90 proof | 74 |
| Beer, light | 8 | Liquor, 94 proof | 77 |
| Brandy | 75 | Liquor, 100 proof | 83 |
| Champagne | 26 | Orange juice | 14 |
| Cider, hard | 15 | Pineapple juice | 17 |
| Club soda | 0 | Port | 40 |
| Cola | 12 | Sherry, dry | 40 |
| Cranberry juice | 19 | Sherry, sweet | 43 |
| Cream | 106 | Tomato juice | 6 |
| Diet soda | 0 | Tonic water | 9 |
| Ginger ale | 9 | Vermouth, dry | 30 |
| Lemon and lime juice | 8 | Vermouth, sweet | 42 |
| Liqueurs | 68–110 | Wine, dry | 25 |
| Liquor (gin, rum, tequila, vodka, whiskey), 80 proof | 65 | Wine, sweet | 40 |

# Responsible Drinking

*Drink the first, sip the second, and skip the third.*

KNUTE ROCKNE, AMERICAN FOOTBALL COACH

No, the phrase "responsible drinking" is not an oxymoron, but it is one to live by. For however much we may enjoy wine, beer, or cocktails, it's important to treat alcohol with respect. Excessive drinking can affect your health, your relationships, your career—your life!

Now we've all heard the phrase "Two drinks per day is considered moderate alcohol consumption." But at least to the United States government, that phrase doesn't *necessarily* apply to everyone. According to guidelines issued jointly by the U.S. Department of Agriculture and the U.S. Department of Health and Human Services, moderate drinking is defined as no more than two drinks a day for most men and one drink a day for most women. Studies have shown that there are several physiological factors for why, on average, women become more intoxicated than men after drinking an equal amount of alcohol. One of the primary reasons is a stomach enzyme that breaks down alcohol four times faster in males (except for Japanese and Native American men) than it does in females. That's not to say, of course, that there aren't some women who can drink some men under the table.

**How much *is* a drink?** In the United States, one drink has been standardized as ½ ounce of pure (100 percent) alcohol. Of course, because all drinks are not created equal—beer contains less alcohol than wine and wine less than distilled spirits—the volume per serving is different. Here's how ½ ounce of 100 percent alcohol breaks down: 1¼ ounces of 80-proof liquor (40 percent alcohol); 3 ounces of fortified wine like sherry or port (about 16½ percent alcohol); 4 ounces of wine (12½ percent alcohol); or 12 ounces of beer (4 percent alcohol). Now that you've got that straight, here's something else to consider: Drinks served in bars and restaurants can be over twice as large as the average drink, and many beers contain over 4 percent alcohol.

On the plus side, research has shown that completely abstaining from alcohol may not be the best thing for one's health. According to some scientists, moderate drinkers have lower rates of coronary heart disease (CHD) than those who've never drunk alcohol. This is most likely because alcohol has been proven to interfere with blood-clot formation and to slow down arterial plaque buildup. Psychological studies show that moderate drinking decreases tension, stress, and anxiety; stimulates the appetite (particularly beneficial in the elderly); and improves mood.

Bottom line? Responsible drinking is a *must*—not only for ourselves but also for our friends. Definitely don't drink and drive. And don't let your friends do so either. Remember that in some states a host is held legally responsible for any injuries or damage created by a guest who's been drinking in his/her home.

Here are some tips on how to make parties enjoyable for everyone while helping your friends not drink too much.

- Make moderate, not strong, drinks.

- Don't pressure anyone into drinking who doesn't want to.

- Always serve food with drinks—it slows the absorption of alcohol.

- Have plenty of cold, nonalcoholic beverages on hand—including fruit juices, bottled water, and soft drinks. Remember that carbonated beverages can increase alcohol absorption, while water dilutes it.

- Keep track of how your guests are doing—if someone's getting intoxicated, cut them off from the liquor. If they're already past the point of no return, make sure they don't drive.

*Once in every lifetime one should experience a hangover, so as to abstain from immoderate imbibing for the rest of one's life.*

MAGGIE WALDRON, AMERICAN BUSINESSWOMAN, WRITER

# Blood Alcohol Chart

Blood alcohol concentration (BAC) is a term referring to a person's intoxication level as determined by the alcohol concentration in the blood. The following chart shows the estimated percentage of alcohol in the blood by the number of drinks per hour in relation to body weight. The levels for women, as well as for Japanese and Native American men, will be slightly higher.

| Body Weight | Number of Drinks in an Hour | | | | | | | |
|---|---|---|---|---|---|---|---|---|
| | 1 | 2 | 3 | 4 | 5 | 6 | 7 | 8 |
| 100 lbs. | .038 | .075 | .113 | .150 | .188 | .225 | .263 | .300 |
| 120 lbs. | .031 | .063 | .094 | .125 | .156 | .188 | .219 | .250 |
| 140 lbs. | .027 | .054 | .080 | .107 | .134 | .161 | .188 | .214 |
| 160 lbs. | .023 | .047 | .070 | .094 | .117 | .141 | .164 | .188 |
| 180 lbs. | .021 | .042 | .063 | .083 | .104 | .125 | .146 | .167 |
| 200 lbs. | .019 | .038 | .056 | .075 | .094 | .113 | .131 | .150 |
| 220 lbs. | .017 | .034 | .051 | .068 | .085 | .102 | .119 | .136 |
| 240 lbs. | .016 | .031 | .047 | .063 | .078 | .094 | .109 | .125 |

# State Laws for Driving While Intoxicated

The following information is based on the best available data at the time this book was written. State laws change, however, so readers should verify the information as it applies presently.

| State | Administration per se Law (BAC Level) | Illegal per se Law (BAC Level) | BAC for Younger Drivers | Applicable Age for Younger Drivers |
|---|---|---|---|---|
| AK | 0.10 | 0.10 | NO | |
| AL | NO | 0.10 | NO | |
| AR | NO | 0.10 | 0.02 | Under 21 |
| AZ | 0.10 | 0.10 | 0.00 | Under 21 |
| CA | 0.08 | 0.08 | 0.01 | Under 21 |
| CO | 0.10 | 0.10 | NO | |
| CT | 0.10 | 0.10 | 0.02 | Under 21 |
| DC | 0.10 | 0.10 | 0.00 | Under 21 |
| DE | 0.10 | 0.10 | 0.02 | Under 21 |
| FL | 0.08 | 0.08 | 0.02 | Under 21 |
| GA | 0.10 | 0.10 | 0.04 | Under 18 |
| HI | 0.10 | 0.10 | NO | |
| IA | 0.10 | 0.10 | 0.02 | Under 21 |
| ID | 0.10 | 0.10 | 0.02 | Under 21 |
| IL | 0.08 | 0.08 | 0.00 | Under 21 |
| IN | 0.10 | 0.10 | NO | |
| KS | 0.08 | 0.08 | NO | |
| KY | ALT | 0.10 | NO | |
| LA | 0.10 | 0.10 | 0.04 | Under 18 |
| MA | 0.08 | NO | 0.02 | Under 21 |
| MD | 0.10 | NO | 0.02 | Under 21 |
| ME | 0.08 | 0.08 | 0.00 | Under 21 |
| MI | NO | 0.10 | 0.00 | Under 21 |
| MN | 0.10 | 0.10 | 0.00 | Under 21 |
| MO | 0.10 | 0.10 | NO | |
| MS | 0.10 | 0.10 | 0.08 | Under 21 |
| MT | NO | 0.10 | 0.02 | Under 21 |
| NC | 0.08 | 0.08 | 0.00 | Under 18 |
| ND | 0.10 | 0.10 | NO | |
| NE | 0.10 | 0.10 | 0.02 | Under 21 |
| NH | 0.08 | 0.08 | 0.02 | Under 21 |

| State | Administration per se Law (BAC Level) | Illegal per se Law (BAC Level) | BAC for Younger Drivers | Applicable Age for Younger Drivers |
|---|---|---|---|---|
| NJ | NO | 0.10 | 0.01 | Under 21 |
| NM | 0.08 | 0.08 | 0.02 | Under 21 |
| NV | 0.10 | 0.10 | NO | |
| NY | ALT | 0.10 | NO | |
| OH | 0.10 | 0.10 | 0.02 | Under 21 |
| OK | 0.10 | 0.10 | NO | |
| OR | 0.08 | 0.08 | 0.00 | Under 21 |
| PA | NO | 0.10 | NO | |
| RI | NO | 0.10 | 0.02 | Under 21 |
| SC | NO | NO | NO | |
| SD | NO | 0.10 | NO | |
| TN | NO | NO | 0.02 | Under 21 |
| TX | 0.10 | 0.10 | 0.07 | Under 21 |
| UT | 0.08 | 0.08 | 0.00 | Under 21 |
| VA | 0.08 | 0.08 | 0.02 | Under 21 |
| VT | 0.08 | 0.08 | 0.02 | Under 18 |
| WA | 0.10 | 0.10 | 0.02 | Under 21 |
| WI | 0.10 | 0.10 | 0.00 | Under 19 |
| WV | 0.10 | 0.10 | 0.02 | Under 21 |
| WY | 0.10 | 0.10 | NO | |

**FIGURES FROM THE NATIONAL MOTORISTS ASSOCIATION**

ADMINISTRATION PER SE LAW (BAC LEVEL) refers to state statutes that allow a state's licensing agency to revoke or suspend a driver's license, based either on a specific alcohol (or drug) concentration or on some other criterion related to alcohol or drug use and driving.

ILLEGAL PER SE LAW (BAC LEVEL) refers to state laws that make it a criminal offense to operate a motor vehicle at or above a specified alcohol (or drug) concentration in the blood, breath, or urine.

BAC FOR YOUNGER DRIVERS (under 18 to 21 years) is set lower than that for adults.

NUMERIC VALUES (0.10 to 0.02) indicate the Blood Alcohol Content (BAC) level at which the state's statute takes affect.

NO indicates that a state doesn't have an administrative per se law and/or illegal per se law.

ALT indicates states with an alternative to Blood Alcohol Content (BAC) regulations.

# After the Party—Hangover "Cures"

*Don't be swindled into believing there's any cure for a hangover. I've tried them all: iced tomatoes, hot clam juice, brandy punches. Like the common cold it defies solution. Time alone can stay it. The hair of the dog? That way lies folly. It's as logical as trying to put out a fire with kerosene.*

TALLULAH BANKHEAD, AMERICAN ACTRESS

American entertainer Joe E. Lewis once said, "I'd take a bromo, but I can't stand the noise." Odds are, most of us who've ever had just "one too many" have felt like Joe Lewis at one time or another. Besides the obvious answer of overdrinking, did you ever wonder just what causes a killer hangover? The screaming headache, woolly dry mouth, lurching stomach, and general feeling of "who was driving the semi that hit me?" Of course, how you're affected by alcohol depends on a complicated formula into which must be factored your sex, weight, height, metabolism, body chemistry—and even race.

There is only one surefire way never to get a hangover: Don't drink. Oh, you don't like that one? Well, then, how about: Don't drink too *much.* What's too much? Let's start with the rather disconcerting news flash that our bodies can only burn off about one drink per hour. Actually this amount is slightly less for women (and Japanese and Native American men) because there's an enzyme in their stomach and liver that converts alcohol more slowly than in men. If you read the section "Responsible Drinking," then you know that a "single drink" equals a 12-ounce beer, or 4 ounces of wine, or 3 ounces of sherry or port, or 1¼ ounces of 80-proof liquor. So knocking back three beers in an hour is just the same as downing three Manhattans. They both produce the same result—trouble. Although some people report that mixing drinks (a Martini before dinner, wine with) makes them feel worse, studies have proven that *what* you drink doesn't count as much as the *amount* you drink.

A primary reason you feel so bad after drinking too much is because your poor abused body is extremely dehydrated. Alcohol acts as a diuretic, primarily because in order for the toxins to be flushed through the membranes in the kidneys, they must be diluted in plenty of water. You feel so weak and lethargic partly because the water that's been madly flushing toxins from your system has, in the process, disposed of myriad necessary vitamins and nutrients. Additionally, your system is in a mild state of shock because it's coming off of a sedative "drug" and is therefore supersensitive.

For some people, hangovers are worse if they drink dark liquors (like bourbon and Scotch) because they're sensitive to congeners, miniscule impurities that contribute distinctive characteristics to such spirits. Vodka is the purest, most congener-free distillate, followed by gin. That doesn't mean, however, that if you drink too much vodka or gin you won't get a hangover. Also, people react differently to different congeners, so what affects your friend may not affect you. One thing that seems sure: Imbibing too many sweet liqueurs or blended mixtures is an ironclad guarantee for a hangover.

## TIPS ON HOW TO FORESTALL A HANGOVER

### BEFORE YOU PARTY

- Drink milk—it'll help slow alcohol absorption.
- Take vitamins B and C to get a jump start on replenishing some of the nutrients the alcohol will deplete.
- Eat something—food helps absorb alcohol. The fructose in foods like fruit, honey, and bread aids in slowing down alcohol absorption. Some theorize that fructose also helps replenish dipping blood sugar levels caused by alcohol consumption.
- Don't take aspirin beforehand. Recent studies show that aspirin retards the action of the enzyme that breaks down alcohol, and those who take it can absorb from 40 to 100 percent more alcohol into their blood.

### DURING

- Drink plenty of water—it'll help rehydrate your system.
- If the evening's going to be a long one, alternate between alcoholic and nonalcoholic drinks.
- Although it probably won't be available at most parties, drinking Gatorade replenishes some of the water and the electrolytes being expelled from your system.

**AFTER**

- First of all, know that "the hair of the dog" will *not* cure a hangover. What it *might* do is numb you temporarily, but then your body will simply have to recover from that assault on it, so why bother?

- Before you go to bed, drink more water; take some more vitamins B and C.

- Don't drink coffee—it's also a diuretic and will exacerbate dehydration.

- Eat something to help absorb the alcohol and replenish the nutrients you've lost. And we don't mean potato chips. Eat fruit (like bananas) or vegetables (potatoes are good). Some people swear by tomatoes—a VIRGIN MARY, or pasta with tomato sauce might fill the bill.

- Sleep—something that may be difficult because as the alcohol in your system decreases, your body begins releasing adrenaline, which makes you fidgety and often increases body temperature slightly, making you restless and hot.

- When you wake up, drink more water.

- Go back to sleep and promise the hangover gods you'll never get drunk again!

---

*This "old wives" superstition that a cup of black coffee will "put you back on your feet" with a hangover is either propaganda by the coffee people or the work of dilettante drinkers who get giddy on cooking sherry. A man with a real hangover is in no mood to be told "Just take a cup of black coffee" or "The thing for you is a couple of aspirin." A real hangover is nothing to try out family remedies on. The only cure for a real hangover is death.*

ROBERT BENCHLEY, AMERICAN HUMORIST, ACTOR

# A-to-Z

*Recipes*

*and*

*Definitions*

Unless otherwise indicated, all drink recipes are for one serving.

★ = nonalcoholic drinks.

### Abbey

1½ oz. (3 Tbsp.) gin
1 oz. (2 Tbsp.) fresh orange juice
2 dashes (about ⅛ tsp.) orange bitters
maraschino cherry

Shake liquid ingredients with ice. Strain into chilled glass; garnish with cherry.

### Abbott's Bitters *see* BITTERS

**Abricotine** [ah-bree-koh-TEEN] The brand name of a BRANDY-based apricot LIQUEUR from the French house of Garnier. *See also* APRICOT-FLAVORED SPIRITS.

**absinthe** [AB-sinth] A potent (136 PROOF; 68 percent alcohol), bitter LIQUEUR flavored with a variety of herbs and distilled from the aromatic wormwood plant, which was once believed to cause madness and death. Absinthe is reputed to be an aphrodisiac, but don't get excited, it's banned in the United States—as in most countries—because of the potentially lethal wormwood. Called the "green muse" by some because of its color, this distinctly anise-flavored liqueur becomes milky white when diluted with water. Substitutes for absinthe include ANISETTE, HERBSAINT, OUZO, and PERNOD. *See also* ANISE-FLAVORED SPIRITS.

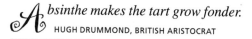

*bsinthe makes the tart grow fonder.*
HUGH DRUMMOND, BRITISH ARISTOCRAT

### Absinthe Special Cocktail

1½ oz. (3 Tbsp.) Pernod or other anise-flavored liqueur
1 oz. (2 Tbsp.) water
1½ tsp. anisette
1 dash (about 1/16 tsp.) orange bitters

Shake ingredients with ice; strain into chilled glass. May be served over crushed ice, if desired.

## Absinthe Suissesse [AB-sinth sweess-EHSS]

1½ oz. (3 Tbsp.) Pernod or other anise-flavored liqueur
1 egg white
1 tsp. white crème de menthe or peppermint schnapps
1 dash (about ¹⁄₁₆ tsp.) anisette
3 drops orange flower water

Shake ingredients with ice; strain into chilled glass.

**Acapulco** Oddly enough, rum is the traditional spirit for this drink, although tequila seems more appropriate for a drink with such a moniker, and is also a delicious substitute.

1¾ oz. (3½ Tbsp.) light rum
½ oz. (1 Tbsp.) Cointreau or Triple Sec
½ oz. (1 Tbsp.) fresh lime juice
1 egg white
1 tsp. sugar
mint sprig

Vigorously shake liquid ingredients and sugar with ice; strain into chilled glass. Add ice cubes; garnish with mint.

## Addington

1½ oz. (3 Tbsp.) sweet vermouth
1½ oz. (3 Tbsp.) dry vermouth
cold club soda
orange or lemon twist

Pour vermouths into chilled glass filled with ice cubes. Top with club soda, stirring lightly. Drop in orange or lemon twist.

**ade** A combination of citrus juice, sweetener, plain or sparkling water, and sometimes liquor, served in a tall glass over ice. Classic nonalcoholic examples are lemonade and limeade. Ades are commonly garnished with fresh fruit.

## Adios, Mother(f****r)

2 oz. (¼ cup) sweet & sour mix
½ oz. (1 Tbsp.) gin
½ oz. (1 Tbsp.) vodka
½ oz. (1 Tbsp.) light rum
½ oz. (1 Tbsp.) blue curaçao
cold club soda

Pour all ingredients except club soda into chilled glass filled with ice cubes. Top with soda, stirring gently.

---

*ℬy the time a bartender knows what drink a man will have before he orders, there is little else about him worth knowing.*

DON MARQUIS, AMERICAN HUMORIST, JOURNALIST, PLAYWRIGHT

---

### Admiral

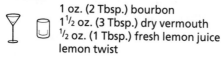

1 oz. (2 Tbsp.) bourbon
1¹/₂ oz. (3 Tbsp.) dry vermouth
¹/₂ oz. (1 Tbsp.) fresh lemon juice
lemon twist

Shake liquid ingredients with ice. Strain into chilled cocktail glass; drop in lemon twist. May also be served over ice in an old-fashioned glass.

### Adonis

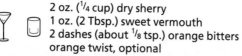

2 oz. (¹/₄ cup) dry sherry
1 oz. (2 Tbsp.) sweet vermouth
2 dashes (about ¹/₈ tsp.) orange bitters
orange twist, optional

Stir or shake liquid ingredients with ice; strain into chilled glass. Drop in orange twist, if desired. May also be served over ice in an old-fashioned glass.

**advocaat** [ad-voh-KAHT] A Dutch brandy-based eggnog-flavored LIQUEUR. The full name is *advocaatenborrel*, Dutch for "advocate's (or lawyer's) drink." *See also* EGGNOG; EGGNOG-FLAVORED SPIRITS.

---

*𝒜 part from cheese and tulips, the main product of [Holland] is advocaat, a drink made from lawyers.*

ALAN COREN, BRITISH HUMORIST, EDITOR

## Affinity #1

1 oz. (2 Tbsp.) Scotch
1 oz. (2 Tbsp.) dry vermouth
1 oz. (2 Tbsp.) sweet vermouth
2 dashes (about ⅛ tsp.) Angostura or orange bitters
maraschino cherry

Stir liquid ingredients with ice; strain into chilled glass. Garnish with cherry.

## Affinity #2

1 oz. (2 Tbsp.) Scotch
1 oz. (2 Tbsp.) dry sherry
1 oz. (2 Tbsp.) ruby port
2 dashes (about ⅛ tsp.) Angostura or orange bitters
maraschino cherry

Stir liquid ingredients with ice; strain into chilled glass. Garnish with cherry.

**Afri-Koko** A West African LIQUEUR flavored with chocolate and coconut. *See also* CHOCOLATE-FLAVORED SPIRITS.

## After 5

½ oz. (1 Tbsp.) Kahlúa
½ oz. (1 Tbsp.) Irish cream liqueur
½ oz. (1 Tbsp.) peppermint schnapps

Pour ingredients into chilled glass in order given.

**After Shock** A cherry-colored, cinnamon-flavored LIQUEUR popular in SHOOTERS.

**age, to; aging** The process of maturing some spirits and wines to produce results that are smoother, more complex, and less harsh and tannic (*see* TANNIN). WHISKEYS, COGNACS, ARMAGNACS, as well as some better BRANDIES and RUMS, all benefit from aging, with many spirits governed by laws regarding minimum aging periods. Spirits that aren't aged include GIN, VODKA, NEUTRAL SPIRITS, and certain brandies and rums. Aging is also beneficial to most fine red and white wines, whereas ROSÉS, light red wines, and most whites are at their best soon after bottling and don't require further aging.

There are different types of aging. **Wood aging** is a process of maturing wine and spirits in barrels or casks prior to bottling. This allows the potables to soften and absorb some of the wood's flavors and tannin. The flavor of the wine or spirit becomes concentrated because of slight evaporation. American whiskeys use new, charred American white-oak barrels for aging. SCOTCH producers often employ barrels that have previously been used to age SHERRY or BOURBON. In modern winemaking, wood aging has become very complex, with considerations such as origin and type of wood used for the barrels, barrelmaking techniques, and container size. Today's container size of choice has become the small oak barrel. The best barrel-oak sources are still being debated—traditionally, winemakers have elected to use French-oak barrels, although some California winemakers prefer American oak.

**Bottle aging** doesn't improve distilled spirits, but it does help develop the nuances of many wines, the length of bottle aging depending on the type of wine. White wines like California CHARDONNAYS do well with a minimum of 6 to 12 months, whereas white BURGUNDIES and SAUTERNES develop better with extended bottle aging. Long-lived red wines—such as CABERNET SAUVIGNON, ZINFANDEL, BORDEAUX, rhône, Barolo, Brunello di Montalcino, and vintage PORT—improve for many years, sometimes decades. Such wines evolve beautifully with bottle aging as their tannins soften and their flavor and bouquet become more intriguing and complex. At some point, however, all wine hits its peak and begins to decline in quality, making bottle aging no longer beneficial.

*Brandy, like man, should gain rather than lose in character with age, but its birth and upbringing determine its characteristics.*

ANDRÉ SIMON, FRENCH GASTRONOME, WRITER

**Aged Whiskey Sours** This recipe was given to us ages ago by Alaskan entrepreneur Connie Bennett, who claimed they were addictive. They are. *See also* SOUR.

**MAKES 1 QUART**

16 oz. (1 pint; 2 cups) bourbon (non sour-mash)
8 oz. (1 cup) fresh orange juice
8 oz. (1 cup) fresh lemon juice
1 cup sugar
half slice orange
maraschino cherry

Combine all ingredients except fruit in a 1½-quart jar or covered pitcher; stir or shake well. Seal tightly and refrigerate for at least 1 month and preferably 3 months. Serve in chilled glass filled with crushed ice; garnish with orange slice and cherry.

**aguardente** [er-gwer-DAYN-ter] The Portuguese term for BRANDY; or, more broadly, for spirits distilled (*see* DISTILLATION) from fruit or vegetables.

**aguardiente; aguardiente de caña** [ah-gwahr-dee-EN-tay; ah-gwahr-dee-EN-tay day KAH-nyah] Spanish for "burned water" (akin to North America's FIREWATER), *aguardiente* is a generic term for any of several potent, low-quality spirits. In Spain the term refers to a BRANDY-based potable made from MARC. The South American *aguardiente de caña* is a coarse liquor based on sugarcane and sometimes flavored with aniseed. *See also* CACHAÇA.

**Airelle** A cranberry-flavored EAU-DE-VIE. *See also* CRANBERRY-FLAVORED SPIRITS.

**A.J.** The initials stand for APPLEJACK, America's apple brandy.

1½ oz. (3 Tbsp.) apple brandy
1½ oz. (3 Tbsp.) unsweetened grapefruit juice
4 dashes (about ¼ tsp.) grenadine

Shake with ice; strain into chilled glass.

★ **Innocent A.J.** Substitute apple juice for the apple brandy.

**akvavit** *see* AQUAVIT

## Alabama

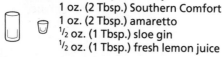

1 oz. (2 Tbsp.) brandy
1 oz. (2 Tbsp.) Cointreau
$1/2$ oz. (1 Tbsp.) fresh lime juice
$1/2$ tsp. sugar
orange twist

Shake liquid ingredients and sugar with ice. Strain into chilled glass; drop in orange twist.

## Alabama Slammer (Slamma)

1 oz. (2 Tbsp.) Southern Comfort
1 oz. (2 Tbsp.) amaretto
$1/2$ oz. (1 Tbsp.) sloe gin
$1/2$ oz. (1 Tbsp.) fresh lemon juice

Shake or stir first 3 ingredients with ice. Strain into chilled glass filled with ice; add lemon juice. May also be served sans ice in a SHOT GLASS.

## Alaska

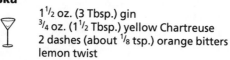

$1 1/2$ oz. (3 Tbsp.) gin
$3/4$ oz. ($1 1/2$ Tbsp.) yellow Chartreuse
2 dashes (about $1/8$ tsp.) orange bitters
lemon twist

Shake liquid ingredients with ice. Strain into chilled glass; drop in lemon twist.

---

*I have made an important discovery . . . that alcohol, taken in sufficient quantities, produces all the effects of intoxication.*

OSCAR WILDE, ANGLO-IRISH PLAYWRIGHT, CRITIC

---

**alcohol** 1. A colorless, intoxicating liquid produced by DISTILL-ING the fermented extraction of fruits, vegetables (like potatoes), and grains. Pure ethyl alcohol (also called *grain alcohol*) is the only alcohol suitable for drinking. Because it's caustic and flammable, ethyl alcohol is tempered with water to reduce its potency. In the United States, the average amount of alcohol in

DISTILLED SPIRITS is 40 percent (80 PROOF). 2. A general term for any alcoholic liquor. *See also* Calories Count! page 42.

**When cooking with alcohol,** remember that the old saw that it "completely evaporates when heated" has been proven invalid. In fact, cooked food can retain from 5 to 85 percent of the original alcohol, depending on how it was prepared (baked, simmered, boiled, etc.) and at what temperature and how long it was cooked. Remember, for those who are alcohol sensitive, even a trace of alcohol can cause a problem.

**ale** A category of alcoholic beverages brewed from barley MALT and HOPS. In this process the yeast rises to the top of the FERMENTATION tank (rather than falling to the bottom, as with BEER). Ale is typically stronger than beer and, because of the hops, more bitter flavored. **Pale ale,** which originated in England, has a flavor that's fairly balanced between the hops and malted barley. The term "pale" refers to the relatively light to deep amber color compared to that of darker ales like PORTER or STOUT. **India pale ale,** originally produced in England for export to British soldiers stationed in India, was at that time brewed in a hearty style so that it could endure the long sea voyage. Today's versions tend to be more bitter than regular pale ale. **Brown ale** is lightly hopped, very full bodied, slightly sweet, and dark brown in color. The color and flavor are derived from caramelized malts. **Scotch ale** is amber to dark brown in color, full bodied, and has a strong malty flavor. Although this ale originated in Scotland, it's now produced in other countries, including Belgium and France. *See also* TRAPPIST BEER.

*It is said that beer drinkers are slow, and a little stupid; that they have an ox-like placidity not quite favourable to any brilliant intellectual display. But there are times when this placidity is what the labouring brain most needs. After the agitation of too active thinking there is safety in a tankard of ale.*

PHILIP G. HAMERTON, BRITISH AUTHOR

**Alexander** This creamy concoction makes a heady dessert drink. For true decadence substitute a small scoop of ice cream for the cream and zap the mixture in a blender. Pure sin!

1 oz. (2 Tbsp.) gin
1 oz. (2 Tbsp.) white crème de cacao
1 oz. (2 Tbsp.) half & half or cream
freshly grated nutmeg

Shake liquid ingredients with ice. Strain into chilled glass; sprinkle with nutmeg.

➤ **Alexander's Sister** Substitute crème de menthe for the crème de cacao.

➤ **Brandy Alexander** Substitute brandy for gin and dark crème de cacao for the white.

### Alexander's Sister *see* ALEXANDER

### Alfonso Special

1½ oz. (3 Tbsp.) Grand Marnier
¾ oz. (1½ Tbsp.) gin
¾ oz. (1½ Tbsp.) dry vermouth
4 dashes (about ¼ tsp.) sweet vermouth
2 dashes (about ⅛ tsp.) Angostura bitters

Stir or shake with ice; strain into chilled glass.

**Algonquin** [al-GONG-kwin] New York's famous Algonquin Hotel is the origin of this eponymous cocktail.

2 oz. (¼ cup) blended whiskey
1 oz. (2 Tbsp.) dry vermouth
1 oz. (2 Tbsp.) unsweetened pineapple juice

Shake ingredients with ice; strain into chilled cocktail glass, or serve over ice cubes in an old-fashioned glass.

**Alizé de France** [ah-lee-ZAY deuh FRAHNSS] A bright yellow French COGNAC-based LIQUEUR with an exotic and refreshingly tart passion-fruit flavor. **Alizé Red Passion** has a rich red color produced in part by the addition of cranberry juice.

**Aliziergeist** [ah-lih-TSEER-gighst] An Alsatian fruit BRANDY made from serviceberries, the brownish fruit of the Mediterranean service tree. *See also* FRUIT-FLAVORED SPIRITS.

**Allasch** Latvian in origin, this extremely sweet LIQUEUR is flavored with almonds, aniseed, and cumin. Its flavor is similar to, although not as complex as, that of KÜMMEL.

**Allegheny** [al-lih-GAY-nee]

> 1 oz. (2 Tbsp.) bourbon
> 1 oz. (2 Tbsp.) dry vermouth
> 1 1/2 tsp. blackberry brandy
> 1 1/2 tsp. fresh lemon juice
> lemon twist

Shake liquid ingredients with ice. Strain into chilled glass; drop in lemon twist.

---

*At four I sought my whirling bed, at eight I woke with such a head! It is no time for mirth or laughter—the cold, grey dawn the morning after.*

GEORGE ADE, AMERICAN HUMORIST

---

**Allen Cocktail**

> 1 1/2 oz. (3 Tbsp.) gin
> 3/4 oz. (1 1/2 Tbsp.) maraschino liqueur
> 1 1/2 tsp. fresh lemon juice

Shake ingredients with ice; strain into chilled glass.

**Allies**

> 1 oz. (2 Tbsp.) gin
> 1 oz. (2 Tbsp.) dry vermouth
> 2 dashes (about 1/8 tsp.) kümmel

Stir or shake with ice; strain into chilled glass.

**All-White Frappé**

> 1 oz. (2 Tbsp.) white crème de cacao
> 1 oz. (2 Tbsp.) anisette
> 1 oz. (2 Tbsp.) peppermint schnapps
> 1 oz. (2 Tbsp.) fresh lemon juice

Shake ingredients with ice; strain into chilled glass over crushed ice.

**almond-flavored spirits** *See* AMARETTO; CRÈME DE NOYAUX

**almond syrup** *See* ORGEAT SYRUP; SYRUPS, FLAVORED

**amaretto** [am-ah-REHT-toh] An almond-flavored LIQUEUR, most renditions of which are flavored with the kernels of apricot pits. This style of liqueur originated in Italy, and Amaretto di Saronno (from Saronno) is undoubtedly the most well known. Amaretto is also produced in the United States. *See also* NUT-FLAVORED SPIRITS.

**amaro** [ah-MAH-roh] Italian for bitter or very DRY, used to describe certain wines as well as myriad bitter Italian LIQUEURS.

### American Beauty

³/₄ oz. (1¹/₂ Tbsp.) brandy
³/₄ oz. (1¹/₂ Tbsp.) dry vermouth
³/₄ oz. (1¹/₂ Tbsp.) fresh orange juice
4 dashes (about ¹/₄ tsp.) white crème de menthe
2 dashes (about ¹/₈ tsp.) grenadine
1 oz. (2 Tbsp.) ruby port

Shake all ingredients except port with ice. Strain into chilled glass. Float port on top by slowly pouring it over the back (rounded) side of a spoon; don't mix.

### American Flyer

1¹/₂ oz. (3 Tbsp.) light rum
1¹/₂ tsp. fresh lime juice
¹/₂ tsp. powdered sugar
cold dry champagne

Shake all ingredients except champagne with ice. Strain into chilled glass; top with champagne.

### Americano

1¹/₂ oz. (3 Tbsp.) sweet vermouth
1¹/₂ oz. (3 Tbsp.) Campari
cold club soda
lemon or orange slice

Pour vermouth and Campari into chilled glass filled with ice cubes; add club soda, stirring gently. Garnish with lemon or orange slice.

**Amer Picon** [ah-MEHR pee-KAWN] Also known simply as *Picon,* this French VERMOUTH-style APÉRITIF is extremely bitter (*amer* is French for "bitter"). Amer Picon is dark reddish brown in color and flavored with gentian, orange, and cinchona bark, which yields QUININE—hence, the bitterness. It's generally taken with CLUB SODA, but is used in other cocktails, such as the following namesake drink, as well as the PICON COCKTAIL, PICON FIZZ, QUEBEC, and SANCTUARY.

### Amer Picon Cocktail

2 oz. (¼ cup) Amer Picon
2 tsp. fresh lime juice
1 tsp. grenadine
orange twist

Shake liquid ingredients with crushed ice. Strain into chilled glass; drop in orange twist.

*I always keep a supply of stimulant handy in case I see a snake . . . which I also keep handy.*

W.C. FIELDS, AMERICAN COMEDIAN, ACTOR

**Amontillado** [ah-mon-the-LAH-doh] *see* SHERRY

**Amoroso** [ah-muh-ROH-soh] *see* SHERRY

### Anchors Aweigh

1 oz. (2 Tbsp.) bourbon
1 oz. (2 Tbsp.) cream
2 tsp. Triple Sec
2 tsp. peach brandy
2 tsp. maraschino liqueur
⅛ tsp. maraschino cherry juice

Shake ingredients with ice; strain into chilled glass.

**Andalusia** [an-duh-LOO-zhuh]

1½ oz. (3 Tbsp.) dry sherry
½ oz. (1 Tbsp.) light rum
½ oz. (1 Tbsp.) brandy
2 dashes (about ⅛ tsp.) Angostura bitters

Stir ingredients with ice; strain into chilled glass.

**Anesone** [ah-nay-SOH-nay] An anise-flavored Italian LIQUEUR that's often used as an ABSINTHE substitute. *See also* ANISE-FLAVORED SPIRITS.

**Angel Face**

1 oz. (2 Tbsp.) gin
½ oz. (1 Tbsp.) apricot brandy
½ oz. (1 Tbsp.) apple brandy

Shake ingredients with ice; strain into chilled glass.

**Angel's Delight** *See* Floating and Layering Techniques, page 30.

1½ tsp. grenadine
1½ tsp. Triple Sec
1½ tsp. sloe gin
1½ tsp. half & half

Pour grenadine into chilled glass. Add remaining ingredients in order given, slowly pouring each one over the back (rounded) side of a spoon so that it floats on top of the one below. Don't mix.

**Angel's Kiss** *See* Floating and Layering Techniques, page 30.

1½ tsp. white crème de cacao
1½ tsp. sloe gin
1½ tsp. brandy
1½ tsp. half & half

Pour crème de cacao into chilled glass. Add remaining ingredients in order given, slowly pouring each one over the back (rounded) side of a spoon so that it floats on top of the one below. Don't mix.

**angel's share** The amount of wine or spirit (such as BOURBON) that vanishes during barrel AGING as a small portion of the liquid evaporates through the pores of the wood.

**Angel's Tip** *See* Floating and Layering Techniques, page 30.

1 oz. (2 Tbsp.) dark crème de cacao
$^1/_2$ oz. (1 Tbsp.) cream

Pour crème de cacao into chilled glass. Float cream on top by slowly pouring it over the back (rounded) side of a spoon; don't mix.

**Angel's Tit** *See* Floating and Layering Techniques, page 30.

1 $^1/_2$ tsp. white crème de cacao
1 $^1/_2$ tsp. maraschino liqueur
1 $^1/_2$ tsp. half & half
maraschino cherry

Pour crème de cacao into chilled glass. Add remaining liquid ingredients in order given, slowly pouring each one over the back (rounded) side of a spoon so that it floats on top of the one below. Don't mix. Spear cherry with toothpick; lay across top of glass.

**Angler's Cocktail**

1 $^1/_2$ oz. (3 Tbsp.) gin
2 dashes (about $^1/_8$ tsp.) Angostura bitters
2 dashes (about $^1/_8$ tsp.) orange bitters
1 dash (about $^1/_{16}$ tsp.) grenadine

Shake ingredients with crushed ice; strain into chilled glass filled with ice cubes.

**Angostura bitters** [ang-uh-STOOR-ah] The most widely known BITTERS, Angostura was formulated by German surgeon Johann Gottlieb Benjamin Siegert, who served under Marshal von Blücher at the Battle of Waterloo. Dr. Siegert emigrated to Angostura (now Ciudad Bolívar), Venezuela, in 1918, and became the surgeon general in Simón Bolívar's army. He created the bitter elixir (based on angostura bark, gentian root, RUM, and other ingredients) as a tonic to stimulate the troops' lagging appetites and improve their health. Although still taken as a DIGESTIF, today Angostura bitters are more apt to be used as a flavoring in foods and drinks—indeed, they're indispensable in many potables, including the MANHATTAN, OLD-FASHIONED, and PINK GIN. At 90 PROOF, Angostura bitters are the most potent among this genre.

**anise-flavored spirits** *see* ABSINTHE; ANESONE; ANISETTE; ARAK; DANZIGER GOLDWASSER; HERBSAINT; OPAL NERA; OUZO; PASTIS; PERNOD; RAKI; SAMBUCA

**anisette** [AN-ih-seht] A clear, very sweet anise-flavored LIQUEUR made from expressed aniseeds. *See also* ANISE-FLAVORED SPIRITS.

> *A man's not drunk if he can lay on the floor without holding on.*
>
> JOE E. LEWIS, AMERICAN ENTERTAINER

**Ankle Breaker** This title of this 151-PROOF rum drink forecasts what'll happen if you have one too many.

   1½ oz. (3 Tbsp.) 151-proof rum
   1 oz. (2 Tbsp.) cherry brandy
   1 oz. (2 Tbsp.) fresh lime juice
   1½ tsp. sugar syrup

Shake ingredients with crushed ice; strain into chilled glass.

★**Annabanana** *see* ANNA'S BANANA

**Anna's Banana**

   1½ oz. (3 Tbsp.) vodka
   1 oz. (2 Tbsp.) fresh lime juice
   ½ small ripe banana
   1 tsp. honey or orgeat syrup
   ½ cup crushed ice
   lime slice

Combine all ingredients except lime slice in a blender. Cover and process at medium speed until smooth, about 15 seconds. Pour into chilled glass; garnish with lime slice.

   ★**Annabanana** Omit vodka, use a whole banana; increase lime juice to 3 Tbsp. and crushed ice to 1 cup.

**apéritif** [ah-perhr-ih-TEEF] 1. A light alcoholic drink taken before lunch or dinner. Although such libations were once ostensibly consumed to "stimulate the appetite," today they are simply enjoyed for premeal conviviality. Among the many popular apéritifs are AMER PICON, CHAMPAGNE, DUBONNET, KIR, LILLET, and SHERRY. 2. The word "apéritif" is also used to describe a style of drink made expressly for this purpose.

**Aperitivo** [ah-pay-ree-TEE-voh]

1½ oz. (3 Tbsp.) gin
1 oz. (2 Tbsp.) Sambuca
4 dashes (about ¼ tsp.) orange bitters

Stir or shake with crushed ice; strain into chilled glass.

**appellation** [ap-uh-LAY-shuhn; *Fr.* ah-pehl-lah-SYAW*N*] A term in the wine world that describes a designated grape-growing area controlled by governmental (federal, local, or both) rules and regulations regarding which grape varieties do best in particular climates and soils, viticultural and winemaking practices, allowable yields per acre, alcohol content of the wine, and so on. Such regulations vary from country to country, but are analogous in their goal to encourage the production of quality wines.

**Apple Blow Fizz**

2 oz. (¼ cup) apple brandy
1 egg white
1 tsp. sugar
1 tsp. fresh lemon juice
cold club soda

Shake all ingredients except club soda with ice. Strain into chilled glass, add 3 ice cubes, and top with soda; stir gently.

　✸**Apple Juice Fizz** Substitute apple juice for the apple brandy.

**apple brandy** A generic name for any BRANDY distilled from apples. *See* APPLEJACK; CALVADOS

**Apple Brandy Cocktail**

1½ oz. (3 Tbsp.) apple brandy
1 tsp. grenadine
1 tsp. fresh lemon juice

Shake ingredients with ice; strain into chilled glass.

**Apple Brandy Highball** *see* HIGHBALL

**Apple Buck** *see* BUCK

## Applecar

1 oz. (2 Tbsp.) apple brandy
1 oz. (2 Tbsp.) Triple Sec
$^1/_2$ oz. (1 Tbsp.) fresh lemon juice

Shake ingredients with ice; strain into chilled glass.

### Apple Daiquiri *see* DAIQUIRI

### apple-flavored spirits *see* APPLEJACK; BERENTZEN; CALVADOS

**applejack** The American term for a potent (80 to 100 PROOF) apple BRANDY that must be AGED 2 years in wooden casks before being bottled. CALVADOS is the well-known French apple brandy. *See also* APPLE-FLAVORED SPIRITS.

---

*Mike and Stan were sitting in a bar when Mike said, "Hey, pal, we both love wine, women, and song, but if you were forced to choose between wine and women, which would it be?" Stan thought for a minute, then said, "I dunno, man, but I guess it could depend on the vintage of the wine . . . and the woman."*

---

### ★ Apple Juice Fizz *see* APPLE BLOW FIZZ

### Apple Swizzle *See also* SWIZZLE; SWIZZLE STICK.

1$^1/_2$ oz. (3 Tbsp.) apple brandy
1 oz. (2 Tbsp.) light rum
$^3/_4$ oz. (1$^1/_2$ Tbsp.) fresh lime juice
1 tsp. powdered sugar
2 to 4 dashes (about $^1/_8$ to $^1/_4$ tsp.) Angostura bitters
lime slice

Combine all ingredients except lime slice in chilled glass filled with crushed ice. Rub a swizzle stick rapidly back and forth between your palms (or stir rapidly with a long spoon), until ingredients are mixed. Garnish with lime slice.

**Apricot Brandy** A generic term for any BRANDY distilled from apricots. *See also* APRICOT-FLAVORED SPIRITS.

## Apricot Cocktail

1½ oz. (3 Tbsp.) apricot brandy
¾ oz. (1½ Tbsp.) fresh lemon juice
¾ oz. (1½ Tbsp.) fresh orange juice
1½ tsp. gin or vodka

Shake ingredients with ice; strain into chilled glass.

★**Apricot Mocktail** Substitute apricot nectar for the apricot brandy.

**apricot-flavored spirits** *see* APRICOT BRANDY; ABRICOTINE; APRY; CREME D'ABRICOTS

## Apricot Lady

1½ oz. (3 Tbsp.) light rum
1 oz. (2 Tbsp.) apricot brandy
1 egg white
½ oz. (1 Tbsp.) Triple Sec
½ oz. (1 Tbsp.) fresh lime juice
orange slice

Shake liquid ingredients with 3 ice cubes. Pour drink with ice into chilled glass; garnish with orange slice.

★**Apricot Mocktail** *see* APRICOT COCKTAIL

**Apry** [AH-pree] A fruity but not overly sweet apricot-flavored LIQUEUR made by the French house of Marie Brizard. *See also* APRICOT-FLAVORED SPIRITS.

**aquavit; akvavit** [AHK-wah-veet; AHK-vah-veet] This Scandinavian original is a potent, colorless liquor distilled from either potatoes or grain. Aquavits go through a second DISTILLATION to add flavor, the most common being caraway, coriander, or dill. Serve aquavit icy cold (store it in the freezer), STRAIGHT UP in small, chilled glasses. It should be taken in one gulp.

**aqua vitae** [AHK-wuh VEE-tee] Latin for "water of life," this term describes a clear distilled BRANDY. *See also* EAU-DE-VIE.

**Aqueduct** [AK-wih-duct]

1 1/2 oz. (3 Tbsp.) vodka
1 1/2 tsp. Triple Sec
1 1/2 tsp. apricot brandy
1/2 oz. (1 Tbsp.) fresh lime juice
orange twist

Shake liquid ingredients with ice. Strain into chilled glass; drop in orange twist.

**arak; arrack; arrak** [EH-rahk; eh-RAK] 1. Arabic in origin, the word "arak" is used generically throughout Asia and the Middle East to describe a potent liquor distilled from any of various ingredients, including dates, grains, grapes, and sundry palm saps. In some Middle Eastern countries, arak has a strong licorice flavor. 2. A pungently aromatic yet light-bodied RUM from Java. *See also* ANISE-FLAVORED SPIRITS; SWEDISH PUNSCH.

**Armagnac** [ahr-muhn-YAK] Hailed as one of the world's two great BRANDIES (the other being COGNAC), Armagnac comes from the region of Gascony, near Condom, a town southeast of Bordeaux. Traditionally, Armagnac is distilled (*see* DISTILLATION) once (as opposed to Cognac's double distillation) and at a relatively low temperature. This single distillation leaves more flavoring elements and produces a hearty, full-flavored spirit redolent of the fruit's CHARACTER. Armagnacs are AGED in black oak (for up to 40 years), which imparts more flavor and allows for faster aging than the Limousin oak used for Cognac. Although Armagnacs generally don't have the finesse of the finest Cognacs, they're silky smooth and fuller flavored. Despite the fact that Armagnac was first made at least 200 years before Cognac, the latter outsells Armagnac today by almost seven to one.

**aroma** In general, aroma refers to a distinctive odor characteristic of a specific liquor, wine, or food. In the world of wine, the word "aroma" traditionally refers to the fruity smell of the grape variety. In today's broader parlance, this term is a synonym for *bouquet,* the complex fragrance that a wine develops through

FERMENTATION and AGING, specifically bottle aging. *See also* NOSE.

### aromatic wine *see* WINE

### Artillery

2 oz. (¼ cup) gin
1 oz. (2 Tbsp.) sweet vermouth
Shake ingredients with ice; strain into chilled glass.

---

*What is the special quality of sparkling wine? Why does the very sight of its bulky bottle, the muffled pop of its cork coming out, act as the starting pistol for smiles and laughter?*

HUGH JOHNSON, BRITISH WINE AND SPIRITS WRITER

---

### Artillery Punch

**MAKES TWENTY-FIVE 6-OUNCE SERVINGS**

32 oz. (1 quart; 4 cups) bourbon
32 oz. (1 quart; 4 cups) dry red wine (Cabernet Sauvignon, Burgundy, etc.)
32 oz. (1 quart; 4 cups) strong black tea
16 oz. (1 pint; 2 cups) dark rum
16 oz. (1 pint; 2 cups) fresh orange juice
8 oz. (1 cup) brandy
8 oz. (1 cup) gin
8 oz. (1 cup) fresh lemon juice
sugar
1 orange, sliced
1 lemon, sliced

Stir together all liquid ingredients; sweeten with sugar to taste. Cover and refrigerate overnight. Pour into punch bowl over a block of ice (*see* Punch Bowl Ice, page 17). Float orange and lemon slices on surface.

**Asbach Uralt** [AHS-bahk OOR-ahlt] A highly esteemed German BRANDY that, like ARMAGNAC and COGNAC, is AGED in oak barrels.

**Asti Spumante** [AH-stee spoo-MAHN-teh] From Asti, a northern Italy wine-growing district in the Piedmont region, this sparkling white wine is sweet and relatively low in alcohol. It's made from muscat (*moscato*) grapes. Asti Spumante is typically served as a dessert wine, but can also be served as an APÉRITIF. *Spumante* is the Italian word for "sparkling."

**Aurum** [OW-rum] A BRANDY-based, orange-flavored Italian LIQUEUR. *See also* CITRUS-FLAVORED SPIRITS; ORANGE-FLAVORED SPIRITS.

### Aviation

1 ¹/₂ oz. (3 Tbsp.) gin
¹/₂ oz. (1 Tbsp.) fresh lemon juice
¹/₂ tsp. apricot brandy
¹/₂ tsp. maraschino liqueur

Shake ingredients with ice; strain into chilled glass.

**B-52** *See* Floating and Layering Techniques, page 30.

¹/₂ oz. (1 Tbsp.) Kahlúa
¹/₂ oz. (1 Tbsp.) Irish cream liqueur
¹/₂ oz. (1 Tbsp.) Grand Marnier

Pour Kahlúa into chilled glass. Add remaining ingredients in order given, slowly pouring each one over the back (rounded) side of a spoon so that it floats on top of the one below. Don't mix.

**BAC; BAL** *see* BLOOD ALCOHOL CONCENTRATION

**Bacardi** [bah-KAHR-dee] This classic cocktail is a variation of the DAIQUIRI. In 1936, a court ruling declared that it was illegal to make this cocktail with any rum other than Bacardi. We won't tell if you don't.

1 ¹/₂ oz. (3 Tbsp.) light (Bacardi!) rum
¹/₂ oz. (1 Tbsp.) fresh lime juice
¹/₂ tsp. grenadine

Shake ingredients with ice; strain into chilled glass.

➤ **Bacardi Special** Add ³/₄ oz. (1¹/₂ Tbsp.) gin.

**Bacchanalia** [bak-uh-NAY-lee-uh] Named for Bacchus, the Greek and Roman god of wine, vegetation, and fertility, a Bacchanalia is—in the most ribald sense—a drunken orgy. A participant in the revelry is called a **bacchanal.**

**back** A bar term referring to a potable served with another primary drink, as in the BMW, which is a BLOODY MARY served with a beer to be sipped alternatively with it or to back it up.

### Bahama Mama

1 oz. (2 Tbsp.) light rum
1 oz. (2 Tbsp.) gold rum
1 oz. (2 Tbsp.) dark rum
1 oz. (2 Tbsp.) coconut liqueur
2 oz. (¹/₄ cup) fresh orange juice
3 oz. (³/₈ cup) unsweetened pineapple juice
¹/₄ tsp. grenadine
maraschino cherry
orange slice

Shake liquid ingredients with ice. Strain into chilled glass; garnish with cherry and orange slice.

*There comes a time in every woman's life when the only thing that helps is a glass of champagne.*
BETTE DAVIS, AMERICAN ACTRESS (IN THE FILM *OLD ACQUAINTANCE*)

**Bailey's Irish Cream** *see* IRISH CREAM LIQUEURS

**Banana Banshee** *see* BANSHEE

**Banana Daiquiri** *see* DAIQUIRI

**banana-flavored spirits** *see* CAYMANA; CRÈME DE BANANE

**B & B** A topaz-colored amalgam of BÉNÉDICTINE and BRANDY, this spicy, herbal LIQUEUR offers the best of both spirits in flavor and texture. B & B is more like a flavored brandy than most liqueurs because it's relatively DRY. *See also* HERB-FLAVORED SPIRITS.

**Banshee** This drink is also called a *Banana Banshee*.

1 oz. (2 Tbsp.) white crème de cacao
1 oz. (2 Tbsp.) crème de banane
1 oz. (2 Tbsp.) cream

Shake ingredients with ice; strain into chilled glass.

**barback** A bartender's assistant or apprentice, responsible for all the things a bartender doesn't want to do, like preparing the garnishes, stocking ice and glassware, and so on.

**Barbados Rum** *see* RUM

**Bärenjäger** [BEH-rehn-YAY-ger] German for "bear hunter," Bärenjäger is a honey-flavored VODKA-based LIQUEUR.

**barfly** One who spends an excessive amount of time in bars.

**Barnum**

1½ oz. (3 Tbsp.) gin
½ oz. (1 Tbsp.) apricot brandy
4 dashes (about ¼ tsp.) Angostura bitters
¼ tsp. fresh lemon juice

Shake ingredients with ice; strain into chilled glass.

**barspoon** A long-handled stainless-steel spoon used for stirring drinks in a mixing glass. *See also* Bar Equipment, page 4.

**Barton Special**

1½ oz. (3 Tbsp.) apple brandy
¾ oz. (1½ Tbsp.) Scotch
¾ oz. (1½ Tbsp.) gin
lemon twist

Shake liquid ingredients with ice. Strain into chilled glass. Add 2 ice cubes and lemon twist.

**Bay Breeze**

4 oz. (½ cup) unsweetened pineapple juice
1½ oz. (3 Tbsp.) vodka
1 oz. (2 Tbsp.) cranberry juice

Pour all ingredients into chilled glass filled with ice cubes; stir well.

★ **Beach Breeze** Omit vodka; increase cranberry juice to 2 oz. (¹/₄ cup).

## Beachcomber

1¹/₂ oz. (3 Tbsp.) light rum
¹/₂ oz. (1 Tbsp.) Triple Sec or Cointreau
¹/₂ oz. (1 Tbsp.) fresh lime juice
1 dash (about ¹/₁₆ tsp.) maraschino liqueur
lime slice

Dip chilled glass rim in water, shake off excess water, then dip rim into granulated sugar. Shake liquid ingredients with ice. Strain into glass; garnish with lime slice.

## Beauty Spot

1 dash (about ¹/₁₆ tsp.) grenadine
1 oz. (2 Tbsp.) gin
¹/₂ oz. (1 Tbsp.) dry vermouth
¹/₂ oz. (1 Tbsp.) sweet vermouth
1 tsp. fresh orange juice

Put grenadine in bottom of chilled glass. Shake remaining ingredients with ice; strain into glass. Don't stir.

---

*Nothing ever tasted better than a cold beer on a beautiful afternoon with nothing to look forward to but more of the same.*

HUGH HOOD

---

**beer** A generic term for low-alcohol beverages brewed from a MASH of malted barley and other cereals (like corn, rye, or wheat), flavored with HOPS, and fermented with yeast. Technically, beers are only those beverages where the yeast sinks to the bottom of the tank during FERMENTATION. Such bottom-fermented brews ferment at colder temperatures for longer periods of time, which produces a lighter, crisper-tasting beverage. ALE—a generic category for top-fermented beers where the yeast rises to the top of the tank—is stronger flavored and higher in alcohol. Beverages that fall into the bottom-fermented beer category include BOCK BEER, LAGER, MALT LIQUOR, PILSNER, and VIENNA BEER. PORTER, STOUT, and WHEAT BEER are all top fermented and are therefore considered ales. To add to the confusion, some states don't allow the words "beer" or "lager" to be used for brews containing over 5 percent alcohol, so the word "ale" is used to describe these beers.

The four ingredients that play the primary roles in beermaking are water, MALT, hops, and yeast. Water is critical because it comprises nine-tenths of a beer's volume. The quality and composition of the water from different beermaking regions contribute greatly to the character of the finished product. Malt, which is made from germinated grain (usually barley), provides beer with a slightly sweet character. How malt is treated—dried but not roasted, lightly roasted, heavily roasted, and so on—impacts a beer's flavor. Hops convey an agreeably bitter, DRY flavor that balances the malt's sweetness. Specially cultivated yeast (each brewer has his favorite strain) is used for brewing, with different yeasts producing different results. LAMBIC BEER utilizes wild yeast for fermentation.

Most beer in the United States ranges from 3.2 to 8 percent alcohol. Some European beers are below 3 percent alcohol, while others range as high as 13 percent. In the United States, the term **light beer** refers to a brew with reduced calories and usually less alcohol. In Europe this term is used to distinguish between pale and dark lagers. **Ice beer** (called *Eisbock* in Germany) is lagered at such cold temperatures (32°F—the freezing point of water) that ice crystals form. When this frozen water is extracted, the resulting beer has a much higher alcohol concentration, with some German ice beers reaching 13 percent alcohol. Beer, unlike most wines, should not be aged but consumed as fresh as possible. Most lighter-style beers (such as lager and Pilsner) should be served at about 45°F; colder temperatures cloud beer and diminish its flavor. Stronger ales should be served at about 55°F so their more complex flavors can be savored. *See also* BITTER; DORTMUNDER; FRUIT BEER; MÜNCHENER SAKE; TRAPPIST BEER.

## beer buster

1½ oz. (3 Tbsp.) icy-cold vodka
2 dashes (about ⅛ tsp.) Tabasco sauce
1 (12 oz.) bottle of cold beer

Stir together vodka and Tabasco in chilled mug; add beer.

**Beer Mug** *see* Glassware, page 8

**Bee's Knees**

1 1/2 oz. (3 Tbsp.) gold rum
1/2 oz. (1 Tbsp.) fresh orange juice
1/2 oz. (1 Tbsp.) fresh lime juice
1 tsp. Triple Sec
1 tsp. powdered sugar
orange twist

Shake all ingredients except orange twist with ice. Strain into chilled glass; drop in orange twist.

**Bellini** [behl-LEE-nee] An APÉRITIF created in 1943 at Venice's renowned Harry's Bar in honor of the illustrious Venetian painter Giovanni Bellini. White peaches (specified in the original recipe) can be hard to find sometimes, but any variety of fresh peach (or even nectarine) offers more flavor than canned peach nectar. Although some recipes call for lemon juice to keep the peach from darkening, it's not really necessary and detracts from the flavor. At Harry's Bar the Bellini is customarily made with Prosecco, an Italian SPARKLING WINE.

1 medium ripe peach, peeled and puréed, or 3 oz.
(3/8 cup) peach nectar
4 to 6 oz. (1/2 to 3/4 cup) icy-cold dry champagne or other
dry sparkling wine
peach slice

Pour peach purée into chilled glass. Slowly add champagne; stir gently. Garnish with peach slice.

**Belmont Cocktail**

2 oz. (1/4 cup) gin
3/4 oz. (1 1/2 Tbsp.) cream
1 1/2 tsp. raspberry syrup

Shake ingredients with ice; strain into chilled glass.

*It is a known fact that beer drinkers will eat pretty much anything; Exhibit A is "Slim Jims." You could put a dish of salted mothballs in front of beer drinkers, and they would snork them up.*

DAVE BARRY, AMERICAN HUMORIST

## Belmont Stakes

1 1/2 oz. (3 Tbsp.) vodka
3/4 oz. (1 1/2 Tbsp.) gold rum
1/2 oz. (1 Tbsp.) strawberry liqueur
1/2 oz. (1 Tbsp.) fresh lime juice
3/4 tsp. grenadine
orange slice

Shake liquid ingredients with ice. Strain into chilled glass; garnish with orange slice.

**bender** A drinking spree. Anyone who says they're "going on a bender" is caught in the act of premeditation.

**Bénédictine D.O.M.** [ben-eh-DIHK-teen] Referred to by some as "the world's oldest LIQUEUR," this seductively piquant elixir is named after the Bénédictine monks of the Abbey of Fécamp, Normandy, who first began making it in 1510. Bénédictine is COGNAC-based and flavored with a complex formula of myriad aromatics. Its flavor is a delicate balance of honey, citrus peel, and herbs such as basil, rosemary, and sage. The D.O.M. on each bottle stands for *Deo Optimo Maximo,* "To God Most Good, Most Great," a Bénédictine dedication. *See also* HERB-FLAVORED SPIRITS.

## Bennett Cocktail

1 1/2 oz. (3 Tbsp.) gin
2 tsp. fresh lime juice
1 tsp. powdered sugar
2 dashes (about 1/8 tsp.) Angostura or orange bitters

Shake ingredients with ice; strain into chilled glass.

**Berentzen** [beh-REHNT-zehn] An apple-flavored LIQUEUR from Germany. *See also* APPLE-FLAVORED SPIRITS.

## Bermuda Highball *See also* HIGHBALL.

1 oz. (2 Tbsp.) gin
1 oz. (2 Tbsp.) dry vermouth
1 oz. (2 Tbsp.) brandy
cold club soda or ginger ale
lemon twist

Put 2 to 3 ice cubes in chilled glass. Add gin, vermouth, and brandy. Top with club soda or ginger ale, stirring gently; drop in lemon twist.

> *I am prepared to believe that a dry martini slightly impairs the palate, but think what it does for the soul.*
>
> ALEC WAUGH, ENGLISH AUTHOR

## Bermuda Rose

1 ½ oz. (3 Tbsp.) gin
½ oz. (1 Tbsp.) fresh lime juice
1 ½ tsp. apricot brandy
1 ½ tsp. grenadine

Shake ingredients with ice; strain into chilled glass over ice.

## berry-flavored spirits *see* BLACKBERRY BRANDY; BLACK-BERRY-FLAVORED SPIRITS; BLACK CURRANT–FLAVORED SPIRITS; CHERRY-FLAVORED SPIRITS; CRANBERRY-FLAVORED SPIRITS; LILLEHAMMER; RASPBERRY-FLAVORED SPIRITS

## Between the Sheets

1 oz. (2 Tbsp.) Cointreau or Triple Sec
1 oz. (2 Tbsp.) brandy
1 oz. (2 Tbsp.) light rum
1 oz. (2 Tbsp.) fresh lemon or lime juice
lemon or lime twist

Shake liquid ingredients with ice. Strain into chilled glass; drop in lemon or lime twist.

## Bijou Cocktail [BEE-zhoo]

1 oz. (2 Tbsp.) gin
1 oz. (2 Tbsp.) sweet vermouth
1 oz. (2 Tbsp.) green Chartreuse
1 dash (about $^1/_{16}$ tsp.) orange bitters
1 maraschino cherry, optional

Stir liquid ingredients with ice. Strain into chilled glass; garnish with cherry, if desired.

## Billy Taylor

2 oz. (¼ cup) gin
1 oz. (2 Tbsp.) fresh lime juice
1 tsp. powdered sugar
cold club soda

Shake all ingredients except club soda with ice. Strain into chilled glass filled with ice cubes. Top with soda; stir gently.

## Biscayne [bihs-KAYN]

1½ oz. (3 Tbsp.) gin
¾ oz. (1½ Tbsp.) light rum
¾ oz. (1½ Tbsp.) Forbidden Fruit liqueur
¾ oz. (1½ Tbsp.) fresh lime juice
lime slice

Shake all ingredients except lime slice with ice. Strain into chilled glass; garnish with lime slice.

## Bishop, The

Back in the eighteenth century, the classic Bishop was a warm mulled wine (often PORT) simmered with a roasted clove-studded orange. Conjecture suggests that the name comes from the burgundy-red color of a bishop's robes. Today's versions of this drink are more likely iced—both are refreshing in their own way.

1 oz. (2 Tbsp.) fresh lemon juice
1 oz. (2 Tbsp.) fresh orange juice
1½ tsp. powdered sugar
pinch of ground cloves
about 6 oz. (¾ cup) red Burgundy or Cabernet
    Sauvignon
orange and lemon slices

Combine lemon and orange juices, sugar, and cloves in chilled glass; stir to dissolve sugar. Add 3 ice cubes; pour in wine, stirring to mix. Garnish with orange and lemon slices.

➤ **The Cardinal** Substitute Bordeaux for the Burgundy.

➤ **The Pope** Substitute champagne for the Burgundy.

➤ **Classic Hot Bishop** Heat all ingredients except citrus slices just until warm (don't boil). Pour into mug; garnish with orange and lemon slices. *See also* Hot Drinks, page 29.

## Bismark *see* BLACK VELVET

**bitter** 1. A popular, golden-brown English ALE, so named for its bitter essence, derived from HOPS. *See also* BEER. 2. A distinctive flavor characteristic of beer, contributed by hops.

*Give me another drink and
I'll tell you all you want to know.*
FATS WALLER, AMERICAN JAZZ MUSICIAN, COMPOSER

**bitters** A general term for any of many aromatic mixtures based on a DISTILLATION of herbs, barks, flowers, seeds, roots, and plants. They generally have a high alcohol content and, true to their name, are bitter or bittersweet in taste. Bitters come in various flavors (including apricot, orange, and peach) and have long been used as DIGESTIFS, appetite stimulants, and hangover cures. They're used in myriad mixed drinks, as well as to enhance the flavor of many food preparations. The most popular bitters are AMER PICON, ANGOSTURA BITTERS, FERNET BRANCA, and PÉY-CHAUD'S BITTERS. Among other bitters from around the world are: **Abbott's Bitters** from the United States (Baltimore, Maryland); **Boonekamp bitters** from Holland; **Gammel Dansk** from Denmark; **orange bitters,** the most well known (such as Holloway's) coming from England; **Stonsdorfer** and **Underberg bitters** from Germany; and **Unicum bitters** from Vienna.

### Bittersweet

1½ oz. (3 Tbsp.) dry vermouth
1½ oz. (3 Tbsp.) sweet vermouth
1 dash (about 1/16 tsp.) Angostura bitters
1 dash (about 1/16 tsp.) orange bitters
orange twist

Shake liquid ingredients with ice. Strain into chilled glass; drop in orange twist.

**blackberry brandy** A generic term for any BRANDY distilled from blackberries. *See also* BERRY-FLAVORED SPIRITS; BLACK-BERRY-FLAVORED SPIRITS.

**blackberry-flavored spirits** *see* BERRY-FLAVORED SPIRITS; ECHTE KROATZBEERE

**black currant–flavored spirits** *see* BERRY-FLAVORED SPIRITS; CRÈME DE CASSIS; DRACULA'S POTION

### Black Hawk

1 1/2 oz. (3 Tbsp.) bourbon
1 1/2 oz. (3 Tbsp.) sloe gin
1 maraschino cherry

Stir liquid ingredients with ice. Strain into chilled glass; garnish with cherry.

### Blackjack

1 1/2 oz. (3 Tbsp.) brandy
1 1/2 oz. (3 Tbsp.) very cold strong coffee
3/4 oz. (1 1/2 Tbsp.) kirsch
lemon twist

Shake liquid ingredients with ice. Strain into chilled glass filled with ice cubes; drop in lemon twist.

### Black Magic

1 1/2 oz. (3 Tbsp.) vodka
3/4 oz. (1 1/2 Tbsp.) Kahlúa
1 dash (about 1/16 tsp.) fresh lemon juice
lemon twist

Stir liquid ingredients with ice. Strain into chilled glass filled with ice cubes; drop in lemon twist.

### Black Russian

2 oz. (1/4 cup) vodka
1 oz. (2 Tbsp.) Kahlúa or Tia Maria

Pour ingredients into chilled glass filled with ice cubes; stir well.

➤**White Russian** Float 1/2 oz. (1 Tbsp.) cream on top by slowly pouring it over the back (rounded) side of a spoon; don't mix.

**Blackthorn** The name of this cocktail comes from its primary ingredient, sloe gin, which is flavored with the fruit of the blackthorn tree, the sloe plum.

1 ½ oz. (3 Tbsp.) sloe gin
1 oz. (2 Tbsp.) sweet vermouth
2 dashes (about ⅛ tsp.) orange bitters
lemon twist

Stir liquid ingredients with ice. Strain into chilled glass; drop in lemon twist.

**Black Velvet** A "champagne in mourning" mixture created in 1861 to commemorate German-born Prince Albert, Queen Victoria's consort, who died of typhoid fever at age 42. Black Velvet is also known as *Bismark* and *Champagne Velvet*.

6 oz. (¾ cup) cold Guinness
6 oz. (¾ cup) cold dry champagne or other dry sparkling wine

Pour both ingredients at once into chilled glass; don't stir.

*I like to start off my day with a glass of champagne. I like to wind it up with champagne, too. To be frank, I also like a glass or two in between. It may not be the universal medicine . . . but it does you less harm than any other liquid.*

FERNAND POINT, FRENCH RESTAURATEUR

★ **Blameless Bull** *see* BLOODY BULL

**Blanche**

1 oz. (2 Tbsp.) Cointreau or Triple Sec
1 oz. (2 Tbsp.) anisette
1 oz. (2 Tbsp.) Triple Sec

Shake ingredients with ice; strain into chilled glass.

**Blarney Stone**

2 oz. (¼ cup) Irish whiskey
1 tsp. Triple Sec
1 tsp. anisette
½ tsp. maraschino liqueur
1 dash (about ¹⁄₁₆ tsp.) Angostura bitters
orange twist

Shake liquid ingredients with ice. Strain into chilled glass; drop in orange twist.

**blend** *n.* Shorthand in the liquor world for a potable created from two or more DISTILLATES. The term is most often used relating to BLENDED WHISK(E)Y.

## blended whisk(e)y *see* WHISKEY

## Blinker

4 oz. (¹/₂ cup) cold unsweetened grapefruit juice
2 oz. (¹/₄ cup) rye whiskey
¹/₂ oz. (1 Tbsp.) grenadine

Shake ingredients with ice. Strain into chilled glass filled with ice cubes.

## Blizzard

3 oz. (³/₈ cup) bourbon
1 oz. (2 Tbsp.) cranberry juice
¹/₂ oz. (1 Tbsp.) fresh lemon juice
1 Tbsp. sugar
¹/₂ cup crushed ice

Combine all ingredients in a blender. Cover and process at medium speed until smooth, about 20 seconds; pour into chilled glass.

**Blond Bombshell** A BLOODY MARY rendition we created one summer when yellow tomatoes were abundant and we wanted something different to serve at a party. Although we prefer gin in this drink, RUM or VODKA also work well.

MAKES 4 DRINKS

1 lb. yellow tomatoes, cored and quartered
6 oz. (³/₄ cup) gin
2 oz. (¹/₄ cup) fresh lemon or lime juice
1 oz. (2 Tbsp.) white-wine Worcestershire sauce
¹/₂ to 1 tsp. green Tabasco sauce
¹/₄ tsp. *each* celery salt and white pepper
8 ice cubes
4 yellow tomato wedges, optional

Place tomatoes in blender; cover and process at medium speed until puréed. Add remaining ingredients except tomato wedges.

Cover and process about 15 seconds, or until ice breaks into large chunks. Pour into chilled glasses; garnish with tomato wedges.

**blood alcohol concentration; BAC** A term referring to a person's intoxication level determined by the alcohol concentration in the blood. This concentration is ascertained by the weight of alcohol in a specific volume of blood. Factors computed to establish the blood alcohol concentration include the individual's weight and metabolism as well as the amount of alcohol ingested within a specific amount of time. Also called *BAL* (blood alcohol level). *See also* Blood Alcohol Chart, page 45.

### Blood and Sand

³/₄ oz. (1¹/₂ Tbsp.) Scotch
³/₄ oz. (1¹/₂ Tbsp.) cherry brandy
³/₄ oz. (1¹/₂ Tbsp.) sweet vermouth
³/₄ oz. (1¹/₂ Tbsp.) fresh orange juice

Shake ingredients with ice; strain into chilled glass.

### Bloodhound

1 oz. (2 Tbsp.) gin
¹/₂ oz. (1 Tbsp.) dry vermouth
¹/₂ oz. (1 Tbsp.) sweet vermouth
¹/₂ oz. (1 Tbsp.) strawberry liqueur
fresh strawberry

Shake liquid ingredients with ice. Strain into chilled glass; garnish with strawberry.

### Bloody Brain *see* BRAIN HEMORRHAGE

### Bloody Brew

1¹/₂ oz. (3 Tbsp.) vodka
4 oz. (¹/₂ cup) beer
4 oz. (¹/₂ cup) tomato juice
salt to taste
dill pickle spear

Combine all ingredients except pickle in chilled glass filled with ice cubes. Stir well; garnish with pickle.

### Bloody Bronx *see* BRONX COCKTAIL

## Bloody Bull

1½ oz. (3 Tbsp.) vodka
3 oz. (³⁄₈ cup) tomato or V-8 juice
3 oz. (³⁄₈ cup) beef broth, beef bouillon, or beef
    consommé
1½ tsp. fresh lemon juice
⅛ tsp. black pepper
3 ice cubes
lime wedge

Shake all ingredients except lime wedge with ice. Pour into chilled glass; garnish with lime.

★ **Blameless Bull** Omit vodka; increase tomato juice and beef broth to ½ cup each.

## Bloody Maria (Tequila Maria) *see* BLOODY MARY

---

*The human intellect owes its superiority over that of the lower animals in great measure to the stimulus which alcohol has given to imagination.*

SAMUEL BUTLER, ENGLISH NOVELIST

---

## Bloody Marie *see* BLOODY MARY

**Bloody Mary** Shortened to "Bloody" by those in a hurry, this immensely popular drink has undergone as many permutations as Michael Jackson's face. Its creation is attributed to bartender Pete Petiot, who was trying out vodka concoctions while working at Harry's New York Bar in Paris in 1921. Many insist that Petiot's original drink was a simple blend of tomato juice, vodka, and ice. In 1933, the Bloody Mary was introduced to the United States when Vincent Astor of the St. Regis Hotel brought Petiot to New York as head barman of the hotel's King Cole Bar. It's said that the name "Bloody Mary" (briefly changed by Astor to "Red Snapper" so as not to offend hotel patrons) alluded to Mary Tudor, queen of England and Ireland, for her bloody persecution of Protestants.

Today you'll find a variety of nontraditional Bloody Marys made with GIN, SLIVOVITZ, WHISKEY, and RUM. No matter how you make it, there's little doubt that even Petiot would have ever guessed that the result of his experimenting with vodka would produce, hands down, America's most popular alcoholic drink. *See also* BLOND BOMBSHELL; BLOODY BULL; BMW.

2 oz. ($^{1}/_{4}$ cup) vodka
4 oz. ($^{1}/_{2}$ cup) tomato juice
$^{1}/_{2}$ oz. (1 Tbsp.) fresh lemon juice
$^{1}/_{4}$ tsp. Worcestershire sauce
$^{1}/_{8}$ to $^{1}/_{4}$ tsp. Tabasco sauce
pinch of celery salt
pinch of black pepper
salt to taste
$^{1}/_{2}$ tsp. horseradish, optional
celery stalk with leaves or lime wedge

Shake all ingredients except celery or lime wedge with ice. Strain into chilled glass; garnish with celery or lime.

➤ **Bloody Maria** (*also called* **Tequila Maria**) Substitute tequila for the vodka.

➤ **Bloody Marie** Reduce lemon juice to 1 tsp.; add $^{1}/_{2}$ tsp. anisette.

✷ **Virgin Mary** (*also called* **Contrary Mary**) Omit liquor; add more tomato juice, if desired.

## Blue Angel

$^{1}/_{2}$ oz. (1 Tbsp.) blue curaçao
$^{1}/_{2}$ oz. (1 Tbsp.) brandy
$^{1}/_{2}$ oz. (1 Tbsp.) crème de vanille or parfait amour
$^{1}/_{2}$ oz. (1 Tbsp.) cream
1 dash (about $^{1}/_{16}$ tsp.) fresh lemon juice

Shake ingredients with ice; strain into chilled glass.

**Blue Blazer** A spectacular flaming drink created at San Francisco's El Dorado Saloon by bartender Jerry Thomas, known as the "professor" for his genius in creating new and inventive combinations. *See also* Hot Drinks, page 29.

3 oz. ($^{3}/_{8}$ cup) boiling water
1$^{1}/_{2}$ tsp. sugar or honey
3 oz. ($^{3}/_{8}$ cup) warm blended whiskey
lemon twist

Heat two mugs by filling with hot water and letting stand 3 minutes. In one mug, combine boiling water and sugar or honey, stirring to dissolve. Pour warm whiskey (*see* Flaming Drinks, page 29) into the other mug. Ignite whiskey and, while it's blazing, slowly and carefully pour whiskey into water. Slowly pour the mixture back and forth from one mug to the other until flame dies out. Drop in lemon twist.

### Blue Hawaiian

1 oz. (2 Tbsp.) light rum
1 oz. (2 Tbsp.) blue curaçao
1 oz. (2 Tbsp.) cream of coconut
2 oz. ($^1/_4$ cup) unsweetened pineapple juice
1 cup crushed ice
pineapple slice
maraschino cherry

Combine all liquid ingredients with ice in a blender. Cover and process at medium speed for 15 seconds. Pour into chilled glass; garnish with pineapple and cherry.

### Blue Margarita *see* MARGARITA

### Blue Monday

2 oz. ($^1/_4$ cup) vodka
1$^1/_2$ oz. (3 Tbsp.) blue curaçao
lemon twist

Shake liquid ingredients with cracked ice. Strain into chilled glass; drop in lemon twist.

### Blue Moon

1$^1/_2$ oz. (3 Tbsp.) gin
$^3/_4$ oz. (1$^1/_2$ Tbsp.) blue curaçao
lemon twist

Shake ingredients with cracked ice; strain into chilled glass and drop in lemon twist.

### Blue Shark

1$^1/_2$ oz. (3 Tbsp.) vodka
1$^1/_2$ oz. (3 Tbsp.) tequila
$^1/_2$ oz. (1 Tbsp.) blue curaçao

Shake ingredients with ice; strain into chilled cocktail glass or over ice cubes in an old-fashioned glass.

**blush wine** A generic name for American wines that are known as ROSÉS or *blanc de noirs,* particularly in France. Most blush wines are slightly sweet (although some are vinified DRY) and vary in color from pale pink to apricot to salmon. Such wines are typically made from red grapes, but the skins are left in contact with the juice for only 2 to 3 days after pressing, thereby transferring the barest amount of color to the wine. Some producers create blush wines by simply mixing red and white wines. Blush wines are known variously as *Blanc de Pinot Noir, Cabernet Blanc, White Zinfandel,* and *Pinot Vin Gris.*

**BMW** A combo made famous at Cindy Pawlcyn's Buckeye Roadhouse in Mill Valley, California, the BMW is a "BLOODY MARY with" a beer BACK.

---

*I envy people who drink—at least they know what to blame everything on.*

OSCAR LEVANT, AMERICAN COMPOSER, PIANIST

---

**Bobby Burns** A Scotch-based libation named after famed Scottish poet and songwriter Robert Burns of "Auld Lang Syne" and "Comin' Thro' the Rye" fame. It can also be made with equal amounts of sweet and dry vermouth.

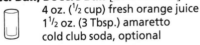

1 1/2 oz. (3 Tbsp.) Scotch
1 1/2 oz. (3 Tbsp.) sweet vermouth
1 1/2 tsp. Bénédictine
lemon twist

Stir liquid ingredients with ice; strain into chilled glass and drop in lemon twist.

**Bocci Ball; Boccie Ball** [BAHCH-ee]

4 oz. (1/2 cup) fresh orange juice
1 1/2 oz. (3 Tbsp.) amaretto
cold club soda, optional

Pour orange juice and amaretto into chilled glass filled with ice cubes. If desired, add a splash of club soda, stirring gently.

**bock beer** A full-bodied, slightly sweet, usually dark-colored German BEER with a malty (*see* MALT) flavor strongly evocative of HOPS. American bock beers are generally less bitter and lighter in both color and BODY than their German counterparts. Originally, bock beer was brewed in the fall, AGED through the winter, and celebrated in the spring at traditional Bavarian bock-beer festivals. There's no longer any seasonal connection to bock beer. **Eisbock** is a strong German "ice beer" that's lagered at such cold temperatures (32°F) that some of the water freezes. After the ice crystals are removed, the beer's ALCOHOL concentration is higher (about 13 percent). *See also* BEER.

**body** The perception of texture or weight of a wine or DISTILLED SPIRIT in the mouth, body is a combination of elements including alcohol, glycerol, and acid. A wine with a rich, complex, well-rounded, lingering flavor is considered full bodied; one that's watery or lacking in body is called light bodied or thin; a medium-bodied wine ranks in between. Not all wines strive to be full bodied, for example, those whose hallmark may be finesse, such as CHAMPAGNE. These same body characteristics also apply to distilled spirits—it's the mouth-feel combined with AROMA and taste that provide an enjoyable tasting experience.

**Boilermaker** This "he-man" combo dates back to the 1920s, when it was named after the brawny, tough men who repaired boilers and other heavy metal equipment.

1 1/2 oz. (3 Tbsp.) whiskey
8 oz. (1 cup) beer

Pour whiskey into a shot glass. Serve beer in a frosted mug or glass as a chaser. Or drop whiskey-filled shot glass into beer-filled mug.

**Bolero** [boh-LEH-roh]

1 1/2 oz. (3 Tbsp.) light rum
3/4 oz. (1 1/2 Tbsp.) apple brandy
1/2 tsp. sweet vermouth

Stir ingredients with ice; strain into chilled glass.

**Bombay Cocktail**

1 oz. (2 Tbsp.) brandy
1 oz. (2 Tbsp.) dry vermouth
1/2 oz. (1 Tbsp.) sweet vermouth
1/2 tsp. Cointreau
1 dash (about 1/16 tsp.) Pernod or other anise-flavored liqueur

Stir ingredients with ice; strain into chilled glass.

## Bombay Punch

MAKES ABOUT FORTY 6-OUNCE SERVINGS

juice of 12 lemons (about 2$^1/_4$ cups)
powdered sugar
1 quart brandy
1 quart dry sherry
4 oz. ($^1/_2$ cup) Triple Sec or Cointreau
4 oz. ($^1/_2$ cup) maraschino liqueur
2 quarts (8 cups) cold club soda
4 (750 ml) bottles cold dry champagne
fresh fruit slices

Pour lemon juice into a large punch bowl; add sugar to taste, stirring well to dissolve. Stir in brandy, sherry, Triple Sec, and maraschino liqueur; cover and refrigerate until ready to serve. Just before serving, add a block of ice (*see* Punch Bowl Ice, page 17); gently stir in club soda and champagne. Garnish with fruit slices.

## Bonnie Prince

1$^1/_2$ oz. (3 Tbsp.) gin
$^1/_2$ oz. (1 Tbsp.) Lillet blanc
$^1/_2$ tsp. Drambuie
orange twist

Shake liquid ingredients with ice. Strain into chilled glass; drop in orange twist.

## Boomerang

1$^1/_2$ oz. (3 Tbsp.) gin
1 oz. (2 Tbsp.) dry vermouth
1 dash (about $^1/_{16}$ tsp.) Angostura bitters
1 dash (about $^1/_{16}$ tsp.) maraschino liqueur
lemon twist

Stir liquid ingredients with ice. Strain into chilled glass; drop in lemon twist.

## Boonekamp bitters *see* BITTERS

*When I sell liquor, it's bootlegging. When my customers serve it on Lakeshore Drive, it's hospitality.*

AL CAPONE, AMERICAN GANGSTER

**bootleg; bootlegger** *n*. An illegally made alcoholic beverage. The word "bootleg" originated in seventeenth-century America, deriving from the practice of hiding a liquor bottle in the leg of one's boot. *See also* MOONSHINE. **bootleg** *v*. To make, sell, or transport alcoholic beverages (or cd's, tapes, etc.) illegally. A **bootlegger** is one who engages in bootlegging.

**booze** *n*. Slang for alcoholic beverages. **booze, to** *v*. Slang for drinking in excess. A **boozer** is one who tipples excessively—or **boozes it up,** or gets **boozed-up.**

**Bordeaux** [bohr-DOH] An area in southwest France considered by most wine enthusiasts as the world's greatest wine-producing region, not only because of the superiority of the wines, but also because of the large annual quantity (500 to 750 million bottles) produced. The wide popularity of Bordeaux wines in the United Kingdom (where they're called CLARETS) can be traced back to 1152 to 1453, a period when the English acquired this part of France through a royal marriage, then lost it in the Hundred Years' War.

The most celebrated of the Bordeaux wines are the reds, which comprise over 75 percent of the production. Nevertheless, the region's rich, sweet white wines from Sauternes are world renowned, and its DRY white wines from Graves have a serious following. The five main Bordeaux districts with individual AP-PELLATIONS are Pomerol, Saint-Emilion, Graves, Sauternes, and the MÉDOC (which has many individual appellations, including Margaux, Pauillac, Saint-Estèphe, and Saint-Julien). The primary red grape varieties used in Bordeaux are CABERNET SAUVIGNON, Cabernet Franc, MERLOT (with almost twice as much acreage as Cabernet Sauvignon), and occasionally Malbec and Petit Verdot. The primary white grapes are SAUVIGNON BLANC, Sémillon, and Muscadelle. Bordeaux winemakers typically blend grape varieties for their wines, as opposed to the prevailing practice in the United States of producing VARIETAL WINES. It should be noted, however, that American vintners are now making more blended wines, which are called MERITAGE wines when approved Bordeaux grape varieties are used. In general, the vineyards of Saint-Emilion and Pomerol are planted more heavily in Merlot and thus produce softer, more supple wines. On the other hand, the vineyards of

Médoc and Graves favor Cabernet varieties, which create more intense, TANNIC, and long-lived wines. Some of the more famous châteaux in Bordeaux are Haut-Brion, Lafite-Rothschild, Latour, Margaux, Mouton Rothschild, and Pétrus.

*No, Agnes, a Bordeaux is not a house of ill-repute.*
GEORGE BAIN, CANADIAN AUTHOR

### Bosom Caresser Some things are better left unsaid.
1 ¹/₂ oz. (3 Tbsp.) brandy
³/₄ oz. (1 ¹/₂ Tbsp.) Madeira
¹/₂ oz. (1 Tbsp.) Triple Sec
1 tsp. grenadine
1 egg yolk, optional

Vigorously shake ingredients with ice; strain into chilled glass.

### Boston Cocktail
1 ¹/₂ oz. (3 Tbsp.) gin
1 ¹/₂ oz. (3 Tbsp.) apricot brandy
1 ¹/₂ tsp. grenadine
1 tsp. fresh lemon juice
lemon twist

Shake liquid ingredients with ice. Strain into chilled glass; drop in lemon twist.

### Boston Cooler
2 oz. (¹/₄ cup) light rum
¹/₂ oz. (1 Tbsp.) fresh lemon juice
1 tsp. powdered sugar
cold club soda
lemon twist

Shake rum, lemon juice, and sugar with ice. Strain into chilled glass over ice cubes. Top with club soda, stirring gently; drop in lemon twist.

### Boston Sidecar *see* SIDECAR

### Boston Sour *see* SOUR

### bottled by *see* WINE LABEL TERMS

**Bottled-in-Bond**   A phrase sometimes used on labels of WHISKEY (and other DISTILLED SPIRITS). It refers to the Bottled in Bond Act of 1894, which allows producers to bottle and store their distilled spirits in U.S. Treasury Department–bonded warehouses without paying excise taxes on them until they're shipped to the retailer. The conditions necessary for such a designation include: The whiskey must be produced at one plant during a single distilling season, be 100 PROOF (50 percent alcohol), and AGED for at least 4 years. Contrary to some beliefs, such labeling does not ensure a high degree of quality.

**bottle sizes** *see* Sizes of Wine and Spirit Bottles, page 22

**bouquet** *see* AROMA

**bourbon**   This all-American corn-based WHISKEY gets its name from Bourbon County, Kentucky, the primary producer and shipper during the late 1700s and the 1800s. All bourbon is based on MASH — grain that's ground or crushed before being steeped in hot water and fermented (*see* FERMENTATION). There are two types of mash used for bourbon: **sweet mash,** which starts the fermentation process from scratch with fresh yeast; and **sour mash,** which combines a new batch of sweet mash with a portion of the residue from the previous fermentation, a technique similar to that used in making sourdough bread. The resulting liquor is often labeled **sour-mash bourbon.**

   **Straight bourbon** is distilled from a mash of at least 51 percent but not more than 79 percent corn; over 80 percent and it must be labeled **corn whiskey.** Straight bourbon must also be AGED in new, charred-oak barrels for a minimum of 2 years (although most bourbons are aged for 4 years or more), must not be over 160 PROOF (80 percent alcohol), and can only use water to reduce the alcohol level. Most bourbons are 80 proof, although some of the newer high-end examples (sometimes called small-batch or single-barrel bourbons) are considerably higher.

   **Single-barrel bourbon,** now being produced to compete with SINGLE-MALT SCOTCHES, comes from a single barrel; the number of the barrel is typically printed on the label. **Small-batch bourbon** generally refers to bourbon blended from selected barrels. The resulting spirit is of high quality, although there's no specific requirement that only small batches be produced. Jim Beam Brands, Inc. (now called James B. Beam Distilling Co.) created the expression in the 1980s to describe their process of blending whiskeys of different maturity levels.

Bourbon can legally be made in any part of the United States, but most of it comes from Kentucky, the state where it was first produced. Popular brands include A.H. Hirsch, Ancient Age, Baker's, Blanton's, Booker's, Elijah Craig, I.W. Harper, Jim Beam, Knob Creek, Maker's Mark, Old Charter, Old Crow, Old Fitzgerald, Old Forester, Old Grand Dad, and Wild Turkey. *See also* TENNESSEE WHISKEY.

**Bourbon à la Crème** Combining the ingredients of this drink in advance and letting them stand allows the perfumy flavor of the vanilla bean to permeate the mixture. If you're the impatient sort, use vanilla extract—the pure, not the artificial, version, please. Whatever you do, don't throw out the vanilla bean after using it. Simply rinse it off, let it dry thoroughly, and wrap it tightly for future use.

2 oz. (¼ cup) bourbon
1 oz. (2 Tbsp.) dark crème de cacao
1 to 2 vanilla beans or ¼ to ½ tsp. pure vanilla extract

Combine all ingredients in shaker; cover and refrigerate at least 1 hour. Add ice and shake well; strain into chilled glass.

**Bourbon Collins** *see* TOM COLLINS

**Bourbon Crusta** *see* CRUSTA

**Bourbon Daisy** *see* DAISY

**Bourbon Milk Punch** *see* MILK PUNCH

> *ℬourbon does for me what the
> piece of cake did for Proust.*
> WALKER PERCY, AMERICAN WRITER

**Bourbon Rickey** *see* RICKEY

**Bourbon Sling** *see* SLING

**Bourbon Stinger** *see* STINGER

**bowl** Akin to PUNCH, a bowl contains liquor, wine, spices and, sometimes, fruit. Bowl ingredients are typically combined ahead of time so their flavors can "marry"; occasionally they're heated, as with the WASSAIL BOWL. An effervescent liquid (such as SPARKLING WINE or water, GINGER ALE, etc.) is sometimes added just before serving.

**bracer** In cocktail parlance, a bracer is a stimulating—usually alcoholic—drink.

### Brain Hemorrhage *Also called* Bloody Brain.

1 oz. (2 Tbsp.) peach schnapps
$^1/_2$ oz. (1 Tbsp.) Irish cream liqueur
2 to 3 drops grenadine

Pour first 2 ingredients into glass; top with grenadine.

**Branca Menta** [BRAHNG-kuh MAYN-tah] A bitter Italian LIQUEUR flavored with peppermint. *See also* MINT-FLAVORED SPIRITS.

**branch water** A term first used in the 1800s referring to pure, clean water from a tiny stream, which was called a "branch." An order for "bourbon and branch" is a nostalgic request for BOURBON and water.

### Brandied Madeira

1 oz. (2 Tbsp.) brandy
1 oz. (2 Tbsp.) Madeira
$^1/_2$ oz. (1 Tbsp.) dry vermouth
lemon twist

Stir liquid ingredients with ice. Strain into chilled glass over ice cubes; drop in lemon twist.

### Brandied Port

1 oz. (2 Tbsp.) brandy
1 oz. (2 Tbsp.) tawny port
$^1/_2$ oz. (1 Tbsp.) fresh lemon juice
$1^1/_2$ tsp. maraschino liqueur
orange slice

Shake liquid ingredients with ice. Strain into chilled glass over ice cubes; garnish with orange slice.

**brandy** A liquor distilled from wine or other FERMENTED fruit juice. The name "brandy" comes from the Dutch *brandewijn* ("burned [distilled] wine"), referring to the technique of heating the wine during DISTILLATION. A number of subcategories fall under the broad definition of brandy, including fruit brandy, GRAPPA, MARC, POMACE, and EAU-DE-VIE (*eau-de-vie de vin* is French for brandy). *Eaux-de-vie* and fruit brandies can be made from almost any fruit, including apples, apricots, blackberries, cherries, elderberries, pears, plums, raspberries, and strawberries. Brandies made from apples and grapes are generally AGED in wood, which contributes flavor and color. Those made from other fruits are less likely to be aged in this fashion and are typically colorless.

The finest brandies traditionally come from COGNAC, followed by those from ARMAGNAC—both in southwestern France. Spain also produces some top-quality brandies, such as the Brandy de Jerez Solera Gran Reservas; in the United States some wonderful examples come from several producers, including Bonny Doon, Carneros Alambic, Creekside Vineyards, and Germain-Robin. *See also* AGUARDENTE; ALIZIERGEIST; APPLE-JACK; APRICOT BRANDY; AQUA VITAE; ASBACH URALT; BLACK-BERRY BRANDY; CACHAÇA; CALVADOS; CHERRY BRANDY; KIRSCH; METAXA; PEACH BRANDY; PISCO; RAKI; SLIVOVITZ.

*Nothing sets a person up more than having something turn out just the way it's supposed to be, like falling into a Swiss snowdrift and seeing a big dog come up with a little cask of brandy round its neck.*

CLAUD COCKBURN, BRITISH AUTHOR, JOURNALIST

**Brandy Alexander** *see* ALEXANDER

**Brandy Buck** *see* BUCK

**Brandy Cassis**

1½ oz. (3 Tbsp.) brandy
1 oz. (2 Tbsp.) fresh lemon juice
½ oz. (1 Tbsp.) crème de cassis
lemon twist

Shake liquid ingredients with ice. Strain into chilled glass; drop in lemon twist.

**Brandy Cobbler** *see* COBBLER

**Brandy Collins** *see* TOM COLLINS

**Brandy Crusta** *see* CRUSTA

**Brandy Daisy** *see* DAISY

**Brandy Eggnog** *see* EGGNOG

**Brandy Fix** *see* FIX

**Brandy Gump**

1 1/2 oz. (3 Tbsp.) brandy
1/2 oz. (1 Tbsp.) fresh lemon juice
1/2 tsp. grenadine

Shake ingredients with ice; strain into chilled glass.

**Brandy Manhattan** *see* MANHATTAN

**Brandy Milk Punch** *see* MILK PUNCH

**Brandy Old-Fashioned** *see* OLD-FASHIONED

*Mixing brandy and water spoils two good things.*

CHARLES LAMB, ENGLISH WRITER

**Brandy Rickey** *see* RICKEY

**Brandy Sangaree** *see* SANGAREE

**Brandy Shrub** *see* SHRUB

**Brandy Sling** *see* SLING

**Brandy Smash** *see* SMASH

**brandy snifter** *see* Glassware, page 8

**Brandy Sour** *see* SOUR

### Brass Monkey

4 oz. (½ cup) fresh orange juice
¾ oz. (1½ Tbsp.) vodka
½ oz. (1 Tbsp.) light rum
½ oz. (1 Tbsp.) Galliano, optional

Pour first 3 ingredients into a chilled glass filled with ice; stir well. If desired, float Galliano on top by slowly pouring it over the back (rounded) side of a spoon; don't mix.

### Brave Bull

1½ oz. (3 Tbsp.) tequila
1 oz. (2 Tbsp.) Kahlúa or Tia Maria
lemon twist

Pour liquid ingredients into chilled glass filled with ice cubes. Stir well; drop in lemon twist.

### Brazil Cocktail

1½ oz. (3 Tbsp.) dry vermouth
1½ oz. (3 Tbsp.) dry sherry
1 dash (about ¹⁄₁₆ tsp.) Angostura bitters
1 dash (about ¹⁄₁₆ tsp.) Pernod or other anise-flavored liqueur
lemon twist

Stir liquid ingredients with ice. Strain into chilled glass; drop in lemon twist.

### Bronx Cheer

2 oz. (¼ cup) apricot brandy
6 to 8 oz. (¾ to 1 cup) raspberry soda
orange twist
2 to 3 fresh raspberries

Pour brandy into chilled glass filled with ice cubes. Top with soda, stirring gently. Drop in orange twist and raspberries.

### Bronx Cocktail

1½ oz. (3 Tbsp.) gin
¾ oz. (1½ Tbsp.) fresh orange juice
½ oz. (1 Tbsp.) dry vermouth
½ oz. (1 Tbsp.) sweet vermouth
orange slice

Shake liquid ingredients with ice; strain into chilled cocktail glass or serve over ice in an old-fashioned glass. Garnish with orange slice.

➤ **Bloody Bronx** Substitute blood-orange juice for regular orange juice.

➤ **Bronx Silver** Add 1 egg white; shake vigorously.

➤ **Dry Bronx Cocktail** Substitute an additional $\frac{1}{2}$ oz. dry vermouth for the sweet vermouth.

➤ **Golden Bronx** Add 1 egg yolk; shake vigorously.

**Bronx Silver** *see* BRONX COCKTAIL

### Bronx Terrace Cocktail

1$\frac{1}{2}$ oz. (3 Tbsp.) gin
$\frac{3}{4}$ oz. (1$\frac{1}{2}$ Tbsp.) fresh lime juice
$\frac{1}{2}$ oz. (1 Tbsp.) dry vermouth
maraschino cherry

Shake liquid ingredients with ice. Strain into chilled glass; garnish with cherry.

**brown ale** *see* ALE

### Brown Cocktail

1 oz. (2 Tbsp.) light rum
1 oz. (2 Tbsp.) gin
$\frac{3}{4}$ oz. (1$\frac{1}{2}$ Tbsp.) dry vermouth

Stir ingredients with ice; strain into chilled glass.

**brut** [BROOT] A term applied to the driest (*see* DRY) CHAMPAGNE. Brut champagnes are less sweet than those labeled "extra dry."

*And when you wanna loosen up rather than introspect or perceive like a sonafagun, booze has it over dope going away. Not just the way the Beach Boys have it over Tommy James, but the way God has it over an apartment house.*

RICHARD MELTZER, AMERICAN WRITER

**Buck** Dating back to the 1890s, a buck is essentially a RICKEY made with GINGER ALE. Although traditionally made with gin, this sugarless drink can be made with almost any liquor plus lemon or lime juice. The buck's distinguishing feature is that, after being squeezed to extract the juice, the citrus shell is traditionally put in the glass.

### Gin Buck *(the original)*

juice of ¼ to ⅓ lemon (about 1 Tbsp.)
1½ oz. (3 Tbsp.) gin
cold ginger ale
lemon slice

Squeeze lemon juice into chilled glass filled with ice cubes; drop in lemon shell, if desired. Add gin; top with ginger ale, stirring gently. Garnish with lemon slice.

➤ **Apple Buck** Substitute apple brandy for the gin; add a slice or spear of candied ginger.

➤ **Brandy Buck** Substitute brandy for the gin, add 1½ tsp. white crème de menthe; garnish with 3 seedless grapes.

➤ **Greek Buck** Substitute Metaxa for the gin, add 1 tsp. ouzo; garnish with lemon slice.

➤ **New Orleans Buck** Substitute 2 Tbsp. orange juice plus 1 tablespoon fresh lime juice for the lemon juice; substitute rum for the gin. Garnish with lime slice.

➤ **Orange Buck** Substitute 2 Tbsp. orange juice plus 1 tablespoon fresh lime juice for the lemon juice. Garnish with orange slice.

➤ **Peach Buck** Substitute vodka for the gin and add 1½ Tbsp. peach brandy. Garnish with peach slice.

**Buck's Fizz** This libation is neither a true BUCK nor a FIZZ, but refreshing nevertheless. Some Buck's Fizz recipes simply combine orange juice and champagne, à la MIMOSA. This version was created in 1921 by John McGarry, a bartender at London's Buck's Club.

1 tsp. grenadine
about 1½ oz. (3 Tbsp.) cold fresh orange juice
about 6 oz. (¾ cup) cold dry champagne
orange slice

Pour grenadine and orange juice into chilled glass. Gently add champagne; garnish with orange slice. May also be served in a collins glass over ice.

**Buckshot** Labeled the "Original Wild West Liqueur," this heady, amber-colored LIQUEUR gets its snap from chile peppers. It has a spicy peach flavor and is often used for SHOOTERS.

### Bulldog Cocktail

1 1/2 oz. (3 Tbsp.) cherry brandy
3/4 oz. (1 1/2 Tbsp.) light rum
2 tsp. fresh lime juice

Shake ingredients with ice; strain into chilled glass.

### Bulldog Highball *See also* HIGHBALL.

1 1/2 oz. (3 Tbsp.) gin
1 1/2 oz. (3 Tbsp.) fresh orange juice
cold ginger ale

Put 2 to 3 ice cubes in chilled glass. Add gin and orange juice; top with ginger ale, stirring gently.

### Bullfrog

1 1/2 oz. (3 Tbsp.) vodka
2 tsp. Triple Sec
6 oz. (3/4 cup) lemonade or limeade
lemon or lime slice

Pour vodka, Triple Sec, and lemon- or limeade into chilled glass filled with ice cubes; stir well. Garnish with citrus slice.

**Bullshot** Appreciated by many as a tasty "hair of the dog" libation for the morning after, the Bullshot is equally enjoyable even before the dog bites.

2 oz. (1/4 cup) vodka or gin
4 oz. (1/2 cup) cold beef bouillon
1 tsp. fresh lemon juice
1/2 tsp. Worcestershire sauce
2 dashes (about 1/8 tsp.) Tabasco sauce, optional
salt and freshly ground pepper
lemon slice

Pour first 4 ingredients (and Tabasco sauce, if desired) into chilled glass filled with ice. Salt and pepper to taste; stir well. Garnish with lemon slice.

➤ **Cock 'n' Bull Shot** Substitute 2 oz. (¼ cup) cold chicken bouillon for 2 oz. of the beef bouillon.

➤ **Hot Bullshot** In a small saucepan, combine all ingredients except vodka and lemon slice; bring to a boil. Pour into heated mug; add vodka and lemon garnish. *See also* Hot Drinks, page 29.

★ **Naked Bullshot** Omit liquor; increase bouillon to ⅔ cup.

## Bull's Milk

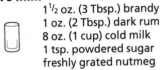

1½ oz. (3 Tbsp.) brandy
1 oz. (2 Tbsp.) dark rum
8 oz. (1 cup) cold milk
1 tsp. powdered sugar
freshly grated nutmeg

Shake all ingredients except nutmeg with ice. Strain into chilled glass; sprinkle with nutmeg.

**Burgundy** [BER-gun-dee] 1. One of the world's most famous wine-growing areas, located in eastern France, southeast of Paris. The Burgundy region has established a reputation over centuries for fine wines, which vary considerably from region to region. Burgundy, known in France as *Bourgogne,* consists of five basic regions—Chablis, the Côte d'Or (divided into Côte de Beaune and Côte de Nuits), the Côte Chalonnaise, the Mâconnais, and Beaujolais. The focus in Burgundy is on three grape varieties: Pinot Noir and Gamay for red wines, Chardonnay for whites. Although the PINOT NOIR and CHARDONNAY wines get most of the attention, there are more Gamay-based wines produced in Beaujolais than in all of Burgundy. Among the notable wines from this region are CHABLIS, Fleurie, Gevrey-Chambertin, Meursault, Montagny, and Pouilly-Fuissé, 2. Burgundy is also a generic name for ordinary, inexpensive red wines made outside of France in countries like Australia, South Africa, and the United States. Although many of the bulk producers in these countries are starting to call them "red table wine," the word "Burgundy" still appears on some wine bottle labels.

### Bushranger

1½ oz. (3 Tbsp.) Dubonnet rouge
1½ oz. (3 Tbsp.) light rum
2 dashes (about ⅛ tsp.) Angostura bitters
lemon twist

Shake liquid ingredients with ice. Strain into chilled glass; garnish with lemon twist.

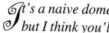

*It's a naive domestic Burgundy without any breeding, but I think you'll be amused by its presumption.*

JAMES THURBER, AMERICAN HUMORIST AND WRITER

**Bushwhacker** Every bartender seems to have his/her own (sometimes distinctly different) recipe for this libation. The following is one of the most popular.

2 oz. (¼ cup) half & half
1½ oz. (3 Tbsp.) Kahlúa or Tia Maria
1½ oz. (3 Tbsp.) cream of coconut
¾ oz. (1½ Tbsp.) light rum
½ oz. (1 Tbsp.) dark crème de cacao
1 cup crushed ice

Combine all ingredients in a blender. Cover and process at medium speed until smooth, about 15 seconds. Pour into chilled glass.

**butler's friend** *see* Bar Equipment (Corkscrews), page 4

**Buttery Nipple** This SHOOTER can be found in many forms, and it is called by several names—*Butterball* and *Buttery Guns*, to cite just two. The key ingredients—butterscotch schnapps and Irish cream liqueur—are integral to the mix, however, no matter what else is added.

½ oz. (1 Tbsp.) Irish cream liqueur
½ oz. (1 Tbsp.) butterscotch schnapps
½ oz. (1 Tbsp.) vodka

Pour ingredients into glass.

**B.V.D.** No, the initials don't stand for a brand of men's under-wear, but for the original combination of liquors, purportedly a mixture of equal parts BRANDY, VERMOUTH, and DUBON-NET. Order a B.V.D. today and you're more likely to get this concoction, which might be more appropriately be called an R.V.G.

 ¾ oz. (1½ Tbsp.) light rum
 ¾ oz. (1½ Tbsp.) dry vermouth
 ¾ oz. (1½ Tbsp.) gin

Stir ingredients with ice; strain into chilled glass.

**Byrrh** [BIHR] A dry, slightly bitter French APÉRITIF with a touch of orange.

### Byrrh Cassis

 2 oz. (¼ cup) Byrrh
 1 oz. (2 Tbsp.) crème de cassis
 cold club soda

 Mix Byrrh and cassis in chilled wineglass. Add ice cubes; top with club soda, stirring gently.

### Byrrh Cocktail

 1 oz. (2 Tbsp.) Byrrh
 1 oz. (2 Tbsp.) dry vermouth
 1 oz. (2 Tbsp.) rye whiskey

Shake ingredients with ice; strain into chilled glass.

### Cabaret [ka-buh-RAY]

 1½ oz. (3 Tbsp.) gin
 1½ oz. (3 Tbsp.) Dubonnet rouge
 4 dashes (about ¼ tsp.) Angostura bitters
 4 dashes (about ¼ tsp.) Pernod or other anise-flavored
  liqueur
 maraschino cherry

Shake all ingredients except cherry with ice. Strain into chilled glass; garnish with cherry.

*Never refuse wine. It is an odd but universally held opinion that anyone who doesn't drink must be an alcoholic.*

P. J. O'ROURKE, AMERICAN WIT, AUTHOR

**Cabernet Sauvignon** [ka-behr-NAY soh-vihn-YOHN; *Fr.* kah-bair-NAY soh-vee-NYAWN] This most successful and popular of the top-quality red-wine grapes is the basis for most of California's superb red wines, and it is the primary grape of the majority of the top vineyards in Bordeaux's Médoc and Graves districts. Cabernet Sauvignon wines are renowned for their intensely fruity flavor (variously described as cherry, black cherry, black currant [cassis], and raspberry), structure, complexity, and longevity. In BORDEAUX, Cabernet Sauvignon grapes are typically blended with one or more other grape varieties, including MERLOT, Cabernet Franc, Petit Verdot, or Malbec. In California these wines are typically made with 100 percent Cabernet Sauvignon grapes, although some American vintners have begun blending in other grapes, as they do in Bordeaux. Among the legion of fine Cabernet Sauvignon–based wines made throughout the world are: France's Château Lafite-Rothschild, Château Latour, Château Mouton-Rothschild, and Château Margaux; California's Beaulieu Vineyards, Caymus Vineyards, Heitz Wine Cellars, and Robert Mondavi Winery.

**Cablegram**

2 oz. (¼ cup) blended whiskey
½ oz. (1 Tbsp.) fresh lemon juice
1 tsp. powdered sugar
ginger ale

Mix first 3 ingredients in chilled glass filled with ice cubes. Top with ginger ale, stirring gently.

**Cachaça** [kah-SHAH-sah] A Brazilian BRANDY made with sugarcane; also called *pinga* (PEEN-gah). Though there are hundreds of different cachaças made in Brazil, in the United States the most common brands are Cachaça de Caricé, Néga Fulô, and Pitù. The CAIPIRINHA is Brazil's most popular cachaça-based drink.

**Cactus Juice** A MARGARITA-flavored LIQUEUR made with 100 percent agave TEQUILLA, TRIPLE SEC, and various herbal flavorings.

**Cádiz** [ka-DIHZ]

³/₄ oz. (1¹/₂ Tbsp.) blackberry brandy
³/₄ oz. (1¹/₂ Tbsp.) dry sherry
¹/₂ oz. (1 Tbsp.) Triple Sec
¹/₂ oz. (1 Tbsp.) cream

Shake ingredients with ice; strain into chilled glass filled with ice cubes.

**Café  Amaretto**  [ka-FAY  am-ah-REHT-toh]  *See  also*  Hot Drinks, page 29.

1 oz. (2 Tbsp.) amaretto
¹/₂ oz. (1 Tbsp.) brandy, optional
about 6 oz. (³/₄ cup) hot coffee
dollop of whipped cream

Pour amaretto and brandy (if desired) into warmed mug. Stir in coffee; top with whipped cream.

---

*A guy walks into his doctor and says, "Doc, you gotta help me, I can't remember anything!" The doc asks, "How long have you had this problem?" The guys says, "What problem?"*

---

**Café Diablo (Diable)** [ka-FAY dee-AH-blow (dee-AH-BLAY)] *See also* Hot Drinks, page 29.

1 oz. (2 Tbsp.) cognac
¹/₂ oz. (1 Tbsp.) Cointreau
2 whole cloves
One 3-inch strip orange peel
One 3-inch strip lemon peel
about 6 ounces hot coffee

In a small saucepan over medium heat, combine all ingredients except coffee; stir often while mixture heats. (Or combine ingredients in an 8-oz. glass measuring cup; microwave just until warm.) While liquor mixture is heating, pour coffee into warmed mug. Just when bubbles begin to form around edge of pan, use a long-handled match to ignite alcohol mixture (see Flaming Drinks, page 29). Pour it flaming into coffee.

### Café Romano [ka-FAY roh-MAH-noh]

1 oz. (2 Tbsp.) Sambuca
1 oz. (2 Tbsp.) Kahlúa or Tia Maria
1 oz. (2 Tbsp.) cream

Shake ingredients with ice; strain into chilled glass.

### Café Royale [ka-FAY roy-AHL] *See also* Hot Drinks, page 29.

1 sugar cube
$^1/_2$ oz. (1 Tbsp.) brandy
about 8 oz. very hot coffee
1 Tbsp. cream, optional

Soak the sugar cube in the brandy. Pour the coffee into a mug or cup. Set the brandy-filled spoon across the top of the mug so that the bowl of the spoon rests over the hot coffee. Allow the brandy to warm for 1 to 2 minutes. Ignite the brandy-soaked sugar cube (*see* Flaming Drinks, page 29). When the flame burns out, stir the brandied sugar cube into the coffee. If desired, float the cream on top by slowly pouring it over the back (rounded) side of a spoon; don't mix.

---

*. . . cocktail parties . . . are an anathema. They are expensive. They are dull. They are good for a time, like a dry Martini, and like that all-demanding drink they can lift you high and then drop you hideously into a slough of boredom, morbidity, and indigestion.*

M.F.K. FISHER, AMERICAN AUTHOR

---

### Caipirinha [ki-pee-REEN-yah] Brazilian for "drink of farmers."

Brazil's most popular spirited potable, the Caipirinha is based on that country's potent sugarcane BRANDY, CACHAÇA. Be prepared for a jolt! Substituting VODKA makes it a *Caipiroska;* RUM makes it a *Caipirissima.*

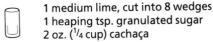

1 medium lime, cut into 8 wedges
1 heaping tsp. granulated sugar
2 oz. (¼ cup) cachaça

Place lime wedges, peel side down, in chilled glass. Add sugar; use a wooden pestle or spoon to crush lime wedges, squeezing out juice and blending in sugar. Fill glass with crushed ice; add cachaça and stir well.

### Cajun Martini *see* MARTINI

**Calisay** [KAH-lee-say] Made in Barcelona, Spain, Calisay is a slightly bitter, herbal LIQUEUR used both as an APÉRITIF and an after-dinner drink.

### Calisay Cocktail

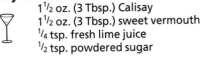

1½ oz. (3 Tbsp.) Calisay
1½ oz. (3 Tbsp.) sweet vermouth
¼ tsp. fresh lime juice
½ tsp. powdered sugar

Shake ingredients with ice; strain into chilled glass.

**call drink** Bartender lingo for a drink ordered with specific ingredients, such as a "Belvedere (VODKA) Collins" rather than the generic "vodka Collins."

**calories in alcohol** *see* Calories Count! page 42

**Calvados** [KAL-vah-dohs; kal-vah-DOHS] A specialty of France's Normandy region, this dry apple BRANDY is considered one of the world's greatest. Calvados is double-distilled in a pot still (*see* DISTILLATION), then AGED in Limousin oak for a minimum of 1 year; some is aged for 40 years. The best Calvados comes from the *Pays d'Auge appellation contrôlée,* a designation that is noted on the label. In the United States, apple brandy is called APPLEJACK. *See also* APPLE-FLAVORED SPIRITS.

**Campari** [kahm-PAH-ree] A popular bitter APÉRITIF created in the nineteenth century in Milan, Italy, by restaurateur Gaspare Campari. This bright red spirit is made with a variety of herbs and fruits and AGED in oak. Regular Campari has an astringent, bittersweet flavor; sweet Campari is also available. Campari is usually taken over ice with a spritz of CLUB SODA.

### Campari Cooler

2 oz. ($^{1}/_4$ cup) fresh orange juice
1$^{1}/_2$ oz. (3 Tbsp.) Campari
2 tsp. raspberry syrup
cold club soda
long spiral of orange peel

Pour first 3 ingredients into chilled glass filled with ice cubes; stir well. Top with club soda, stirring gently. Arrange orange spiral so half of it is inside the glass and half hangs over the rim.

### Canadian Apple

1$^{1}/_2$ oz. (3 Tbsp.) Canadian whisky
$^{1}/_2$ oz. (1 Tbsp.) apple brandy
1 tsp. fresh lemon juice
1 tsp. powdered sugar
1 to 2 pinches of ground cinnamon

Shake all ingredients with ice. Strain into chilled glass over ice cubes.

### Canadian Cherry

1$^{1}/_2$ oz. (3 Tbsp.) Canadian whisky
$^{1}/_2$ oz. (1 Tbsp.) cherry brandy
1$^{1}/_2$ tsp. fresh lemon juice
1$^{1}/_2$ tsp. fresh orange juice

Frost rim of chilled glass by moistening with cherry brandy, then dipping rim into granulated sugar. Shake ingredients with ice; strain into glass over ice cubes.

### Canadian Cocktail

1$^{1}/_2$ oz. (3 Tbsp.) Canadian whisky
1$^{1}/_2$ tsp. Triple Sec
1 dash (about $^{1}/_{16}$ tsp.) Angostura bitters
1 tsp. sugar

Shake ingredients with ice; strain into chilled glass.

### Canadian Old-Fashioned *see* OLD-FASHIONED

### Canadian Pineapple

1$^{1}/_2$ oz. (3 Tbsp.) Canadian whisky
2 tsp. unsweetened pineapple juice
2 tsp. fresh lemon juice

1 tsp. maraschino liqueur
1 pineapple spear or ½ pineapple slice

Shake liquid ingredients with ice. Strain into chilled glass; garnish with pineapple spear or slice.

---

*hampagne's funny stuff. I'm used to whiskey. Whiskey is a slap on the back, and champagne's a heavy mist before my eyes.*

JIMMY STEWART, AMERICAN ACTOR (IN THE FILM *THE PHILADELPHIA STORY*)

---

**Canadian whisky** A BLENDED WHISKY produced in Canada and made from rye, corn, barley (malted and unmalted), and/or wheat. It's wood aged a minimum of 3 years, with an average of 4 to 6 years. The casks used for AGING can be new, or previously used for BOURBON, BRANDY, or SHERRY, all of which lend their individual characteristics. Some producers create their blends before aging, while others age the individual DISTILLATES first, then blend the whiskies after aging. Canadian whisky is smoother and lighter (although some think not as rich) than its cousins RYE and Bourbon. Dropping the *e* from the word "whiskey" is traditionally British and is used in the Canadian and Scottish spelling of the word.

**Cape Codder**

2 oz. (¼ cup) vodka
4 to 6 oz. (½ to ¾ cup) cranberry juice
½ oz. (1 Tbsp.) fresh lime juice
lime wedge

Shake liquid ingredients with ice. Strain into chilled glass over ice cubes; garnish with lime wedge.

➤ **Variation** Use only 4 oz. (½ cup) cranberry juice; top with club soda, stirring gently.

**Capri** [ka-PREE]

1 oz. (2 Tbsp.) crème de cacao
1 oz. (2 Tbsp.) crème de banane
¾ oz. (1½ Tbsp.) cream

Shake ingredients with cracked ice; strain into chilled glass over ice cubes.

**Caprinatura** [kah-pree-nah-TOOR-ah] A lemon-flavored, sweetly tart Italian LIQUEUR with a milky yellow-green color. Caprinatura is often served over ice with club soda. *See also* CITRUS-FLAVORED SPIRITS; LEMON-FLAVORED SPIRITS.

**Capucello** [kah-poo-CHEL-loh] A creamy Dutch LIQUEUR with a nutty, coffeelike flavor, intended to be reminiscent of cappuccino. SEE ALSO COFFEE-FLAVORED SPIRITS.

**Cara Sposa** [KAH-rah SPOH-sah]

1 oz. (2 Tbsp.) Kahlúa or Tia Maria
1 oz. (2 Tbsp.) Triple Sec
$^{1}/_{2}$ oz. (1 Tbsp.) cream
$^{1}/_{2}$ cup cracked ice

Combine all ingredients in a blender. Cover and process at medium speed until smooth, about 15 seconds. Pour into chilled glass.

**carbonated water** *see* CLUB SODA

*drink no more than a sponge.*
FRANÇOIS RABELAIS, FRENCH HUMANIST, WRITER

**Cardinal, The** *see* BISHOP, THE

**Caribbean Champagne** [kair-uh-BEE-uhn; kuh-RIHB-bee-uhn]

$^{1}/_{2}$ tsp. light rum
$^{1}/_{2}$ tsp. crème de banane
1 to 2 dashes ($^{1}/_{16}$ to $^{1}/_{8}$ tsp.) orange bitters
about 4 oz. ($^{1}/_{2}$ cup) cold dry champagne
banana slice

Pour first 3 ingredients into chilled glass. Slowly top with champagne, stirring gently if necessary. Garnish with banana slice.

**Carroll Cocktail**

$1^{1}/_{2}$ oz. (3 Tbsp.) brandy
$^{3}/_{4}$ oz. ($1^{1}/_{2}$ Tbsp.) sweet vermouth
maraschino cherry

Stir liquid ingredients with ice. Strain into chilled glass; garnish with cherry.

**Caruso** [kuh-ROO-soh]

> 1 1/2 oz. (3 Tbsp.) gin
> 1 oz. (2 Tbsp.) dry vermouth
> 1/2 oz. (1 Tbsp.) green crème de menthe

Stir ingredients with ice; strain into chilled glass.

**Casablanca** [kas-uh-BLANG-kuh; kah-suh-BLAHNG-kuh]

> 2 oz. (1/4 cup) light rum
> 1 1/2 tsp. Triple Sec
> 1 1/2 tsp. maraschino liqueur
> 1 1/2 tsp. fresh lime juice

Shake ingredients with ice; strain into chilled glass.

**Casino** [ka-SEE-noh]

> 2 oz. (1/4 cup) gin
> 1/4 tsp. maraschino liqueur
> 1/4 tsp. fresh lemon juice
> 2 dashes (about 1/8 tsp.) orange bitters
> maraschino cherry

Shake liquid ingredients with ice. Strain into chilled glass; garnish with cherry.

**cask** 1. A large, strong, barrel-shaped, leakproof container generally used for storing wines and other spirits. Most wine casks are made of oak. 2. The quantity that such a container holds.

**cat beer** American slang for milk.

> *Anybody that can't get drunk by midnight ain't trying.*
> TOOTS SHOR, AMERICAN RESTAURATEUR, HOTELIER

**Caymana** Made in Ireland, Caymana is a rich, cream-colored, banana-flavored LIQUEUR. *See also* BANANA-FLAVORED SPIRITS.

**Cement Mixer** The stand time for this SHOOTER allows the lime juice to curdle (okay, coagulate, if you prefer) the Irish cream . . . and this is appealing?

> 1 oz. (2 Tbsp.) Irish cream liqueur
> 1 1/2 tsp. fresh lime juice

Pour ingredients into chilled glass; let stand 10 seconds.

**Centerbe** [chehn-TEHR-beh] Said to be made with over 100 herbs, this Italian LIQUEUR has an assertive peppermint flavor. It's also called *Mentuccia. See also* HERB-FLAVORED SPIRITS; MINT-FLAVORED SPIRITS.

**Certosa** [chehr-TOH-sah] An herbal LIQUEUR from Italy.

**Chablis** [sha-BLEE; shah-BLEE; *pl.* sha-BLEEZ] A white wine made in the United States, Australia, South Africa, and France. French Chablis—made from grapes grown in a small area surrounding the town of Chablis and considered one of the world's great white wines—is made entirely from CHARDONNAY grapes and is therefore the only *true* Chablis. French Chablis is crisp, DRY, and lightly fruity. Non-French wines labeled "Chablis" are often inexpensive, sweet to medium-sweet white (also pink!) potables made from various white (and sometimes even red) grapes.

**Chambord** [sham-BORD (BOR)] A garnet-colored French LIQUEUR with an intense black-raspberry flavor. *See also* RASPBERRY-FLAVORED SPIRITS.

*ℐf you're given champagne at lunch, there's a catch somewhere.*

LORD LYONS, BRITISH ARISTOCRAT

**champagne; Champagne** [sham-PAYN; *Fr.* shah(m)-PAH-nyuh] *True* champagne comes only from France's northernmost wine-growing area, the Champagne region, just 90 miles northeast of Paris. Contrary to what some believe, Dom Pérignon, the seventeenth-century cellarmaster of the French Abbey of Hautvillers, didn't invent champagne but is credited for greatly improving the process by using thicker bottles and tying the corks down with string to prevent bottles and corks from exploding. He's also celebrated for developing the art of blending wines to create champagnes with superior flavor. Today, some champagne makers mix 30 or more different base wines to create their own unique blend (*cuvée*).

Although the word "champagne" is used for some non-

French SPARKLING WINES, most countries bow to French tradition by not placing it on their labels. Italy calls their sparkling wines SPUMANTE, Germany calls theirs SEKT, while in other regions of France such wines are referred to as *vins mousseux* ("frothy" or "sparkling wines"). In the United States and some South American countries, it's legal to use the word "champagne" on the label, although most top-quality sparkling-wine producers simply indicate that the wines were made by the *méthode champenoise,* a traditional French technique requiring a second FERMENTATION (in the bottle) during which the bottles are rotated some 100 turns. It's this special *méthode champenoise* plus the use of premium grapes that make truly good champagnes and other sparkling wines so expensive.

Champagne comes in a variety of styles and can be light, fruity, toasty, or yeasty, and DRY or sweet. **Vintage champagnes** are made from the best grapes of a better-than-average harvest year and must be aged for 3 years prior to release. Wines from the declared vintage year must comprise at least 80 percent of the *cuvée,* with the balance coming from reserve wines of prior years. **Nonvintage champagnes** (75 to 80 percent of those produced) are blends of 2 or more years, meticulously made to reflect a definitive house style. The salmon-pink **rosé champagnes** are generally made by adding a small amount of red still wine to the *cuvée,* although some producers *macerate* the juice with red grape skins to give the wine its color. The pale pink **blanc de noirs champagnes** are made entirely from red Pinot Noir and/or Meunier grapes. **Blanc de blancs champagnes** are made entirely from CHARDONNAY grapes and are typically the lightest in color. **Crémant champagnes,** made with only slightly more than half the pressure of standard sparkling wines, have a creamier mouthfeel.

A sparkling-wine label indicates the level of sweetness: **brut** (bone dry to almost dry—less than 1.5 percent sugar); **extra sec or extra dry** (slightly sweeter—1.2 to 2 percent sugar); **sec** (medium sweet—1.7 to 3.5 percent sugar); **demi-sec** (sweet—3.3 to 5 percent sugar); and **doux** (very sweet—over 5 percent sugar). The last two champagnes are considered dessert wines. *See also* Opening Wine and Champagne Bottles, page 25.

> *I drink [champagne] when I'm happy and when I'm sad. Sometimes I drink it when I'm alone. When I have company I consider it obligatory. I trifle with it if I'm not hungry and drink it when I am. Otherwise I never touch it—unless I'm thirsty.*
>
> LILY BOLLINGER, FRENCH CHAMPAGNE HEIR

## Champagne Cocktail

1 sugar cube
1 to 2 dashes ($\frac{1}{16}$ to $\frac{1}{8}$ tsp.) Angostura bitters
cold dry champagne
lemon twist

Place sugar cube in chilled glass; sprinkle with bitters. Top with champagne; drop in lemon twist.

➤ **London Special** Substitute a long strip of orange peel for the lemon twist, arranging it so half is inside the glass and half hangs over the rim.

## Champagne Collins *see* FRENCH 75

## Champagne Cup

MAKES ABOUT EIGHT 6-OUNCE SERVINGS

6 *each* strawberries, orange slices, and peach slices (or other fruit in season)
4 oz. ($\frac{1}{2}$ cup) brandy
2 oz. ($\frac{1}{4}$ cup) Cointreau
1 (750 ml) bottle cold dry champagne
16 oz. (1 pint; 2 cups) cold club soda
8 long strips cucumber peel
8 mint sprigs

In a large glass pitcher, combine fruit, brandy, and Cointreau. Fill pitcher about halfway with ice cubes. Slowly pour in champagne and soda, stirring gently. Pour into chilled glasses; garnish each serving with strip of cucumber peel and mint sprig.

**champagne glass** *see* Glassware, page 8

*For some reason, you can't just pick up champagne and drink it—someone has to be very witty and give a toast.*

GARY MERRILL, AMERICAN ACTOR (IN THE FILM *ALL ABOUT EVE*)

## Champagne Punch

MAKES ABOUT TWENTY 6-OUNCE SERVINGS

juice of 12 lemons (about 2¼ cups)
powdered sugar
16 oz. (1 pint; 2 cups) brandy
8 oz. (1 cup) maraschino liqueur
8 oz. (1 cup) Triple Sec
2 (750 ml) bottles cold dry champagne
16 oz. (1 pint; 2 cups) cold club soda
fresh fruit slices

Pour lemon juice into a large punch bowl; add sugar to taste, stirring well to dissolve. Stir in brandy, maraschino liqueur, and Triple Sec; cover and refrigerate until ready to serve. Just before serving, add a block of ice (see Punch Bowl Ice, page 17); gently stir in champagne and soda. Garnish with fruit.

▶ **Claret Punch** Substitute claret (red Bordeaux) or Cabernet Sauvignon for the champagne.

**champagne stopper** *see* Bar Equipment, page 4

**Champagne Velvet** *see* BLACK VELVET

## Chapala [chuh-PAH-luh]

1½ oz. (3 Tbsp.) tequila
½ oz. (1 Tbsp.) fresh orange juice
½ oz. (1 Tbsp.) fresh lemon juice
2 tsp. grenadine
½ tsp. Triple Sec
orange slice

Shake liquid ingredients with ice. Strain into chilled glass over ice; garnish with orange slice.

## Chapel Hill

1 1/2 oz. (3 Tbsp.) bourbon
1/2 oz. (1 Tbsp.) Triple Sec
1/2 oz. (1 Tbsp.) fresh lemon juice
orange twist

Shake liquid ingredients with ice. Strain into chilled glass; drop in orange twist.

**character** A term used in the wine and spirit world to describe a potable with distinctive, obvious features, pertaining either to its style or—in the case of wine—its grape variety.

**Chardonnay** [shar-dn-AY; shar-doh-NAY] A top-rate, easy-to-grow, and versatile white-wine grape from which a broad spectrum of wines with diverse characteristics are produced. Chardonnay's flavors are variously described as buttery, creamy, nutty, and smoky—the fruit range can include apple, lemon, melon, and pineapple. As with many popular wines, Chardonnay's reputation was established in France, particularly in the BURGUNDY and CHAMPAGNE regions. California has passionately adopted this grape and prominent Chardonnay wines are produced by myriad wineries, including Acacia, Chalone, Kistler, Robert Mondavi, Mount Eden, and Stony Hill. There are hundreds of American wineries producing Chardonnay in other parts of the country as well. Australia makes some excellent Chardonnays from several wineries, including Petaluma and Leeuwin Estate. The Chardonnay grape is also called Beaunois, Gamay Blanc, Melon d'Arbois, and Pinot Chardonnay. It's sometimes mistakenly referred to as *Pinot Blanc,* a different variety.

## Charles Cocktail

1 1/2 oz. (3 Tbsp.) brandy
1 1/2 oz. (3 Tbsp.) sweet vermouth
2 dashes (about 1/8 tsp.) Angostura bitters

Stir ingredients with ice; strain into chilled glass.

*People may say what they like about Christianity; the religious system that produced green Chartreuse can never really die.*

SAKI (H. H. MUNRO), SCOTTISH AUTHOR

**Chartreuse** [shar-TROOZ] An aromatic LIQUEUR created by the sixteenth-century Carthusian monks of France's La Grande Chartreuse. One of the world's most famous herbal liqueurs, Chartreuse is still produced in Grenoble under the monastery's direction. It's made from an exotic formula of 130 different herbs and spices, then AGED in oak. This inimitable liqueur comes in two versions. **Green** (*verte*) **Chartreuse,** which gets its pale yellow-green color from chlorophyll, is 110 PROOF (55 percent alcohol), and has a minty, spicy flavor that's more intense and aromatic than its golden counterpart. **Yellow** (*jaune*) **Chartreuse** is lower in alcohol (43 percent), lighter in body, sweeter (thanks to the addition of honey), and has a pale yellow color, attributable to saffron. **Chartreuse V.E.P.** (*Vieillissement Exceptionnellement Prolongé*—"Exceptionally Prolonged Aging") describes limited lots of both green and yellow Chartreuse that have been oak aged for 12 years. The aging produces mellow, incredibly complex liqueurs with slightly lowered (1 percent) alcohol levels. *See also* HERB-FLAVORED SPIRITS.

**chaser** A beverage drunk immediately after drinking another (usually alcoholic), as in the original BOILERMAKER, where a SHOT of WHISKEY is followed by a beer "chaser."

**château bottled** *see* WINE LABEL TERMS

**Chatham** [CHAT-uhm]
  1½ oz. (3 Tbsp.) gin
  2 tsp. ginger brandy
  1 tsp. fresh lemon juice
  ½-inch chunk of crystallized ginger

Shake liquid ingredients with ice. Strain into chilled glass; drop in ginger.

**Chelsea Sidecar** *see* SIDECAR

**Chéri-Suisse** [shay-REE SWEES] A Swiss LIQUEUR that tastes like chocolate-covered cherries. *See also* CHOCOLATE-FLAVORED SPIRITS.

**Cherry Blossom**

2 oz. (¼ cup) brandy
1 oz. (2 Tbsp.) kirsch or other cherry brandy
2 tsp. fresh lemon juice
1½ tsp. grenadine
1½ tsp. Triple Sec

Frost rim of chilled glass by moistening with cherry brandy, then dipping rim into granulated sugar. Shake ingredients with ice; strain into glass.

**cherry brandy** 1. A generic term for any BRANDY distilled from cherries. 2. A term sometimes applied to any of various cherry-flavored LIQUEURS. *See also* CHERRY-FLAVORED SPIRITS.

*I hate to advocate drugs, alcohol, violence, or insanity to anyone, but they've always worked for me.*

HUNTER S. THOMPSON, AMERICAN WRITER, JOURNALIST

**Cherry Cobbler** *see* COBBLER

**Cherry Daiquiri** *see* DAIQUIRI

**cherry-flavored spirits** *see* BERRY-FLAVORED SPIRITS; CHERRY MARNIER; KIRSCH; MARASCHINO LIQUEUR; PETER HEERING

**Cherry Heering** *see* PETER HEERING

**Cherry Marnier** [mahr-NYAY] A BRANDY-based, medium-sweet, cherry-flavored LIQUEUR with a kiss of almond. *See also* CHERRY-FLAVORED SPIRITS.

**Cherry Rum**

1½ oz. (3 Tbsp.) light rum
¾ oz. (1½ Tbsp.) cherry brandy
½ oz. (1 Tbsp.) cream

Shake ingredients with ice; strain into chilled glass.

**Chianti** [kee-AHN-tee; KYAHN-tee] 1. A large, well-known wine-producing area in Tuscany in central Italy. Chianti produces sturdy, DRY red wines from four traditional grape varieties—Sangiovese, Canaiolo, Trebbiano, and Malvasia—with CABERNET SAUVIGNON added to some blends. Chianti wines were once instantly recognizable by their squat, straw-covered bottles (*fiaschi*); but today, better-quality Chiantis are produced in the traditional Bordeaux-type bottle. Among these better wines are those from the Chianti Classico region, which are usually identifiable by a black rooster (*gallo nero*) on the label. The word "Riserva" on the label indicates a Chianti wine of superior quality that has been aged for at least 3 years before being released. 2. A generic name for ordinary, inexpensive, non-Italian red wine made in countries like Argentina and the United States.

## Chicago

lemon wedge
1½ oz. (3 Tbsp.) brandy
2 dashes (about ⅛ tsp.) Triple Sec
1 dash (about 1/16 tsp.) Angostura bitters
cold dry champagne

Frost rim of chilled glass by moistening it with the lemon wedge, then dipping rim into granulated sugar. Shake brandy, Triple Sec, and bitters with ice. Strain into glass; top with champagne, stirring gently.

➤ **Chicago Cocktail** Use a chilled cocktail glass; omit champagne.

## Chicago Fizz

1½ oz. (3 Tbsp.) white rum
1½ oz. (3 Tbsp.) ruby port
2½ tsp. fresh lemon juice
1 tsp. powdered sugar
1 egg white
cold club soda

Shake all ingredients except club soda with ice. Strain into chilled glass over ice cubes. Top with soda, stirring gently.

**Chi-Chi** [SHE-she] Two entirely different drinks bear this name—one is a PIÑA COLADA made with VODKA instead of rum, and the other is the following concoction.

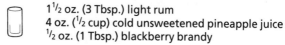

　　1 ½ oz. (3 Tbsp.) light rum
　　4 oz. (½ cup) cold unsweetened pineapple juice
　　½ oz. (1 Tbsp.) blackberry brandy

Shake rum and pineapple juice with ice; strain into chilled glass filled with ice. Float blackberry brandy on top by slowly pouring it over the back (rounded) side of a spoon; don't mix.

**chilling glasses** *see* Chilling Glasses, page 24

**chimney glass** *see* Glassware, page 8

**China-Martini** [KEE-nahr mahr-TEE-nee] No, this is not a MAR-TINI from China. As you might guess from the pronunciation, China-Martini is Italian, made by the famous house of Martini & Rossi. It's a syrupy, bittersweet LIQUEUR, characterized by a de-cidedly herbal-QUININE flavor. *See also* HERB-FLAVORED SPIRITS.

*An alcoholic is someone you don't like who drinks as much as you do.*

DYLAN THOMAS, WELSH POET

**Chip Shot**

　　1 ½ oz. (3 Tbsp.) hot coffee
　　¾ oz. (1 ½ Tbsp.) Tuaca
　　¾ oz. (1 ½ Tbsp.) Irish cream liqueur

Pour coffee into mug. Add remaining ingredients, stirring well.

**Chip Shot Shooter**

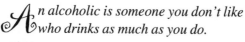

　　¾ oz. (1 ½ Tbsp.) Tuaca
　　¾ oz. (1 ½ Tbsp.) Irish cream liqueur
　　1 oz. (2 Tbsp.) hot coffee

Pour ingredients into glass in order given.

**Chocolate-Covered Cherry** *See* Floating and Layering Tech-niques, page 30.

1 maraschino cherry, optional
$^1/_2$ oz. (1 Tbsp.) grenadine
$^1/_2$ oz. (1 Tbsp.) Kahlúa
$^1/_2$ oz. (1 Tbsp.) Irish cream liqueur

If using cherry, drop it into chilled glass; pour grenadine into glass. One by one, add remaining ingredients in order given, slowly pouring each one over the back (rounded) side of a spoon so that it floats on top of the one below. Don't stir.

### Chocolate Eggnog *See also* EGGNOG.

MAKES ABOUT EIGHT 6-OUNCE SERVINGS

4 eggs, separated
$^1/_2$ cup packed brown sugar
$^2/_3$ cup unsweetened cocoa powder
1 tablespoon pure vanilla extract
12 oz. (1$^1/_2$ cups) milk
4 oz. ($^1/_2$ cup) light rum or brandy
$^1/_8$ teaspoon salt
12 oz (1$^1/_2$ cups) whipping cream, whipped to
    soft-peak stage
$^1/_4$ to $^1/_3$ cup grated semisweet chocolate

In a large bowl, beat together egg yolks, sugar, cocoa, and vanilla until thick and smooth. Slowly stir in milk and rum, mixing well. Refrigerate, covered, until just before serving, at least 2 hours so mixture becomes very cold. Beat egg whites with salt until soft peaks form. Fold whipped cream into chocolate mixture, then gently fold in egg whites. Serve immediately, garnished with grated chocolate.

★ **Chocolate Un-nog** Substitute 4 oz. ($^1/_2$ cup) more milk for the rum.

**chocolate-flavored spirits** *see* AFRI-KOKO; CHÉRI-SUISSE; CHOCOLAT ROYALE; CORDIAL MÉDOC; CRÈME DE CACAO; FRAGONARD LIQUEUR DE COGNAC X.O.; GODIVA CHOCOLATE LIQUEUR; SABRA; TRUFFLES; VANDERMINT

**Chocolate Martini** Some ask why? Others, why not? Also known as *Chocotini* this interesting cocktail is certainly more appropriate served after dinner than before. Using white crème de cacao creates a clear cocktail; Godiva Chocolate Liqueur produces a brown libation. *See also* MARTINI.

1 Tbsp. sweetened cocoa powder
tiny chocolate truffle or other chocolate candy
2 oz. (¹/₄ cup) vodka
1 to 1¹/₂ oz. (2 to 3 Tbsp.) crème de cacao or Godiva
    Chocolate Liqueur

Moisten rim of chilled glass with a little crème de cacao, then dip rim into cocoa powder. Drop candy into bottom of glass. Stir or shake vodka and liqueur with ice; strain into glass.

➤ **White Chocolate Martini** Dip glass rim into powdered sugar instead of cocoa powder; substitute White Chocolate Godiva for the crème de cacao; garnish with white chocolate truffle.

---

*Liquor is not a necessity. It is a means of momentarily side-stepping necessity.*

CLIFTON FADIMAN, AMERICAN AUTHOR

---

### Chocolate Rum

1 oz. (2 Tbsp.) light rum
2 tsp. white crème de cacao
2 tsp. white crème de menthe
2 tsp. cream
1 tsp. 151-proof rum

Shake first 4 ingredients with ice; strain into chilled cocktail glass or into an old-fashioned glass over ice cubes. Float 151-proof rum on top by slowly pouring it over the back (rounded) side of a spoon; don't mix.

### ★ Chocolate Un-nog *see* CHOCOLATE EGGNOG

### Chocolat Royale Made by the famous French house of Marie Brizard, this LIQUEUR is rich and creamy with an intense milk-chocolate flavor. *See also* CHOCOLATE-FLAVORED SPIRITS.

### Chocotini *see* CHOCOLATE MARTINI

**Chrysanthemum** [krih-SAN-thuh-muhm]

2 oz. (¹/₄ cup) dry vermouth
1¹/₂ oz. (3 Tbsp.) Bénédictine
¹/₄ tsp. Pernod or other anise-flavored liqueur
orange twist

Shake liquid ingredients with ice. Strain into chilled glass; drop in orange twist.

**church key** Slang for a small metal can and bottle opener. *See also* Bar Equipment, page 4.

**cider** A beverage made by pressing the juice from fruit (generally apples). FERMENTED cider is called *hard cider* and ranges widely in alcohol content. Unfermented cider is called *sweet cider.* Cider can be consumed straight or diluted with water. Apple cider is also used to make BRANDY, such as the famous CALVADOS. *See also* MULLED WINE.

**Cider Cup**

MAKES ABOUT EIGHT 6-OUNCE SERVINGS

32 oz. (1 quart; 4 cups) cold apple cider
6 oz. (³/₄ cup) Calvados or other brandy
4 oz. (¹/₂ cup) Triple Sec
12 oz. (1¹/₂ cups) cold club soda
1¹/₂ Tbsp. powdered sugar
8 apples slices, brushed lightly with lemon juice
8 mint sprigs

Fill a large glass pitcher halfway with ice cubes. Add all ingredients except apples and mint; stirring gently. Pour into chilled glasses; garnish each serving with apple slice and mint.

➤**Wine Cup** Substitute Cabernet Sauvignon or Zinfandel for the cider. Garnish with strawberries instead of apples.

★**Soft Cider Cup:** Substitute ³/₄ cup cold strong tea for the brandy and ¹/₂ cup orange juice for the Triple Sec.

**Cider Grog** *see* GROG

**Cider Smash** *see* SMASH

**cinnamon-flavored spirits** *see* AFTER SHOCK; GOLDSCHLAGER

**Cinzano** [cheen-TSAH-noh] The brand name of an Italian VER-MOUTH.

**citrus-flavored spirits** *see* CAPRINATURA; COINTREAU; CU-RAÇAO; FORBIDDEN FRUIT; GRAND MARNIER; LEMON-FLAVORED SPIRITS; MANDARINE NAPOLÉON; ORANGE-FLAVORED SPIRITS; ROCK AND RYE; TRIPLE SEC; VAN DER HUM

**citrus reamer** *see* Bar Equipment, page 4

**citrus spout** *see* Bar Equipment, page 4

**citrus stripper** *see* Bar Equipment, page 4

**Clamato Cocktail** *see* CLAM DIGGER

**Clam Digger** Clamato juice is a commercially available combo of clam and tomato juice.

> 2 oz. ($^1/_4$ cup) vodka
> 6 oz. ($^3/_4$ cup) Clamato juice (or 3 oz. *each* tomato juice and clam juice)
> 2 tsp. fresh lemon juice
> $^1/_4$ tsp. Tabasco sauce
> $^1/_4$ tsp. Worcestershire sauce
> pinch of freshly ground pepper
> lemon slice

Shake all ingredients except lemon slice with ice. Strain into chilled glass over ice cubes; garnish with lemon slice.

> ➤ **Clamato Cocktail** Omit all seasonings and simply use vodka and Clamato juice.

> ★ **Sober Clam Digger** Substitute $^1/_4$ cup more Clamato for the vodka.

**claret** [KLAR-eht] 1. The English use the word "claret" for France's red BORDEAUX wines. 2. Elsewhere, "claret" is sometimes used as a general reference to light red wines, although the word itself has no legal definition.

**Claret Cobbler** *see* COBBLER

**Claret Cup** *see* CIDER CUP

**Claret Punch** *see* CHAMPAGNE PUNCH

## Claridge

1 oz. (2 Tbsp.) gin
1 oz. (2 Tbsp.) dry vermouth
$^{1}/_{2}$ oz. (1 Tbsp.) apricot brandy
$^{1}/_{2}$ oz. (1 Tbsp.) Triple Sec or Cointreau

Shake ingredients with ice; strain into chilled glass.

## Classic Cocktail

lemon wedge
$1^{1}/_{2}$ oz. (3 Tbsp.) brandy
$1^{1}/_{2}$ tsp. maraschino liqueur
$1^{1}/_{2}$ tsp. Triple Sec
1 tsp. fresh lemon juice
lemon twist

Frost rim of chilled glass by moistening it with the lemon wedge, then dipping rim into granulated sugar. Shake remaining ingredients except lemon twist with ice. Strain into chilled glass; drop in lemon twist.

### Classic Hot Bishop *see* BISHOP, THE

## Cloister [KLOY-ster]

$1^{1}/_{2}$ oz. (3 Tbsp.) gin
2 tsp. yellow Chartreuse
2 tsp. unsweetened grapefruit juice
1 tsp. fresh lemon juice
$^{1}/_{2}$ tsp. powdered sugar

Shake ingredients with ice; strain into chilled glass.

## Clover Club

$1^{1}/_{2}$ oz. (3 Tbsp.) gin
$^{3}/_{4}$ oz. (1$^{1}/_{2}$ Tbsp.) fresh lemon or lime juice
2 tsp. grenadine
1 egg white

Vigorously shake ingredients with ice; strain into chilled glass.

---

*Water taken in moderation cannot hurt anybody.*
MARK TWAIN, AMERICAN AUTHOR, HUMORIST

**club soda** One of many names for water that has been highly charged with carbon dioxide, which produces effervescence. Such water is also referred to as *carbonated water, soda water,* and sometimes *sparkling water,* the latter of which may be naturally carbonated. Club soda is also occasionally called *seltzer water,* although true seltzer is a naturally effervescent water named after the town of its origin—Nieder Seltzers in Germany's Wiesbaden region. Manmade (carbon dioxide injected) "seltzer" was created during the latter half of the eighteenth century. Because soda waters contain a small amount of sodium bicarbonate, they often help neutralize an acidic stomach.

**cobbler** Cobblers date back to at least 1809 when a "sherry cobbler" was mentioned in Washington Irving's *History of New York.* Although cobblers were originally wine-based potables, today's versions use any of various liquors or LIQUEURS. All cobblers are served over crushed or cracked ice, sometimes mixed with fruit syrup, and classically garnished with fresh fruit and mint sprigs.

### Brandy Cobbler

1 tsp. powdered sugar
2 oz. (¼ cup) cold club soda
2 oz. (¼ cup) brandy
orange slice or other fruit in season
maraschino cherry

Dissolve sugar with a little of the club soda. Fill chilled glass three-quarters full with cracked or crushed ice. Add brandy and remaining soda, stirring gently. Garnish with fruit; serve with 2 straws.

➤ **Cherry Cobbler** Substitute gin for the brandy and add ¾ oz. (1½ Tbsp.) cherry brandy.

➤ **Gin Cobbler** Substitute gin for the brandy.

✸ **Peach Cobbler** Substitute peach nectar for the brandy.

➤ **Rum Cobbler** Substitute rum for the brandy; add pineapple spear to garnish.

➤ **Scotch Cobbler** Substitute Scotch for the brandy and add ½ tsp. *each* Cointreau and brandy; add mint sprig to garnish.

➤ **Sherry Cobbler** Use a large wineglass. Substitute 3 oz. ($^3/_8$ cup) sweet sherry for 2 oz. brandy and add $^1/_2$ tsp. Cointreau.

➤ **Wine Cobbler** Use a large wineglass. Substitute 4 oz. ($^1/_2$ cup) Cabernet Sauvignon or Zinfandel for 2 oz. brandy. Omit cherry.

**Cock 'n' Bull Shot** *see* BULLSHOT

**cocktail** Any alcoholic beverage that combines two or more ingredients, including MIXERS.

**cocktail glass** *see* Glassware, page 8

---

*If you were to ask me if I'd ever had the bad luck to miss my daily cocktail, I'd have to say that I doubt it; where certain things are concerned, I plan ahead.*

LUIS BUÑUEL, SPANISH FILMMAKER

---

**cocktail onions** *see* Ingredients, page 18

**cocktail shaker** *see* Bar Equipment, page 7

**cocktail stick** *see* SWIZZLE STICK

**coconut cream** *see* COCONUT MILK; CREAM OF COCONUT

**coconut-flavored spirits** *see* MALIBU

**coconut milk** An unsweetened, milklike liquid made by processing water with coconut meat. Coconut milk is commonly available in Asian markets and many supermarkets. Some Asian markets carry a more concentrated **coconut cream,** which is not to be confused with the extremely sweet CREAM OF COCONUT.

**coconut syrup** *see* SYRUPS, FLAVORED

**coffee drinks** *see* BLACKJACK; CAFÉ AMARETTO; CAFÉ DIABLO; CAFÉ ROYALE; IRISH COFFEE; ITALIAN COFFEE; JAMAICAN COFFEE; MEXICAN COFFEE

## Coffee Eggnog *See also* EGGNOG.

6 oz. (³/₄ cup) milk
1¹/₂ oz. (3 Tbsp.) Kahlúa
1¹/₂ oz. (3 Tbsp.) blended whiskey
1 oz. (2 Tbsp.) cream
1 egg
¹/₂ tsp. instant coffee
¹/₂ cup cracked ice
freshly grated nutmeg or ground cinnamon

Combine all ingredients except nutmeg in a blender. Cover and process at medium speed until smooth, about 15 seconds. Pour into chilled glass; sprinkle lightly with nutmeg or cinnamon.

## coffee-flavored spirits *see* CAPUCELLO; COPA DE ORO; KAHLÚA; KAHLÚA ROYALE CREAM LIQUEUR; KAMORA; PASHA; PATRON XO CAFÉ; TIA MARIA; TIRAMISU

## Coffee Grasshopper *see* GRASSHOPPER

**Cognac** [KOHN-yak; KON-yak; *Fr.* kaw-NYAK] Considered the finest of all BRANDIES, Cognac hails from in and around western France's town of Cognac. It's made primarily from Trebbiano grapes (known in France as Ugni Blanc and Saint-Emilion) and double-DISTILLED immediately after FERMENTATION. Freshly distilled Cognac is strong, sharp, and harsh, and requires wood AGING (usually in Limousin oak) to mellow and enhance both AROMA and flavor. Stars on a Cognac label vary in significance from producer to producer—three stars usually indicate longer aging and therefore higher quality than one or two stars. Older Cognacs are labeled V.S. (Very Superior), V.S.O.P. (Very Superior Old Pale), and V.V.S.O.P. (Very, Very, Superior Old Pale). Since French authorities have difficulty keeping track of Cognac's aging time, there's a limit to what producers can claim on the label—the maximum is 7 years. The terms "X.O.," "Extra," and "Reserve," generally indicate the oldest Cognac produced by a particular house. Labels indicating "Fine Champagne" mean that 60 percent of the grapes came from a superior grape-growing section called Grande Champagne; "Grande Fine Champagne" tells you all the grapes came from that eminent area.

*ℭognac . . . a sense of amusement, charm, excitement, all combined into the purest of pleasure.*

ROY ANDRIES DE GROOT, BRITISH-BORN AMERICAN WRITER,

SCREENWRITER, DIRECTOR

**Cointreau** [KWAHN-troh] Made by France's Cointreau family since the mid-nineteenth century, Cointreau is considered the world's most distinguished orange-flavored LIQUEUR. It's made with the peel of sour oranges native to the Caribbean island of Curaçao, as well as with sweet orange peel from Spain. Cointreau is clear and colorless with an intensely exotic, mildly bitter orange flavor. *See also* CITRUS-FLAVORED SPIRITS; ORANGE-FLAVORED SPIRITS.

**Colada** *see* PIÑA COLADA

**Cold Deck**

1½ oz. (3 Tbsp.) brandy
¾ oz. (1½ Tbsp.) sweet vermouth
1½ tsp. crème de menthe

Shake ingredients with ice; strain into chilled glass.

**Collins** A refreshing, lemony drink akin to a tall SOUR. The most popular collins is the TOM COLLINS, after which all subsequent collinses were patterned. These popular drinks spawned the tall, eponymous COLLINS GLASS. *See also* CHAMPAGNE COLLINS; RUM COLLINS; VODKA COLLINS; WHISKEY COLLINS.

**collins glass** *see* Glassware, page 8

**Colonial**

1½ oz. (3 Tbsp.) gin
½ oz. (1 Tbsp.) unsweetened grapefruit juice
1 tsp. maraschino liqueur
stuffed green olive

Shake liquid ingredients with ice. Strain into chilled glass; garnish with olive.

## Commodore Cocktail

1 1/2 oz. (3 Tbsp.) bourbon
3/4 oz. (1 1/2 Tbsp.) white crème de cacao
1/2 oz. (1 Tbsp.) fresh lemon juice

Shake ingredients with ice; strain into chilled glass.

*I'm a Christian, but that doesn't mean I'm a long-faced square. I like a little bourbon.*

LILLIAN CARTER, MOTHER OF JIMMY CARTER, 39TH UNITED STATES PRESIDENT

## Commonwealth

1 1/2 oz. (3 Tbsp.) Canadian whisky
1/2 oz. (1 Tbsp.) Van der Hum, Crystal Comfort, or Grand
    Marnier
1 tsp. fresh lemon juice
orange twist

Shake liquid ingredients with ice. Strain into chilled glass; drop in orange twist.

## Continental

1 3/4 oz. (3 1/2 Tbsp.) light rum
1/2 oz. (1 Tbsp.) green crème de menthe
1/2 oz. (1 Tbsp.) fresh lime juice
1/2 tsp. powdered sugar

Shake ingredients with ice; strain into chilled glass.

**Contrary Mary** Another name for the drink Virgin Mary (*see* BLOODY MARY).

**cooler** A tall, iced drink of wine or liquor mixed with a carbonated beverage and often garnished with a long, continuous spiral of citrus peel. *See also* BOSTON COOLER, CAMPARI COOLER; COUNTRY CLUB COOLER; CURAÇAO COOLER; HARVARD COOLER; IRISH COOLER; KLONDIKE COOLER; PINEAPPLE COOLER; REMSEN COOLER; ROCK AND RYE COOLER; SCOTCH COOLER.

**Copa de Oro** [KOH-pah day OH-roh] A very sweet, dark brown Mexican LIQUEUR with a coffeelike flavor. *See also* COFFEE-FLAVORED SPIRITS.

**cordial** *see* LIQUEUR

**Cordial Campari** An Italian LIQUEUR that combines the flavors of CAMPARI and raspberries.

**cordial glass** *see* Glassware, page 8

**Cordial Médoc** [may-DAWK] A French COGNAC-based LIQUEUR that combines the flavors of orange and chocolate. *See also* MÉDOC; ORANGE-FLAVORED SPIRITS.

**Cordless Screwdriver** *see* SCREWDRIVER

**corenwijn** Dutch for "corn wine," this triple-distilled SCHNAPPS-style spirit is based on equal parts rye, corn, and barley. Wood AGING for several years adds a distinctive flavor that makes *corenwijn* a favorite of the Dutch.

**Corkscrew**

1½ oz. (3 Tbsp.) light rum
½ oz. (1 Tbsp.) dry vermouth
½ oz. (1 Tbsp.) peach-flavored liqueur or brandy
lime slice

Shake liquid ingredients with ice. Strain into chilled glass; garnish with lime.

**corkscrews; corkpullers** Instruments used to extract a cork from a wine bottle. *See* Bar Equipment, page 4.

**corn whiskey** *see* BOURBON

**Corpse Reviver** The colorful name of this drink comes from the fact that it's purportedly good for the morning after . . . but we all know the "hair of the dog" doesn't *really* shed a hangover. The name seems to inspire bartenders, which is undoubtedly why this drink has at least three versions.

### Corpse Reviver #1

1 oz. (2 Tbsp.) brandy
1 oz. (2 Tbsp.) apple brandy
1 oz. (2 Tbsp.) sweet vermouth

### Corpse Reviver #2

1 oz. (2 Tbsp.) brandy
1 oz. (2 Tbsp.) Fernet Branca
1 oz. (2 Tbsp.) white crème de menthe

### Corpse Reviver #3

1 oz. (2 Tbsp.) gin
1 oz. (2 Tbsp.) Swedish punsch
1 oz. (2 Tbsp.) Cointreau
$^3/_4$ oz. (1$^1/_2$ Tbsp.) fresh lemon juice
2 dashes (about $^1/_8$ tsp.) Pernod or other anise-
flavored liqueur

With any of the above formulas, shake ingredients with ice;
strain into chilled glass.

**Cosmopolitan** Shortened to "Cosmo" by enthusiasts, this drink
made a spirited comeback during the raging cocktail revival of
the nineties. Sugar-frosting the rim is optional.

2 oz. ($^1/_4$ cup) vodka, plain or citron flavored
1 oz. (2 Tbsp.) Cointreau or Triple Sec
1 oz. (2 Tbsp.) cranberry juice
$^1/_2$ oz. (1 Tbsp.) fresh lime juice

If desired, frost rim of chilled glass by moistening with a little
cranberry juice, then dipping rim into granulated sugar. Shake ingredients with ice; strain into chilled glass.

### Costa Del Sol [KOH-stah dehl SOHL]

2 oz. ($^1/_4$ cup) gin
1 oz. (2 Tbsp.) Cointreau
1 oz. (2 Tbsp.) apricot brandy

Shake ingredients with ice; strain into chilled glass.

## Country Club Cooler

2 oz. ($^1/_4$ cup) dry vermouth
$^1/_2$ tsp. grenadine
cold club soda or ginger ale
long spiral of orange or lemon peel

Pour vermouth and grenadine into chilled glass filled with ice cubes. Top with club soda, stirring gently. Arrange citrus spiral so half of it is inside the glass and half hangs over the rim.

## Cowboy

2 oz. ($^1/_4$ cup) rye whiskey
1 oz. (2 Tbsp.) cream

Shake ingredients with ice; strain into chilled glass.

**cranberry-flavored spirits** *See* AIRELLE; BERRY-FLAVORED SPIRITS

**cream-based spirits** *see* CRÈME DE GRAND MARNIER; EGGNOG-FLAVORED SPIRITS; IRISH CREAM LIQUEURS; LIQUEUR

**cream liqueurs** *see* LIQUEUR

**cream of coconut** A thick, extremely sweet mixture of coconut paste, water, and sugar. Cream of coconut, which is used in drinks like PIÑA COLADA, is commonly available in supermarkets and liquor stores.

*When I read about the evils of drinking,
I gave it up . . . reading, that is.*
HENNY YOUNGMAN, AMERICAN COMEDIAN

**cream sherry** *see* SHERRY

★ **Creamsicle** *see* DREAMSICLE

**Creamy London Fog** *see* LONDON FOG

## Creamy Orange

1 oz. (2 Tbsp.) cream sherry
1 oz. (2 Tbsp.) fresh orange juice
½ oz. (1 Tbsp.) brandy
½ oz. (1 Tbsp.) cream

Shake ingredients with ice; strain into chilled glass.

**creamy screwdriver** *see* SCREWDRIVER

**crème d'abricots** [krehm dah-bree-KOH] Sweet apricot-flavored LIQUEUR. *See* APRICOT-FLAVORED SPIRITS.

**crème d'amande** [krehm dah-MAHND] An almond-flavored LIQUEUR with a pale pink color. The American version is simply called *crème de almond. See also* ALMOND-FLAVORED SPIRITS; NUT-FLAVORED SPIRITS.

**crème d'ananas** [krehm dah-nah-NAHS] A sweet pineapple-flavored LIQUEUR.

*Two drunks are walking along a railroad track when one says, "All these stairs are killing me." The other guy replies, "It's not the stairs that kill me, it's these low railings."*

**crème de** [krehm deuh] Designation used for extremely sweet (about 50 percent sugar) LIQUEURS, including CRÈME DE BANANE, CRÈME DE CACAO, CRÈME DE CASSIS, and CRÈME DE MENTHE. Such potables are thicker than other spirits, but do not contain cream.

**crème de almond** [krehm deuh AL-mond] *see* CRÈME D'AMANDE

**crème de banane; crème de banana** [krehm deuh bah-NAHN] A sweet LIQUEUR with an intense banana flavor. *See also* BANANA-FLAVORED SPIRITS.

**crème de cacao** [krehm deuh kah-KAH-oh] A dark, chocolate-flavored LIQUEUR delicately scented with vanilla. **White crème**

**de cacao** is a clear, colorless form of the same liqueur. *See also* CHOCOLATE-FLAVORED SPIRITS.

**crème de cassis** [krehm deuh kah-SEES] This black currant-flavored LIQUEUR is an essential ingredient in KIR. *See also* BLACK CURRANT–FLAVORED SPIRITS.

**crème de fraise** [krehm deuh FREHZ] A strawberry-flavored LIQUEUR.

**crème de framboise** [krehm deuh frahm-BWAHZ] A raspberry-flavored LIQUEUR. *See also* RASPBERRY-FLAVORED SPIRITS.

**Crème de Grand Marnier** [krehm deuh GRAN mahr-NYAY] A very sweet cream-based LIQUEUR with a flavor reminiscent of bubblegum and mint. *See also* GRAND MARNIER.

*Drinking makes such fools of people,*
*and people are such fools to begin with,*
*that it's compounding a felony.*

ROBERT BENCHLEY, AMERICAN HUMORIST, ACTOR

**crème de mandarines** [krehm deuh mahn-dah-REEN] A LIQUEUR flavored with mandarin oranges. *See also* ORANGE-FLAVORED SPIRITS.

**crème de menthe** [krehm deuh MENTH (MAHNTH)] A mint-flavored LIQUEUR that comes in two colors—green and clear, the latter called **white crème de menthe.** There's no discernible flavor difference between the green and white versions. *See also* MINT-FLAVORED SPIRITS.

**crème de noya** *see* CRÈME DE NOYAUX

**crème de noyaux; crème de noyau; crème de noya** [krehm deuh nwah-YOH] A sweet pink LIQUEUR with a flavor reminiscent of almonds. *Noyaux* is French for "fruit pits," which are, in fact, the primary flavoring ingredient in this cordial. *See also* ALMOND-FLAVORED SPIRITS; NUT-FLAVORED SPIRITS.

**crème de rose** [krehm deuh ROSE] An exotically scented, rose-flavored LIQUEUR. *See also* FLOWER-FLAVORED SPIRITS.

**crème de vanille (vanilla)** [krehm deuh vah-NEEY] A smooth, rich vanilla-flavored LIQUEUR. *See also* VANILLA-FLAVORED SPIRITS.

**crème de violette** [krehm deuh vee-oh-LEHT] An amethyst-colored LIQUEUR flavored with the essence of violets. *See also* CRÈME YVETTE; FLOWER-FLAVORED SPIRITS.

**crème yvette** [krehm ih-VEHT (ee-VEHT)] A violet-flavored LIQUEUR named after French actress Yvette Gilbert. *See also* CRÈME DE VIOLETTE; FLOWER-FLAVORED SPIRITS.

**creole** [KREE-ohl]

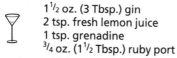

> 1 ½ oz. (3 Tbsp.) light rum
> 1 tsp. fresh lemon juice
> 1 to 2 dashes (about ¹/₁₆ to ⅛ tsp.) Tabasco sauce
> cold beef bouillon
> salt and pepper

Shake first 3 ingredients with ice; strain into chilled glass over ice cubes. Top with bouillon; add salt and pepper to taste, stirring well.

**Crimson**

> 1 ½ oz. (3 Tbsp.) gin
> 2 tsp. fresh lemon juice
> 1 tsp. grenadine
> ¾ oz. (1 ½ Tbsp.) ruby port

Shake all ingredients except port with ice. Strain into chilled glass. Float port on top by slowly pouring it over the back (rounded) side of a spoon; don't mix.

**Crusta** This drink was invented in the mid-1800s by the owner of a New Orleans bar, Santina's Saloon. Although brandy is traditional for crustas other potables may be substituted. The sugar-coated glass rim and long spiral of citrus peel gives this cocktail its style.

### Brandy Crusta

peel of 1 lemon or orange, colored portion only,
cut in a continuous spiral
2 oz. (¹/₄ cup) brandy
¹/₂ oz. (1 Tbsp.) lemon juice
2 tsp. Cointreau
1 tsp. maraschino liqueur

Dip chilled glass rim in water, shake off excess water, then dip rim into granulated sugar. Place peel in glass, draping about 2 inches of it over the rim. Shake remaining ingredients with about ¹/₂ cup crushed ice (or 2 cubes). Strain into chilled glass.

▶ **Variations:** Substitute bourbon, gin, or rum for the brandy.

**Crystal Comfort** Made in the United States, this crystal-clear, slightly sweet LIQUEUR has a lively orange-tangerine flavor. *See also* ORANGE-FLAVORED SPIRITS.

**Cuarenta Y Tres** [kwah-RAYN-tah ee TRAYSS] Spanish for "43," Cuarenta Y Tres is a bright yellow, extremely sweet, and viscous LIQUEUR with a vanilla-citrus flavor. This libation is also called *Licor 43,* because it is said to be made with 43 different ingredients.

**Cuba Libre** [KYOO-bah LEE-bray] A fancy name for Rum and Coke.

¹/₂ lime
2 oz. (¹/₄ cup) light rum
cold cola

Squeeze lime juice directly into chilled glass; drop in lime shell. Add ice cubes, then rum; top with cola, stirring gently.

▶ **Cuba Libre Supreme** Substitute Southern Comfort for the rum.

### Cuban Special

1¹/₂ oz. (3 Tbsp.) light rum
¹/₂ oz. (1 Tbsp.) fresh lime juice
¹/₂ oz. (1 Tbsp.) unsweetened pineapple juice
2 tsp. Triple Sec
pineapple slice or spear

Shake all ingredients except pineapple slice with ice. Strain into chilled glass; garnish with pineapple.

**cup** A chilled punch-style drink made with WINE, CHAMPAGNE, or CIDER mixed with BRANDY, an orange-flavored LIQUEUR such as CURAÇAO, and CLUB SODA. Cups are made as individual drinks, or for several servings, poured from a pitcher into wineglasses or punch cups, then garnished with fruit slices and often cucumber peel. *See also* CHAMPAGNE CUP; CIDER CUP; STIRRUP CUP.

**curaçao** [KYOOR-uh-soh] A generic term for several orange-flavored LIQUEURS whose essence is derived from the dried peel of bitter oranges grown on an island of the Netherlands Antilles in the southern Caribbean Sea. Although most curaçaos are amber in color, several are tinted blue and a few are colorless. COINTREAU is arguably the world's preeminent curaçao, with TRIPLE SEC sharing that spotlight. *See also* CITRUS-FLAVORED SPIRITS; ORANGE-FLAVORED SPIRITS.

### Curaçao Cooler

1 oz. (2 Tbsp.) dark rum
1 oz. (2 Tbsp.) curaçao (Triple Sec or Cointreau)
1 oz. (2 Tbsp.) fresh lime juice
cold club soda
orange slice

Shake all ingredients except soda and orange slice with ice. Pour into chilled glass. Top with club soda; garnish with orange slice.

**Cynar** [CHEE-nahr] A bitter Italian APÉRITIF made from arti-chokes and a medley of herbs and other flavorings. Cynar is served over ice, either PLAIN or with a spritz of CLUB SODA.

---

*A heavyset guy walks into a bar with a duck under his arm and sits down next to a whiskered old drunk. The old man raises his head from the bar and says, "Where'd you get that pig?" The man, clearly irritated, said haughtily, "That's not a pig, you fool, it's a duck." The drunk snorted loudly, "I was talkin' to the duck!"*

---

**Daiquiri** [DAK-uh-ree] Legend tells us that American mining engineer Jennings Cox invented the Daiquiri for visitors in 1896, naming it in honor of the nearby village of Daiquiri in eastern Cuba. That simple inspiration has become one of America's most popular drinks, with infinite renditions, as the following variations make obvious. If desired, the rim of the glass can be moistened with lime juice and sugar-frosted. *See also* BACARDI.

## Classic Daiquiri

1¹/₂ oz. (3 Tbsp.) light rum
³/₄ oz. (1¹/₂ Tbsp.) fresh lime juice
1 tsp. powdered sugar
lime slice

Shake liquid ingredients with ice. Strain into chilled glass; garnish with lime slice.

➤ **Apple Daiquiri** Add ¹/₂ oz. (1 Tbsp.) Calvados or other apple brandy; garnish with an apple slice brushed lightly with lime juice.

➤ **Banana Daiquiri** Increase lime juice to 3 Tbsp. and add ¹/₂ oz. (1 Tbsp.) Triple Sec (or banana-flavored liqueur), 1 small ripe banana, and 1 cup crushed ice. Combine ingredients in a blender. Cover and process at medium speed until smooth, about 15 seconds. Pour into chilled large wineglass; garnish with lime and serve with straw.

➤ **Cherry Daiquiri** Add ¹/₂ oz. (1 Tbsp.) cherry brandy and ¹/₂ tsp. kirsch; garnish with lime.

➤ **Derby Daiquiri** Add 1 oz. (2 Tbsp.) fresh orange juice; garnish with orange slice.

➤ **Frozen Daiquiri** Add ¹/₂ oz. (1 Tbsp.) Triple Sec and 1 cup crushed ice. Combine all ingredients in a blender. Cover and process at medium speed until smooth, about 15 seconds. Pour into chilled glass; garnish with lime.

➤ **Frozen Fruit Daiquiri** Prepare as for frozen daiquiri, adding ¹/₂ cup chopped fruit (melon, peaches, or strawberries). If desired, substitute 1 tablespoon flavored brandy or liqueur (such as peach brandy for peach daiquiris) for the Triple Sec.

➤ **Passion Daiquiri** Add ¹/₂ oz. (1 Tbsp.) passion-fruit juice; garnish with lime.

**Daisy** Created in the 1850s, this American drink typically contains grenadine or some kind of fruit syrup and a small amount (no more than 1 to 2 ounces) of club soda. Daisies are served over crushed or cracked ice, although early versions were presented STRAIGHT UP. Traditionally they're served in an iced metal mug, although a highball glass is more commonly used today.

**Bourbon Daisy** (*arguably the original*)
2 oz. (¹/₄ cup) bourbon
¹/₂ oz. (1 Tbsp.) fresh lemon juice
2 tsp. grenadine or raspberry syrup
¹/₂ tsp. powdered sugar, optional
cold club soda
2 tsp. Southern Comfort
orange slice

Shake first 4 ingredients with ice; strain into chilled mug or glass three-quarters full of crushed or cracked ice. Top with a little club soda, stirring gently. Float Southern Comfort on top by slowly pouring it over the back (rounded) side of a spoon; don't mix. Garnish with orange slice or other fresh fruit; serve with straw.

➤ **Brandy Daisy** Substitute brandy for the bourbon; omit Southern Comfort.

➤ **Gin Daisy** Substitute gin for the bourbon; omit Southern Comfort.

➤ **Rum Daisy** Substitute rum for the bourbon; omit Southern Comfort.

➤ **Star Daisy** Substitute 1 oz. (2 Tbsp.) *each* gin and apple brandy for the bourbon; omit Southern Comfort.

## Damn the Weather
1¹/₂ oz. (3 Tbsp.) gin
¹/₂ oz. (1 Tbsp.) sweet vermouth
¹/₂ oz. (1 Tbsp.) fresh orange juice
1 tsp. Triple Sec

Shake ingredients with ice; strain into chilled glass.

**Dancing Leprechaun** *See also* LEPRECHAUN.

1¹/₂ oz. (3 Tbsp.) Irish whiskey
³/₄ oz. (1¹/₂ Tbsp.) Drambuie
³/₄ oz. (1¹/₂ Tbsp.) fresh lemon juice
cold ginger ale
lemon twist

Shake liquid ingredients with ice. Strain into chilled glass over ice cubes; drop in lemon twist.

*God invented liquor so the Irish wouldn't rule the world.*
IRISH SAYING

**Danish Gin Fizz** *See also* GIN FIZZ.

2 oz. (1/4 cup) gin
1/2 oz. (1 Tbsp.) Peter Heering
1/2 oz. (1 Tbsp.) fresh lime juice
1 tsp. kirsch
1 tsp. powdered sugar
cold club soda
lime slice
maraschino cherry

Shake first 5 ingredients with ice. Strain into chilled glass over 2 to 3 ice cubes. Top with club soda, stirring gently. Garnish with fruit.

**Danziger Goldwasser** [DAHNG-tsih-gehr GOLT-vahs-sehr] A full-bodied, clear LIQUEUR in which flecks of edible shimmering gold airily float. It's also called simply *Goldwasser,* German for "gold water." Although the original Goldwasser hails from Danzig (now Gdansk), Poland, this potable is now made in several European countries. It's variously flavored, depending on the country of origin—the German version has a caraway-aniseed flavor; the French rendition tastes more of orange zest and spices.

**dash** A measure equal to approximately ¹/₁₆ teaspoon.

**dead soldier** Slang for an empty liquor bottle, so named because it's performed its duty and is now gone.

**Deauville** [DOH-vihl]

$^3/_4$ oz. ($1^1/_2$ Tbsp.) brandy
$^3/_4$ oz. ($1^1/_2$ Tbsp.) apple brandy
$^3/_4$ oz. ($1^1/_2$ Tbsp.) Cointreau or Triple Sec
$^1/_2$ oz. (1 Tbsp.) fresh lemon juice

Shake ingredients with ice; strain into chilled glass.

**decant; decanting** [dee-KANT] Decanting is done either to separate a wine from sediment deposited during the AGING process, or to allow it to breathe (aerate) in order to enhance its flavor. When decanting an older wine, care should be taken not to disturb the sediment. A wine basket (also called *cradle* or *Burgundy basket*) can be used to move the bottle in a horizontal position (so as not to disturb the sediment) from where it was stored to where it will be decanted. This keeps the sediment from disseminating throughout the wine. If you don't have such a basket, stand the bottle upright for an hour so the sediment can settle to the bottom. Once the foil and cork are removed, gently wipe the mouth of the bottle. Then begin slowly pouring the wine into a DECANTER, placing a strong light (a candle is charming, a flashlight more practical) behind or below the neck of the bottle. The light lets you see the first signs of sediment, at which point you stop pouring. There are also silver or pewter funnels with extremely fine filters that work great for decanting. All such items are available in fine wine stores.

**decanter** A glass container into which wine is decanted (*see* DE-CANT). A decanter can be a simple carafe, but is generally more elegant and often made of hand-cut crystal.

**Delmonico**

$1^1/_2$ oz. (3 Tbsp.) gin
$^1/_2$ oz. (1 Tbsp.) brandy
$^1/_2$ oz. (1 Tbsp.) dry vermouth
$^1/_2$ oz. (1 Tbsp.) sweet vermouth
2 dashes (about $^1/_8$ tsp.) Angostura bitters
lemon twist

Stir or shake liquid ingredients with ice. Strain into chilled glass; drop in lemon twist.

*I've made it a rule never to drink by daylight and never to refuse a drink after dark.*

H. L. MENCKEN, AMERICAN JOURNALIST, AUTHOR

**Delmonico glass** *see* Glassware, page 8

### Delta

1¹/₂ oz. (3 Tbsp.) blended whiskey
¹/₂ oz. (1 Tbsp.) Southern Comfort
2 tsp. fresh lime juice
1 tsp. powdered sugar
orange slice
peach slice, brushed lightly with lime or lemon juice

Shake all ingredients except fruit slices with ice. Strain into chilled glass; garnish with fruit.

**Demerara rum** [dim-uh-REHR-uh; dim-uh-RAHR-uh] *see* RUM

### Dempsey

1 oz. (2 Tbsp.) gin
1 oz. (2 Tbsp.) apple brandy
¹/₂ tsp. Pernod or other anise-flavored liqueur
¹/₂ tsp. grenadine
1 cup cracked ice

Shake ingredients together; strain into chilled glass.

### Depth Bomb

1¹/₂ oz. (3 Tbsp.) brandy
1¹/₂ oz. (3 Tbsp.) apple brandy
¹/₂ tsp. grenadine
¹/₂ tsp. fresh lemon juice

Shake ingredients with ice; strain into chilled glass over ice cubes.

### Depth Charge

1½ oz. (3 Tbsp.) peppermint schnapps (preferably cold)
12 oz (1½ cups) cold beer

Pour schnapps into frosted mug or glass; add beer.

### Derby Daiquiri *see* DAIQUIRI

**Diablo** [dee-AH-blow] *Diablo* is Spanish for "devil," although there's nothing particularly devilish about this combination. *See also* EL DIABLO.

1½ oz. (3 Tbsp.) white port
1 oz. (2 Tbsp.) dry vermouth
¼ tsp. fresh lemon juice
lemon twist

Shake liquid ingredients with ice. Strain into chilled glass; drop in lemon twist.

### Diana

2 oz. (¼ cup) white crème de menthe
2 to 3 tsp. brandy

Fill a small wineglass with crushed ice; pour in crème de menthe. Float brandy on top by slowly pouring it over the back (rounded) side of a spoon; don't mix.

**digestif** [dee-zheh-STEEF] A French term, also broadly used in English, for a spirited potable taken either after a meal, as a NIGHTCAP or—particularly with bitter potions like FERNET BRANCA—to aid digestion. Digestifs are also called *after-dinner drinks*. Among the many drinks one finds in the capacious category of digestifs are B & B, PINK GIN, and VELVET HAMMER. The only common denominator among these libations is that they all contain spirits of some sort.

### Dinah

1½ oz. (3 Tbsp.) blended whiskey
½ oz. (1 Tbsp.) fresh lemon juice
½ tsp. powdered sugar
mint sprig

Shake all ingredients except mint with ice. Strain into chilled glass; garnish with mint.

## Diplomat

1 $\frac{1}{2}$ oz. (3 Tbsp.) dry vermouth
$\frac{1}{2}$ oz. (1 Tbsp.) sweet vermouth
$\frac{1}{2}$ tsp. maraschino liqueur
2 dashes (about $\frac{1}{8}$ tsp.) Angostura bitters
lemon twist
maraschino cherry

Shake all ingredients except lemon twist and cherry with ice. Strain into chilled glass; drop in lemon twist and cherry.

**dipsomania; dipsomaniac** [DIP-soh-MAY-nee-uh] An irresistible craving for an alcoholic drink. A **dipsomaniac** is the one doing the craving.

**Dirty Martini** *see* MARTINI

## HAT GOES AROUND . . .

*Next time you hear someone say they invented the Dirty Martini, call their bluff. What's true is that this rather murky potable was a favorite of Franklin Delano Roosevelt over a half century ago. History records FDR serving a Dirty Martini to Joseph Stalin in 1943. Maybe that's why the Soviet leader often seemed so dour.*

**distillate** [DIHS-tl-it; DIHS-tl-ate] *see* DISTILLATION *n.*

**distillation** *v.* The process of separating a liquid's components by heating it to the point of vaporization and collecting the cooled condensate (vapor that reverts to liquid through condensation) in order to obtain a purified and/or concentrated form. The apparatus that performs distillation is called a "still," of which there are two types—pot still and continuous still.

The **pot still** (in France, called an **alembic** or **alambic**) consists of a copper or copper-lined pot with a large, rounded bottom and long, tapering neck connected by a copper pipe to a condenser (a cooled spiral tube). As the fermented (*see*

FERMENTATION) liquid (WINE for brandy, MASH for whiskey) in the pot comes to a boil, it vaporizes. The vapor rises up into the still's condenser, where it cools and returns to a liquid state. This condensation (condensate), which has a higher alcohol concentration than the original mixture, is collected in a receiving compartment. However, because alcohol boils at 173.3°F, water at 212°F, and a mixture of the two at a temperature somewhere in between, the condensed liquid still contains some water. This means that redistilling (often several times) may be necessary to achieve the appropriate alcohol level—COGNAC and SCOTCH WHISKY are distilled twice, for example, while IRISH WHISKEY undergoes three distillations. In this case, several pot stills may be lined up, distilling the condensate produced by the first pot still through the second pot still, and so on. The pot still, with its painstaking thoroughness, produces distillates that retain the CHARACTER and personality of their source ingredients.

The **continuous still** was considered revolutionary when it was introduced in 1826. It's also known by several other names: **column still, patent still,** and **Coffey still** (after a Scottish tax official, Aeneas Coffey, who made major improvements to it in the early 1830s). Continuous distillation repeatedly recycles a mixture of steam and alcohol until all the spirit is extracted. The continuous still consists of tall copper columns that continually receive cold mash, which trickles down and over a series of steam-producing plates. As the alcohol vaporizes, it becomes part of the steam which, as it rises, goes through the liquid that is flowing down the plates. As the vapor interacts with this liquid, some of the alcohol in the liquid vaporizes and some of the steam converts back to liquid. The vapor is drawn into vents that then take it to a condenser and receiver. If the tower or column has enough plates, a very high level of alcohol concentration can be attained in this one continuous process. Sometimes two or more towers or columns are used so that higher levels of alcohol or different levels of alcohol concentration can be produced. A single continuous still performs much like the redistilling process with multiple pot stills, and whereas the pot still works in relatively small batches, the continuous still has an uninterrupted flow of incoming material and outgoing product. The continuous still brought mass production to distillers and dramatically expanded Scotland's whisky industry in the 1800s.

**distillation; distilled spirits; distillate** *n*. The end product of the distillation process. Distilled spirits include BRANDY, GIN, RUM, TEQUILA, VODKA, and WHISKEY. These liquors are based on cereal grains, fruit, and sometimes vegetables, which are fermented before beginning the distillation process. After distillation, many are flavored in some way, either with added ingredients, or by barrel AGING, or both. In the United States, each type of distilled spirit must meet strict federal standards relating to the ingredients used (which must be FDA approved) as well as how the liquor is made, labeled (to reflect the contents accurately), advertised, and sold. *See also* ALCOHOL.

*Civilization begins with distillation.*
WILLIAM FAULKNER, AMERICAN NOVELIST

**distilled spirits** *see* DISTILLATION

**distiller's beer** *see* MASH

## Dixie

1 oz. (2 Tbsp.) gin
1 oz. (2 Tbsp.) fresh orange juice
$^1/_2$ oz. (1 Tbsp.) dry vermouth
$^1/_2$ oz. (1 Tbsp.) Pernod or other anise-flavored liqueur
2 dashes (about $^1/_8$ tsp.) grenadine

Shake ingredients with ice; strain into chilled glass.

## Dixie Whiskey

2 oz. ($^1/_4$ cup) bourbon
$^1/_2$ tsp. white crème de menthe
$^1/_4$ tsp. Triple Sec
1 dash (about $^1/_{16}$ tsp.) Angostura bitters
$^1/_2$ tsp. powdered sugar

Shake ingredients with ice; strain into chilled glass.

**Dortmunder** [DORT-moont-er] Originating in Germany's largest brewing city, Dortmund, this gold-colored BEER is darker and less bitter than PILSNER and stronger and paler than MÜNCH-ENER. It's also called simply "Dort."

**double old-fashioned glass** *see* Glassware, page 8

**Double Standard Sour** *see* SOUR

**Dracula's Potion** A German SCHNAPPS with a gingery black-currant flavor.

**dram** 1. A small drink—as in the Scottish usage "a wee dram." 2. A unit of weight in the U.S. Customary System, equivalent to about $^1/_{16}$ ounce. From the Greek *drachmê* (*drachma*), a unit of currency.

---

*Lastly (and this is, perhaps, the golden rule), no woman should marry a teetotaller. . . .*

ROBERT LOUIS STEVENSON, BRITISH WRITER

---

**Drambuie** [dram-BOO-ee] Gaelic for "the drink that satisfies," this Scottish LIQUEUR was first made on the Isle of Skye from a recipe purportedly passed down from Bonnie Prince Charlie. Drambuie is based on SCOTCH WHISKY and sweetened with heather honey. It has a deep golden color and a sweetly spicy, herbal/whisky flavor with overtones of licorice. *See also* WHISK(E)Y-BASED LIQUEURS.

**Dream Cocktail**

$1^1/_2$ oz. (3 Tbsp.) brandy
$^3/_4$ oz. ($1^1/_2$ Tbsp.) Cointreau or Triple Sec
$^1/_2$ tsp. anisette

Shake ingredients with ice; strain into chilled glass.

**Dreamsicle** One of Sharon's favorite childhood memories is of the summertime ice cream truck ambling down the street with a payload of frozen goodies, including her favorite, the Dreamsicle—a heavenly alliance of vanilla and orange. Here's that memory translated to a grown-up drink, along with a nonalcoholic version for those so inclined.

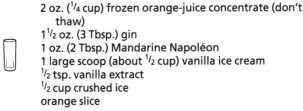

2 oz. (¹/₄ cup) frozen orange-juice concentrate (don't thaw)
1¹/₂ oz. (3 Tbsp.) gin
1 oz. (2 Tbsp.) Mandarine Napoléon
1 large scoop (about ¹/₂ cup) vanilla ice cream
¹/₂ tsp. vanilla extract
¹/₂ cup crushed ice
orange slice

Combine all ingredients except orange slice in a blender. Cover and process at medium speed until smooth, about 15 seconds. Pour into chilled glass; garnish with orange slice.

★ **Creamsicle** Omit liquors; increase orange-juice concentrate to ¹/₂ cup and use 2 scoops ice cream.

**dry** A term used to describe a wine or other spirited beverage that isn't sweet. In wines, dry is also referred to as SEC (*see* SEC).

### Dubarry Cocktail

1¹/₂ oz. (3 Tbsp.) gin
³/₄ oz. (1¹/₂ Tbsp.) dry vermouth
¹/₂ tsp. anisette
1 dash (about ¹/₁₆ tsp.) Angostura bitters
orange slice

Stir liquid ingredients with ice. Strain into chilled glass; garnish with orange slice.

**Dubonnet** [doo-buh-NAY] An aromatic, wine-based APÉRITIF of which there are two styles: **Dubonnet rouge** (also called simply *red*), the richer of the two, is red-wine based and flavored with QUININE; **Dubonnet blanc** (also called *blond*) is a drier (*see* DRY), VERMOUTH-style apéritif. Dubonnet originated in France, but is now also made in the United States.

### Dubonnet Cocktail

1 oz. (2 Tbsp.) Dubonnet rouge
³/₄ oz. (1¹/₂ Tbsp.) gin
1 dash (about ¹/₁₆ tsp.) orange bitters
lemon twist

Stir liquid ingredients with ice. Strain into chilled glass; drop in lemon twist.

*A* drunk at a bar said to a man sitting next to him,
*"One drink always makes me drunk." The other guy
says, "You're kidding—only one?" The drunk reels back
in his seat, "Yeah, and it's usually the sixth."*

### Dubonnet Fizz

2 oz. ($^1$/4 cup) Dubonnet rouge
1 oz. (2 Tbsp.) fresh orange juice
$^1$/2 oz. (1 Tbsp.) cherry brandy
$^1$/2 oz. (1 Tbsp.) fresh lemon juice
cold club soda
lemon slice
maraschino cherry

Shake first 4 ingredients with ice; strain into chilled glass over ice cubes. Top with club soda, stirring gently. Garnish with fruit.

### Duchess

$^3$/4 oz. (1$^1$/2 Tbsp.) anisette
$^3$/4 oz. (1$^1$/2 Tbsp.) sweet vermouth
$^3$/4 oz. (1$^1$/2 Tbsp.) dry vermouth

Shake ingredients with ice; strain into chilled glass.

**Dutch courage** Also referred to as *Irish courage,* any alcoholic drink taken to bolster one's nerve. The term originated in the late seventeenth century when British soldiers stationed in the Netherlands first tasted GIN and dubbed it "Dutch courage" for its restorative powers.

**Earl Grey English Liqueur** A syrupy, russet-colored, tea-flavored LIQUEUR from England.

### Earthquake

1 oz. (2 Tbsp.) rye whiskey
1 oz. (2 Tbsp.) gin
1 oz. (2 Tbsp.) Pernod or other anise-flavored liqueur

Shake ingredients with ice; strain into chilled glass.

## East India

1¹/₂ oz. (3 Tbsp.) brandy
1¹/₂ tsp. Cointreau
1¹/₂ tsp. unsweetened pineapple juice
1 dash (about ¹/₁₆ tsp.) Angostura bitters
lemon twist
maraschino cherry

Shake liquid ingredients with ice. Strain into chilled glass; drop in twist and cherry.

## East India *see* SHERRY

## East Indian (Special)

1¹/₂ oz. (3 Tbsp.) dry sherry
1¹/₂ oz. (3 Tbsp.) dry vermouth
2 dashes (about ¹/₈ tsp.) orange bitters

Shake ingredients with ice; strain into chilled glass.

**Eau-de-vie;** *pl.* **Eaux-de-vie** [oh-deuh-VEE] French for "water of life," *eau-de-vie* describes any of many colorless, potent spirits distilled (*see* DISTILLATION) from fermented (*see* FERMENTATION) fruit juice. Some of the better-known *eaux-de-vie* are FRAMBOISE (distilled from raspberries), KIRSCH (cherries), and POIRE WILLIAMS (pears). In France *eau-de-vie de vin* is BRANDY, whereas *eau-de-vie de cidre* is CALVADOS. *See also* AIRELLE; FRAISE DES BOIS; MIRABELLE; QUETSCH.

**Echte Kroatzbeere** [ehkht KROHTZ-bay-rer] German for "genuine blackberry," *Echte Kroatzbeere* is a clear, ruby-colored LIQUEUR that tastes like the wild blackberries from which it's made.

## Eclipse

maraschino cherry
1¹/₂ tsp. grenadine
1¹/₂ oz. (3 Tbsp.) sloe gin
1 oz. (2 Tbsp.) gin
orange twist

Drop cherry into chilled glass; add grenadine. Shake gins with ice; strain into glass by slowly pouring over the back (rounded) side of a spoon so that the gin mixture floats on the grenadine. Drop in orange twist.

★ **Egg Cream** *see* EGG CREAM SPECIAL

**Egg Cream Special** A spirited version of the famous New York concoction in which there are—surprise—no eggs or cream, but simply equal parts chocolate syrup and milk, mixed with club soda. Our boozy rendition *does* use cream to create the richness that's missing because liquor replaces the milk. The darker and richer the chocolate syrup, the better this drink.

> 1½ oz. (3 Tbsp.) dark chocolate syrup
> 1½ oz. (3 Tbsp.) brandy, rum, or gin
> 1 oz. (2 Tbsp.) cold cream or half & half
> cold club soda

Stir chocolate syrup, liquor, and cream together until well blended. Top with club soda, stirring vigorously to create a foamy head.

★ **Egg Cream** Substitute 4 to 6 oz. (½ to ¾ cup) cold milk for the liquor and cream.

**Egghead**

> 4 oz. (½ cup) fresh orange juice
> 1½ oz. (3 Tbsp.) vodka
> 1 egg
> ½ cup crushed ice

Combine all ingredients in a blender. Cover and process at medium speed until smooth, about 15 seconds. Pour into chilled glass over ice cubes.

★ **Smart Head** Omit vodka; increase orange juice to ⅔ cup.

*Memorial services are the cocktail parties of the geriatric set.*

HAROLD MACMILLAN, BRITISH POLITICIAN

**eggnog; nog** A creamy, egg-rich concoction commonly liberally laced with rum, brandy, or bourbon (or a combination of liquors). The eggnog is named after whatever liquor it contains, such as "Brandy Eggnog" or "Sherry Eggnog." Alcohol-free versions have long been served to fortify growing children and convalescents.

Homemade eggnog's calorie and cholesterol count can be reduced by substituting nonfat evaporated milk for the cream or whole milk, and by using 2 egg whites for each whole egg. The sweetness of any eggnog can be reduced and the texture lightened by folding in stiffly beaten egg whites just before serving. Leftover homemade eggnog should be tightly covered and refrigerated for use within 2 days. *See also* CHOCOLATE EGGNOG; COFFEE EGGNOG; EGGNOG-FLAVORED SPIRITS.

**Eggnog for One** Since this libation isn't typically served over ice, chilling all the ingredients beforehand will create a colder drink. Alternatively, the ingredients may be shaken with ice and strained into the glass, but that slightly dilutes the mix.

> 1 egg
> 2 tsp. sugar
> 1/4 tsp. pure vanilla extract
> pinch of salt
> 2 oz. (1/4 cup) brandy, bourbon, rum, sherry, or other liquor
> 6 oz. (3/4 cup) very cold milk
> freshly grated nutmeg

Beat egg, sugar, vanilla, and salt until smooth and light; pour into chilled glass. Stir in liquor and milk, mixing well; sprinkle lightly with nutmeg.

➤ **Hot Eggnog** Heat milk just until it simmers (do not boil). Gradually whisk milk into beaten-egg mixture. Pour into a warm heatproof mug. *See also* Hot Drinks, page 29.

★ **Nogless Eggnog** Substitute 2 oz. (1/4 cup) more milk for the liquor.

### Party Eggnog

MAKES ABOUT THIRTY 6-OUNCE SERVINGS

12 eggs, separated
1 cup sugar
16 oz. (1 pint; 2 cups) brandy
16 oz. (1 pint; 2 cups) bourbon or dark rum
32 oz. (1 quart; 4 cups) milk
1 tablespoon pure vanilla extract
32 oz. (1 quart; 4 cups) whipping cream
$^1/_2$ tsp. salt
freshly grated nutmeg

Beat egg yolks with the sugar until creamy and light. Stir in brandy, bourbon, milk, and vanilla; cover and refrigerate for at least 4 hours, or until very cold. Whip cream until it forms soft mounds; fold into eggnog mixture. May be refrigerated for 1 to 2 hours at this point. Just before serving, beat egg whites and salt to the soft-peak stage; fold into eggnog. Sprinkle with nutmeg.

**eggnog-flavored spirits** *see* ADVOCAAT; VOV ZABAJONE

**eggs** *see* Ingredients, page 13

### Egg Sour *See also* SOUR.

$1^1/_2$ oz. (3 Tbsp.) brandy
$1^1/_2$ oz. (3 Tbsp.) Cointreau
1 oz. (2 Tbsp.) fresh lemon juice
1 tsp. powdered sugar
1 egg
maraschino cherry

Vigorously shake all ingredients except cherry with ice. Pour into chilled glass over ice cubes; garnish with cherry.

**Eisbock** [EYESS-bahk] *see* BEER; BOCK BEER

### El Diablo *See also* DIABLO.

$^1/_2$ lime
$1^1/_2$ oz. (3 Tbsp.) tequila
$^1/_2$ oz. (1 Tbsp.) crème de cassis
cold ginger ale

Put 3 to 4 ice cubes in chilled glass. Squeeze lime juice into glass and drop in lime shell; add tequila and crème de cassis. Top with ginger ale, stirring gently.

## Electric Lemonade

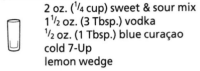

2 oz. (¼ cup) sweet & sour mix
1½ oz. (3 Tbsp.) vodka
½ oz. (1 Tbsp.) blue curaçao
cold 7-Up
lemon wedge

Pour first 3 ingredients into chilled glass filled with ice cubes. Top with 7-Up, stirring well. Garnish with lemon wedge.

➤**Variation** Substitute ½ oz. (1 Tbsp.) each vodka, gin, and rum for the 1½ oz. vodka.

---

*A cocktail or several, before dinner, enabled me to laugh wholeheartedly at things which had long since ceased being laughable.*

JACK LONDON, AMERICAN AUTHOR

---

## El Presidente #1

1½ oz. (3 Tbsp.) light rum
¾ oz. (1½ Tbsp.) dry vermouth
1 dash (about ¹⁄₁₆ tsp.) Angostura bitters

Stir ingredients with ice; strain into chilled glass.

## El Presidente #2

1½ oz. (3 Tbsp.) light rum
½ oz. (1 Tbsp.) fresh lime juice
½ oz. (1 Tbsp.) unsweetened pineapple juice
1 tsp. grenadine

Shake ingredients with ice; strain into chilled glass.

## El Salvador

1½ oz. (3 Tbsp.) light rum
¾ oz. (1½ Tbsp.) Frangelico
½ oz. (1 Tbsp.) fresh lime juice
1 tsp. grenadine

Shake ingredients with ice; strain into chilled glass.

### Emerald Isle Cocktail

2 oz. ($^{1}/_{4}$ cup) gin
1 tsp. green crème de menthe
2 dashes (about $^{1}/_{8}$ tsp.) Angostura bitters
green maraschino cherry, optional

Stir liquid ingredients with ice. Strain into chilled glass; garnish with cherry, if desired.

### Emerson

1 $^{1}/_{2}$ oz. (3 Tbsp.) gin
1 oz. (2 Tbsp.) sweet vermouth
$^{1}/_{2}$ oz. (1 Tbsp.) fresh lime juice
1 tsp. maraschino liqueur

Shake ingredients with ice; strain into chilled glass.

### Empire

1 $^{1}/_{2}$ oz. (3 Tbsp.) gin
$^{1}/_{2}$ oz. (1 Tbsp.) apple brandy
$^{1}/_{2}$ oz. (1 Tbsp.) apricot brandy

Stir ingredients with ice; strain into chilled glass.

**enology** [ee-NAHL-uh-jee] The science or study of making wines. An expert in the field is an **enologist** or **enologue.** Also spelled *enology.*

**enophile** [EE-nuh-file] Someone who enjoys wine, commonly referred to as a connoisseur. Also spelled *oenophile.*

**Escorial Green (Grün)** [ehs-KOR-ee-uhl (GREWN)] Best served chilled, this Bavarian herb-flavored LIQUEUR is—you guessed it—green colored. *See also* HERB-FLAVORED SPIRITS.

**estate bottled** *see* WINE LABEL TERMS

### Everybody's Irish

2 oz. ($^{1}/_{4}$ cup) Irish whiskey
1 tsp. green crème de menthe
1 tsp. green Chartreuse
stuffed green olive

Stir liquid ingredients with ice. Strain into chilled glass; garnish with olive.

➤ **Shamrock** Add $^1/_2$ oz. (1 Tbsp.) dry vermouth.

**Evian** [ay-vee-AHN] A famous French mineral water, it's the namesake of the spa town at the foot of Mont Blanc from which it hails.

**eye-opener; eyeopener** American slang for an alcoholic drink taken early in the day to wake up those who are sluggish—for whatever reason.

### Eye-Opener

1$^1/_2$ oz. (3 Tbsp.) light rum
1 tsp. Cointreau
1 tsp. white crème de cacao
$^1/_2$ tsp. Pernod or other anise-flavored liqueur
1 egg yolk
$^1/_2$ tsp. powdered sugar

Vigorously shake ingredients with ice; strain into chilled glass.

**Falernum** [fuh-LER-num] Made in the West Indies, Falernum is a syrupy sweetener with a flavor reminiscent of lime, ginger, and almonds. *See also* SYRUPS, FLAVORED.

### Fallen Angel

2 oz. ($^1/_4$ cup) gin
$^3/_4$ oz. (1$^1/_2$ Tbsp.) fresh lemon or lime juice
1 tsp. white crème de menthe
1 dash (about $^1/_{16}$ tsp.) Angostura bitters
maraschino cherry

Shake liquid ingredients with ice. Strain into chilled glass; garnish with cherry.

### Fancy Brandy

2 oz. ($^1/_4$ cup) brandy
$^1/_2$ tsp. Cointreau or Triple Sec
2 dashes (about $^1/_8$ tsp.) Angostura bitters
$^1/_2$ tsp. powdered sugar
lemon twist

Shake liquid ingredients with ice. Strain into chilled glass; drop in lemon twist.

➤ **Fancy Gin** Substitute gin for the brandy.

➤ **Fancy Whiskey** Substitute blended whiskey for the brandy.

### Fantasio

1 ¹/₂ oz. (3 Tbsp.) brandy
³/₄ oz. (1 ¹/₂ Tbsp.) dry vermouth
1 tsp. white crème de menthe
1 tsp. maraschino liqueur

Shake ingredients with ice; strain into chilled glass.

### Farmer's Cocktail

1 ¹/₂ oz. (3 Tbsp.) gin
³/₄ oz. (1 ¹/₂ Tbsp.) dry vermouth
³/₄ oz. (1 ¹/₂ Tbsp.) sweet vermouth
2 dashes (about ¹/₈ tsp.) Angostura bitters

Stir ingredients with ice; strain into chilled glass.

---

*The only way to get rid of a temptation is to yield to it.*

OSCAR WILDE, ANGLO-IRISH PLAYWRIGHT, CRITIC

---

### Favorite Cocktail

³/₄ oz. (1 ¹/₂ Tbsp.) gin
³/₄ oz. (1 ¹/₂ Tbsp.) dry vermouth
³/₄ oz. (1 ¹/₂ Tbsp.) apricot brandy
¹/₄ tsp. fresh lemon juice

Shake ingredients with ice; strain into chilled glass over ice cubes.

**fermentation; fermenting** The natural process whereby yeast enzymes convert sugars from grain, fruit, and vegetables into alcohol. In wine, for example, the sugars in grape juice are converted into alcohol, while RUM utilizes molasses made from sugarcane. With WHISKEYS, a MASH is made from cereal grains, such as corn, rye, or barley—diastase enzymes convert the grain's starches into sugar, which is subsequently converted by yeast to alcohol.

**Fernet Branca** [FAYR-nay BRAHN-kah] An extremely astringent, very brown Italian BITTERS. Long known as a DIGESTIF, Fernet Branca originated in Milan in the early 1800s. As with most such elixirs, Fernet Branca is made from a secret formula, but this one purportedly includes some 40 ingredients, including rhubarb, chamomile, and myrrh. Although many use it primarily as a hangover cure and stomach soother, Italians enjoy 80-PROOF Fernet Branca as an APÉRITIF, either STRAIGHT or ON THE ROCKS.

### Ferrari [feh-RAHR-ree]

2 oz. (¼ cup) dry vermouth
1 oz. (2 Tbsp.) amaretto
lemon twist

Pour vermouth and amaretto into chilled glass filled with ice cubes; stir well. Garnish with lemon twist.

### Fifth Avenue

1 oz. (2 Tbsp.) dark crème de cacao
1 oz. (2 Tbsp.) apricot brandy
½ oz. (1 Tbsp.) cream

Pour crème de cacao into chilled glass. Add remaining ingredients in order given, slowly pouring each one over the back (rounded) side of a spoon so that it floats on top of the one below. Don't mix.

### Fifty-Fifty

1½ oz. (3 Tbsp.) gin
1½ oz. (3 Tbsp.) dry vermouth
stuffed green olive

Stir liquid ingredients with ice. Strain into chilled glass; garnish with olive.

### Fine and Dandy

1½ oz. (3 Tbsp.) gin
½ oz. (1 Tbsp.) Triple Sec or Cointreau
½ oz. (1 Tbsp.) fresh lemon juice
1 dash (about 1/16 tsp.) Angostura bitters
maraschino cherry

Shake liquid ingredients with ice. Strain into chilled glass; garnish with cherry.

**finger** As a unit of measurement, this term refers to the breadth of a finger, approximately three-quarters of an inch. Order "three fingers of SCOTCH" and you'll get a little over 2 inches of liquor (sans ice), typically served in a HIGHBALL or OLD-FASHIONED GLASS.

**fining** A winemaking procedure that improves a wine's clarity by removing microscopic elements (like protein particles) and reduces bitterness and astringency by removing phenolic compounds like TANNINS. The most frequently used fining agents are activated carbon, activated charcoal, bentonite, casein, egg whites, gelatin, isinglass, nylon, and polyvinyl poly-pyrrolidone (PVPP). When added to wine, fining agents capture suspended particles by absorption or coagulation, causing them to settle to the bottom of the container. Once the particles sink, the wine is separated from this sediment through racking (siphoning), filtering, or centrifuging. In addition to clarifying wines, various fining agents can also be used to remove color from white wines, deodorize wines with an off odor, and reduce acids.

**finish** The final impression of flavor and texture that remains in the mouth after a potable is swallowed.

**fino; fino amontillado** [FEE-noh ah-mon-the-LAH-doh] *see* SHERRY

**Fino Martini** *see* MARTINI

**fiore d'alpi** [FYOH-ray DAHL-pee] Italian for "alpine flowers," *fiore d'alpi* describes any of several sweet Italian LIQUEURS that use mountain herbs as their flavor base. Each bottle of this style of liqueur contains a small tree branch heavily encrusted with sparkling sugar crystals. These liqueurs are also called *Flor Alpina* and *Mille Fiori. See also* HERB-FLAVORED SPIRITS.

**Fireman's Sour** *see* SOUR

**firewater** A nineteenth-century term for strong liquor (usually WHISKEY), thought to have been translated from *ishkodewaaboo,* the Ojibwa word for whiskey.

*When I have one martini, I feel bigger, wiser, taller. When I have a second, I feel superlative. When I have more, there's no holding me.*

WILLIAM FAULKNER, AMERICAN NOVELIST

**Fish House Punch** Legend tells us that this punch dates back to 1732, when it was created for the members of Philadelphia's State in Schuylkill Fishing Club by Captain Samuel Morris. The recipe has undergone numerous permutations—one substitutes cold water for the tea, another uses 1½ quarts dark rum and 1 pint brandy. The following version is arguably one of the most popular.

MAKES ABOUT TWENTY-FIVE 6-OUNCE SERVINGS

juice of 12 lemons (about 2¼ cups)
about 1 cup sugar
48 oz. (1½ quarts; 6 cups) brandy
32 oz. (1 quart; 4 cups) cold strong tea
16 oz. (1 pint; 2 cups) dark rum
16 oz. (1 pint; 2 cups) peach brandy
32 oz. (1 quart; 4 cups) cold club soda
2 fresh peaches, peeled and sliced, optional

Combine lemon juice and sugar in a large punch bowl, stirring well to dissolve. Stir in brandy, tea, rum, and peach brandy; cover and refrigerate until ready to serve. Just before serving, add a block of ice (see Punch Bowl Ice, page 17); gently stir in club soda and garnish with fruit, if desired.

**Fix** This smaller version of the COBBLER always includes lemon juice and plenty of crushed ice, and is traditionally served in an OLD-FASHIONED GLASS.

## Brandy Fix

½ oz. (1 Tbsp.) fresh lemon juice
1 tsp. powdered sugar
2 oz. (¼ cup) brandy
lemon slice

Combine lemon juice and sugar in chilled glass, stirring to dissolve sugar. Fill with crushed or cracked ice; add brandy and stir. Garnish with lemon slice.

➤ **Gin Fix** Substitute gin for the brandy.

➤ **Irish Fix** Substitute Irish whiskey for the brandy, add ½ oz. (1 Tbsp.) *each* Irish Mist and pineapple juice. Garnish with lemon slice and pineapple spear.

➤ **Rum Fix** Substitute rum for the brandy.

**fizz** "Fizzy water" (CLUB SODA) is what gives this drink its name. The technique to making it is to shake all the ingredients together with ice, then strain the mixture into an ice-filled glass, and top it off with fizz (soda). Because fizzes vary widely in their ingredients, see individual listings for: APPLE BLOW FIZZ; BUCK'S FIZZ; CHICAGO FIZZ; DANISH GIN FIZZ; DUBONNET FIZZ; GIN FIZZ; GOLDEN FIZZ; GRAND ROYAL FIZZ; IMPERIAL FIZZ; JAPANESE FIZZ; MORNING GLORY FIZZ; OSTEND FIZZ; PEACH BLOW FIZZ; PICON FIZZ; PINEAPPLE FIZZ; RAMOS FIZZ; ROYAL GIN FIZZ; RUBY FIZZ; SILVER FIZZ; SLOE GIN FIZZ.

**flaming drinks** *see* BLUE BLAZER; CAFÉ DIABLO; CAFÉ ROYALE

## Flamingo

1½ oz. (3 Tbsp.) gin
½ oz. (1 Tbsp.) apricot brandy
½ oz. (1 Tbsp.) fresh lime juice
1 tsp. grenadine

Shake ingredients with ice; strain into chilled glass.

**flavored vodka** *see* INFUSED VODKA; VODKA

**flip** The original flip was made by plunging a hot fireplace poker ("flip iron" or "iron flip dog") into a concoction of rum, beer, sweetener, and spices and stirring vigorously, thereby heating and blending the drink. Adding beaten eggs to the poker-stirred potion changed the old-time flip to a *yard of flannel,* referring to the roughened surface caused by the cooked eggs. Today's flip always includes an egg and, depending on the version, may be served hot or cold. *See also* PERNOD FLIP; SEVILLA FLIP; STREGA FLIP.

**float** *v.* To slowly pour a liquid (such as LIQUEUR or cream) over another liquid so that it floats on top of it. In the case of a POUSSE-CAFÉ, several liquids are floated, one on top of the other, so as not to mix them together. *See also* Floating and Layering Techniques, page 30. **float** *n.* A small amount of liquid (such as liqueur or cream) that sits atop another liquid without becoming mixed in.

**Flor Alpina** *see* FIORE D'ALPI

### Florida

1 ½ oz. (3 Tbsp.) fresh orange juice
¾ oz. (1 ½ Tbsp.) gin
2 tsp. Triple Sec
2 tsp. kirsch
1 tsp. fresh lemon juice
orange slice

Shake liquid ingredients with ice. Strain into chilled glass; garnish with orange slice.

**flower-flavored spirits** *see* CRÈME DE ROSE; CRÈME DE VIOLETTE; CRÈME YVETTE

**flute glass** *see* Glassware, page 8

### Flying Dutchman

2 oz. (¼ cup) gin
½ tsp. Triple Sec
1 dash (about ¹⁄₁₆ tsp.) orange bitters

Pour ingredients into chilled glass filled with ice cubes; stir well.

*Alcohol: An excellent preservative for almost anything . . . except secrets.*

### Flying Grasshopper

1 ½ oz. (3 Tbsp.) vodka
½ oz. (1 Tbsp.) white crème de menthe
½ oz. (1 Tbsp.) green crème de menthe

Shake ingredients with cracked ice; strain into chilled glass over ice cubes.

## Flying Scotsman

1 1/2 oz. (3 Tbsp.) Scotch
1 1/2 oz. (3 Tbsp.) sweet vermouth
1/4 tsp. powdered sugar
1 dash (about 1/16 tsp.) Angostura bitters

Stir ingredients with ice; strain into chilled glass over ice cubes.

## Fog Cutter

1 1/2 oz. (3 Tbsp.) light rum
1 1/2 oz. (3 Tbsp.) fresh orange juice
1 oz. (2 Tbsp.) fresh lemon juice
1/2 oz. (1 Tbsp.) brandy
1/2 oz. (1 Tbsp.) gin
1 1/2 tsp. orgeat syrup
1 tsp. sweet sherry

Shake all ingredients except sherry with ice. Strain into chilled glass; float sherry on top by slowly pouring it over the back (rounded) side of a spoon; don't mix.

## Foghorn

2 oz. (1/4 cup) gin
1/2 oz. (1 Tbsp.) fresh lime juice
cold ginger ale
lime slice

Put 4 to 5 ice cubes in chilled glass; add gin, lime juice, and ginger ale, stirring lightly. Garnish with lime slice.

**Forbidden Fruit** A tangy, brandy-based American LIQUEUR flavored with honey, oranges, and pomelo (also called "shaddock"), a grapefruit-like fruit. *See also* CITRUS-FLAVORED SPIRITS.

**fortified wine** *see* WINE

## Fort Lauderdale

1 1/2 oz. (3 Tbsp.) light rum
1/2 oz. (1 Tbsp.) sweet vermouth
2 tsp. fresh lime juice
2 tsp. fresh orange juice
orange slice

Shake liquid ingredients with ice. Strain into chilled glass over ice cubes; garnish with orange slice.

### Fox River

2 oz. ($^1/_4$ cup) rye whiskey
$^1/_2$ oz. (1 Tbsp.) crème de cacao
4 dashes (about $^1/_4$ tsp.) Angostura or peach bitters
lemon twist

Shake liquid ingredients with ice. Strain into chilled glass; drop in lemon twist.

**Fragonard Liqueur de Cognac X.O.** [frah-gaw-NAHR] A CO-GNAC-based, silky-smooth French LIQUEUR with a creamy chocolate flavor and hints of nuts and fruit. *See also* CHOCO-LATE-FLAVORED SPIRITS.

**fraise des bois** [frehz day BWAH] 1. A colorless, strawberry-flavored EAU-DE-VIE. *Fraise* is French for "strawberry." 2. The name of a tiny, intensely sweet wild strawberry from France.

**framboise** [frahm-BWAHZ] A potent, colorless EAU-DE-VIE distilled from raspberries. *Framboise* is French for "raspberry." *See also* RASPBERRY-FLAVORED SPIRITS.

**Frangelico** [fran-JELL-ih-koh] Made in northern Italy, Frangelico is a clear, golden-colored LIQUEUR with a buttery hazelnut flavor that has hints of vanilla and white chocolate. *See also* NUT-FLAVORED SPIRITS.

### Frankenjack Cocktail

1 oz. (2 Tbsp.) gin
$^1/_2$ oz. (1 Tbsp.) dry vermouth
$^1/_2$ oz. (1 Tbsp.) apricot brandy
1 tsp. Triple Sec or Cointreau
maraschino cherry

Shake liquid ingredients with ice. Strain into chilled glass; garnish with cherry.

**frappé** [fra-PAY] A drink made by pouring a spirit—usually a LIQUEUR—over crushed or shaved ice in an OLD-FASHIONED GLASS. A frappé is usually served as an after-dinner drink. *See also* ALL-WHITE FRAPPÉ; PERNOD FRAPPÉ.

**frappé glass** *see* Glassware, page 8

### Freddy Fudpucker

1 oz. (2 Tbsp.) tequila
4 to 6 oz. (¹/₂ to ³/₄ cup) fresh orange juice
¹/₂ oz. (1 Tbsp.) Galliano

Pour tequila and orange juice into chilled glass filled with ice cubes; stir well. Float Galliano on top by slowly pouring it over the back (rounded) side of a spoon; don't mix.

➤ **Variation** Add ¹/₂ oz. (1 Tbsp.) Kahlúa or Tia Maria; shake ingredients with ice and strain into chilled glass over ice cubes.

**French** In British cocktail lingo, to order a drink "French" (such as a "VODKA and French") means you want it mixed with dry VERMOUTH. The jargon comes from the days when Italians produced only sweet vermouths while the French vermouths were DRY. Now, of course, both countries produce both styles.

### French Connection

2 oz. (¹/₄ cup) brandy
1 oz. (2 Tbsp.) amaretto

Pour into chilled glass over ice cubes; stir well.

**French 75** This potent cocktail is said to have been named after the powerful French 75-millimeter howitzer cannon, which also delivers quite a punch.

1 oz. (2 Tbsp.) lemon juice
2 oz. (¹/₄ cup) cognac
1 tsp. sugar
about 4 oz. (¹/₂ cup) cold dry champagne

Shake all ingredients except champagne with ice; strain into chilled glass. Add 2 ice cubes; top with champagne, stirring gently.

➤ **Champagne Collins** Substitute gin for the cognac.

*I like [champagne] because it always tastes as though my foot is asleep.*

ART BUCHWALD, AMERICAN HUMORIST

**Friesengeist** [FREET-zehn-gighst] A potent mint LIQUEUR from Germany. *See also* MINT-FLAVORED SPIRITS.

**Frisco Sour** *see* SOUR

**frost, to** *see* Chilling Glasses; Frosting Glasses; Frosting Glass Rims with Sugar or Salt, page 24

**Frostbite**

2 oz. (¼ cup) cream
1½ oz. (3 Tbsp.) tequila
¾ oz. (1½ Tbsp.) blue curaçao
½ oz. (1 Tbsp.) crème de cacao

Shake ingredients with cracked ice; strain into chilled glass.

**frosted glass** A term used in two ways. The first refers to a glass that has been placed in the freezer until it is so cold it becomes "frosty" when removed (after about 1 hour). The second way to make a glass frosted is by coating the rim with salt or sugar. *See* Chilling Glasses; Frosting Glass Rims with Sugar or Salt, page 24.

**Froth Blower Cocktail**

2 oz. (¼ cup) gin
1 egg white
1 tsp. grenadine

Vigorously shake ingredients with ice; strain into chilled glass.

**Froupe** [FROOP]

1½ oz. (3 Tbsp.) brandy
1½ oz. (3 Tbsp.) sweet vermouth
1 tsp. Bénédictine

Stir ingredients with ice; strain into chilled glass.

**Frozen Berkley**

1½ oz. (3 Tbsp.) light rum
½ oz. (1 Tbsp.) brandy
2 tsp. passion-fruit syrup or juice
1 tsp. fresh lemon or lime juice
½ cup crushed ice

Combine all ingredients in a blender. Cover and process at medium speed until smooth, about 15 seconds. Pour into chilled glass.

**Frozen Daiquiri** *see* DAIQUIRI

**Frozen Margarita** *see* MARGARITA

**Frozen Matador**

> 2 oz. (¹/₄ cup) unsweetened pineapple juice
> 1¹/₂ oz. (3 Tbsp.) tequila
> ¹/₂ oz. (1 Tbsp.) fresh lime juice
> ¹/₂ cup crushed ice
> pineapple spear

Shake all ingredients except pineapple spear with ice. Pour into chilled glass; garnish with pineapple.

**fruit beer** Mild ALES flavored with fruit concentrates. *See also* BEER.

**fruit brandy** *see* BRANDY

**fruit-flavored spirits** *see* listings for individual fruits (BERRY-FLAVORED SPIRITS, ORANGE FLAVORED SPIRITS, ETC.)

**fruit syrups** *see* SYRUPS, FLAVORED

★ **Fuzzless Navel** *see* FUZZY NAVEL

**Fuzzy Navel**

> 2 oz. (¹/₄ cup) peach schnapps
> about 6 oz. (³/₄ cup) fresh orange juice
> orange slice

Pour peach schnapps and orange juice into chilled glass filled with ice cubes; stir well. Garnish with orange slice.

> ★ **Fuzzless Navel** Substitute peach nectar for the peach schnapps.

**Galliano** [gal-LYAH-noh] Also referred to as *Liquore Galliano,* this Italian herbal LIQUEUR is a brilliant saffron-yellow color. Its nuances of herbs, flowers, and spices add up to an intriguingly unique taste sensation. Liquore Galliano is very sweet and has a thick, syrupy texture. It gained notoriety in the United States when the HARVEY WALLBANGER was introduced in the late 1960s. *See also* HERB-FLAVORED SPIRITS.

**Galliano Stinger** *see* STINGER

**Gammel Dansk** *see* BITTERS

**Gauguin** [goh-GA*N*]

2 oz. (¹/₄ cup) light rum
¹/₂ oz. (1 Tbsp.) passion-fruit syrup
¹/₂ oz. (1 Tbsp.) fresh lemon juice
¹/₂ oz. (1 Tbsp.) fresh lime juice
¹/₂ cup crushed ice
maraschino cherry

Combine all ingredients except cherry in a blender. Cover and process at medium speed until smooth, about 15 seconds. Pour into chilled glass; garnish with cherry.

**Gazette**

1¹/₂ oz. (3 Tbsp.) brandy
³/₄ oz. (1¹/₂ Tbsp.) sweet vermouth
1 tsp. fresh lemon juice
¹/₂ tsp. powdered sugar

Shake ingredients with ice; strain into chilled glass.

---

*You know you've had too much to drink when you can light candles on a birthday cake by blowing on them!*

---

**Genever** *see* GIN

**Genoa** There are two entirely different drinks called "Genoa," so if this isn't the one you're thinking of, see GENOA VODKA.

³/₄ oz. (1¹/₂ Tbsp.) gin
³/₄ oz. (1¹/₂ Tbsp.) grappa
2 tsp. Sambuca
2 tsp. dry vermouth
stuffed green olive

Stir liquid ingredients with ice. Strain into chilled glass over ice cubes; garnish with olive.

## Genoa Vodka

2 oz. (¼ cup) fresh orange juice
1½ oz. (3 Tbsp.) vodka
¾ oz. (1½ Tbsp.) Campari
orange slice

Shake liquid ingredients with ice; strain into chilled glass over ice cubes. Garnish with orange slice.

## Gentle Bull

1½ oz. (3 Tbsp.) tequila
¾ oz. (1½ Tbsp.) Kahlúa
¾ oz. (1½ Tbsp.) cream

Shake ingredients with ice; strain into chilled glass.

## Gibson *see* MARTINI

*A well-made Martini or Gibson, correctly chilled and nicely served, has been more often my true friend than any two-legged creature.*

M.F.K. FISHER, AMERICAN AUTHOR

## Gilroy

1 oz. (2 Tbsp.) gin
1 oz. (2 Tbsp.) cherry brandy
½ oz. (1 Tbsp.) dry vermouth
½ oz. (1 Tbsp.) fresh lemon juice
4 dashes (about ¼ tsp.) orange bitters

Shake ingredients with ice; strain into chilled glass.

## Gimlet [GIHM-liht] The British say that the secret of a truly good gimlet is thorough mixing with ice. If you substitute fresh lime juice for the ROSE'S LIME JUICE, add 1 teaspoon confectioners' sugar. If desired, the rim of the glass may frosted by dipping it in lime juice, then granulated sugar. Chill the sugar-frosted glass thoroughly before preparing the drink.

2 oz. (¼ cup) gin
½ oz. (1 Tbsp.) Rose's lime juice
lime slice, optional

Shake liquid ingredients with ice. Strain into chilled glass; garnish with lime.

**gin** A distilled (*see* DISTILLATION) liquor made from grain and flavored primarily with juniper berries. According to most historians, the "Father of Gin" was Dutchman Franciscus de la Böe, a University of Leiden professor of medicine, also known as Doctor Sylvius. It was 1650 when the good Doctor developed an alcohol-based medicinal infused with juniper berries—oil of juniper having known therapeutic properties as an appetite stimulant, stomach soother, fever reducer, and sedative, to name just a few. The Dutch called this potion *jenever* (juniper), the French, *genièvre*. British soldiers stationed in the Netherlands during the late seventeenth century tagged gin "Dutch courage" for its restorative powers and brought it home, where it fast became the rage and is still an English favorite.

In the most basic terms, gin is first distilled until it achieves a desired alcohol level, then redistilled with juniper berries and other botanicals to extract the desired flavors. Distilled water is then added to adjust the alcohol concentration to somewhere between 80 and 95 PROOF. Gin producers closely guard their secret recipes, which can contain numerous botanicals, including angelica, anise, calamus root, caraway seed, cardamom, cassia bark, cinnamon, citrus peel, coriander seeds, fennel, ginger, licorice, and orris root.

There are two primary styles of gin—Dutch and dry. **Dutch gin,** also known as *Hollands, Genever, Jenever,* and *Schiedam* gin, is typically made from equal parts of malted (*see* MALT) barley, corn, and rye. This style of gin is slightly sweet, has a malty CHARACTER, and is generally fuller flavored than dry gin. There are two styles of Dutch gin: *Oude* ("old") has a stronger flavor, due to a higher proportion of barley than the *Jonge* ("young") style, which is lighter in flavor and texture. **Dry gin**—the style of choice for most of the gin-drinking world—is made primarily from corn with a small percentage of malted barley and other grains. This gin is typically DRY (not sweet), aromatic, and moderately light in flavor and BODY. Dry gins made in England (where this style originated) commonly have a slightly higher alcohol content and are more flavorful than American-made gins. Labels indicating "English Dry Gin," "London Dry Gin," or "London Extra Dry Gin" allude to the gin's style, not where it was produced. **Plymouth gin** (also called *Plym*) is a dry gin made only in Plymouth, England; it is fuller bodied and stronger flavored than the London style. **Flavored gins** are infused with added flavorings, such as almond, lemon, lime, mint, and so on, and are labeled appropriately. In order for these potables to be labeled "gin," however, the fundamental flavoring agent must be juniper berries. **Golden gin** has been AGED briefly in wood (although aging is not standard practice for most gins), which contributes a light golden color to the normally colorless spirit. **Old Tom gin,** a sweetened English-made gin that was fashionable in England from the 1700s to mid-1800s, is hard to find outside of Britain. SLOE GIN is not actually gin, but a LIQUEUR. Popular gin brands include Beefeater, Boodles, Bombay (and Bombay Sapphire), Bradburn's, Gilbey's, Gordon's, Seagram's, and Tanqueray. *See also* STEINHÄGER.

*I never drink anything stronger than gin before breakfast.*

W. C. FIELDS, AMERICAN ACTOR

## Gin Aloha

1½ oz. (3 Tbsp.) gin
1½ oz. (3 Tbsp.) Triple Sec
½ oz. (1 Tbsp.) unsweetened pineapple juice
2 dashes (about ⅛ tsp.) orange bitters

Shake ingredients with ice; strain into chilled glass.

**Gin and Bitters** *see* PINK GIN

**Gin and French** *see* GIN AND IT

**Gin and It** The "It" stands for *It*alian vermouth; the French version of the drink uses dry vermouth. Whichever rendition you choose, it is an iceless drink.

1 1/2 oz. (3 Tbsp.) gin
3/4 oz. (1 1/2 Tbsp.) sweet vermouth

Pour gin and vermouth into glass, stirring well.

➤ **Gin and French** Substitute dry vermouth for the sweet vermouth.

## Gin and Sin

1 1/2 oz. (3 Tbsp.) gin
1 1/2 oz. (3 Tbsp.) fresh orange juice
1 oz. (2 Tbsp.) fresh lemon juice
2 dashes (about 1/8 tsp.) grenadine

Shake ingredients with ice; strain into chilled glass.

★ **Ginless Sin** Omit gin; increase orange juice to 1/4 cup, lemon juice to 2 1/2 Tbsp., and grenadine to 1/4 tsp.

## Gin and Tonic

2 oz. (1/4 cup) gin
4 to 6 oz. (1/2 to 3/4 cup) tonic water
lime wedge

Pour gin into chilled glass filled with ice cubes. Top with tonic, stirring gently; garnish with lime.

**Gin Buck** *see* BUCK

**Gin Cobbler** *see* COBBLER

## Gin Cocktail

2 oz. (1/4 cup) gin
2 dashes (about 1/8 tsp.) orange bitters
lemon twist

Stir liquid ingredients with ice; strain into chilled glass. Drop in lemon twist.

**Gin Crusta** *see* CRUSTA

**Gin Daisy** *see* DAISY

**Gin Fix** *see* FIX

**Gin Fizz** One of the most popular members of the FIZZ family, the gin fizz has several variations, four of which follow. *See also* DANISH GIN FIZZ; RAMOS FIZZ.

2 oz. (¹/₄ cup) gin
1 oz. (2 Tbsp.) fresh lemon juice
1 tsp. powdered sugar
cold club soda

Shake all ingredients except club soda with ice. Strain into chilled glass filled with ice cubes. Top with soda, stirring gently.

➤ **Golden Fizz** Add 1 egg yolk to first 3 ingredients; shake vigorously.

➤ **Royal Gin Fizz** Add 1 whole egg to first 3 ingredients; shake vigorously.

➤ **Silver Fizz** Add 1 egg white to first 3 ingredients; shake vigorously.

➤ **Sloe Gin Fizz** Substitute sloe gin for the gin.

**ginger ale** A carbonated, ginger-flavored SOFT DRINK.

★ **Ginger Julep** *See also* JOCOSE JULEP; MINT JULEP.

8 medium to large fresh mint leaves
1 tsp. sugar
1 tsp. water
1 tsp. grenadine
4 to 6 oz. (¹/₂ to ³/₄ cup) cold ginger ale
3 mint sprigs

Muddle mint leaves, sugar, water, and grenadine in chilled julep cup or collins glass until leaves are crushed and sugar is dissolved. Fill glass with crushed ice. Top with ginger ale, stirring well. Add more crushed ice to within ¹/₂ inch of rim; garnish with mint sprigs and serve with a straw.

★ **Ginger-Lime Rickey** *see* LIME RICKEY

★ **Gin-Gin**

¹/₂ -inch piece of fresh gingerroot or crystallized ginger
1 oz. (2 Tbsp.) ginger-flavored syrup
cold ginger ale
mint sprig

Smash ginger with a mallet or other heavy utensil; drop into chilled glass. Add ginger syrup; fill glass with ice cubes. Top with ginger ale, stirring well. Garnish with mint.

⭐ **Ginless Sin** *see* GIN AND SIN

**Gin Milk Punch** *see* MILK PUNCH

**Gin Remsen Cooler** *see* REMSEN COOLER

**Gin Rickey** *see* RICKEY

**Gin Sangaree** *see* SANGAREE

**Gin Sidecar** *see* SIDECAR

**Gin Sling** *see* SLING

---

*Gin was mother's milk to her.*
GEORGE BERNARD SHAW, IRISH ESSAYIST, DRAMATIST

---

**Gin Smash** *see* SMASH

**Gin Sour** *see* SOUR

**Gin Swizzle** *see* SWIZZLE

### Girl Scout Cookie

¾ oz. (1½ Tbsp.) peppermint schnapps
¾ oz. (1½ Tbsp.) dark crème de cacao
½ oz. (1 Tbsp.) cream

Shake ingredients with ice; strain into chilled old-fashioned glass over ice cubes or into shot glass.

### Glad Eye(s)

2 oz. (¼ cup) Pernod or other anise-flavored liqueur
1 oz. (2 Tbsp.) peppermint schnapps

Stir ingredients with cracked ice; strain into chilled glass.

**glasses, chilling** *see* Chilling Glasses, page 24

**Glayva** A Scottish LIQUEUR based on SCOTCH WHISKY, Glayva is flavored with herbs and honey. *See also* WHISK(E)Y-BASED LIQUEURS.

*I don't have a drinking problem
except when I can't get one.*

TOM WAITS, AMERICAN SINGER

## Gloom Chaser

³/₄ oz. (1¹/₂ Tbsp.) Grand Marnier
³/₄ oz. (1¹/₂ Tbsp.) Cointreau or Triple Sec
³/₄ oz. (1¹/₂ Tbsp.) grenadine
³/₄ oz. (1¹/₂ Tbsp.) fresh lemon juice

Shake ingredients with ice; strain into chilled glass.

## Godchild

1 oz. (2 Tbsp.) vodka
1 oz. (2 Tbsp.) amaretto
1 oz. (2 Tbsp.) cream

Shake ingredients with cracked ice; strain into chilled glass.

## Godfather

2 oz. (¹/₄ cup) Scotch or bourbon
1 oz. (2 Tbsp.) amaretto

Pour ingredients into chilled glass filled with ice cubes; stir well.

**Godiva Chocolate Liqueur** Made by the same company famous for its chocolate candies, this ultra-velvety LIQUEUR comes in two versions. **Chocolate Godiva** is a medium brown color and has an ultrarich chocolate flavor tinged with anise and spices. **White Chocolate Godiva** is milky white and has a much lighter, vanilla–milk chocolate flavor akin to a cream liqueur, which is logical because white chocolate isn't really chocolate at all. *See also* CHOCOLATE-FLAVORED SPIRITS.

## Godmother

2 oz. (¹/₄ cup) vodka
1 oz. (2 Tbsp.) amaretto

Pour ingredients into chilled glass filled with ice cubes; stir well.

### Golden Bronx *see* BRONX COCKTAIL

### Golden Cadillac

2 oz. (¹/₄ cup) white crème de cacao
1 oz. (2 Tbsp.) Galliano
1 oz. (2 Tbsp.) half & half
¹/₂ cup crushed ice

Combine all ingredients in a blender. Cover and process at medium speed until smooth, about 15 seconds. Pour into chilled glass.

### Golden Daze

1¹/₂ oz. (3 Tbsp.) gin
1 oz. (2 Tbsp.) fresh orange juice
³/₄ oz. (1¹/₂ Tbsp.) apricot brandy

Shake ingredients with ice; strain into chilled glass.

### Golden Dream

1¹/₂ oz. (3 Tbsp.) Galliano
³/₄ oz. (1¹/₂ Tbsp.) Triple Sec or Cointreau
³/₄ oz. (1¹/₂ Tbsp.) fresh orange juice
³/₄ oz. (1¹/₂ Tbsp.) half & half

Shake ingredients with ice; strain into chilled glass.

*No one at the office knew Ralph was a drinker until one day when he came to work sober.*

### Golden Fizz *see* GIN FIZZ

### Golden Slipper

1 oz. (2 Tbsp.) apricot brandy
1 oz. (2 Tbsp.) yellow Chartreuse
1 egg yolk

Vigorously shake ingredients with ice; strain into chilled glass.

### Goldfinger

1¹/₂ oz. (3 Tbsp.) vodka
1 oz. (2 Tbsp.) unsweetened pineapple juice
³/₄ oz. (1¹/₂ Tbsp.) Galliano

Shake ingredients with ice; strain into chilled glass.

**Goldschlager** [GOLT-shlah-gehr] Made in Switzerland, this clear LIQUEUR has bits of gold leaf floating in it. Goldschlager has a tangy-sweet, intensely cinnamon flavor. *See also* CINNAMON-FLAVORED SPIRITS.

---

*The worst thing about some men is that when they are not drunk they are sober.*

WILLIAM BUTLER YEATS, IRISH POET, PLAYWRIGHT

---

**Goldwasser** *see* DANZIGER GOLDWASSER

### Golf Cocktail

2 oz. (¹/₄ cup) gin
³/₄ oz. (1 ¹/₂ Tbsp.) dry vermouth
2 dashes (about ¹/₈ tsp.) Angostura bitters

Stir ingredients with ice; strain into chilled glass.

**gomme syrup** [GAWM] *see* SUGAR SYRUP

**Gorilla Sweat** Make sure to put a spoon in the glass (*see* Hot Drinks, page 29) to absorb the heat when you add the hot water. If the butter's at room temperature rather than right out of the fridge your gorilla will "sweat" a lot faster.

1¹/₂ oz. (3 Tbsp.) tequila
¹/₂ tsp. sugar
about 4 oz. (¹/₂ cup) boiling water
¹/₂ Tbsp. butter
freshly grated nutmeg
cinnamon stick

Pour tequila into glass; add sugar. Slowly stir in water; drop in butter. Sprinkle lightly with nutmeg; add cinnamon stick for stirring.

**grain alcohol** *see* ALCOHOL

**grain spirits** *see* NEUTRAL SPIRIT

**grain whisk(e)y** *see* NEUTRAL SPIRIT; SCOTCH WHISKY

**Grand Marnier** [GRAN mahr-NYAY] This grande dame of orange-flavored LIQUEURS is made by the famed French liqueur house Marnier-Lapostelle. COGNAC-based and flavored with Haitian bitter orange peel, exotic spices, and vanilla, amber-colored Grand Marnier is rich but not overly sweet. **Grand Marnier Cuvée du Centenaire** is a special-edition liqueur with a darker amber color and a deeper, more complex flavor. The exquisite **Grand Marnier Cuvée Spéciale Cent Cinquantenaire,** which is blended with X.O. Cognac, is packaged in a hand-painted bottle. *See also* CITRUS-FLAVORED SPIRITS; CRÈME DE GRAND MARNIER; ORANGE-FLAVORED SPIRITS.

**Grand Passion** Although gin is traditional for this drink, RUM makes it truly exotic.

> 2 oz. ($1/4$ cup) gin
> 1 oz. (2 Tbsp.) passion-fruit juice
> 1 dash (about $1/16$ tsp.) Angostura bitters

Shake ingredients with ice; strain into chilled glass.

**Grand Royal Fizz**

> 2 oz. ($1/4$ cup) gin
> 1 oz. (2 Tbsp.) fresh orange juice
> $3/4$ oz. ($1 1/2$ Tbsp.) fresh lemon juice
> 2 tsp. half & half
> 1 tsp. maraschino liqueur
> $1/2$ tsp. powdered sugar
> cold club soda

Shake all ingredients except club soda with ice. Strain into chilled glass filled with ice cubes. Top with soda, stirring gently.

**Granville**

> $1 1/2$ oz. (3 Tbsp.) gin
> $1 1/2$ tsp. Grand Marnier
> $1 1/2$ tsp. Calvados
> $1 1/2$ tsp. fresh lemon juice

Shake ingredients with ice; strain into chilled glass.

## Grapefruit Cocktail

1½ oz. (3 Tbsp.) gin
1½ oz. (3 Tbsp.) unsweetened grapefruit juice
1½ tsp. maraschino liqueur
maraschino cherry

Shake liquid ingredients with ice. Strain into chilled glass; garnish with cherry.

**grappa** [GRAHP-pah] Made commercially since the eighteenth century, grappa is the Italian counterpart to France's MARC. This colorless, high-alcohol EAU-DE-VIE is distilled from the residue (grape skins and seeds) left in the wine press after the juice is removed to make wine. There are hundreds of highly individual, markedly different styles of this fiery distillation, which can have great CHARACTER and depth. There are also aged grappas that are complex in flavor due to being AGED in a series of containers made of different woods, including oak, birch, and juniper.

**Grasshopper** *See also* FLYING GRASSHOPPER.

1 oz. (2 Tbsp.) white crème de cacao
1 oz. (2 Tbsp.) green crème de menthe
1 oz. (2 Tbsp.) cream

Shake ingredients with ice; strain into chilled glass.

➤ **Coffee Grasshopper** (also called *Mexican Grasshopper*) Substitute Kahlúa or Tia Maria for the crème de cacao.

*A grasshopper jumped into a bar. The bartender looked at him and said, "Hey, there's a drink named after you." Looking surprised, the grasshopper said, "You gotta be kiddin' . . . you have a drink called Ralph?"*

## Great Secret

2 oz. ($^1/_4$ cup) gin
$^1/_2$ oz. (1 Tbsp.) Lillet blanc
2 dashes (about $^1/_8$ tsp.) Angostura bitters
orange twist

Shake liquid ingredients with ice. Strain into chilled glass; drop in orange twist.

## Greek Buck *see* BUCK

## Greenback

2 oz. ($^1/_4$ cup) gin
$^1/_2$ oz. (1 Tbsp.) green crème de menthe
$1^1/_2$ tsp. fresh lime juice

Shake ingredients with ice; strain into chilled glass over ice cubes.

## Green Devil

$1^1/_2$ oz. (3 Tbsp.) gin
$^3/_4$ oz. ($1^1/_2$ Tbsp.) green crème de menthe
$^1/_2$ oz. (1 Tbsp.) fresh lime juice
mint sprig

Shake liquid ingredients with ice. Strain into chilled glass over ice cubes; garnish with mint.

## Green Dragon

$1^1/_2$ oz. (3 Tbsp.) gin
$^3/_4$ oz. ($1^1/_2$ Tbsp.) green crème de menthe
$^3/_4$ oz. ($1^1/_2$ Tbsp.) kümmel
$^3/_4$ oz. ($1^1/_2$ Tbsp.) fresh lemon juice
4 dashes (about $^1/_4$ tsp.) orange bitters

Shake ingredients with ice; strain into chilled glass.

## Green Lizard

$^3/_4$ oz. ($1^1/_2$ Tbsp.) green Chartreuse
$^3/_4$ oz. ($1^1/_2$ Tbsp.) 151-proof rum

Pour Chartreuse into glass. Layer rum on top by slowly pouring over the back (rounded) side of a spoon so that it floats; don't mix.

## Green Room

1 ½ oz. (3 Tbsp.) dry vermouth
½ oz. (1 Tbsp.) brandy
2 drops Cointreau
orange twist

Shake liquid ingredients with ice. Strain into chilled glass; drop in orange twist.

## Green Russian *see* STINGER

## ✴ Grenada Sunset *see* TEQUILA SUNRISE

**grenadine** [GREHN-uh-deen; grehn-uh-DEEN] A sweet, deep red, pomegranate-flavored syrup that was once made exclusively from pomegranates grown on the Caribbean island of Grenada. Today, other fruit-juice concentrates are sometimes used to make this syrup. Grenadine is used both for sweetening and for coloring drinks. Some brands contain a small amount of alcohol, while others are alcohol free. *See also* SYRUPS, FLAVORED.

## Greyhound

1 ½ oz. (3 Tbsp.) vodka
6 to 8 oz. (¾ to 1 cup) unsweetened grapefruit juice
Pour vodka into glass filled with ice cubes; top with grapefruit juice, stirring well.

**Grog** A libation named after eighteenth-century British Admiral Edward Vernon, whose nickname was "Old Grog," alluding to the thick grogram cape he favored. Old Grog purportedly watered his crew's rum ration to extend it. It was found that heating the brew comforted cold sailors; at the turn of the century lemon or lime juice was added to grog to forestall scurvy. According to John Mariani in his *Dictionary of American Food and Drink,* the eighteenth-century slang term "grog blossoms" alludes to the broken blood vessels in the nose caused by imbibing too much alcohol. *See also* Hot Drinks, page 29.

2 oz. (¹/₄ cup) Jamaican rum
¹/₂ oz. (1 Tbsp.) fresh lemon juice
1 sugar cube or 1 tsp. sugar
3 to 5 whole cloves
about 6 oz. (³/₄ cup) boiling water
1 cinnamon stick

In a warm mug, combine rum, lemon juice, sugar, and cloves. Top with hot water, stirring with cinnamon stick until sugar dissolves.

➤ **Cider Grog** Substitute hot apple cider for the hot water.

**grog on** An Australian colloquialism for steady drinking or partying.

**Grown, Produced, and Bottled By** *see* WINE LABEL TERMS

*A motorcycle cop sees a man driving a pickup truck full of penguins. He pulls the guy over and says, "Sorry, sir, but you can't legally possess penguins in this town. You'll have to take them to the zoo." The man shrugs, nods okay, and drives away. The next day the officer sees the guy again, his truck full of penguins wearing sunglasses. He pulls the guy over again and says, "All right, young man, I told you yesterday to take these penguins to the zoo. What's going on?" The guy smiles proudly: "I did, officer. And today I'm taking them to the beach."*

**Guinness** This Irish brew is the most famous and widely distributed STOUT in the world. *See also* BEER.

**Gypsy**

2 oz. (¹/₄ cup) vodka
¹/₂ oz. (1 Tbsp.) Bénédictine
1 tsp. fresh lemon juice
1 tsp. fresh orange juice
orange slice

Shake liquid ingredients with ice. Strain into chilled glass over ice cubes; garnish with orange slice.

### Gypsy Cocktail

1 ½ oz. (3 Tbsp.) gin
1 oz. (2 Tbsp.) sweet vermouth
maraschino cherry

Stir liquid ingredients with ice. Strain into chilled glass; garnish with cherry.

### Happy Apple

3 oz. (³⁄₈ cup) apple cider
1 ½ oz. (3 Tbsp.) rum
½ oz. (1 Tbsp.) fresh lemon juice
lime twist

Shake liquid ingredients with ice. Strain into chilled glass over ice cubes; drop in lime twist.

**happy hour** In America, the "happy hour" is cocktail hour, with participants often gathering at the local "watering hole" (bar) right after work.

### Harbor Lights

³⁄₄ oz. (1 ½ Tbsp.) brandy
³⁄₄ oz. (1 ½ Tbsp.) Galliano

Shake ingredients with ice; strain into chilled glass.

### Harlem

1 ½ oz. (3 Tbsp.) gin
³⁄₄ oz. (1 ½ Tbsp.) unsweetened pineapple juice
½ tsp. maraschino liqueur
2 to 3 pineapple chunks

Shake liquid ingredients with ice. Strain into chilled glass over ice; garnish with pineapple chunks speared with cocktail pick.

## Harvard Cocktail

1 1/2 oz. (3 Tbsp.) brandy
3/4 oz. (1 1/2 Tbsp.) sweet vermouth
2 tsp. fresh lemon juice
1 tsp. grenadine
1 dash (about 1/16 tsp.) Angostura bitters

Shake ingredients with ice; strain into chilled cocktail glass or over ice cubes in an old-fashioned glass.

## Harvard Cooler

2 oz. (1/4 cup) apple brandy
1/2 oz. (1 Tbsp.) fresh lemon juice
1 tsp. powdered sugar
cold club soda
long spiral of lemon peel

Combine first 3 ingredients in chilled glass, stirring to dissolve sugar. Add 3 to 4 ice cubes; top with club soda, stirring gently. Arrange lemon spiral so half of it is inside the glass and half hangs over the rim.

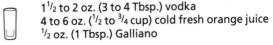

*A mixture of brandy and water spoils two good things.*
CHARLES LAMB, ENGLISH WRITER

**Harvey Wallbanger** A Harvey Wallbanger is a SCREWDRIVER with a Galliano FLOAT, a combination that became wildly popular in the late sixties and the 1970s. Although many attribute its origin to a brilliant marketing coup by the makers of Galliano, the more colorful tale is that it was named after a California surfer dude (Harvey) who, after a particularly bad day on the waves, was prone to console himself with so many Galliano-spiked Screwdrivers that he staggered into the walls. (We didn't make this up!)

1 1/2 to 2 oz. (3 to 4 Tbsp.) vodka
4 to 6 oz. (1/2 to 3/4 cup) cold fresh orange juice
1/2 oz. (1 Tbsp.) Galliano

Combine vodka and orange juice in chilled glass filled with ice cubes. Float Galliano on top by slowly pouring it over the back (rounded) side of a spoon; don't mix. Alternatively, the vodka and orange juice can be shaken with ice and strained into a cocktail glass; float Galliano on top.

### Hasty

1 1/2 oz. (3 Tbsp.) gin
1/2 oz. (1 Tbsp.) dry vermouth
1 tsp. grenadine
1/4 tsp. Pernod or other anise-flavored liqueur

Stir or shake with ice; strain into chilled glass.

### Havana Club

1 1/2 oz. (3 Tbsp.) light rum
1/2 oz. (1 Tbsp.) dry vermouth

Shake ingredients with crushed ice; strain into chilled glass.

### Havana Cocktail

3 oz. (3/8 cup) unsweetened pineapple juice
1 1/2 oz. (3 Tbsp.) light rum
1 tsp. fresh lemon juice

Shake ingredients with ice; strain into chilled glass.

### Havana Special

2 oz. (1/4 cup) unsweetened pineapple juice
1 1/2 oz. (3 Tbsp.) light rum
1 1/2 tsp. maraschino liqueur

Shake ingredients with crushed ice; strain into chilled glass.

### Hawaiian Cocktail

2 oz. (1/4 cup) gin
1/2 oz. (1 Tbsp.) Triple Sec
1/2 oz. (1 Tbsp.) unsweetened pineapple juice

Shake ingredients with ice; strain into chilled glass.

### Hawaiian Punch

6 oz. (³/₄ cup) unsweetened pineapple juice
³/₄ oz. (1 ¹/₂ Tbsp.) Southern Comfort
¹/₂ oz. (1 Tbsp.) sloe gin
¹/₂ oz. (1 Tbsp.) amaretto

Pour all ingredients into chilled glass filled with ice cubes; stir well.

### Hawthorne strainer *see* Bar Equipment, page 6

### Heatwave

1 oz. (2 Tbsp.) dark rum
¹/₂ oz. (1 Tbsp.) peach schnapps
about 6 oz. (³/₄ cup) unsweetened pineapple juice
2 tsp. grenadine

Pour rum and peach schnapps into chilled glass filled with ice cubes. Top with pineapple juice, stirring well. Float grenadine on top by slowly pouring it over the back (rounded) side of a spoon; don't mix.

### Heering *see* PETER HEERING

### herb-flavored spirits *see* B & B; BÉNÉDICTINE; CENTERBE; CERTOSA; CHARTREUSE; CHINA-MARTINI; ESCORIAL GREEN; FIORE D'ALPI; GALLIANO; IZARRA; JÄGERMEISTER; KÜMMEL; STREGA

### Herbsaint An anise-flavored LIQUEUR that was developed in New Orleans and is still primarily produced there. *See also* ANISE-FLAVORED SPIRITS.

### high Slang for inebriated.

### Highball Although the origin of the word "highball" is obscure, the most popular story is that the name is derived from a nineteenth-century railroad signal (raising a ball on a pole) that indicated "full speed ahead" to a train's engineer. The term is said to have been coined by New York bartender Patrick Duffy, for the speed with which the drink can be assembled. High-balls—classically a simple mixture of whiskey and CLUB

SODA—are traditionally served in a tall (highball) glass over ice, as opposed to a LOWBALL, which is typically served an OLD-FASHIONED GLASS. *See also* BERMUDA HIGHBALL; BULLDOG HIGHBALL; LEAPFROG HIGHBALL; PRESBYTERIAN.

2 oz. (¹/₄ cup) bourbon, rye, or Scotch
cold club soda or ginger ale
lemon twist, optional

Pour whiskey into chilled glass filled with ice cubes. Top with club soda or ginger ale, stirring gently. Drop in lemon twist, if desired.

➤ **Apple Brandy Highball** Substitute apple brandy for the whiskey.

➤ **Rum Highball** Substitute rum for the whiskey.

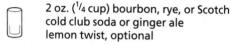

*Alcohol is like love. The first kiss is magic, the second is intimate, the third is routine. After that you take the girl's clothes off.*

RAYMOND CHANDLER, AMERICAN AUTHOR

**highball glass** *see* Glassware, page 8

## Highland Fling

2 oz. (¹/₄ cup) Scotch
1 oz. (2 Tbsp.) sweet vermouth
2 to 4 dashes (about ¹/₈ to ¹/₄ tsp.) orange bitters
green olive

Shake liquid ingredients with ice. Strain into chilled glass; drop in olive.

**hock** A British term for white wine (DRY or sweet) from Germany's Rhine regions. The word is a derivation of *Hochheim,* a town on the River Main.

### Hoffman House Cocktail

1 1/2 oz. (3 Tbsp.) gin
3/4 oz. (1 1/2 Tbsp.) dry vermouth
2 dashes (about 1/8 tsp.) orange bitters
green olive

Stir liquid ingredients with ice. Strain into chilled glass; drop in olive.

### Hole-in-One

2 oz. (1/4 cup) Scotch
3/4 oz. (1 1/2 Tbsp.) dry vermouth
1/4 tsp. fresh lemon juice
1 dash (about 1/16 tsp.) orange bitters

Shake ingredients with ice; strain into chilled glass.

### Hollands gin *see* GIN

### Homestead

2 oz. (1/4 cup) gin
1 oz. (2 Tbsp.) sweet vermouth
orange slice

Stir liquid ingredients with ice. Strain into chilled glass; garnish with orange slice.

### Honeybee

2 oz. (1/4 cup) light rum
1 Tbsp. honey
2 tsp. fresh lemon juice

Shake ingredients with cracked ice; strain into chilled glass.

### honey-flavored spirits *see* BÄRENJÄGER

### Honeymoon

1 1/2 oz. (3 Tbsp.) apple brandy
1 oz. (2 Tbsp.) fresh lemon juice
3/4 oz. (1 1/2 Tbsp.) Bénédictine
1 tsp. Triple Sec

Shake ingredients with ice; strain into chilled glass.

### Honolulu Cocktail #1

1 1/2 oz. (3 Tbsp.) gin
1/2 tsp. fresh orange juice
1/2 tsp. fresh lemon juice
1/2 tsp. unsweetened pineapple juice
1/2 tsp. powdered sugar
1 dash (about 1/16 tsp.) Angostura bitters

Shake ingredients with ice; strain into chilled glass.

### Honolulu Cocktail #2

1 oz. (2 Tbsp.) gin
1 oz. (2 Tbsp.) Bénédictine
3/4 oz. (1 1/2 Tbsp.) maraschino liqueur

Shake ingredients with ice; strain into chilled glass.

**hooch** Slang for liquor that's either BOOTLEG or just plain cheap. The word was broadly used for PROHIBITION-era WHISKEY, although it dates back to the late 1800s. The origin of the term is Admiralty Island, Alaska, where the inhabitants of the Tlingit Indian village *Hoochinoo* (*Hootchinoo*) illegally made and sold alcoholic beverages.

### Hoopla

3/4 oz. (1 1/2 Tbsp.) brandy
3/4 oz. (1 1/2 Tbsp.) Lillet blanc
3/4 oz. (1 1/2 Tbsp.) Cointreau or Triple Sec
3/4 oz. (1 1/2 Tbsp.) fresh lemon juice

Shake ingredients with ice; strain into chilled glass.

**hops** Conelike flowers which, after being dried, are used to impart a pleasantly bitter flavor to BEER and ALE.

### Hop Toad

1 oz. (2 Tbsp.) light rum
1 oz. (2 Tbsp.) apricot brandy
2 tsp. fresh lime juice

Shake ingredients with ice; strain into chilled glass.

**Horse's Neck** There are two versions of this drink—one with a "kick," one without. Both are refreshing and quick to make.

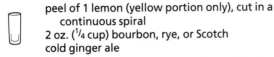

peel of 1 lemon (yellow portion only), cut in a
    continuous spiral
2 oz. (¼ cup) bourbon, rye, or Scotch
cold ginger ale

Drape lemon spiral over rim of chilled glass, allowing excess to
hang inside glass. Add 3 to 4 ice cubes. Pour in whiskey; top with
ginger ale, stirring gently.

★**Kickless Horse's Neck** Omit whiskey. Place sugar cube
    soaked in ¼ tsp. grenadine in bottom of chilled glass before
    adding ice cubes and filling with ginger ale.

---

*I misremember who first was cruel enough to nurture the
cocktail party into life. But perhaps it would be not too
much to say, in fact it would be not enough to say, that it
was not worth the trouble.*

DOROTHY PARKER, AMERICAN WRITER

---

**Hot Brick Toddy** *See also* Hot Drinks, page 29.

1 tsp. powdered sugar
1 tsp. butter
⅛ tsp. ground cinnamon
4 to 6 oz. (½ to ¾ cup) boiling water
2 oz. (¼ cup) blended whiskey

In warmed mug, combine sugar, butter, cinnamon, and a splash
of hot water; stir to melt butter. Add whiskey and additional hot
water to taste.

**Hot Buttered Rum (Bourbon; Comfort)** Though classically
made with water, this drink takes on a whole new personality
when hot milk is used. *See also* Hot Drinks, page 29.

1 tsp. brown sugar
about 6 oz. (¾ cup) boiling water
2 oz. (¼ cup) dark rum
1 Tbsp. butter
freshly grated nutmeg

Combine sugar and water in warmed mug. Stir in rum; float butter on top. Sprinkle lightly with nutmeg.

➤ **Hot Buttered Bourbon** Substitute bourbon for the rum.

➤ **Hot Buttered Comfort** Substitute Southern Comfort for the rum.

**hot drinks** *see* Hot Drinks, page 29. *See also* BLUE BLAZER; CAFÉ AMARETTO; CAFÉ DIABLO; CAFÉ ROYALE; CLASSIC HOT BISHOP (*see* BISHOP, THE); GORILLA SWEAT; HOT BRICK TODDY; HOT BULLSHOT (*see* BULLSHOT); HOT BUTTERED RUM; HOT EGGNOG (*see* EGGNOG); HOT MILK PUNCH; HOT SPICED WINE (*see* MULLED WINE); HOT TODDY; IRISH COFFEE; ITALIAN COFFEE; JAMAICAN COFFEE; MEXICAN COFFEE; MULLED CIDER; MULLED WINE; NIGHTCAP; TOM AND JERRY; WASSAIL

### Hot Eggnog *see* EGGNOG

### Hot Milk Punch *see* MILK PUNCH

### Hot Pants

1 ¹/₂ oz. (3 Tbsp.) tequila
¹/₂ oz. (1 Tbsp.) peppermint schnapps
¹/₂ oz. (1 Tbsp.) unsweetened grapefruit juice
1 tsp. powdered sugar

Frost rim of chilled glass by moistening with water, then dipping rim into salt. Shake ingredients with ice; strain into glass.

### Hot Spiced Wine *see* MULLED WINE

### Hot Toddy *See also* HOT BRICK TODDY; Hot Drinks, page 29; TODDY.

¹/₂ lemon slice
3 whole cloves
1 tsp. granulated or brown sugar
pinch of freshly grated nutmeg
2 oz. (¹/₄ cup) blended whiskey, rum, or other liquor
about 6 oz. (³/₄ cup) boiling water
1 cinnamon stick

Stud lemon slice with cloves; drop into mug. Add sugar, nutmeg, and liquor; top with water. Stir with cinnamon stick, leaving it in drink as garnish.

*As a cure for the cold, take your toddy to bed, put one bowler hat at the foot, and drink until you see two.*
SIR ROBERT BRUCE LOCKHART, BRITISH WRITER, DIPLOMAT

## Hudson Bay

1 oz. (2 Tbsp.) gin
1/2 oz. (1 Tbsp.) cherry brandy
1/2 oz. (1 Tbsp.) fresh orange juice
1 1/2 tsp. 151-proof rum
1 tsp. fresh lime juice
lime slice

Shake liquid ingredients with ice. Strain into chilled glass; garnish with lime slice.

## Hula-Hula

1 1/2 oz. (3 Tbsp.) gin
3/4 oz. (1 1/2 Tbsp.) fresh orange juice
1/2 tsp. powdered sugar or 1 1/2 tsp. Triple Sec

Shake ingredients with ice; strain into chilled glass.

## Hunter's Cocktail

1 1/2 oz. (3 Tbsp.) rye whiskey
1/2 oz. (1 Tbsp.) cherry brandy
maraschino cherry

Pour liquid ingredients into chilled glass filled with ice cubes; stir well. Garnish with cherry.

## Huntress Cocktail

1 oz. (2 Tbsp.) bourbon
1 oz. (2 Tbsp.) cherry liqueur
3/4 oz. (1 1/2 Tbsp.) half & half
1 tsp. Triple Sec

Shake ingredients with ice; strain into chilled glass.

## Huntsman

1 1/2 oz. (3 Tbsp.) vodka
1/2 oz. (1 Tbsp.) dark rum
1/2 oz. (1 Tbsp.) fresh lime juice
1/2 tsp. powdered sugar

Shake ingredients with ice; strain into chilled glass.

**Hurricane** Pat O'Brien's famous French Quarter bar in New Orleans gave birth to this libation, which became so popular that a special glass was created to contain it.

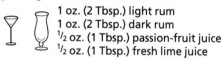

1 oz. (2 Tbsp.) light rum
1 oz. (2 Tbsp.) dark rum
1/2 oz. (1 Tbsp.) passion-fruit juice
1/2 oz. (1 Tbsp.) fresh lime juice

Shake ingredients with cracked ice; strain into chilled cocktail glass or into a hurricane glass over ice.

➤**Variation** Add 1 oz. (2 Tbsp.) unsweetened pineapple juice.

**Hurricane glass** *see* Glassware, page 8

**ice, general** *see* Ingredients (Ice Tips), page 16

**ice beer** *see* BEER

**ice crusher** *see* Bar Equipment, page 6; Ingredients (Ice Tips), page 16

## Ideal

1 1/2 oz. (3 Tbsp.) gin
1 oz. (2 Tbsp.) dry vermouth
1 tsp. unsweetened grapefruit juice
4 dashes (about 1/4 tsp.) maraschino liqueur
maraschino cherry

Shake liquid ingredients with ice. Strain into chilled glass; garnish with cherry.

## Imperial Cocktail

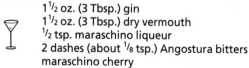

1 1/2 oz. (3 Tbsp.) gin
1 1/2 oz. (3 Tbsp.) dry vermouth
1/2 tsp. maraschino liqueur
2 dashes (about 1/8 tsp.) Angostura bitters
maraschino cherry

Stir liquid ingredients with ice. Strain into chilled glass; garnish with cherry.

## Imperial Fizz

1 1/2 oz. (3 Tbsp.) bourbon or rye
1/2 oz. (1 Tbsp.) light rum
3/4 oz. (1 1/2 Tbsp.) fresh lemon juice
1 tsp. powdered sugar
cold club soda

Shake all ingredients except club soda with ice. Strain into chilled glass filled with ice cubes; top with soda.

## Imperial stout *see* STOUT

## Inca

1 oz. (2 Tbsp.) gin
1 oz. (2 Tbsp.) dry vermouth
1 oz. (2 Tbsp.) sweet vermouth
1 oz. (2 Tbsp.) dry sherry
1 dash (about 1/16 tsp.) Angostura bitters
1 dash (about 1/16 tsp.) orgeat syrup

Stir ingredients with ice; strain into chilled glass.

*Alcohol is the anesthesia by which we endure the operation of life.*

GEORGE BERNARD SHAW, IRISH ESSAYIST, DRAMATIST

## Income Tax Cocktail

1 1/2 oz. (3 Tbsp.) gin
1/2 oz. (1 Tbsp.) fresh orange juice
2 tsp. dry vermouth
2 tsp. sweet vermouth
2 dashes (about 1/8 tsp.) Angostura bitters

Shake ingredients with ice; strain into chilled glass.

## Independence Swizzle *See also* SWIZZLE; SWIZZLE STICK.

1 tsp. honey
3/4 oz. (1 1/2 Tbsp.) fresh lime juice
2 oz. (1/4 cup) dark rum
2 to 4 dashes (about 1/8 to 1/4 tsp.) Angostura bitters
lime slice

Combine honey and about $\frac{1}{2}$ tablespoon of the lime juice in chilled glass, stirring until honey dissolves. Add remaining lime juice, rum, and bitters; fill with crushed ice. Rub a swizzle stick rapidly back and forth between your palms (or stir rapidly with a long-handled spoon) until ingredients are mixed. Garnish with lime slice.

**India ale** *see* ALE

**Indian River**

1 $\frac{1}{2}$ oz. (3 Tbsp.) blended whiskey
$\frac{1}{2}$ oz. (1 Tbsp.) unsweetened grapefruit juice
1 tsp. sweet vermouth
1 tsp. raspberry liqueur

Shake ingredients with cracked ice; strain into chilled glass.

**inebriant** [in-EE-bree-uhnt] *n.* An intoxicant; **inebriant** *adj.* Something intoxicating.

**inebriate; inebriated** [in-EE-bree-ate(d)] *n.* An intoxicated person or a habitual drunkard. Someone in this condition is *inebriated.* **inebriate** *v.* To make drunk.

**infused vodka (gin, rum, or tequila)** True, there are many commercially bottled flavored vodkas; however, not only is it fun to make your own, but you get a bonus in personalized flavors. Although any liquor can be flavor infused (*see* INFUSION), vodka is the most logical alcohol to work with because it has the most neutral taste. Any of the following recipes, however, can be also tried with GIN, RUM, or TEQUILA.

*Tips for infusions:* Begin with a good-quality vodka (although premium brands would be wasted); start with a small amount—you can always make a larger batch once you perfect the flavors. Use fresh ingredients, including spices—dried herbs, canned fruit, or old spices won't give your vodka a flavor worth the bother. Always use scrupulously clean containers with screw-top lids. If the final flavor is too strong, simply dilute it with more (unflavored) vodka. Experiment with flavor combinations and intensities—once you find the perfect one, write it down.

The following combinations are for 16 oz. (1 pint; 2 cups) vodka; double the amounts for a quart of vodka. Put flavorings in a clean 1-quart jar with a screw-top lid; pour in 1 pint vodka. Secure lid tightly; shake 3 or 4 times. Set in a cool, dark place for 24 hours; refrigeration isn't necessary (note: fresh-fruit infusions will take at least 1 week for flavor to develop). Check for flavor; let stand another 24 hours, or until flavor reaches desired intensity. Shake mixture several times a day during infusion. When vodka is ready, strain through a paper coffee filter into a clean container; the vodka should be clear. Seal tightly; refrigerate indefinitely.

**Cherry/Berry** 1 cup sun-dried cherries, cranberries, or blueberries, plus large strips of peel (colored portion only) from ½ medium orange or 1 small lemon, optional

**Citron** large strips of peel (colored portion only) from 2 large lemons, 2 medium oranges, 1 large grapefruit, or 5 limes

**Coconut** 1 cup unsweetened dried coconut (available at health food stores)

**Fruit** 2 cups fresh raspberries, chopped strawberries, peaches, pineapple, or dried apricots

**Ginger-Lemon** 8 (⅛ inch thick) slices peeled fresh gingerroot, plus large strips of peel (colored portion only) from 1 large lemon

**Herbed** ½ cup fresh herbs, such as basil, dill, oregano, tarragon, or thyme (leave herbs on their stems)

**Jalapeño** 1 jalapeño pepper, quartered, plus 1 chipotle (smoked jalapeño pepper)

**Pepper** 12 *each* black peppercorns and white peppercorns, plus large strips of peel (colored portion only) from ½ medium lemon, optional

**Seed** 1 Tbsp. anise, fennel, or caraway seed

**Spiced** 1 cinnamon stick, 10 allspice berries, and 5 whole cloves
**Vanilla** 2 fresh vanilla beans, split lengthwise

---

*This man's sitting at a bar nursing his drink when suddenly he hears a voice, "Hey, nice tie—goes great with your shirt." The man looks around—no one's there, so he goes back to his drink. All at once he hears another voice. "You look like a million bucks in that suit—bet it cost you a mint." The man whips around and looks behind him—doesn't see a soul. He's turning back to his drink, when suddenly he hears yet another voice. "Nice, haircut, Jack. Makes you look like a movie star—who's your barber?" By now completely mystified, the guy calls the bartender over. "Look, I keep hearing these voices saying nice things about me, but no one's here—am I going crazy or is this some kind of trick?" The bartender grins at him and says, "Hey, man, that's just the peanuts—they're complimentary."*

---

**infusion** [in-FYOO-zhun] In the world of cocktails, infusions are spirits (VODKA, GIN, TEQUILA, and the like) that have been flavored with various ingredients, including herbs, chiles, spices, and fruit. After the liquor and flavorings have steeped together for a period of days (sometimes weeks), the liquid is strained and used in various drinks. *See also* INFUSED VODKA.

★ **Innocent A.J.** *see* A.J.

### International Cocktail

1 1/2 oz. (3 Tbsp.) cognac
2 tsp. Cointreau
2 tsp. anisette
1 tsp. vodka

Shake ingredients with ice; strain into chilled glass.

## IRA

1 oz. (2 Tbsp.) Irish whiskey
1 oz. (2 Tbsp.) Irish cream liqueur

Shake ingredients with ice; strain into chilled glass.

---

*nly Irish coffee provides in a single glass
all four essential food groups—
alcohol, caffeine, sugar, and fat.*

ALEX LEVINE

---

## Irish Coffee *See also* Hot Drinks, page 29.

1½ oz. (3 Tbsp.) Irish whiskey
1 tsp. sugar
about 6 oz. (¾ cup) hot coffee
heavy whipping cream or whipped cream

Combine first 3 ingredients in warm mug, stirring to combine. Float cream on top by slowly pouring it over the back (rounded) side of a spoon; don't mix. Or top with a large dollop of whipped cream.

➤ **Iced Irish Coffee** Substitute cold coffee for hot; serve over ice cubes (*see* Flavored Ice Cubes, page 17, for coffee-flavored cubes) in an old-fashioned or collins glass.

## Irish coffee mug *see* Glassware, page 8

## Irish Cooler

2 oz. Irish whiskey
cold club soda
long spiral of lemon peel

Pour whiskey into chilled glass filled with ice cubes. Top with club soda, stirring gently. Arrange lemon spiral so half of it is inside the glass and half hangs over the rim.

## Irish courage *see* DUTCH COURAGE

**Irish cream liqueurs** Any of several LIQUEURS that, depending on the brand, can range in texture from creamy to milky, in color from beige to pale brown, and in flavor from spiced toffee to honeyed chocolate. Among the more popular brands are Bailey's (the original), Carolans, O'Casey's, and St. Brendan's. There are also a couple of "light" Irish creams available, all with about 2 percent less alcohol, slightly fewer calories, and a lighter texture. All of which, to most people, adds up to less satisfying quaffing. Why not just drink less of the real thing, which is eminently more pleasing?

### Irish Eyes (Are Smiling)

2 oz. ($^1/_4$ cup) green crème de menthe
2 oz. ($^1/_4$ cup) heavy cream
1 oz. (2 Tbsp.) Irish whiskey

Shake ingredients with ice; strain into chilled glass.

### Irish Fix *see* FIX

### Irish Kilt

2 oz. ($^1/_4$ cup) Irish whiskey
1 oz. (2 Tbsp.) Scotch
1 oz. (2 Tbsp.) fresh lemon juice
$^1/_2$ to 1 oz. (1 to 2 Tbsp.) sugar syrup
4 dashes (about $^1/_4$ tsp.) orange bitters

Shake ingredients with cracked ice; strain into chilled glass.

**Irish Mist** Made from a formula dating back over 1,200 years, this Irish LIQUEUR comes from the town of Tullamore. Irish Mist is based on IRISH WHISKEY and flavored with herbs and honey. *See also* WHISK(E)Y-BASED LIQUEURS.

**Irish Shillelagh** [shih-LAY-lee; shih-LAY-luh] Traditionally made of blackthorn or oak, a shillelagh (or *shillalah*) is a cudgel that packs a wallop when used the right way . . . as does this drink!

$1^1/_2$ oz. (3 Tbsp.) Irish whiskey
$^1/_2$ oz. (1 Tbsp.) light rum
$^1/_2$ oz. (1 Tbsp.) sloe gin
$^1/_2$ oz. (1 Tbsp.) fresh lemon juice
1 tsp. powdered sugar
1 peach slice
3 raspberries
1 maraschino cherry

Shake all ingredients except fruit with ice. Strain into chilled glass over 2 to 3 ice cubes. Garnish with fruit.

**Irish stout** *see* STOUT

---

*Give an Irishman lager for a month, and he's a dead man. An Irishman is lined with copper, and the beer corrodes it. But whiskey polishes the copper and is the saving of him.*

MARK TWAIN, AMERICAN AUTHOR

---

**Irish whiskey** Although Scots would argue the point, there is strong foundation to the theory that the Irish have been distilling whiskey for nearly 900 years (although not from the ubiquitous Irish potato, as was once opined). This whiskey is made primarily from barley (malted or unmalted), as well as corn, rye, wheat, and oats. Irish whiskeys are triple-distilled (*see* DISTILLATION) for extra smoothness and AGED in casks for a minimum of 4 (but usually 7 to 8) years. The casks more often than not have been used for aging BOURBON, SHERRY, or RUM, whose flavors contribute uniquely individual nuances to the Irish whiskey. Although overshadowed by their Scottish neighbors, the Irish are advancing into the premium market with their own SINGLE-MALT whiskeys. Irish whiskeys on the market include Bushmills (Old Bushmills), Connemara, Jameson, John Power & Son, Tullamore Dew, and Tyrconnell. *See also* IRISH CREAM LIQUEURS; WHISK(E)Y-BASED LIQUEURS.

**Italian Coffee** There are undoubtedly as many versions of this drink as there are Italians. Their common denominator is the amaretto. *See also* Hot Drinks, page 29.

³/₄ oz. (1¹/₂ Tbsp.) brandy
³/₄ oz. (1¹/₂ Tbsp.) amaretto
about 6 oz. (³/₄ cup) hot espresso or very strong coffee
heavy whipping cream or whipped cream

Combine first 3 ingredients in warm mug, stirring to combine. Float cream on top by slowly pouring it over the back (rounded) side of a spoon; don't mix. Or top with a large dollop of whipped cream.

### Italian Stallion

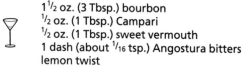

1 1/2 oz. (3 Tbsp.) bourbon
1/2 oz. (1 Tbsp.) Campari
1/2 oz. (1 Tbsp.) sweet vermouth
1 dash (about 1/16 tsp.) Angostura bitters
lemon twist

Stir liquid ingredients with ice. Strain into chilled glass; drop in lemon twist.

**Izarra** [ih-ZAHR-ruh] An ARMAGNAC-based LIQUEUR flavored with herbs grown in the French Pyrénées. Izarra comes in green and yellow varieties, the green being the stronger and less sweet of the two. *See also* HERB-FLAVORED SPIRITS.

**Jack Daniel's** One of the best-known distilleries in the United States, famous for its Tennessee WHISKEY.

### Jack-in-the-Box

2 oz. (1/4 cup) apple brandy
1 oz. (2 Tbsp.) unsweetened pineapple juice
1 oz. (2 Tbsp.) fresh lemon juice
2 to 4 dashes (about 1/8 to 1/4 tsp.) Angostura bitters

Shake ingredients with ice; strain into chilled cocktail glass or in an old-fashioned glass filled with ice cubes.

★ **Jill-in-the-Box** Substitute apple juice for the apple brandy.

### Jack Rose

2 oz. (1/4 cup) apple brandy
1/2 oz. (1 Tbsp.) fresh lime juice
2 to 4 dashes (about 1/8 to 1/4 tsp.) grenadine

Shake ingredients with ice; strain into chilled glass.

## Jade

1 1/2 oz. (3 Tbsp.) gold rum
1/2 oz. (1 Tbsp.) fresh lime juice
1/2 tsp. green crème de menthe
1/2 tsp. Triple Sec
1 tsp. powdered sugar
lime slice

Shake all ingredients except lime slice with ice. Strain into chilled glass; garnish with lime slice.

**Jägermeister** [YAY-ger-my-ster] Made in Wulfenbuttel, Germany, this reddish-brown LIQUEUR has an intensely bitter herbal CHARACTER, edged with cola and a touch of chocolate in the aftertaste. Fifty-six different herbs plus fruits, spices, barks, resins, and seeds make up the complicated formula, which has been used since at least 1878. Serving Jägermeister ("hunt master") icy cold helps tame its assertive flavor. *See also* HERB-FLAVORED SPIRITS.

*Why don't we slip out of those wet clothes
and into a dry Martini?*

ROBERT BENCHLEY, AMERICAN HUMORIST, CRITIC, ACTOR

## Jamaica Glow

1 1/2 oz. (3 Tbsp.) gin
1/2 oz. (1 Tbsp.) dry red wine (Cabernet Sauvignon, Burgundy, etc.)
1/2 oz. (1 Tbsp.) dark rum
1/2 oz. (1 Tbsp.) fresh orange juice

Shake ingredients with ice; strain into chilled glass.

**Jamaican Coffee** *See also* Hot Drinks, page 29.

1 oz. (2 Tbsp.) Jamaican rum
1 oz. (2 Tbsp.) Tia Maria or other coffee liqueur
about 6 oz. (3/4 cup) hot coffee
heavy whipping cream or whipped cream
ground allspice

Combine first 3 ingredients in warm mug, stirring to combine. Float cream on top by slowly pouring it over the back (rounded) side of a spoon; don't mix. Or top with a large dollop of whipped cream. Sprinkle lightly with allspice.

### Jamaican rum *see* RUM

### Japanese Fizz

2 oz. (¼ cup) blended whiskey
½ oz. (1 Tbsp.) ruby port
2 tsp. fresh lemon juice
1 tsp. powdered sugar
cold club soda
pineapple stick
orange slice

Shake first 4 ingredients with ice; strain into glass over ice cubes. Top with club soda, stirring gently. Garnish with fruit.

### Jell-O Shot

The fact that Jell-O Shots found an audience in the nineties is testament to the adage "different strokes for different folks." Enthusiasts evidently go for the admittedly strange semi-solid, jiggly texture with an alcoholic kick. Oh well, that just means more MARTINIS for the rest of us!

MAKES ABOUT NINE 1½-OUNCE SHOTS

1 (3 ounce) package any flavor Jell-O gelatin
6 oz. (¾ cup) boiling water
6 oz. (¾ cup) vodka, gin, rum, or other spirit

Pour gelatin into medium bowl. Add boiling water; stir until gelatin is dissolved. Stir in liquor; refrigerate until cool. Pour into glasses; refrigerate until set. Serve cold.

### Jelly Bean

1 oz. (2 Tbsp.) blackberry brandy
1 oz. (2 Tbsp.) anisette

Shake ingredients with ice; strain into chilled old-fashioned glass over ice cubes or into a shot glass.

### Jenever *see* GIN

*What's the difference between a bartender and God?
God doesn't think he's a bartender!*

### Jersey Lightning

2 oz. (¹/₄ cup) apple brandy
1 oz. (2 Tbsp.) sweet vermouth
³/₄ oz. (1¹/₂ Tbsp.) fresh lime juice

Shake ingredients with ice; strain into chilled glass.

### Jewel Cocktail

1 oz. (2 Tbsp.) gin
1 oz. (2 Tbsp.) green Chartreuse
1 oz. (2 Tbsp.) sweet vermouth
2 dashes (about ¹/₈ tsp.) orange bitters
maraschino cherry

Shake liquid ingredients with ice. Strain into chilled glass; garnish with cherry.

**jigger** 1. Also called a SHOT GLASS, a jigger is a small drinking glass–shaped vessel used both to measure and serve liquor. The average jigger is 1¹/₂ ounces; others range in size from 1 to 3 ounces. *See also* Glassware, page 8. 2. The amount of liquid such a measure holds, as in "a jigger" of WHISKEY, VODKA, etc. Also called a SHOT.

 **Jill-in-the-Box** *see* JACK-IN-THE-BOX

### Jockey Club

1¹/₂ oz. (3 Tbsp.) gin
2 tsp. fresh lemon juice
¹/₄ tsp. white crème de cacao
1 dash (about ¹/₁₆ tsp.) Angostura bitters

Shake ingredients with ice; strain into chilled glass.

**Jocose Julep** [joh-KOHSS] Dictionaries define "jocose" as someone or something characterized by humor, joking, comedy . . . well, you get the drift. We can't find anything that chronicles just how this drink got this name—maybe because drinking more than one can turn you into a real comedian. *See also* GINGER JULEP; JULEP; MINT JULEP.

2¹/₂ oz. (¹/₄ cup plus 1 Tbsp.) bourbon
1 oz. (2 Tbsp.) fresh lime juice
¹/₂ oz. (1 Tbsp.) green crème de menthe
1 tsp. sugar
5 mint leaves
cold club soda
mint sprig

Combine all ingredients except club soda and mint sprig in a blender. Cover and process at medium speed until smooth, about 15 seconds. Pour into chilled glass over ice cubes. Top with soda, stirring gently; garnish with mint sprig.

**Johannesberg Riesling** *see* RIESLING

**John Collins** *see* TOM COLLINS

### Johnny Cocktail

1¹/₂ oz. (3 Tbsp.) sloe gin
³/₄ oz. (1¹/₂ Tbsp.) Triple Sec
1 tsp. Pernod or other anise-flavored liqueur

Shake ingredients with ice; strain into chilled glass.

**jolt** American slang for a drink, as in "Let's go have a jolt or two."

### Joulouville [JOO-loo-vihl]

1 oz. (2 Tbsp.) gin
¹/₂ oz. (1 Tbsp.) apple brandy
¹/₂ oz. (1 Tbsp.) fresh lemon juice
1¹/₂ tsp. sweet vermouth
2 dashes (about ¹/₈ tsp.) grenadine

Shake ingredients with ice; strain into chilled glass.

### Journalist

1¹/₂ oz. (3 Tbsp.) gin
1¹/₂ tsp. dry vermouth
1¹/₂ tsp. sweet vermouth
¹/₂ tsp. Triple Sec
¹/₂ tsp. fresh lemon juice
1 dash (about ¹/₁₆ tsp.) Angostura bitters

Shake ingredients with ice; strain into chilled glass.

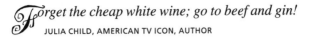

*orget the cheap white wine; go to beef and gin!*
JULIA CHILD, AMERICAN TV ICON, AUTHOR

## Judge, Jr. Cocktail

¾ oz. (1½ Tbsp.) gin
¾ oz. (1½ Tbsp.) light rum
2½ tsp. fresh lemon juice
1 tsp. grenadine

Shake ingredients with ice; strain into chilled glass.

## Judgette Cocktail

¾ oz. (1½ Tbsp.) gin
¾ oz. (1½ Tbsp.) dry vermouth
¾ oz. (1½ Tbsp.) peach brandy
1 tsp. fresh lime juice
maraschino cherry

Shake liquid ingredients with ice. Strain into chilled glass; garnish with cherry.

**juicer** *see* Bar Equipment, page 6

**julep** The word "julep" comes from the Persian *julâb,* which means "rosewater." In fifteenth-century England the word was used to describe a sugar syrup that was variously flavored and often mixed with medication. According to John Mariani's *Dictionary of American Food and Drink,* julep first appeared in print in the United States in John Davis's 1803 tome *Travel's of Four Years and a Half in the United States of America* described as: "A dram of spiritous liquor that has mint in it, taken by Virginians in the morning." *See also* GINGER JULEP; JOCOSE JULEP; MINT JULEP.

**jungle juice** Slang for an alcoholic beverage of dubious origin and quality. The term is said to have originated with American troops in the tropics, who created "jungle juice" by fermenting anything they could find, including coconuts, mangoes, and bananas.

## Jupiter Cocktail

1½ oz. (3 Tbsp.) gin
¾ oz. (1½ Tbsp.) dry vermouth
1 tsp. parfait amour or crème de violette
1 tsp. fresh orange juice

Shake ingredients with ice; strain into chilled glass.

**Kahana Royale** [kah-HAH-nah roy-YAHL] A Hawaiian LIQUEUR with the flavor of macadamia nuts. *See also* NUT-FLAVORED SPIRITS.

**Kahlúa; Kahlúa Licor de Café** [kah-LOO-ah] A mahogany-colored, coffee-flavored LIQUEUR produced in Mexico for more than a half century. Kahlúa, arguably the most popular liqueur of its kind, has a rich and complex roasted-coffee flavor layered with vanilla and semisweet chocolate. *See also* COFFEE-FLAVORED SPIRITS; KAHLÚA ROYALE CREAM LIQUEUR.

*There are people who strictly deprive themselves of each and every eatable, drinkable, and smokable which has in any way acquired a shady reputation. They pay this price for health. And health is all they get for it.*

MARK TWAIN, AMERICAN AUTHOR, HUMORIST

**Kahlúa Mudslide** One of several like-named, sweet, low-alcohol (6.5 percent) LIQUEURS made in the United States, all of which share a milky texture and milky-beige color. Kahlúa Mudslide has a faint coffee flavor, **Kahlúa and Milk** has a slightly more prominent coffee flavor than the "Mudslide," **Kahlúa Toasted Almond** tastes of candied almonds, and **Kahlúa Raspberry Brownie** has a raspberry-chocolate flavor. These liqueurs are sold in four-packs of 200-ml bottles, as well as the standard 750-ml bottle.

**Kahlúa Royale Cream Liqueur** [kah-LOO-ah roy-YAHL] A CREAM LIQUEUR with a café-au-lait color, a smooth, satiny texture, and a kiss-of-coffee flavor. *See also* COFFEE-FLAVORED SPIRITS; KAHLÚA.

### Kahlúa Toreador [kah-LOO-ah TOR-ee-uh-dor]

2 oz. (¹/₄ cup) brandy
1 oz. (2 Tbsp.) Kahlúa
1 egg white

Vigorously shake ingredients with ice; strain into chilled glass.

### Kamikaze [kah-mih-KAH-zee] The slang definition for this word is "a person who acts in a wildly reckless or destructive way" but—compared to some other libations—this long-popular SHOOTER isn't particularly ruinous. Today, the Kamikaze is often served UP in a COCKTAIL GLASS or ON THE ROCKS in an OLD-FASHIONED GLASS. Whether you use ROSE'S LIME JUICE or fresh squeezed is a matter of personal taste—ours is for the latter.

³/₄ oz. (1¹/₂ Tbsp.) vodka
³/₄ oz. (1¹/₂ Tbsp.) Triple Sec
³/₄ oz. (1¹/₂ Tbsp.) fresh lime juice or Rose's lime juice

Shake ingredients with ice; strain into chilled cocktail glass, a large shot glass, or over ice in an old-fashioned glass.

### Kamora A chocolate-brown, satiny-textured Mexican LIQUEUR with the flavor of coffee scented with cocoa and mint. Kamora also comes in vanilla- and hazelnut-flavored renditions. *See also* COFFEE-FLAVORED SPIRITS.

### Kangaroo

1¹/₂ oz. (3 Tbsp.) vodka
³/₄ oz. (1¹/₂ Tbsp.) dry vermouth
lemon twist

Stir liquid ingredients with ice. Strain into chilled glass; drop in lemon twist.

### Kentucky Cocktail

2 oz. (¹/₄ cup) bourbon
1¹/₂ oz. (3 Tbsp.) unsweetened pineapple juice

Shake ingredients with ice; strain into chilled glass.

### Kentucky Colonel Cocktail

1¹/₂ oz. (3 Tbsp.) bourbon
2 tsp. Bénédictine
lemon twist

Stir liquid ingredients with ice. Strain into chilled glass; drop in lemon twist.

### Key Lime Pie

½ oz. (1 Tbsp.) Cuarenta Y Tres
½ oz. (1 Tbsp.) Rose's lime juice
½ oz. (1 Tbsp.) half & half

Shake ingredients with ice; strain into chilled glass.

### ☀ Kickless Horse's Neck *see* HORSE'S NECK

### King Cole Cocktail

1 orange slice
1 pineapple slice
½ tsp. sugar
2 oz. (¼ cup) blended whiskey

Muddle fruit with sugar in chilled glass. Add whiskey and ice cubes, stirring well.

### King's Peg

2 oz. (¼ cup) brandy
about 6 oz. (¾ cup) cold dry champagne

Pour brandy into chilled glass filled with ice cubes. Add champagne, stirring gently.

---

*𝓑urgundy makes you think of silly things, Bordeaux makes you talk of them, and Champagne makes you do them.*

JEAN-ANTHELME BRILLAT-SAVARIN, FRENCH GASTRONOME, WRITER

---

### Kingston #1

1½ oz. (3 Tbsp.) Jamaican rum
¾ oz. (1½ Tbsp.) gin
½ oz. (1 Tbsp.) fresh lime or lemon juice
½ tsp. grenadine

Shake ingredients with ice; strain into chilled glass.

## Kingston #2

1¹/₂ oz. (3 Tbsp.) Jamaican rum
¹/₂ oz. (1 Tbsp.) kümmel
¹/₂ oz. (1 Tbsp.) fresh orange juice
2 dashes (about ¹/₈ tsp.) Pimento Dram

Shake ingredients with ice; strain into chilled glass.

## Kingston Cocktail

1¹/₂ oz. (3 Tbsp.) Jamaican rum
1 oz. (2 Tbsp.) Kahlúa or Tia Maria
1 tsp. fresh lime juice

Shake ingredients with ice; strain into chilled glass.

**Kir** [KEER] An APÉRITIF purportedly named for Canon Félix Kir, mayor of Dijon and a famous French war hero. We like just a "kiss" of cassis in this drink, but have seen recipes calling for a few drops to 2 tablespoons! Remember, the more cassis, the sweeter the drink.

¹/₄ tsp. to 1 Tbsp. crème de cassis
6 oz. (³/₄ cup) cold dry white wine (Chardonnay,
    Sauvignon Blanc, etc.)
lemon twist

Pour cassis and wine into chilled glass filled with ice cubes; stir well and drop in lemon twist.

---

*Champagne, if you are seeking the truth,
is better than a lie detector.*

GRAHAM GREENE, ENGLISH NOVELIST

---

## Kir Royale [KEER roy-AL]

¹/₄ to ¹/₂ tsp. crème de cassis
6 oz. (³/₄ cup) cold dry champagne

Pour cassis into chilled glass. Slowly add champagne; don't stir.

**kirsch; kirschwasser** [KEERSH; KEERSH-vah-ser] A DRY, clear EAU-DE-VIE made from cherries, including their pits. From the German *kirsch,* ("cherry") and *wasser,* ("water").

## Kiss Me Quick

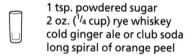

1 1/2 oz. (3 Tbsp.) Pernod or other anise-flavored liqueur
1/4 tsp. Cointreau
1/4 tsp. Angostura bitters
cold club soda

Shake all ingredients except club soda with ice. Strain into chilled glass filled with ice cubes. Top with soda, stirring gently.

## Klondike Cooler

1 tsp. powdered sugar
2 oz. (1/4 cup) rye whiskey
cold ginger ale or club soda
long spiral of orange peel

Stir sugar and whiskey together in chilled glass until sugar dissolves. Add 3 to 4 ice cubes; top with ginger ale or club soda, stirring gently. Arrange orange spiral so half of it is inside the glass and half hangs over the rim.

## Knickerbocker Cocktail [NIHK-er-bahk-er] Some renditions of this cocktail use only 2 teaspoons of dry vermouth; however, this version seems to be the most widely made.

2 oz. (1/4 cup) gin
1 oz. (2 Tbsp.) dry vermouth
1/2 tsp. sweet vermouth
lemon twist

Stir liquid ingredients with ice. Strain into chilled glass; drop in lemon twist.

## Knickerbocker Special Cocktail

2 oz. (1/4 cup) light rum
1 tsp. raspberry syrup or grenadine
1 tsp. fresh lime juice
1 tsp. fresh orange juice
1/2 tsp. Triple Sec
1/2 pineapple slice

Shake liquid ingredients with ice. Strain into chilled glass; garnish with pineapple slice.

## Knockout Cocktail

³/₄ oz. (1 ¹/₂ Tbsp.) gin
³/₄ oz. (1 ¹/₂ Tbsp.) dry vermouth
¹/₂ oz. (1 Tbsp.) Pernod or other anise-flavored liqueur
1 tsp. white crème de menthe
maraschino cherry

Stir liquid ingredients with ice. Strain into chilled glass; garnish with cherry.

## Kretchma Cocktail

1 oz. (2 Tbsp.) vodka
1 oz. (2 Tbsp.) white crème de cacao
¹/₂ oz. (1 Tbsp.) fresh lemon juice
¹/₄ tsp. grenadine

Shake ingredients with ice; strain into chilled glass.

**kümmel** [KIM-uhl] Created in Holland and now also produced in Germany, kümmel is a colorless LIQUEUR flavored with a panoply of herbs and seeds, including caraway, cumin, and fennel. Its name comes from the Middle High German *kümmel,* which means "cumin seed." *See also* HERB-FLAVORED SPIRITS.

## Kup's Indispensable Cocktail

1 ¹/₂ oz. (3 Tbsp.) gin
¹/₂ oz. (1 Tbsp.) dry vermouth
¹/₂ oz. (1 Tbsp.) sweet vermouth
1 dash (about ¹/₁₆ tsp.) Angostura bitters
orange twist

Stir liquid ingredients with ice. Strain into chilled glass; drop in orange twist.

## Kyoto Cocktail #1 [kee-OH-toh]

1 ¹/₂ oz. (3 Tbsp.) gin
¹/₂ oz. (1 Tbsp.) dry vermouth
¹/₂ oz. (1 Tbsp.) apricot brandy
¹/₂ oz. (1 Tbsp.) Triple Sec
maraschino cherry

Shake liquid ingredients with ice. Strain into chilled glass over ice cubes; garnish with cherry.

## Kyoto Cocktail #2

1 1/2 oz. (3 Tbsp.) gin
1/2 oz. (1 Tbsp.) dry vermouth
1/2 oz. (1 Tbsp.) melon liqueur
1/4 tsp. fresh lemon juice

Shake ingredients with cracked ice; strain into chilled glass.

---

*It is, of course, true that we can be intemperate in eating as well as in drinking, but the results of the intemperance would appear to be different. After a fifth helping of rice-pudding one does not become over-familiar with strangers, nor does an extra slice of ham inspire a man to beat his wife.*

A. A. MILNE, ENGLISH AUTHOR, DRAMATIST

---

## Ladies' Cocktail

2 oz. (1/4 cup) blended whiskey
1/8 tsp. Pernod or other anise-flavored liqueur
1/8 tsp. anisette
1/8 tsp. Angostura bitters
pineapple spear

Shake liquid ingredients with ice. Strain into chilled glass; garnish with pineapple.

## Lady Be Good

1 1/2 oz. (3 Tbsp.) brandy
1/2 oz. (1 Tbsp.) white crème de menthe
1/2 oz. (1 Tbsp.) sweet vermouth

Shake ingredients with ice; strain into chilled glass.

## Ladyfinger

1 1/2 oz. (3 Tbsp.) gin
3/4 oz. (1 1/2 Tbsp.) kirsch
3/4 oz. (1 1/2 Tbsp.) cherry brandy

Shake ingredients with ice; strain into chilled glass.

**lager** [LAH-guhr] A general style of beer that was originally stored and AGED (lagered) in its cask or vat for 1 to 3 months until free of sediment and crystal clear, after which carbonation was added before the beer was bottled. Modern production techniques complete this process much more quickly. Lagers—which are light flavored, bubbly, and pale golden in color—rank as America's most popular beer. *See also* BEER.

**lagering; lagered** A beermaking term for the period of time a beer is stored, during which the temperature is gradually reduced, a process that mellows and clarifies the beer.

**La Grande Passion** A pale golden French LIQUEUR with the exotic flavor of tropical fruit and an elegant, silky texture. *See also* PASSION FRUIT–FLAVORED SPIRITS.

**La Jolla** [lah HOY-yuh]
  1½ oz. (3 Tbsp.) brandy
  ½ oz. (1 Tbsp.) crème de banane
  2 tsp. fresh lemon juice
  1 tsp. fresh orange juice
Shake ingredients with ice; strain into chilled glass.

**lambic beer** A WHEAT BEER produced in a small area southwest of Brussels. This Belgian brew is produced from 60 to 70 percent malted barley and 30 to 40 percent wheat. The MASH is traditionally made in the winter when conditions are just right for a wild yeast called *Brettanomyces* to start spontaneous FERMENTATION. Lambics are AGED in casks anywhere from several months to several years. Younger lambic beers can be sour and slightly cloudy, while older versions mellow and lose much of their sour CHARACTER. A light, fruity essence is sometimes infused into lambics when fruits (such as cherries or raspberries) are added to the beer during aging. *See also* BEER.

*Teetotallers seem to die the same as others,
so what's the use of knocking off the beer?*

A. P. HERBERT, BRITISH AUTHOR, POLITICIAN

### Lawhill Cocktail

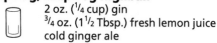

1 ½ oz. (3 Tbsp.) blended whiskey
¾ oz. (1 ½ Tbsp.) dry vermouth
¼ tsp. maraschino liqueur
¼ tsp. Pernod or other anise-flavored liqueur
1 dash (about ¹⁄₁₆ tsp.) Angostura bitters

Stir ingredients with ice; strain into chilled glass.

### Leapfrog; Leapfrog Highball

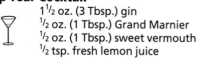

2 oz. (¼ cup) gin
¾ oz. (1 ½ Tbsp.) fresh lemon juice
cold ginger ale

Pour gin and lemon juice into chilled glass over ice cubes. Top with ginger ale, stirring gently.

### Leap Year Cocktail

1 ½ oz. (3 Tbsp.) gin
½ oz. (1 Tbsp.) Grand Marnier
½ oz. (1 Tbsp.) sweet vermouth
½ tsp. fresh lemon juice

Shake ingredients with cracked ice; strain into chilled glass.

### Leave-It-to-Me Cocktail #1

1 oz. (2 Tbsp.) gin
½ oz. (1 Tbsp.) dry vermouth
½ oz. (1 Tbsp.) apricot brandy
¼ tsp. fresh lemon juice
1 dash (about ¹⁄₁₆ tsp.) grenadine

Shake ingredients with ice; strain into chilled glass.

### Leave-It-to-Me Cocktail #2

1 ½ oz. (3 Tbsp.) gin
1 ½ tsp. fresh lemon juice
1 tsp. raspberry syrup
¼ tsp. maraschino liqueur

Shake ingredients with ice; strain into chilled glass.

**Lemon Drop Shooter** This immensely popular drink started out as a SHOOTER, but those who want to savor it slowly can make the "sipper" version. Either way, put the vodka in the freezer for a couple of hours to become icy cold. Using Absolut Citron vodka will particularly please lemon lovers.

> lemon wedge
> sugar
> 2 oz. (¼ cup) icy-cold vodka

Thoroughly coat lemon wedge with sugar; pour vodka into chilled glass. Knock the vodka back in one gulp, then suck on the sugar-coated lemon.

## Lemon Drop Sipper

> 2 tsp. fresh lemon juice
> about 2 tsp. sugar
> 2 oz. (¼ cup) icy-cold vodka
> lemon slice

Frost rim of chilled glass by moistening with a little lemon juice, then dipping rim into granulated sugar. Shake remaining lemon juice, 1 tsp. of the sugar, and vodka with ice. Strain into glass; garnish with lemon slice.

**lemon-flavored spirits** *see* CAPRINATURA; CITRUS-FLAVORED SPIRITS

**Leprechaun** [LEHP-rih-kon] Legend has it that if you can catch one of the Irish elves after which this drink is named, he'll lead you to treasure. *See also* DANCING LEPRECHAUN.

> 2 oz. (¼ cup) Irish whiskey
> cold tonic water
> lemon twist

Pour whiskey into chilled glass filled with ice cubes. Top with tonic water, stirring gently; drop in lemon twist.

---

*It is not brandy, it is not wine, it is Jameson's Irish Whiskey. It fills the heart with joy divine, and makes the fancy frisky.*
JAMES THOMSON, BRITISH POET

**leverpull** *see* Bar Equipment (Corkscrews), page 4

**Liberty Cocktail**

1 1/2 oz. (3 Tbsp.) apple brandy
3/4 oz. (1 1/2 Tbsp.) light rum
1/4 tsp. powdered sugar

Stir ingredients with ice; strain into chilled glass.

**Licor 43** *see* CUARENTA Y TRES

**licorice-flavored spirits** *see* ANISE-FLAVORED SPIRITS

**light beer** *see* BEER

**light whiskey** *see* WHISKEY

**Lillehammer** [LIHL-luh-hah-mer] Produced in Denmark, this clear, cherry-red LIQUEUR is made from lingonberries and has a irresistibly sweet-tart berry flavor. *See also* BERRY-FLAVORED SPIRITS.

**Lillet** [lee-LAY; lih-LAY] Hailing from the French village of Podensac and made since the late 1800s, Lillet is a medley of wine, BRANDY, fruit, and herbs. This APÉRITIF comes in two styles— **Lillet blanc,** based on white wine, is drier (*see* DRY) than the red-wine version, **Lillet rouge.** Both are traditionally served ON THE ROCKS in an OLD-FASHIONED GLASS, garnished with a twist of orange.

**Lillet Cocktail**

1 1/2 oz. (3 Tbsp.) Lillet blanc
1/2 oz. (1 Tbsp.) gin
lemon twist

Shake liquid ingredients with ice. Strain into chilled cocktail glass or over ice cubes in an old-fashioned glass. Drop in lemon twist.

➤ **Lillet Noyaux** Add 1 tsp. crème de noyaux before shaking.

**Limbo**

2 oz. (1/4 cup) light rum
1 oz. (2 Tbsp.) fresh orange juice
1/2 oz. (1 Tbsp.) crème de banane

Shake ingredients with ice; strain into chilled glass.

★ **Lime Rickey** *See also* RICKEY.

2 oz. (¹/₄ cup) lime-flavored syrup
¹/₂ oz. (1 Tbsp.) fresh lime juice
cold club soda
lime wedge
maraschino cherry, optional

Pour first 2 ingredients into chilled glass over ice cubes. Top with club soda, stirring gently. Garnish with lime wedge and cherry, if desired.

★ **Ginger-Lime Rickey** Substitute ginger ale for the club soda.

> *We frequently hear of people dying from too much drinking. . . . But the blame is always placed on whiskey. Why this should be I could never understand. You can die from drinking too much of anything—coffee, water, milk, soft drinks. . . . And so long as the presence of death lurks with anyone who goes through the simple act of swallowing, I will make mine whiskey.*
>
> W. C. FIELDS, AMERICAN COMEDIAN, ACTOR

**Linstead**

1¹/₂ oz. (3 Tbsp.) blended whiskey
1¹/₂ oz. (3 Tbsp.) unsweetened pineapple juice
¹/₄ tsp. Pernod or other anise-flavored liqueur
¹/₄ tsp. fresh lemon juice
¹/₂ tsp. sugar

Shake ingredients with ice; strain into chilled glass.

**liqueur** [lih-KYOOR; lih-KER] Simply put, a liqueur is a sweetened spirit flavored with seeds, fruits, herbs, flowers, nuts, spices, roots, leaves, and barks. The spirit base can be anything from BRANDY to RUM to WHISKEY, and may be flavored in four different ways: *distillation*—alcohol and flavoring agents are blended before being distilled (*see* DISTILLATION); *infusion*—flavorings are steeped in hot water, which is then mixed with the alcohol base; *maceration*—flavoring agents are steeped directly in the alcohol base; *percolation*—alcohol is dripped through the flavoring agents, thereby extracting their essences. **Proprietary liqueurs** (such as BÉNÉDICTINE, GALLIANO, and SOUTHERN COMFORT) are made exclusively by specific liqueur houses with secret formulas, some of which have been closely guarded for centuries. **Generic liqueurs** (like AMARETTO and CRÈME DE MENTHE) are made by various producers using fairly standard recipes. Quality brands are typically flavored with the finest ingredients, essential oils, and extracts, while less expensive examples sometimes use artificial flavorings. **Cream liqueurs** are flavored mixtures that have been homogenized with cream, resulting in a rich, velvety smooth, creamy mixture that requires no refrigeration. Liqueurs range widely in alcohol content, from about 15 percent (for some IRISH CREAM LIQUEURS) to 55 percent (green CHARTREUSE), although a few "baby liqueurs" like KAHLÚA MUDSLIDE contain only 6.5 percent alcohol. Although the word "liqueur" is common usage today, these potables are also called *cordials* and, less frequently, *ratafias. See also* ABRICOTINE; ABSINTHE; ADVOCAAT; AFRI-KOKO; AFTER SHOCK; ALIZÉ DE FRANCE; ALLASCH; AMARETTO; AMARO; ANISETTE; APRY; AURUM; B & B; BÄRENJÄGER; BÉNÉDICTINE D.O.M.; BERENTZEN; BRANCA MENTA; BUCKSHOT; CACTUS JUICE; CALISAY; CAPRINATURA; CAPUCELLO; CAYMANA; CENTERBE; CERTOSA; CHAMBORD; CHARTREUSE; CHÉRI-SUISSE; CHERRY MARNIER; CHINA-MARTINI; CHOCOLAT ROYALE; COINTREAU; COPA DE ORO; CORDIAL CAMPARI; CORDIAL MÉDOC; CRÈME D'ABRICOTS; CRÈME D'AMANDE; CRÈME D'ANANAS; CRÈME DE BANANE; CRÈME DE CACAO; CRÈME DE CASSIS; CRÈME DE FRAISE; CRÈME DE FRAMBOISE; CRÈME DE GRAND MARNIER; CRÈME DE MANDARINES; CRÈME DE MENTHE; CRÈME DE NOYAUX; CRÈME DE ROSE; CRÈME DE VANILLE; CRÈME DE VIOLETTE; CRÈME YVETTE; CRYSTAL COMFORT; CUARENTA Y TRES; CURAÇAO; DANZIGER GOLDWASSER; DRACULA'S POTION; DRAMBUIE; EARL GREY ENGLISH LIQUOR; ECHTE KROATZBEERE; ESCORIAL GREEN; FIORE D'ALPI; FORBIDDEN FRUIT; FRAGONARD LIQUEUR DE COGNAC X.O.; FRAMBOISE; FRANGELICO; FRIESENGEIST; GALLIANO; GLAYVA; GODIVA CHOCOLATE LIQUEUR; GOLDSCHLAGER; GRAND MARNIER;

HERBSAINT; IRISH CREAM LIQUEURS; IRISH MIST; IZARRA; JÄGERMEISTER; KAHANA ROYALE; KAHLÚA; KAHLÚA MUDSLIDE; KAHLÚA ROYALE CREAM; KAMORA; KÜMMEL; LA GRANDE PASSION; LILLEHAMMER; LIQUEUR D'ANIS; LIQUEUR D'OR; MALIBU; MANDARINE NAPOLÉON; MARASCHINO LIQUEUR; MIDORI; NOCELLO; OPAL NERA; OUZO; PARFAIT AMOUR; PASHA; PASTIS; PATRON XO CAFÉ; PEARLE DE BRILLET; PERNOD; PETER HEERING; PONCHE; PRUNELLE; RATAFIA; ROCK AND RYE; SABRA; SAFARI EXOTIC LIQUEUR; SAMBUCA; SLOE GIN; SOUTHERN COMFORT; STREGA; SWEDISH PUNSCH; TIA MARIA; TIRAMISU; TRIPLE SEC; TRUFFLES; TUACA; VAN DER HUM; VANDERMINT; VOV ZABAJONE; WILD TURKEY LIQUEUR.

*A serious writer does not drink liqueurs.*
ARNOLD BENNETT, BRITISH NOVELIST

**liqueur d'anis** [lee-KER dah-NEES] A generic French term for anise-flavored LIQUEURS.

**Liqueur d'Or** [lee-KER DAWR] A French lemon-flavored LIQUEUR with flakes of gold leaf floating in it. The French word *or* means "gold."

**Liquid Cocaine #1** There seem to be at least a dozen versions of this potent potable. Following are just two. This drink's a real killer if you use 151-proof rum.

- ½ oz. (1 Tbsp.) dark rum
- ½ oz. (1 Tbsp.) Rumple Minze
- ½ oz. (1 Tbsp.) Jägermeister
- ½ oz. (1 Tbsp.) Goldschlager

Shake ingredients with ice; strain into chilled old-fashioned glass over ice cubes or into a shot glass.

**Liquid Cocaine #2**

- ½ oz. (1 Tbsp.) dark rum
- ½ oz. (1 Tbsp.) root-beer schnapps
- ½ oz. (1 Tbsp.) Jägermeister
- ½ oz. (1 Tbsp.) Rumple Minze

Shake ingredients with ice; strain into chilled old-fashioned glass over ice cubes or into a shot glass.

**liquor** Any alcoholic beverage (such as GIN, VODKA, or WHISKEY) produced by DISTILLATION. *See also* ALCOHOL; SPIRITS.

**Liquore Galliano** [lee-KWAW-ray gal-LYAH-noh] *see* GALLIANO

---

*A 95-year-old matriarch was lying in bed close to death, her family members surrounding her. Thinking it might soothe her final minutes, her granddaughter brought her a glass of warm milk, spiced with cinnamon and liberally laced with whiskey. She held the milk up to her grandmother's lips. The old woman took a small sip . . . and then another . . . and another. As her eyes popped open she exclaimed, "Don't sell that cow"!*

---

**Liquore Strega** [lee-KWAW-ray STRAY-gah] *see* STREGA

**Little Devil**

1 oz. (2 Tbsp.) gin
1 oz. (2 Tbsp.) light rum
$^{1}/_{2}$ oz. (1 Tbsp.) Triple Sec
2 tsp. fresh lemon juice

Shake ingredients with ice; strain into chilled glass.

**Little Princess**

1$^{1}/_{2}$ oz. (3 Tbsp.) sweet vermouth
1$^{1}/_{2}$ oz. (3 Tbsp.) light rum

Stir or shake with ice; strain into chilled glass.

### Loch Lomond [LAHK LOH-mond]

1½ oz. (3 Tbsp.) Scotch
1 tsp. powdered sugar
2 to 4 dashes (about ⅛ to ¼ tsp.) Angostura bitters

Shake ingredients with ice; strain into chilled cocktail glass or over ice in an old-fashioned glass.

### Lollipop

¾ oz. (1½ Tbsp.) green Chartreuse
¾ oz. (1½ Tbsp.) Cointreau
¾ oz. (1½ Tbsp.) kirsch
¼ tsp. maraschino liqueur

Shake ingredients with ice; strain into chilled glass.

### London Cocktail

2 oz. (¼ cup) gin
½ tsp. maraschino liqueur
2 dashes (about ⅛ tsp.) orange bitters
½ tsp. powdered sugar
lemon twist

Shake all ingredients except twist with ice. Strain into chilled glass; drop in lemon twist.

### London dry gin *see* GIN

### London Fog

1 oz. (2 Tbsp.) white crème de menthe
1 oz. (2 Tbsp.) anisette
2 dashes (about ⅛ tsp.) Angostura bitters
lemon slice

Shake liquid ingredients with ice. Strain into chilled glass; garnish with lemon slice.

➤ **Creamy London Fog** Omit bitters and lemon slice. Combine crème de menthe, anisette, and 1 scoop (about ½ cup) vanilla ice cream in a blender. Cover and process at medium speed until smooth, about 15 seconds. Pour into chilled glass.

### London Special *see* CHAMPAGNE COCKTAIL

## Lone Tree Cocktail

³/₄ oz. (1¹/₂ Tbsp.) gin
³/₄ oz. (1¹/₂ Tbsp.) dry vermouth
³/₄ oz. (1¹/₂ Tbsp.) sweet vermouth
2 dashes (about ¹/₈ tsp.) orange bitters

Stir ingredients with ice; strain into chilled glass.

**long drink** *see* TALL DRINKS

**Long Island Ice Tea** This potent combo is definitely *not* iced tea. It was invented in the late 1970s by Long Island bartender Robert C. "Rosebud" Butt.

¹/₂ oz. (1 Tbsp.) gin
¹/₂ oz. (1 Tbsp.) light rum
¹/₂ oz. (1 Tbsp.) tequila
¹/₂ oz. (1 Tbsp.) vodka
¹/₂ oz. (1 Tbsp.) Triple Sec
1 oz. (2 Tbsp.) fresh lemon juice
1 tsp. sugar
cold cola
lemon wedge

Shake first 7 ingredients with ice; strain into chilled glass filled with ice cubes. Top with cola, stirring gently; garnish with lemon wedge.

---

*Like a camel I can go without a drink for seven days— and have on several horrible occasions.*

HERB CAEN, AMERICAN COLUMNIST

---

## Los Angeles Cocktail

1¹/₂ oz. (3 Tbsp.) blended whiskey
1¹/₂ tsp. fresh lemon juice
1 tsp. sugar
2 dashes (about ¹/₈ tsp.) sweet vermouth
1 egg

Vigorously shake ingredients with ice; strain into chilled cocktail glass or over ice cubes in an old-fashioned glass.

## Loudspeaker

1 oz. (2 Tbsp.) brandy
1 oz. (2 Tbsp.) gin
¹/₂ oz. (1 Tbsp.) fresh lemon or lime juice
¹/₂ oz. (1 Tbsp.) Triple Sec

Shake ingredients with ice; strain into chilled cocktail glass or in an old-fashioned glass over ice cubes.

## Love Cocktail

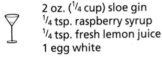

2 oz. (¹/₄ cup) sloe gin
¹/₄ tsp. raspberry syrup
¹/₄ tsp. fresh lemon juice
1 egg white

Shake ingredients with cracked ice; strain into chilled glass.

**lowball** In cocktailese, a lowball is the short version of a HIGH-BALL, typically a WHISKEY–soda water combo over ice, or sometimes whiskey alone ON THE ROCKS, served in an OLD-FASHIONED GLASS.

## Made and Bottled By *see* WINE LABEL TERMS

**Madeira; madeira** [muh-DEER-uh] 1. One of the three best-known FORTIFIED WINES, the others being PORT and SHERRY. True Madeira comes from the Portuguese island of Madeira, which is located some 530 miles southwest of Lisbon and 360 miles due west of Morocco. Madeira's unique flavor is derived through heat and oxidization, elements that would ruin most other wines. This classic evolved centuries ago when wine was transported by lengthy ship voyages, during which time warm temperatures and poor air circulation caused oxidization and—surprise—created wonderful wines. Today, the same conditions are duplicated by "baking" Madeiras in hot rooms or heated tanks (*estufas*) for a minimum of 90 days, a process called *estufagem*. The finer Madeiras are AGED in wooden casks in extremely warm conditions for years, which slowly develops the tangy, slightly bitter, burned-caramel flavor unique to this wine. Madeira ranges in color from pale blond to deep tawny, runs the gamut from very DRY to very sweet, and is commonly fortified to about 20 percent alcohol.

There are four distinct styles of Madeira: **Sercial**—light, dry, and pale golden in color; **Verdelho**—sweeter and stronger; **Boal** (or *Bual*)—fuller and sweeter than the first two; and **Malmsey**—the richest, darkest, and sweetest of the lot. The two lighter styles are typically served as APÉRITIFS, while the heavier, sweeter styles are considered dessert wines. While the four styles of Madeira were originally made from the classic VARIETALS—Sercial, Verdelho, Boal, and Malvasia (Malmsey)—Tinta Negra Mole grapes have been widely used since the late 1800s, particularly in inexpensive versions. In 1986, however, Portugal entered the European Common Market, whose regulations state that any Madeira listing a grape variety on its label must contain at least 85 percent of that grape. This move has prompted replanting of the four classic vines. Wines labeled "Boal-style" or "Sercial-style" most likely contain less than 85 percent of that grape and are made from Tinta Negra Mole. 2. A generic term for American dessert wines that attempt to mimic the flavor of true Madeiras. Such wines cannot compare with the Portuguese originals, but then they're a fraction of the price.

### Madras [MAD-ruhs]

3 oz. (³/₈ cup) cranberry juice
2 oz. (¹/₄ cup) fresh orange juice
1¹/₂ oz. (3 Tbsp.) vodka

Pour into chilled glass filled with ice cubes; stir well.

★ **Maiden Madras** Omit vodka; increase cranberry juice to ¹/₂ cup and orange juice to ¹/₃ cup. Garnish with orange slice.

### ★ Maiden Madras *see* MADRAS

### Maiden's Blush

1¹/₂ oz. (3 Tbsp.) gin
1 tsp. Triple Sec
¹/₂ tsp. grenadine
¹/₄ tsp. fresh lemon juice

Shake ingredients with ice; strain into chilled glass.

### Maiden's Prayer

1 oz. (2 Tbsp.) gin
1 oz. (2 Tbsp.) Cointreau or Triple Sec
¹/₂ oz. (1 Tbsp.) fresh lemon juice
¹/₂ oz. (1 Tbsp.) fresh orange juice

Shake ingredients with ice; strain into chilled glass.

**Mai Tai** This potent, exotic favorite is said to have been invented by Victor Bergeron, the original owner of Trader Vic's restaurant. He purportedly created it for a couple of Tahitian friends who, upon tasting it, exclaimed in Tahitian, "*Maitai!*" ("Out of this world!").

> 1 oz. (2 Tbsp.) light rum
> 1 oz. (2 Tbsp.) dark rum
> 1 oz. (2 Tbsp.) Triple Sec
> $\frac{1}{2}$ oz. (1 Tbsp.) grenadine
> $\frac{1}{2}$ oz. (1 Tbsp.) orgeat syrup
> $\frac{1}{2}$ oz. (1 Tbsp.) fresh lime juice
> pineapple spear
> maraschino cherry

Shake liquid ingredients with ice. Strain into chilled glass over ice cubes. Garnish with pineapple and cherry; serve with straw.

---

*. . . mai tai, a tarted-up cocktail usually garnished with a miniature paper parasol and served to egregious rubes in Sino-Polynesian restaurants.*

JAY JACOBS, AMERICAN AUTHOR, FOOD CRITIC

---

**Malibu** A crystal-clear, RUM-based LIQUEUR with an intense co-conut flavor. Sometimes referred to as *Malibu Rum.*

**Malibu rum** *see* MALIBU

**malt** A grain (typically barley) that's steeped in water, sprouted, dried, and coarsely milled. The characteristics of malt—one of the primary ingredients used to make beer—vary depending on the type of barley, germination time, and drying temperature. In general, malt contributes a mellow, sweet flavor and also influences the CHARACTER and color of whatever it flavors.

**malt liquor** A beer with a relatively high alcoholic content by weight, generally about 5 to 8 percent—some varieties reach as high as 9 percent. Their high alcohol concentrations make such brews ineligible to be labeled "beer" or "lager." *See also* BEER.

**malt whisk(e)y** A WHISKEY made from not less than 51 percent malted barley. *See also* SCOTCH WHISKY; SINGLE-MALT WHISK(E)Y.

*There are two things a Highlander likes naked, and one of them is malt whisky.*

SCOTTISH PROVERB

## Mamie Taylor

2 oz. (¼ cup) Scotch
½ oz. (1 Tbsp.) fresh lime juice
cold ginger ale
lime slice

Pour Scotch and lime juice into chilled glass. Add 3 to 4 ice cubes; top with ginger ale and garnish with lime slice.

## Mañana [mah-NYAH-nah]

1½ oz. (3 Tbsp.) light rum
½ oz. (1 Tbsp.) apricot brandy
1 tsp. fresh lemon juice
1 tsp. grenadine

Shake ingredients with ice; strain into chilled glass.

## Mandarine Napoléon

Made in Belgium from tangerines, this perfumy, BRANDY-based LIQUEUR has a silky texture and candied orange flavor. *See also* CITRUS-FLAVORED SPIRITS.

## Mandeville

1½ oz. (3 Tbsp.) light rum
1 oz. (2 Tbsp.) dark rum
½ oz. (1 Tbsp.) fresh lemon juice
½ oz. (1 Tbsp.) cola
1 tsp. Pernod or other anise-flavored liqueur
¼ tsp. grenadine

Shake ingredients with ice; strain into chilled glass over ice cubes.

## Manhasset

1½ oz. (3 Tbsp.) blended whiskey
½ oz. (1 Tbsp.) fresh lemon juice
1½ tsp. dry vermouth
1½ tsp. sweet vermouth
lemon twist

Shake liquid ingredients with ice. Strain into chilled glass; drop in lemon twist.

**Manhattan** One of the true classic cocktails, the Manhattan is said to have been created in 1874 by a bartender at New York's Manhattan Club for a fête given by Lady Randolph Churchill (Winston's American mum) in honor of New York's newly elected governor Samuel J. Tilden. As with so many classics, this cocktail has undergone myriad permutations over the past 100-plus years, its ingredients and proportions inspiring lively debate among enthusiasts. But whether you prefer classic RYE (or other blended whisk[e]y) or prefer BOURBON, whether you like it served UP or ON THE ROCKS, one thing most of today's bartenders agree on is that bitters are essential.

2 oz. ($^1/_4$ cup) rye whiskey
1 oz. (2 Tbsp.) sweet vermouth
1 to 2 dashes (about $^1/_{16}$ to $^1/_8$ tsp.) Angostura bitters
maraschino cherry

Stir liquid ingredients with ice; strain into chilled cocktail glass. Or pour first 3 ingredients into an old-fashioned glass filled with ice cubes; stir well. Garnish with cherry.

➤ **Brandy Manhattan** Substitute brandy for the whiskey.

➤ **Dry Manhattan** Substitute dry vermouth for the sweet vermouth; garnish with lemon twist.

➤ **Perfect Manhattan** Substitute 1 Tbsp. dry vermouth for 1 Tbsp. of the sweet vermouth.

➤ **Scotch Manhattan** *see* ROB ROY

---

*The cocktail is a pleasant drink; it's mild and harmless I don't think. When you've had one you call for two, and then you don't care what you do.*

GEORGE ADE, AMERICAN HUMORIST

---

**Manzanilla** [man-zuh-NEE-yuh] *see* SHERRY

**maraschino cherry** [mar-uh-SKEE-noh; mar-uh-SHEE-noh] A specially treated cherry that can be made from any variety, the

Royal Anne being the most common. Cherries become "maraschinoized" when macerated in a sugar syrup that's flavored (typically, almond for red cherries, mint for green), then dyed the appropriate color. Harmful dyes that were once used have since been banned by the federal government.

**maraschino liqueur** [mar-uh-SKEE-noh (mar-uh-SHEE-noh) lih-KYOOR] A clear, relatively dry LIQUEUR with a subtle bitter-almond flavor. Maraschino is made from Marasca cherries, including the pits. *See also* CHERRY-FLAVORED SPIRITS.

**marc** [MARK; MAHR] 1. A French term (known as POMACE in English) for the residue (skins, pits, seeds, and pulp) remaining after the juice has been pressed from grapes. 2. A potent BRANDY distilled from this mixture—the French counterpart to GRAPPA (the name used in Italy and California).

**Margarita** History tells us that the Margarita dates back to the early 1930s and (by most accounts) hails from Mexico. However, as happens with most spirited classics, legends abound as to who actually did the deed. Some claim it was first served at Tijuana's Caliente racetrack, others credit Bertita's Bar in Tasca; some say it was invented by Pancho Morales of Tommy's Place in Juárez; and Daniel Negrete said *he* invented it (naming it after his girlfriend) while tending bar in 1936 at Puebla's Garcí Crespo Hotel. Then there's a relatively latecomer, Texan Margarita Sames, who maintains that she created it for guests while living in Acapulco in 1948. What's probably true is that—as with most brilliant ideas—many people got the notion to mix tequila with lime juice and orange-flavored liqueur at about the same time. And for that we all thank them!

### Basic Margarita

1½ oz. (3 Tbsp.) tequila
¾ oz. (1½ Tbsp.) fresh lime juice
½ oz. (1 Tbsp.) Cointreau or Triple Sec
lime wedge or slice

Moisten chilled glass rim with a little lime juice, then dip rim into salt. Shake first 3 ingredients with cracked ice; strain into glass. Garnish with lime.

➤ **Blue Margarita** Substitute blue curaçao for the Cointreau.

➤ **Frozen Margarita** Add 1 cup crushed ice. Combine all ingredients in a blender. Cover and process at medium speed until slushy, about 5 seconds. For a **Frozen Fruit Margarita:** Reduce crushed ice to ½ cup; add ½ cup frozen fruit (such as peach or mango slices or chopped strawberries).

➤ **Melon Margarita** Substitute Midori or other melon-flavored liqueur for the Cointreau; garnish with a wedge of melon instead of lime.

➤ **Peach or Strawberry Margarita** Substitute peach or strawberry liqueur for the Cointreau. Add 4 to 6 peach slices or large strawberries; process all ingredients in blender until smooth, about 15 seconds. Omit lime wedge.

**Margarita-flavored liqueur** *see* CACTUS JUICE

**Margarita glass** *see* Glassware, page 8

**Marsala** [mahr-SAH-lah] One of Italy's most famous FORTIFIED WINES, Marsala comes from the old seaside port city of the same name on the western tip of Sicily. This area's long history of making fortified wine dates back to Roman times, but it wasn't until the late 1700s that Englishman John Woodhouse devised today's conventional techniques for making Marsala. As with SHERRY and MADEIRA, a Marsala gets much of its flavor from oxidization during AGING. Marsala wines are made in various styles—*secco* (DRY), *semisecco* (semisweet), and *dolce* (sweet). The quality levels are: **Fine**—the lowest level, with requirements of at least 17 percent alcohol and 1 year of wood aging; **Superiore**—at least 18 percent alcohol and 2 years of wood aging; **Superiore Riserva**—at least 4 years of aging (Superiore Marsalas may also be labeled *Garibaldi Dolce* [*GD*], *London Particular* [*LP*], or *Superior Old Marsala* [*SOM*]); and **Vergine**—the highest quality, with at least 5 years of wood aging

(Vergine *stravecchio* or *riserva* must be aged a minimum of 10 years). Dry Marsalas, especially the Vergine styles with their distinctively smoky, caramel-toffee flavor, are typically served as APÉRITIFS, whereas many of the semisweet and sweet styles make better dessert wines. The label terms **ambra** and **oro** indicate wines made from white grapes, while **rubino** wines are made from red grapes. **Cremevo** (*Cremevo Zabaione Vino Aromatizzato*)—once called **Marsala Speciali**—is a flavored wine made with 80 percent Marsala, plus various other ingredients like eggs or coffee.

*In the film world, "The Martini" is moviespeak for the last shot of the day.*

**Martinez; Martinez Cocktail** Bar lore abounds about the creation of this cocktail, hailed as the ancestor to the MARTINI. The good folks in Martinez, California, claim it was invented at a local bar in 1849 for a miner who was celebrating having struck gold. Others say it was created by San Francisco bartender "Professor" Jerry Thomas and originally appeared in his 1862 *Bon Vivant's Companion, or How to Mix Drinks* as a "gin cocktail," to be changed to a *Martinez* in the book's 1887 revision. What's true is that early recipes for the Martinez are just a MANHATTAN made with gin. Nevertheless, here is today's updated, drier Martinez. If you can't find the elusive OLD TOM GIN, use regular gin and increase the maraschino liqueur to 1½ teaspoons.

2½ oz. (5 Tbsp.) dry vermouth
1½ oz. (3 Tbsp.) Old Tom gin
¼ tsp. maraschino liqueur
2 dashes (⅛ tsp.) Angostura bitters
lemon twist
maraschino cherry

Shake liquid ingredients with ice. Strain into chilled glass; drop in lemon twist and cherry.

*There is something about a Martini, ere the dining and dancing begin. And to tell you the truth, it is not the vermouth— I think that perhaps it's the gin.*

OGDEN NASH, AMERICAN POET, AUTHOR

**Martini** Arguably *the* most popular cocktail of all time, and certainly the favorite of myriad characters in novels and motion pictures, the Martini is stunning in its simplicity—gin (or VODKA) and dry vermouth. There are numerous stories of its origin, the most popular (and logical) being that it's a descendant of the MARTINEZ, which is, in turn, an offspring of the MANHATTAN. Over the years, that early four-component Martinez recipe has metamorphosed into a two-ingredient, much drier (*see* DRY) *Martini,* which replaces its predecessor's slight sweetness with an icy austerity. At the turn of the century, when popular usage of the word "Martini" took hold, the drink's proportions were equal parts gin and dry vermouth. By about 1915, the ratio was two parts gin to one part vermouth, with four-to-one being the norm by World War II. Today, it's not uncommon to see ratios of six, eight, twelve, or fifteen parts gin to one part vermouth. Bottom line: The less vermouth, the drier the Martini. Of course, according to some, the *ultimate* dry Martini is made by reverently passing a tightly capped bottle of vermouth over a gin-filled glass.

The Martini is enjoying an enthusiastic renaissance—so much so that there have been entire books written on the subject. Recipes abound for everything from Blue (CURAÇAO) Martinis to CHOCOLATE MARTINIS, all of which have classic Martini enthusiasts sadly shaking their heads at such sacrilege. Indeed, the list of "new" Martinis seems to be endless, but are these new drinks really *Martinis*? There are those of us who would answer a resounding "No!," while some suggest that the Martini has evolved from being simply a drink to a drink category, like a COOLER, FIZZ, or HIGHBALL. It's a "stirring" controversy that will undoubtedly go on as long as people with imagination keep creating new drinks and calling them Martinis.

Made properly, a classic Martini can take your breath away

with its icy fire, while simultaneously soothing the stress of the most savage day. **To make a superlative Martini:** 1. The classic Martini only has 2 ingredients, so it's particularly important to use the best you can afford—there are no fruit juices or other flavors to mask inferior potables. 2. Store vermouth in the refrigerator to retain its flavor longer. 3. *Don't* chill the gin or vodka or it won't get diluted enough by the ice to achieve the proper proportions (one-eighth to one-fourth water—it's true!). 4. Energetic stirring or shaking with ice is vital for a smooth and silky result. Stirring produces a crystal-clear Martini, but it'll never get as cold as a shaken Martini. Shaking (James Bond's preference) creates bubbles and tiny ice shards, and therefore a "misty" appearance—which clears in about 60 seconds, so who cares? And, no, Virginia—gin *cannot* be "bruised." 5. Always serve Martinis in a frosty-cold glass (we keep ours on call in the freezer). 6. A classic Martini is served STRAIGHT UP—those who prefer it ON THE ROCKS will get a more diluted drink. 7. Garnish a Martini with a pitted olive (stuffed or not) or a $1/2$-inch-wide twist of lemon peel, with which you may rub the rim of the glass. Substituting a COCKTAIL ONION transforms the Martini into a Gibson. *See also* QUEEN ELIZABETH MARTINI; VESPER, THE.

### Extra-Dry Martini
2 oz. ($1/4$ cup) gin (or vodka)
1 tsp. dry vermouth

### Classic Dry Martini
2 oz. ($1/4$ cup) gin (or vodka)
$1 1/2$ tsp. dry vermouth

### Martini

2 oz. ($1/4$ cup) gin (or vodka)
$1/2$ oz. (1 Tbsp.) dry vermouth

Stir or shake with ice; strain into chilled glass. Garnish as desired with olive or lemon twist.

➤ **Cajun Martini** Substitute Jalapeño-Infused Vodka or Gin (*see* INFUSED VODKA) for the regular gin; garnish with a pickled tomato or okra, or a tiny whole red or green chile (don't bite into it!).

➤ **Dirty Martini** Add 1 to 2 tsp. olive brine.

➤ **Fino Martini** Substitute 2 tsp. fino sherry for the vermouth.

➤ **Gibson** Garnish with a cocktail onion.

➤ **Paisley Martini** Reduce vermouth to 1½ tsp. Add 1 tsp. Scotch; garnish with lemon twist.

➤ **Peggy Cocktail** Add ¼ tsp. each Dubonnet rouge and Pernod.

➤ **Perfect Martini** Use half sweet and half dry vermouth; garnish with orange slice.

➤ **Racquet Club** Add 1 to 2 dashes (about ¹⁄₁₆ to ⅛ tsp.) orange bitters.

➤ **Rolls Royce** Use half dry vermouth and half sweet vermouth; add ¼ tsp. Bénédictine.

➤ **Rumtini** Substitute light rum for the gin; garnish with lime twist.

➤ **Saketini** Substitute sake for the vermouth; garnish with lemon twist or olive.

➤ **Scotini** Substitute Scotch for the vermouth; garnish with lemon twist.

➤ **Sweet Martini** Substitute sweet vermouth for the dry vermouth; garnish with orange slice.

➤ **Tequini** Substitute tequila for the gin.

➤ **Third Degree** Add ½ tsp. Pernod or other anise-flavored liqueur.

**martini glass** *see* Glassware, page 9

**Martinique rum** *see* RUM

**Mary Pickford** The namesake of an actress who began her film career in 1907 and went on to become one of the most popular stars in history. Mary Pickford successfully made the transition from silent to sound films and won an Academy Award in 1929 for *Coquette*. In 1919, she became one of the founders of United Artists, along with D. W. Griffith, Charles Chaplin, and Douglas

Fairbanks, whom she ultimately married. We couldn't find any chronicle of whether Miss Pickford actually liked this sweet drink, or if some creative barkeep simply thought she might have.

1½ oz. (3 Tbsp.) light rum
1½ oz. (3 Tbsp.) unsweetened pineapple juice
¼ tsp. grenadine
¼ tsp. maraschino liqueur

Shake ingredients with ice; strain into chilled glass.

---

*You can no more keep a martini in the refrigerator than you can keep a kiss there. The proper union of gin and vermouth is a great and sudden glory; it is one of the happiest marriages on earth and one of the shortest-lived.*

BERNARD DE VOTO, AMERICAN CRITIC, HISTORIAN

---

**mash** Used in the brewing of beer and DISTILLATION of WHISKEY, mash is MALT or other grain coarsely milled, mixed with hot water, and allowed to ferment in a large vat (mash tub). When FERMENTATION is complete, the liquid is strained off. A second mashing with hot water follows, and the two liquids are combined. The drained liquid is called by any of various names, including *mash, distiller's beer,* and *wort.* There are two types of mash: **Sweet mash,** which starts fermentation from scratch with fresh yeast; and **sour mash,** sometimes used for liquors like BOURBON and TENNESSEE WHISKEY, which combines sweet mash with a portion of the remnants of the previous fermentation, a technique similar to that used in making sourdough bread.

---

*I'm only a beer teetotaler, not a champagne teetotaler.*
GEORGE BERNARD SHAW, IRISH ESSAYIST, DRAMATIST

### Matador

3 oz. (³/₈ cup) unsweetened pineapple juice
1¹/₂ oz. (3 Tbsp.) tequila
¹/₂ oz. (1 Tbsp.) fresh lime juice

Shake ingredients with ice; strain into chilled glass over ice cubes.

### Matinee

1 oz. (2 Tbsp.) gin
2 tsp. Sambuca
2 tsp. fresh lime juice
1¹/₂ tsp. whipping cream
¹/₂ egg white (about 1 Tbsp.) (*see* page 14, How to Divide
    Egg Whites in Half)

Vigorously shake ingredients with ice; strain into chilled glass over ice cubes.

### Maurice

1 oz. (2 Tbsp.) gin
¹/₂ oz. (1 Tbsp.) dry vermouth
¹/₂ oz. (1 Tbsp.) sweet vermouth
¹/₂ oz. (1 Tbsp.) fresh orange juice
2 dashes (about ¹/₈ tsp.) Angostura bitters

Shake ingredients with ice; strain into chilled glass.

### McClelland Cocktail

1¹/₂ oz. (3 Tbsp.) sloe gin
³/₄ oz. (1¹/₂ Tbsp.) Triple Sec
2 dashes (about ¹/₈ tsp.) orange bitters

Shake ingredients with ice; strain into chilled glass.

**mead** This fermented beverage dates back to biblical times and is based on honey. Mead is classically flavored with flowers and spices. It was extremely popular in early England and, although not widely distributed today, is still bottled in England.

**Médoc** *see* BORDEAUX; CORDIAL MÉDOC

### Melon Ball

3 oz. (³/₈ cup) fresh orange juice
1 oz. (2 Tbsp.) vodka
1 oz. (2 Tbsp.) Midori or other melon-flavored liqueur
melon ball, optional

Shake liquid ingredients with ice. Strain into chilled glass over ice cubes. If desired, spear melon ball with pick; drop into drink.

> ➤ **Variation** Substitute unsweetened pineapple juice for the orange juice.

### Melon Ball Shooter

¹/₂ oz. (1 Tbsp.) vodka
¹/₂ oz. (1 Tbsp.) Midori or other melon-flavored liqueur
¹/₂ oz. (1 Tbsp.) unsweetened pineapple juice

Shake ingredients with ice; strain into chilled glass.

### Melon Cocktail

2 oz. (¹/₄ cup) gin
¹/₄ tsp. maraschino liqueur
¹/₄ tsp. fresh lemon juice
maraschino cherry

Shake liquid ingredients with cracked ice. Strain into chilled glass; drop in cherry.

### melon-flavored spirits *see* MIDORI

### Melon Margarita *see* MARGARITA

### Mentuccia [mayn-TOOT-chah] *see* CENTERBE

**Meritage** [MEHR-ih-tihj] The name of this wine classification is a compound of "merit" and "heritage" and rhymes with the latter word, although many people mistakenly try to Frenchify it as *mehr-ih-TAHJ*. This distinctive term was coined in 1988 by a group of American vintners as part of an effort to establish identification standards for a category of quality blended wines made with traditional BORDEAUX grape varieties. In the United States, if wines aren't made with at least 75 percent of a single grape variety (such as CABERNET SAUVIGNON or ZINFANDEL), the variety name cannot appear on the label. This forced many producers to label excellent wines with generic names like "claret" or "red table wine," which caused immense consumer confusion. To be designated Meritage, a wine must be 1. A blend of two or more Bordeaux grape varieties—for red wines: Cabernet Franc, Cabernet Sauvignon, Carmenère, Gros Verdot, Malbec, MERLOT, Petit Verdot, and Saint Macaire; and for whites: SAUVI-

GNON BLANC, Muscadelle, and Sémillon. 2. The winery's best wine of its type. 3. Produced and bottled by a U.S. winery from grapes in a U.S. APPELLATION. 4. Limited in production to a maximum 25,000 cases per VINTAGE.

*This wine is too good for toast-drinking, my dear. You don't want to mix emotions up with a wine like that. You lose the taste.*

ERNEST HEMINGWAY, AMERICAN AUTHOR

**Merlot** [mehr-LOH; mer-LOH] In French, the word *merlot* means "young blackbird," presumably alluding to the grape's beautiful dark-blue color. Much of the wine world views Merlot as simply a blending grape for CABERNET SAUVIGNON or Cabernet Franc. However, the Merlot grape can produce great wines like those of Pomerol's famous Château Pétrus, which makes one of the world's most expensive red wines, most of which are 100 percent Merlot. In the United States, California and Washington are the top producers of Merlot wines, which continue to gain popularity. High-quality Merlot wines are medium to dark red in color, rich, and fruity, with flavor characteristics of black currant, cherry, and mint. Merlots are rounder, more supple, and have a slightly higher alcohol content than Cabernet Sauvignon wines, and can usually be enjoyed much earlier. On the other hand, Merlot wines don't generally AGE as long as Cabernet Sauvignons.

### Merry Widow #1

1¹/₂ oz. (3 Tbsp.) cherry brandy
1¹/₂ oz. (3 Tbsp.) maraschino liqueur
maraschino cherry

Stir liquid ingredients with ice. Strain into chilled glass; drop in cherry.

### Merry Widow #2

1¹/₂ oz. (3 Tbsp.) dry sherry
1¹/₂ oz. (3 Tbsp.) sweet vermouth
lemon twist

Stir liquid ingredients with ice. Strain into chilled glass; drop in lemon twist.

**Merry Widow #3** (sometimes also called **Merry Widower**)

> 1 oz. (2 Tbsp.) gin
> 1 oz. (2 Tbsp.) dry vermouth
> $1/4$ tsp. Pernod or other anise-flavored liqueur
> $1/4$ tsp. Bénédictine
> 1 dash (about $1/16$ tsp.) orange bitters
> lemon twist

Stir liquid ingredients with ice. Strain into chilled glass; drop in lemon twist.

**Metaxa** [muh-TAHK-suh] An amber-colored, sweetened Greek BRANDY with a winelike flavor reminiscent of muscat grapes. Metaxas are based on red grapes and flavored with herbs and spices. Some versions are so sweet they can be considered LIQUEURS. The **Seven-Star Amphora Metaxa** has a more caramelized, nutty flavor, while the dark amber-colored **Metaxa Grande Fine** is the finest of the lot, with a full, rich, almost sherrylike taste.

---

*The cocktail party—a device for paying off obligations to people you don't want to invite to dinner.*

CHARLES MERRILL SMITH, AMERICAN WRITER

---

**Metropolitan #1** This is the classic recipe that's been around for decades.

> $1^1/_2$ oz. (3 Tbsp.) brandy
> $1^1/_2$ oz. (3 Tbsp.) sweet vermouth
> $1/_2$ tsp. sugar syrup
> 1 to 2 dashes (about $1/16$ to $1/8$ tsp.) Angostura bitters
> maraschino cherry

Shake liquid ingredients with ice. Strain into chilled cocktail glass or an old-fashioned glass over ice cubes; drop in cherry.

**Metropolitan #2** Various individuals claim to have invented the nineties version of the Metropolitan, but most people give the credit to Chuck Coggins, bartender at Marion's Continental Restaurant & Lounge in New York City. One look at the ingredients tells you that it's a variation on the popular COSMO-POLITAN.

2 oz. (¼ cup) vodka (plain or Absolut Kurant)
1 oz. (2 Tbsp.) cranberry juice
¾ oz. (1½ Tbsp.) fresh lime juice
lime wedge

Shake liquid ingredients with ice. Strain into chilled glass; garnish with lime wedge.

## Mexicana

1½ oz. (3 Tbsp.) tequila
1½ oz. (3 Tbsp.) unsweetened pineapple juice
1 oz. (2 Tbsp.) fresh lime or lemon juice
1 tsp. grenadine

Shake ingredients with ice; strain into chilled glass over ice cubes.

## Mexican Coffee *See also* Hot Drinks, page 29.

1 oz. (2 Tbsp.) Kahlúa or Tia Maria
½ oz. (1 Tbsp.) tequila
about 6 oz. (¾ cup) hot coffee
dollop of whipped cream

Pour Kahlúa and tequila into warmed mug. Stir in coffee; top with whipped cream.

## Mexican Flag *See* Floating and Layering Techniques, page 30.

½ oz. (1 Tbsp.) grenadine
½ oz. (1 Tbsp.) green crème de menthe
½ oz. (1 Tbsp.) tequila

Pour first ingredient into glass. One by one, add remaining ingredients in order given, slowly pouring each one over the back (rounded) side of a spoon so that each one floats on top of the one below.

**Mexican Grasshopper** *see* GRASSHOPPER (COFFEE)

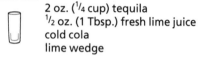

*No doubt alcohol, tobacco, and so forth, are things that a saint must avoid, but sainthood is also a thing that human beings must avoid.*

GEORGE ORWELL, BRITISH WRITER

### Mexicola

2 oz. ($^{1}/_{4}$ cup) tequila
$^{1}/_{2}$ oz. (1 Tbsp.) fresh lime juice
cold cola
lime wedge

Pour tequila and lime juice into chilled glass filled with ice cubes. Top with cola, stirring gently; garnish with lime wedge.

**mezcal** [mehs-KAL] A potent, clear liquor that originated in Oaxaca, a state in southeastern Mexico. The word *mezcal,* sometimes spelled *mescal,* is derived from the Náhuatl *mexcalmetl,* "agave species." Like TEQUILA, mezcal is produced from the agave plant, but whereas tequila must be made from the blue agave, mezcal may be produced from any of several species. Mezcal may also be made anywhere in Mexico, while tequila must be produced from plants grown only in a specified area. A small worm (the *gusano*) can be found in the bottom of bottles labeled *Mezcal de Gusanitos.* The worm, which lives in the agave plant, is said to honor the lucky person who swallows it, endowing him or her with strength. Most mezcal, which has a smoky, peppery CHARACTER, is quite crudely made. It's often flavored and sweetened, presumably to mask its rough flavor. Although mezcal is enjoyed all over Mexico, it's just beginning to catch on in the United States. Among the few brands that are imported are Encantado, Gusano, Miguel de la Mezcal, and Monte Alban. *See also* PULQUE.

### Miami

2 oz. ($^{1}/_{4}$ cup) light rum
1 oz. (2 Tbsp.) white crème de menthe
$^{1}/_{4}$ tsp. fresh lemon juice

Shake ingredients with ice; strain into chilled glass.

### Miami Beach

$^3/_4$ oz. (1$^1/_2$ Tbsp.) Scotch
$^3/_4$ oz. (1$^1/_2$ Tbsp.) dry vermouth
$^3/_4$ oz. (1$^1/_2$ Tbsp.) unsweetened grapefruit juice

Shake ingredients with ice; strain into chilled glass.

### Midnight Cocktail

1$^1/_2$ oz. (3 Tbsp.) apricot brandy
$^3/_4$ oz. (1$^1/_2$ Tbsp.) Triple Sec
$^1/_2$ oz. (1 Tbsp.) fresh lemon juice

Shake ingredients with ice; strain into chilled glass.

> ★ **Midnight Mocktail** Substitute apricot nectar for the apricot brandy and orange juice for the Triple Sec.

★ **Midnight Mocktail** *see* MIDNIGHT COCKTAIL

### Midnight Sun

1$^1/_2$ oz. (3 Tbsp.) aquavit
1 oz. (2 Tbsp.) unsweetened grapefruit juice
$^1/_2$ tsp. grenadine
orange slice

Shake liquid ingredients with ice. Strain into chilled glass; garnish with orange slice.

**Midori** [mih-DOOR-ee] A bright green Japanese LIQUEUR with the taste of honeydew melon.

### Mikado

1$^1/_2$ oz. (3 Tbsp.) brandy
$^1/_4$ tsp. crème de noyaux
$^1/_4$ tsp. Triple Sec
$^1/_4$ tsp. grenadine
1 dash (about $^1/_{16}$ tsp.) Angostura bitters

Shake ingredients with ice; strain into chilled cocktail glass or an old-fashioned glass over ice cubes.

★ **Mild Sea Breeze** *see* SEA BREEZE

**Milk Punch** Almost any liquor is suitable for this "nutritious" drink. Whatever is used then becomes part of the name, such as "Bourbon Milk Punch" or "Brandy Milk Punch."

8 oz. (1 cup) milk
2 oz. (¼ cup) bourbon, brandy, gin, rum, rye, or Scotch
1 tsp. powdered sugar
¼ tsp. pure vanilla extract, optional
freshly grated nutmeg

Shake first 3 (or 4 if you're using the vanilla) ingredients with ice. Strain into chilled collins glass or a large cocktail glass; sprinkle with nutmeg.

➤ **Hot Milk Punch** Heat milk until simmering. Combine liquor, sugar, and vanilla in a heatproof mug; add milk, stirring well. Sprinkle with nutmeg and add a cinnamon stick for stirring. *See also* Hot Drinks, page 29.

**Mille Fiori** *see* FIORE D'ALPI

**Millionaire** Although the classic version of this drink is made with bourbon, gin is becoming a popular alternative.

1½ oz. (3 Tbsp.) bourbon or gin
½ oz. (1 Tbsp.) Pernod or other anise-flavored liqueur
1 egg white

Vigorously shake ingredients with ice; strain into chilled cocktail glass or an old-fashioned glass over ice cubes.

➤ **Variation:** Add 1 tsp. Triple Sec and ¼ tsp. grenadine.

*ℬubbles are the gracenotes of champagne.*
ANONYMOUS

## Million Dollar Cocktail; Million Dollar Baby

1½ oz. (3 Tbsp.) gin
¾ oz. (1½ Tbsp.) sweet vermouth
¾ oz. (1½ Tbsp.) unsweetened pineapple juice
1 tsp. grenadine
1 egg white

Vigorously shake ingredients with cracked ice; strain into chilled glass.

## Mimosa

4 oz. ($^1/_2$ cup) cold fresh orange juice
4 oz. ($^1/_2$ cup) cold dry champagne

Pour orange juice into chilled glass. Slowly add champagne; stir gently.

★ **Mimosa Light** Substitute sparkling white grape juice for the champagne.

## Mind Eraser

$^3/_4$ oz. (1$^1/_2$ Tbsp.) Kahlúa or Tia Maria
$^3/_4$ oz. (1$^1/_2$ Tbsp.) vodka
cold club soda

Pour Kahlúa, then vodka into chilled glass. Top with a splash of club soda. Or shake Kahlúa and vodka with ice; strain into glass and add soda.

**mint-flavored spirits** *see* BRANCA MENTA; CENTERBE; CRÈME DE MENTHE; FRIESENGEIST; MINT JULEP LIQUEUR; VANDERMINT

**Mint Julep** For many people, the first Saturday in May is synonymous with the running of the Kentucky Derby, which simply would not be complete without imbibing at least one bourbon-based mint julep. Decades before bourbon became popular, early American mint juleps (*see* JULEP) were made with BRANDY, which argues the Kentuckian claim that they invented this lively libation. Although the traditional bourbon mint julep is currently the popular favorite, some juleps are still made with brandy as well as with RUM and SCOTCH. The preferred mint julep vessel is a silver julep cup or mug, although a COLLINS GLASS is perfectly acceptable. Hotly contested among true julep aficionados is whether or not to crush (MUDDLE) the mint, with enthusiasts on both sides. Muddling brings out a more assertive mint flavor. *See also* GINGER JULEP; JOCOSE JULEP.

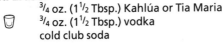

10 to 15 medium to large fresh mint leaves
1 tsp. sugar
1 Tbsp. water
2$^1/_2$ oz. (5 Tbsp.) bourbon
3 mint sprigs

Muddle mint leaves, sugar, and water in chilled julep cup or collins glass until leaves are crushed and sugar is dissolved. Fill glass with crushed ice. Pour in bourbon; stir thoroughly. Add more crushed ice to within ½ inch of rim; garnish with mint sprigs and serve with straw.

**Mint Julep Liqueur** An amber-colored, WHISKEY-based LIQUEUR made by Ancient Age (of Kentucky BOURBON fame). It has a flavor reminiscent of a MINT JULEP, and can be served STRAIGHT or over crushed ice. *See also* MINT-FLAVORED SPIRITS.

**Mirabelle** [mee-rah-BELL; MIH-rah-bell] Made from yellow mirabelle plums, found in France, Germany, and Switzerland, this heady EAU-DE-VIE has a lightly sweet and spicy plum flavor.

*Wine is like sex in that few men will admit not knowing all about it.*

HUGH JOHNSON, BRITISH WINE AND SPIRITS WRITER

**mist** Any drink in which undiluted spirits, such as Grand Marnier, are poured into a glass (typically short) filled with crushed ice, in which case it would be called a "Grand Marnier Mist."

**mixer** Any nonalcoholic liquid, such as CLUB SODA, which is added to a drink containing alcohol.

**mixing glass** *see* Bar Equipment, page 7

**Mocha Mint**

¾ oz. (1½ Tbsp.) coffee-flavored brandy, Kahlúa, or Tia Maria
¾ oz. (1½ Tbsp.) white crème de menthe
¾ oz. (1½ Tbsp.) white crème de cacao

Shake ingredients with ice; strain into chilled glass.

### Mockingbird

1¹/₂ oz. (3 Tbsp.) tequila
1 oz. (2 Tbsp.) fresh lime juice
¹/₂ oz. (1 Tbsp.) white crème de menthe

Shake ingredients with ice; strain into chilled glass.

**mocktail** An 1980s idiom for a nonalcoholic cocktail, such as a SHIRLEY TEMPLE.

### Mojito [moh-HEE-toh]

1 oz. (2 Tbsp.) fresh lime juice
1 tsp. powdered sugar
4 loose mint leaves plus 1 mint sprig
2 oz. (¹/₄ cup) light rum
cold club soda, optional

Combine lime juice, sugar, and loose mint leaves in glass; stir well, crushing mint slightly. Fill glass with crushed ice; stir in rum. If desired, top with club soda, stirring gently. Garnish with mint sprig.

### Monkey Gland

1¹/₂ oz. (3 Tbsp.) gin
1 oz. (2 Tbsp.) fresh orange juice
2 to 4 dashes (about ¹/₈ to ¹/₄ tsp.) grenadine
2 to 4 dashes (about ¹/₈ to ¹/₄ tsp.) Bénédictine

Shake ingredients with ice; strain into chilled glass over ice cubes.

### Montana

2 oz. (¹/₄ cup) brandy
1 oz. (2 Tbsp.) ruby port
¹/₂ oz. (1 Tbsp.) dry vermouth

Pour ingredients into a chilled glass filled with ice cubes; stir.

**Montmartre Cocktail** [maw*n*-MAH*R*-t*r*uh] Named for the picturesque area of Montmartre on the Right Bank of the Seine in Paris.

1¹/₂ oz. (3 Tbsp.) gin
¹/₂ oz. (1 Tbsp.) sweet vermouth
¹/₂ oz. (1 Tbsp.) Triple Sec
maraschino cherry

Shake liquid ingredients with ice. Strain into chilled glass; garnish with cherry.

### Moonlight

2 oz. ($^1/_4$ cup) apple brandy
1 oz. (2 Tbsp.) fresh lemon juice
1 tsp. powdered sugar

Shake ingredients with ice; strain into chilled glass over ice cubes.

**moonshine** Unlawfully distilled American WHISKEY, usually made from corn, and particularly popular during PROHIBITION. Colloquialisms for moonshine include *angel teat, Kentucky (Tennessee, etc.) fire, squirrel whiskey, stump liquor,* and *swamp dew. See also* BOOTLEG.

*efinition of corn "licker": It smells like gangrene starting in a mildewed silo, it tastes like the wrath to come, and when you absorb a deep swig of it you have all the sensations of having swallowed a lighted kerosene lamp. A sudden, violent jolt of it has been known to stop the victim's watch, snap his suspenders, and crack his glass eye right across.*

IRVIN SHREWSBURY COBB, AMERICAN HUMORIST

### Morning Cocktail

1 oz. (2 Tbsp.) brandy
1 oz. (2 Tbsp.) dry vermouth
$^1/_4$ tsp. Pernod or other anise-flavored liqueur
$^1/_4$ tsp. maraschino liqueur
$^1/_4$ tsp. Triple Sec
2 dashes (about $^1/_8$ tsp.) orange bitters
maraschino cherry

Stir or shake liquid ingredients with ice; strain into chilled glass over ice cubes. Garnish with cherry.

### Morning Glory

1 oz. (2 Tbsp.) Scotch
1 oz. (2 Tbsp.) brandy
¼ tsp. Cointreau
⅛ tsp. Pernod or other anise-flavored liqueur
2 dashes (about ⅛ tsp.) Angostura bitters
½ tsp. powdered sugar
cold club soda

Shake all ingredients except club soda with ice. Strain into chilled collins glass over ice cubes; top with soda, stirring gently. Alternatively, strain into cocktail glass; omit ice and soda.

### Morning Glory Fizz

2 oz. (¼ cup) Scotch
¾ oz. (1½ Tbsp.) fresh lemon juice
1 tsp. Pernod or other anise-flavored liqueur
1 tsp. powdered sugar
½ egg white (about 1 Tbsp.) *(See* page 14, How to Divide Egg Whites in Half)
2 dashes (about ⅛ tsp.) Angostura bitters
cold club soda
lemon slice

Vigorously shake all ingredients except club soda and lemon slice with ice; strain into chilled glass filled with ice cubes. Top with soda, stirring gently. Garnish with lemon slice.

---

*When men drink, then they are rich and successful and win lawsuits and are happy and help their friends.*

ARISTOPHANES, GREEK SATIRIST, PLAYWRIGHT

### Morro

1 oz. (2 Tbsp.) gin
½ oz. (1 Tbsp.) golden rum
2 tsp. fresh lime juice
2 tsp. unsweetened pineapple juice
½ tsp. powdered sugar

Frost rim of chilled glass by moistening with water, shaking off the excess, then dipping rim into granulated sugar. Shake ingredients with ice; strain into glass filled with ice cubes.

**Moscow Mule** The classic container for this drink is a copper cup or mug, but it tastes just as good in a COLLINS GLASS or a small BEER MUG. In a pinch, ginger ale may be substituted for the ginger beer.

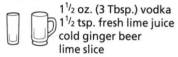

1 1/2 oz. (3 Tbsp.) vodka
1 1/2 tsp. fresh lime juice
cold ginger beer
lime slice

Pour vodka and lime juice into chilled glass filled with ice cubes; stir well. Top with ginger beer, stirring gently. Garnish with lime slice.

### Moulin Rouge [moo-la*n* ROOZH]

1 1/2 oz. (3 Tbsp.) sloe gin
3/4 oz. (1 1/2 Tbsp.) sweet vermouth
2 dashes (about 1/8 tsp.) Angostura bitters

Stir ingredients with ice; strain into chilled glass.

**muddle** *v.* To mash or crush ingredients. **muddler** *n.* A rod (usually wooden) with a broad, rounded, or flattened end. The most well-known muddled drink is the MINT JULEP, in which mint leaves are crushed. *See also* Bar Equipment, page 7; Tricks of the Trade (Muddling), page 29.

### Mudslide

3/4 oz. (1 1/2 Tbsp.) Irish cream liqueur
3/4 oz. (1 1/2 Tbsp.) Kahlúa
3/4 oz. (1 1/2 Tbsp.) vodka

Pour into chilled glass over ice cubes; stir well.

**mull** *n.* A warm drink or PUNCH flavored variously. **mull** *v.* To flavor a beverage by heating it with ingredients like spices, fruit, and sugar.

### Mulled Cider *see* MULLED WINE

**Mulled Wine** There are dozens of styles of this hot, spiced wine—the spices can vary, fruit may or may not be used, and it may be spirited or not. For an almost alcohol-free mulled wine, simply boil the mixture for at least 10 minutes so most of the alcohol burns off. *See also* Hot Drinks, page 29.

MAKES ABOUT FOURTEEN 6-OUNCE SERVINGS

2 (750-ml) bottles dry red wine (Cabernet Sauvignon, Burgundy, etc.)
$^1/_2$ cup packed brown sugar
12 whole cloves
4 cinnamon sticks
peel of 1 large orange, cut into long strips
peel of 1 large lemon, cut into long strips
16 oz. (1 pint; 2 cups) ruby port
16 oz. (1 pint; 2 cups) brandy (*see* Note)

Combine all ingredients except port and brandy in a large pot (not aluminum); bring to a simmer, stirring occasionally. Reduce heat to low; simmer for 10 minutes. Add port and brandy; heat just until steaming (don't boil). Pour into large, heatproof bowl. Ladle into mugs or heatproof punch cups, adding a few spices and citrus strips to each serving. Strain leftover mulled wine, tightly seal, and store in a cool place for at least 6 months.

**Note:** To make mulled wine ahead of time and reheat for individual servings, don't add the brandy. When ready to serve, heat a cup of the mulled wine until very hot, pour into mug or cup, then add 1 oz. (2 Tbsp.) brandy.

➤ **Mulled Cider** Substitute $2^1/_2$ quarts (10 cups) apple cider for the wine; omit port. If desired, substitute $^1/_3$ cup honey for the brown sugar.

**Münchener** [MEWN-chner] A dark LAGER-style BEER with a malty (*see* MALT) flavor. The term "Münchener" is used primarily in Europe to distinguish dark from light lagers.

**Nail Drive** *see* RUSTY NAIL

★ **Naked Bullshot** *see* BULLSHOT

## Navy Grog

1 oz. (2 Tbsp.) light rum
1 oz. (2 Tbsp.) Jamaica rum
1 oz. (2 Tbsp.) 86-proof Demerara rum
$^1/_2$ oz. (1 Tbsp.) fresh lime juice
$^1/_2$ oz. (1 Tbsp.) passion-fruit or guava nectar
$^1/_2$ oz. (1 Tbsp.) unsweetened pineapple juice
$^1/_2$ oz. (1 Tbsp.) orange juice
$^1/_2$ oz. (1 Tbsp.) orgeat syrup
$^1/_2$ cup crushed ice
mint sprig
lime slice

Combine all ingredients except mint and lime slice in a blender. Cover and process at medium speed until smooth, about 15 seconds; pour into chilled glass. Garnish with mint and lime; serve with straw.

**neat** A term referring to a spirit drunk without ice, water, or mixers. Synonymous with *plain*. Therefore, a "SCOTCH, neat" and a "Scotch, plain" are the same thing. *See also* STRAIGHT UP.

---

*The trouble with the world is that everybody in it is three drinks behind.*

HUMPHREY BOGART, AMERICAN ACTOR

---

**Negroni** [neh-GROH-nee] According to legend, this cocktail was created in 1919 when Italian Count Camillo Negroni asked a Florence bartender to add gin to his AMERICANO. Although sweet vermouth is classic for this drink, many prefer it made with dry vermouth.

$^3/_4$ oz. (1$^1/_2$ Tbsp.) gin
$^3/_4$ oz. (1$^1/_2$ Tbsp.) Campari
$^3/_4$ oz. (1$^1/_2$ Tbsp.) sweet or dry vermouth
cold club soda, optional
lemon twist

Stir liquid ingredients with ice; strain into chilled cocktail glass; add splash of soda, if desired. Or combine liquid ingredients in an old-fashioned glass filled with ice cubes; add a splash of soda, if desired. Garnish either style with lemon twist.

➤ **Punt è Mes Negroni** [poont ay MAYSS] Substitute Punt è Mes for the Campari; use sweet vermouth.

**neutral spirit** A colorless, flavorless liquid that is 95 percent (190 PROOF) ALCOHOL. Neutral spirits are used for blending with straight WHISKEYS and as a base for potables such as GIN and VODKA. Neutral spirits that are AGED in wood are called **grain spirits.** The wood aging contributes nuances that produce a mellower flavor. *See also* DISTILLATION.

## Nevada

1¹/₂ oz. (3 Tbsp.) golden rum
1¹/₂ oz. (3 Tbsp.) unsweetened grapefruit juice
³/₄ oz. (1¹/₂ Tbsp.) fresh lime juice
1 dash (about ¹/₁₆ tsp.) Angostura bitters
1¹/₂ tsp. powdered sugar

Shake ingredients with ice; strain into chilled glass.

## Nevins

1¹/₂ oz. (3 Tbsp.) bourbon
¹/₂ oz. (1 Tbsp.) unsweetened grapefruit juice
1¹/₂ tsp. apricot brandy
1¹/₂ tsp. fresh lemon juice
1 dash (about ¹/₁₆ tsp.) Angostura bitters

Shake ingredients with ice; strain into chilled glass.

## Newbury

1 oz. (2 Tbsp.) gin
1 oz. (2 Tbsp.) sweet vermouth
¹/₄ tsp. Cointreau
orange slice

Shake liquid ingredients with cracked ice. Strain into chilled glass; garnish with orange slice.

**New Orleans Buck** *see* BUCK

**New Orleans Fizz** *see* RAMOS FIZZ

### New York Cocktail; New Yorker

2 oz. ($^1/_4$ cup) rye whiskey or bourbon
$^3/_4$ oz. (1$^1/_2$ Tbsp.) fresh lime or lemon juice
1 tsp. powdered sugar
$^1/_8$ tsp. grenadine
lemon twist

Shake liquid ingredients with ice. Strain into chilled glass; drop in lemon twist.

### New York Sour *see* SOUR

**nightcap** A drink (usually alcoholic) taken at the end of an evening, either to top off a festive occasion or just before bedtime—purportedly to induce sleep. Such potables may be served cold or warm, the latter being considered the most soothing for bedtime quaffing.

**Nightcap #1** As you might suspect, there are several versions of this drink. Following are two of the most popular—both may be served cold by substituting cold milk for hot and serving over ice in a HIGHBALL or DOUBLE OLD-FASHIONED GLASS. *See also* Hot Drinks, page 29.

2 oz. ($^1/_4$ cup) light rum
1 to 2 tsp. sugar
about 6 oz. ($^3/_4$ cup) hot milk
freshly grated nutmeg

Combine rum and sugar in warmed mug. Add milk, stirring well; sprinkle with nutmeg.

### Nightcap #2

2 oz. ($^1/_4$ cup) brandy
1 egg yolk
1 to 2 tsp. sugar
4 to 6 oz. ($^1/_2$ to $^3/_4$ cup) hot milk
freshly grated nutmeg

Combine brandy, egg yolk, and sugar in warmed mug; beat with fork until frothy. Add milk, stirring well; sprinkle with nutmeg.

## Nightmare

1 ¹/₂ oz. (3 Tbsp.) gin
¹/₂ oz. (1 Tbsp.) Madeira
¹/₂ oz. (1 Tbsp.) cherry brandy
2 tsp. fresh orange juice

Shake ingredients with ice; strain into chilled glass.

## Ninotchka [nih-NAHCH-kah]

1 ¹/₂ oz. (3 Tbsp.) vodka
¹/₂ oz. (1 Tbsp.) white crème de cacao
¹/₂ oz. (1 Tbsp.) fresh lemon juice

Shake ingredients with ice; strain into chilled glass.

**nip** *n.* In the world of liquor, "nip" refers to a small drink, as in "He always relished a small nip before going to bed." Synonymous with TOT. **nip** *v.* To drink in small sips.

**Nocello** [noh-CHAY-loh] An Italian walnut-flavored LIQUEUR. *See also* NUT-FLAVORED SPIRITS.

**nog** The word "nog" harks back at least to seventeenth-century England and originally referred to a strong East Anglia ALE. Today, it refers to any beverage made with beaten eggs, such as EGGNOG.

**noggin** 1. A mid-seventeenth–century word describing a small cup or mug. 2. The amount of liquid such a small cup would hold (about 5 ounces). 3. Colloquially, the word refers to any kind of alcoholic drink, as in "Let's have another noggin."

## ✸ Nogless Eggnog *see* EGGNOG

**nose** In the wine world "nose" refers to the olfactory sense of wine. Some ENOPHILES use the term as a descriptor for wines with an extremely intense BOUQUET (*see* AROMA), although as commonly used the word doesn't generally connote quality.

## Noyaux, crème de *see* CRÈME DE NOYAUX

**nut-flavored spirits** *see* AMARETTO; CRÈME D'AMANDE; CRÈME DE NOYAUX; FRANGELICO; KAHANA ROYALE; NOCELLO; PRALINE

**Nutty Colada** *see* PIÑA COLADA

---

*A meal without wine . . . is breakfast!*
MOLLY MANN, AMERICAN ENTREPRENEUR

---

**Oatmeal Cookie** Grandmother never made 'em like this! *See* Floating and Layering Techniques, page 30.

½ oz. (1 Tbsp.) butterscotch schnapps
½ oz. (1 Tbsp.) Goldschlager
½ oz. (1 Tbsp.) Irish cream liqueur

Pour schnapps into glass. One by one, add remaining ingredients in order given, slowly pouring each one over the back (rounded) side of a spoon so that each one floats on top of the one below.

➤ **Variation** Add ½ oz. (1 Tbsp.) Jägermeister as top layer. Or shake all ingredients with ice; strain into chilled old-fashioned glass over ice cubes.

**oatmeal stout** *see* STOUT

**Ocho Rios** [OH-choh REE-ohss]

1½ oz. (3 Tbsp.) dark rum
1 oz. (2 Tbsp.) guava nectar
2 tsp. fresh lime juice
2 tsp. cream
½ tsp. sugar
⅓ cup crushed ice

Combine all ingredients in a blender. Cover and process at medium speed until smooth, about 15 seconds. Pour into chilled glass.

★ **Poco Rios** Omit rum; increase guava nectar to 3 oz. (⅜ cup) and cream to ½ ounce (1 Tbsp).

**Old-Fashioned** Another classic cocktail for which the "perfect recipe" is hotly debated. Some like RYE, others BOURBON; some insist on SUGAR SYRUP instead of a sugar cube; others demand a specific brand of bitters. Then there are those who love the fruit garnish while others consider it *déclassé;* and for some an Old-Fashioned would be incomplete without a splash of soda. Whatever your preference, you have a late 1880s bartender of Louisville, Kentucky's exclusive Pendennis Club to thank for this popular concoction. This classic cocktail spawned the squat, eponymous OLD-FASHIONED GLASS.

1 sugar cube or 2 tsp. sugar syrup
1 to 2 dashes (about $^1/_{16}$ to $^1/_8$ tsp.) Angostura bitters
1 tsp. water
2 oz. ($^1/_4$ cup) blended whiskey
lemon twist
orange slice
maraschino cherry

Put first 3 ingredients into chilled glass; muddle until sugar dissolves. (If using sugar syrup, simply stir first 3 ingredients together.) Fill glass with ice cubes; stir in whiskey and lemon twist. Garnish with orange slice and cherry.

➤ **Variation** Add $^1/_{16}$ to $^1/_8$ tsp. Cointreau.

➤ **Brandy Old-Fashioned** Substitute brandy for the whiskey.

➤ **Canadian Old-Fashioned** Substitute Canadian whisky for blended whiskey; add 1 tsp. Cointreau and $^1/_8$ tsp. fresh lemon juice.

## old-fashioned glass *see* Glassware, page 9

## Old Pal

1$^1/_2$ oz. (3 Tbsp.) rye whiskey
$^1/_2$ oz. (1 Tbsp.) sweet vermouth
$^1/_2$ oz. (1 Tbsp.) grenadine

Stir ingredients with ice; strain into chilled glass.

➤ **Variation** For a much drier (*see* DRY) drink substitute dry vermouth for the sweet vermouth and Campari for the grenadine.

## Old Tom Gin *see* GIN

## Olé [oh-LAY]

1 1/2 oz. (3 Tbsp.) tequila
1 oz. (2 Tbsp.) Kahlúa
2 tsp. sugar
1/2 oz. (1 Tbsp.) cream

Stir first 3 ingredients together without ice. Pour into chilled glass filled with crushed ice. Float cream on top by slowly pouring it over the back (rounded) side of a spoon; don't mix.

**oloroso** [oh-loh-ROH-soh] *see* SHERRY

## Olympic

1 oz. (2 Tbsp.) brandy
1 oz. (2 Tbsp.) Triple Sec
1 oz. (2 Tbsp.) fresh orange juice
orange peel

Shake liquid ingredients with ice. Strain into chilled glass; garnish with orange peel.

**onions, cocktail** *see* Ingredients, page 18

**on the rocks; rocks** A term with the general meaning of "served with ice." In bartender lingo, however, "on the rocks" describes a small ROCKS GLASS filled with ice over which 1 1/2 ounces of spirits (either a single liquor or LIQUEUR or a combination of ingredients) are poured. Ordering a "Scotch rocks" would simply be SCOTCH over ice cubes.

---

*Gazing at the typewriter in moments of desperation, I console myself with three thoughts: alcohol at six, dinner at eight, and to be immortal you've got to be dead.*

GYLES BRANDETH, ENGLISH AUTHOR

---

## Opal Cocktail

1 oz. (2 Tbsp.) gin
1/2 oz. (1 Tbsp.) Triple Sec
1/2 oz. (1 Tbsp.) fresh orange juice
1/2 tsp. powdered sugar
2 drops orange flower water

Shake ingredients with ice; strain into chilled glass.

**Opal Nera** [OH-pahl NAY-ruh] An Italian LIQUEUR with an intriguing purple-black color, a satiny texture, and a flavor reminiscent of anise and berries. *See also* ANISE-FLAVORED SPIRITS.

## Opening Cocktail

1¹/₂ oz. (3 Tbsp.) blended whiskey
¹/₂ oz. (1 Tbsp.) sweet vermouth
¹/₂ oz. (1 Tbsp.) grenadine

Shake ingredients with ice; strain into chilled glass.

## Opera

1¹/₂ oz. (3 Tbsp.) gin
¹/₂ oz. (1 Tbsp.) Dubonnet rouge
1 tsp. maraschino liqueur

Stir or shake with ice; strain into chilled glass.

### orange bitters *see* BITTERS

## Orange Blossom

1¹/₂ oz. (3 Tbsp.) gin
1¹/₂ oz. (3 Tbsp.) fresh orange juice
¹/₂ tsp. powdered sugar
orange slice

Shake first 3 ingredients with ice. Strain into chilled glass over ice cubes; garnish with orange slice.

➤ **Variation** Add 2 tsp. Cointreau and 2 drops orange flower water.

### Orange Buck *see* BUCK

**orange-flavored spirits** *see* AURUM; CITRUS-FLAVORED SPIRITS; COINTREAU; CORDIAL MÉDOC; CRÉME DE MANDARINES; CRYSTAL COMFORT; CURAÇAO; GRAND MARNIER; MANDARINE NAPOLÉON; SABRA (with chocolate); TRIPLE SEC

**orange flower water** A DISTILLATION of bitter-orange blossoms with a perfumy orange flavor. Available in supermarkets and liquor stores.

## Orange Oasis

4 oz. ($^{1}/_{2}$ cup) fresh orange juice
1 $^{1}/_{2}$ oz. (3 Tbsp.) gin
$^{1}/_{2}$ oz. (1 Tbsp.) cherry brandy
cold ginger ale

Shake all ingredients except ginger ale with ice. Strain into chilled glass over ice cubes. Top with ginger ale, stirring gently.

**orange syrup** *see* SYRUPS, FLAVORED

## Orgasm

$^{1}/_{2}$ oz. (1 Tbsp.) amaretto
$^{1}/_{2}$ oz. (1 Tbsp.) Irish cream liqueur
$^{1}/_{2}$ oz. (1 Tbsp.) Kahlúa or Tia Maria

Shake ingredients with ice; strain into chilled shot glass or into an old-fashioned glass filled with ice cubes.

➤ **Variation** Add $^{1}/_{2}$ oz. (1 Tbsp.) cream.

➤ **Screaming Orgasm** Add $^{1}/_{2}$ oz. (1 Tbsp.) vodka.

**orgeat syrup** [ohr-ZHAY] An almond-flavored syrup, the original version of which was made from a combination of barley and almonds. Modern-day orgeats are more likely to be a blend of almonds, sugar, and ROSEWATER or ORANGE FLOWER WATER. Also known as *sirop d'amandes*. *See also* SYRUPS, FLAVORED.

## Oriental Cocktail

1 oz. (2 Tbsp.) blended whiskey
$^{1}/_{2}$ oz. (1 Tbsp.) sweet vermouth
$^{1}/_{2}$ oz. (1 Tbsp.) Triple Sec
2 tsp. fresh lime juice

Shake ingredients with ice; strain into chilled glass.

## Ostend Fizz [aws-TEND]

$^{3}/_{4}$ oz. (1 $^{1}/_{2}$ Tbsp.) kirsch
$^{3}/_{4}$ oz. (1 $^{1}/_{2}$ Tbsp.) crème de cassis
2 tsp. fresh lemon juice
cold club soda
lemon slice

Shake first 3 ingredients with ice. Strain into chilled glass filled with ice cubes; top with club soda, stirring gently. Garnish with lemon slice.

**ouzo** [OO-zoh] A crystal-clear LIQUEUR from Greece, ouzo gets its intense licorice flavor from aniseeds. As with similar potables, ouzo turns milky when combined with water or ice. *See also* ANISE-FLAVORED SPIRITS.

### Pacific Pacifier

1 oz. (2 Tbsp.) Cointreau
$^1/_2$ oz. (1 Tbsp.) crème de banane
$^1/_2$ oz. (1 Tbsp.) cream

Shake ingredients with ice; strain into chilled glass filled with crushed ice.

*Here's to Irish, a whiskey with heart,  as smooth as a Leprechaun's touch.  Yet soft in taste as a mother's embrace, with a gentleness saying as much.*

### Paddy Cocktail; Paddy Wagon

1$^1/_2$ oz. (3 Tbsp.) Irish whiskey
1$^1/_2$ oz. (3 Tbsp.) sweet vermouth
2 dashes (about $^1/_8$ tsp.) Angostura bitters

Stir ingredients with ice; strain into chilled cocktail glass or an old-fashioned glass filled with ice cubes.

### Paisley Martini *see* MARTINI

### pale ale *see* ALE

### Pall Mall

1$^1/_2$ oz. (3 Tbsp.) gin
$^1/_2$ oz. (1 Tbsp.) dry vermouth
$^1/_2$ oz. (1 Tbsp.) sweet vermouth
1 tsp. white crème de menthe
1 dash (about $^1/_{16}$ tsp.) orange bitters, optional

Stir ingredients with ice; strain into chilled cocktail glass or an old-fashioned glass filled with ice cubes.

### Palm Beach

1$^1/_2$ oz. (3 Tbsp.) gin
1$^1/_2$ tsp. sweet vermouth
1$^1/_2$ tsp. unsweetened grapefruit juice

Shake ingredients with ice; strain into chilled glass.

### Palmer

2 oz. ($^1/_4$ cup) blended whiskey
$^1/_2$ tsp. fresh lemon juice
1 dash (about $^1/_{16}$ tsp.) Angostura bitters

Stir ingredients with ice; strain into chilled glass.

### Palmetto Cocktail

1$^1/_2$ oz. (3 Tbsp.) light rum
1 oz. (2 Tbsp.) sweet vermouth
2 dashes (about $^1/_8$ tsp.) orange bitters
lemon twist

Stir liquid ingredients with ice. Strain into chilled glass; drop in lemon twist.

### Panama Cocktail

1 oz. (2 Tbsp.) brandy
1 oz. (2 Tbsp.) white crème de cacao
1 oz. (2 Tbsp.) cream

Shake ingredients with ice; strain into chilled glass.

➤ **Variation** Substitute rum or gin for the brandy.

### Panther

1$^1/_2$ oz. (3 Tbsp.) tequila
$^1/_2$ oz. (1 Tbsp.) sweet & sour mix

Shake ingredients with ice; strain into chilled old-fashioned glass over ice cubes or into shot glass.

**Paradis** [pah-rah-DEES] If fresh raspberries aren't in season, use thawed dry-pack berries. Purée raspberries in a blender or food processor; strain through a fine sieve.

1$^1/_2$ Tbsp. strained raspberry purée
cold dry champagne
1 fresh raspberry

Spoon raspberry purée into chilled glass. Top with champagne, stirring gently. Drop in fresh raspberry.

### Paradise Cocktail

1 oz. (2 Tbsp.) apricot brandy
$^3/_4$ oz. (1$^1/_2$ Tbsp.) gin
$^3/_4$ oz. (1$^1/_2$ Tbsp.) fresh orange juice

Shake ingredients with ice; strain into chilled glass.

**parfait amour; parfait d'amour** French for "perfect love," this LIQUEUR can be as capricious as love, its interpretation depending on its origin. The version found most often in Europe is CURAÇAO based and flavored with flowers (roses, violets), almonds, spices, and vanilla. The American rendition is more citrusy, although also flavored with spices and flowers such as violets. Both versions are very sweet and can range in color from pale violet to electric purple.

**parfait glass** *see* Glassware, page 9

**Parisian**

³/₄ oz. (1¹/₂ Tbsp.) gin
³/₄ oz. (1¹/₂ Tbsp.) crème de cassis
³/₄ oz. (1¹/₂ Tbsp.) dry vermouth

Shake ingredients with ice; strain into chilled glass.

**Park Avenue**

1¹/₂ oz. (3 Tbsp.) gin
³/₄ oz. (1¹/₂ Tbsp.) sweet vermouth
¹/₂ oz. (1 Tbsp.) unsweetened pineapple juice

Stir ingredients with ice; strain into chilled glass.

**Party Eggnog** *see* EGGNOG

**Pasha** A coffee-flavored LIQUEUR from Turkey. *See also* COFFEE-FLAVORED SPIRITS.

**Passion Daiquiri** *see* DAIQUIRI

**passion fruit–flavored spirits** *see* ALIZÉ DE FRANCE; LA GRANDE PASSION; SYRUPS, FLAVORED

**⋆ Passion Perfect**

3 oz. (³/₈ cup) passion-fruit nectar
¹/₂ oz. (1 Tbsp.) grenadine
¹/₂ oz. (1 Tbsp.) fresh lime juice
cold ginger ale or club soda
lime slice

Pour first 3 ingredients into a chilled glass filled with ice cubes; stir well. Top with ginger ale, stirring gently; garnish with lime.

**pastis** [pas-TEES] A generic name for any of several clear, strong (90 PROOF) French LIQUEURS, all of which have a pronounced licorice flavor. Similar to PERNOD, pastis is particularly popular in the south of France. As with most anise liqueurs, pastis is typically mixed with water, which turns it milky. The name comes from the French word *pastiche,* or a hodgepodge of ingredients. *See also* ANISE-FLAVORED SPIRITS.

**Patron XO Café** A cola-colored, TEQUILA-based Mexican LIQUEUR that has a bittersweet coffee-chocolate flavor. *See also* COFFEE-FLAVORED SPIRITS.

**peach bitters** *see* BITTERS

**Peach Blow Fizz**
> 2 oz. (¹/₄ cup) gin
> 2 tsp. strawberry liqueur
> 2 tsp. fresh lemon juice
> 2 tsp. cream
> 1 tsp. powdered sugar
> cold club soda
> 1 large strawberry

Shake first 5 ingredients with ice; strain into chilled glass filled with ice cubes. Top with club soda; stir gently. Garnish with strawberry.

**peach brandy** A generic term for any BRANDY distilled from peaches. *See also* PEACH-FLAVORED SPIRITS.

**Peach Buck** *see* BUCK

⭐ **Peach Cobbler** *see* COBBLER

**Peaches and Cream**
> 2 oz. (¹/₄ cup) peach schnapps, liqueur, or brandy
> 1 oz. (2 Tbsp.) cream

Shake ingredients with ice; strain into chilled glass over ice cubes.

> ⭐ **Peachy Creamy** Substitute peach nectar for the peach schnapps.

**peach-flavored spirits** *see* PEACH BRANDY; PEACHTREE; SOUTHERN COMFORT

**Peachtree** A peach-flavored LIQUEUR from Holland. *See also* PEACH-FLAVORED SPIRITS.

★ **Peachy Keen** *see* PEACHES AND CREAM

**pear-flavored spirits** *see* PEARLE DE BRILLET; POIRE WILLIAMS

**Pearle de Brillet** A French EAU-DE-VIE–based LIQUEUR with a seductively perfumy pear flavor. *See also* PEAR-FLAVORED SPIRITS.

**Peggy Cocktail** *see* MARTINI

**Pendennis Club Cocktail** Named after Louisville, Kentucky's famous club, which also lays claim to the invention of the OLD-FASHIONED.

1 ¹/₂ oz. (3 Tbsp.) gin
¹/₂ oz. (1 Tbsp.) apricot brandy
¹/₂ oz. (1 Tbsp.) fresh lime juice
1 to 2 dashes (about ¹/₁₆ to ¹/₈ tsp.) Péychaud's bitters

Shake ingredients with ice; strain into chilled glass.

**Peppermint Patty** *See* Floating and Layering Techniques, page 30.

³/₄ oz. (1 ¹/₂ Tbsp.) crème de cacao
¹/₂ oz. (1 Tbsp.) peppermint schnapps

Pour crème de cacao into glass. Slowly add peppermint schnapps, pouring it over the back (rounded) side of a spoon so that it floats on top; don't mix.

**peppermint schnapps** *see* SCHNAPPS

**perfect** A bar term for drinks made with equal parts dry and sweet VERMOUTH. For instance, a MANHATTAN, which is made with sweet vermouth, becomes a "Perfect Manhattan" when made with equal parts sweet and dry vermouth.

**Perfect Cocktail**

³/₄ oz. (1 ¹/₂ Tbsp.) gin
³/₄ oz. (1 ¹/₂ Tbsp.) dry vermouth
³/₄ oz. (1 ¹/₂ Tbsp.) sweet vermouth
orange twist, optional

Stir liquid ingredients with ice. Strain into chilled glass; garnish with orange twist, if desired.

**Perfect Manhattan** *see* MANHATTAN

**Perfect Martini** *see* MARTINI

**Perfect Rob Roy** *see* ROB ROY

**Pernod** [pehr-NOH] A light, clear, yellow-green LIQUEUR made in France, Pernod has an assertive licorice flavor and is the original ABSINTHE substitute. It's commonly mixed with about four to five parts water, which turns it whitish and cloudy. This style of liqueur is named after Henri-Louis Pernod, who's credited as the first commercial producer of ABSINTHE. *See also* ANISE-FLAVORED SPIRITS.

---

*There is only one really safe, mild, harmless beverage and you can drink as much of that as you like without running the slightest risk, and what you say when you want it is, "Garcon! Un Pernod!"*

ALEISTER CROWLEY, BRITISH OCCULTIST

---

### Pernod Cocktail

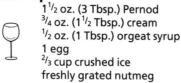

2 to 3 tsp. water
2 to 4 dashes (about $^1/_8$ to $^1/_4$ tsp.) Angostura bitters
$^1/_4$ tsp. powdered sugar
2 oz. ($^1/_4$ cup) Pernod

Put first 3 ingredients into chilled glass; stir well. Fill glass with crushed ice; add Pernod, stirring well.

### Pernod Flip

1 $^1/_2$ oz. (3 Tbsp.) Pernod
$^3/_4$ oz. (1 $^1/_2$ Tbsp.) cream
$^1/_2$ oz. (1 Tbsp.) orgeat syrup
1 egg
$^2/_3$ cup crushed ice
freshly grated nutmeg

Combine all ingredients except nutmeg in a blender. Cover and process at medium speed until smooth, about 15 seconds. Pour into chilled glass; sprinkle with nutmeg.

### Pernod Frappé

1 1/2 oz. (3 Tbsp.) Pernod
2 tsp. anisette
2 dashes (about 1/8 tsp.) Angostura bitters

Shake ingredients with ice; strain into chilled glass filled with crushed ice.

**Peter Heering** Also called *cherry Heering,* this Danish LIQUEUR was invented in the 1830s by Peter Heering. It's ruby red and has a complex black-cherry flavor that's not overly sweet. *See also* CHERRY-FLAVORED SPIRITS.

**Péychaud's bitters** New Orleans apothecary Antoine Péychaud is often credited for creating the first cocktail, based on his family's secret formula for this BRANDY-based BITTERS, which is still popular today.

### Phoebe Snow

1 1/2 oz. (3 Tbsp.) brandy
1 1/2 oz. (3 Tbsp.) Dubonnet rouge
1/4 tsp. Pernod or other anise-flavored liqueur

Shake ingredients with cracked ice; strain into chilled cocktail glass or an old-fashioned glass filled with cracked ice.

### Piccadilly Cocktail

1 1/2 oz. (3 Tbsp.) gin
3/4 oz. (1 1/2 Tbsp.) dry vermouth
1/4 tsp. Pernod or other anise-flavored liqueur
1/4 tsp. grenadine

Stir ingredients with ice; strain into chilled glass.

**pick-me-up** A drink—alcoholic or otherwise—taken to revive one's mood or energy.

**Picon** *see* AMER PICON

**Picon Cocktail** *See also* AMER PICON COCKTAIL.

1 oz. (2 Tbsp.) Amer Picon
1 oz. (2 Tbsp.) sweet vermouth
Shake ingredients with ice; strain into chilled cocktail glass or an old-fashioned glass over ice cubes.

➤**Variation** Substitute dry vermouth for the sweet vermouth.

**Picon Fizz**

1 1/2 oz. (3 Tbsp.) Amer Picon
1/2 oz. (1 Tbsp.) grenadine
cold club soda
1/2 oz. (1 Tbsp.) brandy

Pour first 2 ingredients into chilled glass filled with ice cubes. Top with club soda, stirring gently. Float brandy on top by slowly pouring it over the back (rounded) side of a spoon; don't mix.

*You can't be a Real Country unless you have A BEER and an airline—it helps if you have some kind of a football team, or some nuclear weapons, but at the very least you need A BEER.*

FRANK ZAPPA, AMERICAN ROCK MUSICIAN

**Pilsner; Pilsener** [PIHLZ-nuhr] Although the term "Pilsner" originally referred to a very fine beer brewed in Pilsen, in the Czech Republic, today it describes any pale, light LAGER. Pilsners generally have a mild (some say bland) flavor, although some reflect a pronounced HOPS characteristic. *See also* BEER.

**pilsner glass** *see* Glassware, page 9

**Pimento Dram** A spicy LIQUEUR made from the dried berries of the pimento-pepper tree, found throughout the Caribbean.

**Pimm's Cup**

3 oz. (3/8 cup) Pimm's No. 1
cold 7-Up or lemon-lime soda
1 long strip of cucumber or cucumber peel
lemon slice

Pour Pimm's into chilled glass or mug filled with ice cubes. Top with 7-Up, stirring gently. Garnish with cucumber peel and lemon slice.

➤ **Variation** Add 1 Tbsp. fresh lime juice and 1 tsp. Cointreau.

**Pimm's No. 1** Said to be the original GIN SLING, this bittersweet LIQUEURlike drink, flavored with herbs, spices, and fruit, was invented in the 1880s by London restaurateur James Pimm. It became so popular that Pimm began commercially producing it. Subsequent drinks were also produced: Pimm's No. 2, based on WHISKEY; No. 3 (BRANDY); No. 4 (RUM); No. 5 (RYE); and No. 6 (VODKA). Of these, only the vodka-based version is still available. Pimm's No. 1 is primarily used to make PIMM'S CUP, in which it's diluted with soda.

**Piña Colada** [PEEN-yah koh-LAH-dah] The original Piña Colada (Spanish for "strained pineapple") hails from Puerto Rico, but whether it was created at the Caribe Hotel in the mid-1950s or at the La Barrachina Restaurant a decade later is still in question. One thing's for sure—it became such a rage in the 1970s that a popular song of the times was nicknamed the "Piña Colada song."

> 4 oz. (¹/₂ cup) unsweetened pineapple juice
> 2 oz. (¹/₄ cup) light or gold rum
> 2 oz. (¹/₄ cup) cream of coconut
> ¹/₂ cup crushed ice
> pineapple spear

Combine all ingredients except pineapple spear in a blender. Cover and process at medium speed until smooth, about 15 seconds. Pour into chilled glass; garnish with pineapple spear.

➤ **Chi-Chi** Substitute vodka for the rum. *See also* CHI-CHI.

➤ **Nutty Colada** Substitute amaretto for the rum.

✶ **Sneaky Colada** Omit rum; add ¹/₄ cup pineapple juice, ¹/₂ oz. (1 Tbsp.) cream of coconut, and ¹/₄ cup crushed ice.

## Pineapple Cooler

2 oz. ($^{1}/_{4}$ cup) cold, dry white wine (Chardonnay,
Sauvignon Blanc, etc.)
2 oz. ($^{1}/_{4}$ cup) unsweetened pineapple juice
2 tsp. fresh lemon juice
$^{1}/_{2}$ tsp. powdered sugar
cold club soda
lemon twist

Shake first 4 ingredients with ice. Strain into chilled glass filled
with ice cubes. Top with club soda, stirring gently; drop in lemon
twist.

## Pineapple Fizz

3 oz. ($^{3}/_{8}$ cup) unsweetened pineapple juice
2 oz. ($^{1}/_{4}$ cup) light rum
$^{1}/_{2}$ tsp. powdered sugar
cold club soda

Shake first 3 ingredients with ice; strain into chilled glass filled
with ice cubes; top with club soda, stirring gently.

## pineapple-flavored spirits *see* CRÈME D'ANANAS

## pinga [PEEN-gah] *see* CACHAÇA

## Pink Almond

1 oz. (2 Tbsp.) blended whiskey
$^{1}/_{2}$ oz. (1 Tbsp.) crème de noyaux
$^{1}/_{2}$ oz. (1 Tbsp.) amaretto
$^{1}/_{2}$ oz. (1 Tbsp.) kirsch
$^{1}/_{2}$ oz. (1 Tbsp.) fresh lemon juice
lemon slice

Shake liquid ingredients with ice. Strain into chilled glass; garnish with lemon slice.

**Pink Creole** This recipe calls for a rum-soaked black cherry, but
not to worry if you don't plan ahead, a plain black cherry will be
fine. If you *do* plan ahead, soak the pitted cherries in rum to cover
for at least a week; cover tightly and refrigerate.

1 1/2 oz. (3 Tbsp.) light rum
1/2 oz. (1 Tbsp.) fresh lime juice
1 tsp. grenadine
1 tsp. cream
1 pitted rum-soaked black cherry

Shake liquid ingredients with ice. Strain into chilled glass; drop in cherry.

**Pink Gin** Also referred to simply as *gin and bitters,* this British favorite is served sans ice. For those who prefer a cold drink, put the gin in the freezer for a couple of hours before serving.

1 tsp. Angostura bitters
2 to 3 oz. (4 to 6 Tbsp.) gin
ice water, optional

Pour bitters into chilled glass, swirling to thoroughly coat sides; discard excess. Pour in gin. Serve with a glass of ice water, if desired.

## Pink Lady

2 oz. (1/4 cup) gin
1/2 oz. (1 Tbsp.) cream
1 tsp. grenadine
1 egg white
2 tsp. fresh lemon juice, optional

Vigorously shake ingredients with ice; strain into chilled glass.

## Pink Lemonade

1 1/2 oz. (3 Tbsp.) vodka
1 oz. (2 Tbsp.) sweet & sour mix
1 oz. (2 Tbsp.) cranberry juice
1/2 oz. (1 Tbsp.) Triple Sec
cold 7-Up
lemon wedge

Shake first 4 ingredients with ice; strain into chilled glass over ice cubes. Top with 7-Up, stirring gently; garnish with lemon wedge.

*I drink only to make my friends seem interesting.*
DON MARQUIS, AMERICAN HUMORIST, JOURNALIST

## Pink Panther

1 oz. (2 Tbsp.) gin
³/₄ oz. (1¹/₂ Tbsp.) dry vermouth
³/₄ oz. (1¹/₂ Tbsp.) fresh orange juice
¹/₂ oz. (1 Tbsp.) crème de cassis
1 egg white

Shake ingredients with ice; strain into chilled glass.

## Pink Rose

1¹/₂ oz. (3 Tbsp.) gin
¹/₂ egg white (about 1 Tbsp.) (*See* page 14, How to
    Divide Egg Whites in Half)
1 tsp. cream
1 tsp. fresh lemon juice
¹/₂ tsp. grenadine

Vigorously shake ingredients with ice; strain into chilled glass.

## Pink Squirrel

1 oz. (2 Tbsp.) white crème de cacao
1 oz. (2 Tbsp.) crème de noyaux
1 oz. (2 Tbsp.) cream

Shake ingredients with cracked ice; strain into chilled glass.

**pisco** [PEES-koh] Thought to date back to the Incas, pisco is a South American BRANDY that's briefly AGED in clay jars. Produced primarily in Chile and Peru, most piscos are made from a wine based on the perfumy muscat grape, although some are produced from a blend of Pedro Ximenez, torontel, and muscat grapes. This potable has a spicy, exotic flavor (often compared to that of beeswax) with definitive orange-blossom overtones. It can range in color from clear to pale straw.

## Pisco Punch

2 oz. (¹/₄ cup) pisco
1 tsp. fresh lime juice
1 tsp. unsweetened pineapple juice
2 dashes (about ¹/₈ tsp.) Angostura bitters

½ cup crushed ice
lime slice, optional

Combine all liquid ingredients in a blender. Cover and process at medium speed until smooth, about 15 seconds. Pour into chilled glass; garnish with lime slice, if desired.

## Planter's Cocktail

1½ oz. (3 Tbsp.) dark rum
½ oz. (1 Tbsp.) fresh lemon juice
½ tsp. powdered sugar

Shake ingredients with cracked ice; strain into chilled glass.

## Planter's Punch
This potent drink was created by the Myers Rum Company in the late 1800s.

3 oz. (⅜ cup) fresh orange juice
2 oz. (¼ cup) dark rum
½ oz. (1 Tbsp.) fresh lemon or lime juice
2 tsp. powdered sugar
¼ tsp. grenadine
¼ tsp. Triple Sec
orange slice
maraschino cherry

Shake all ingredients except orange slice and cherry with ice. Strain into chilled glass over ice cubes. Garnish with orange slice and cherry; serve with straw.

★ **Planter's Punchless** Omit liquor; increase orange juice to ½ cup and grenadine to 1 tsp.

## Plaza Cocktail

¾ oz. (1½ Tbsp.) gin
¾ oz. (1½ Tbsp.) dry vermouth
¾ oz. (1½ Tbsp.) sweet vermouth
½ tsp. unsweetened pineapple juice

Shake ingredients with ice; strain into chilled glass.

## plum-flavored spirits *see* MIRABELLE; PRUNELLE; QUETSCH; SLIVOVITZ; SLOE GIN

★ **Poco Rios** *see* OCHO RIOS

**Poire Williams** [pwahr WEEL-yahms (VEEL-yahms)] A crystal-clear, pear-flavored EAU-DE-VIE, the premier brands of which are distinguished by a whole pear inside the bottle. This feat is accomplished by placing a bottle over the budding fruit and attaching it to the tree so the fruit grows inside. After the pear and the bottle are removed from the branch, the bottle is filled with a BRANDY made from the Williams pear. This delectable potable is made in Switzerland and France.

### Poker Cocktail

1½ oz. (3 Tbsp.) light rum
1½ oz. (3 Tbsp.) sweet vermouth

Shake ingredients with ice; strain into chilled glass.

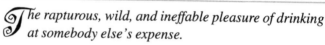

*he rapturous, wild, and ineffable pleasure of drinking at somebody else's expense.*

H. S. LEIGH, ENGLISH AUTHOR

### Polish Sidecar *see* SIDECAR

### Pollyanna

3 orange slices
3 pineapple slices
2 oz. (¼ cup) gin
½ oz. (1 Tbsp.) sweet vermouth
½ tsp. grenadine

Muddle fruit with gin; add vermouth and grenadine. Shake ingredients with ice; strain into chilled glass.

### Polo Cocktail

1½ oz. (3 Tbsp.) gin
¾ oz. (1½ Tbsp.) fresh orange juice
½ oz. (1 Tbsp.) fresh lemon juice

Shake ingredients with ice; strain into chilled glass.

### Polonaise [pahl-uh-NAYZ]

1½ oz. (3 Tbsp.) brandy
½ oz. (1 Tbsp.) blackberry brandy
½ oz. (1 Tbsp.) dry sherry
¼ tsp. fresh lemon juice
1 dash (about 1/16 tsp.) orange bitters

Shake ingredients with ice; strain into chilled glass over ice cubes.

### Polynesian Cocktail [pahl-uh-NEE-zhun]

lime wedge
1¹/₂ oz. (3 Tbsp.) vodka
³/₄ oz. (1¹/₂ Tbsp.) cherry brandy
¹/₂ oz. (1 Tbsp.) fresh lime juice

Frost rim of chilled glass by moistening with lime wedge, then dipping rim into granulated sugar. Shake remaining ingredients with ice; strain into glass. Drop in lime wedge, if desired.

**pomace** [PUH-muss] The residue (skins, pits, seeds, and pulp) that remains after wine grapes have been pressed. Pomace is sometimes processed to make a BRANDY, variously known as pomace brandy, EAU-DE-VIE, MARC (in France), and GRAPPA (in Italy and California).

### Pompano [PAHM-puh-noh]

1¹/₂ oz. (3 Tbsp.) gin
1¹/₂ oz. (3 Tbsp.) unsweetened grapefruit juice
³/₄ oz. (1¹/₂ Tbsp.) dry vermouth
2 to 4 dashes (about ¹/₈ to ¹/₄ tsp.) orange bitters
orange slice

Shake liquid ingredients with ice. Strain into chilled glass; garnish with orange slice.

**Ponche; Ponche Soto** [PAWN-chay SOH-toh] An herb-flavored Spanish LIQUEUR made from SHERRY and BRANDY.

**pony glass** *see* Glassware, page 9

### Poop Deck Cocktail

1 oz. (2 Tbsp.) brandy
1 oz. (2 Tbsp.) ruby port
¹/₂ oz. (1 Tbsp.) blackberry brandy

Shake ingredients with cracked ice; strain into chilled glass.

**Pope, The** *see* BISHOP, THE

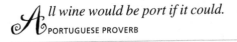

*All wine would be port if it could.*
PORTUGUESE PROVERB

**port; porto** A sweet FORTIFIED WINE whose name derives from the fact that such wines are shipped out of the Portuguese city of Oporto. Today, there's a specific region in northern Portugal's Douro Valley that has exacting regulations for producing quality port wines. There are four basic categories of port: Vintage, Tawny, Ruby, and White. **Vintage ports,** the best and most expensive, must be made from grapes of a single VINTAGE and only from the best "declared" (superior) vintages. A port producer won't make a traditional vintage port in undeclared years but will make other types of port wine. Vintage ports must be bottled within 2 years; the very best can age 50 years or more. **Tawny ports,** tawny in color and ready to drink when bottled, are made from a blend of grapes from several different years and can be AGED in wood for as long as 40 years (labels typically indicate the number of years); low-priced versions are blends of white and ruby ports. **Ruby ports,** generally the least expensive, are made from lower-quality grapes, wood aged for about 2 years, and bottled while still youthful, fruity, and bright red in color. **White ports** are made from white grapes, with the DRY versions undergoing a longer FERMENTATION.

Within the four basic port categories are many types: **Single-quinta ports** are essentially vintage ports made in nondeclared years—they are still considered excellent. **Second-label vintage ports** are produced when the vintage is good but not quite good enough to be declared. **Late Bottled Vintage (LBV) ports** and **Colheita ports** (also called *Single Vintage Ports* or *Dated Ports*) are made from single-vintage grapes that aren't as high quality as those for vintage ports. LBVs are aged in wood from 4 to 6 years and are considered high-quality ruby ports; Colheita ports have been wood aged at least 7 years and fall into the tawny-port category. Both are ready to drink when bottled and do not have the aging potential of Vintage ports. **Crusted ports**—a blend of two or three wines from different vintages—are aged for 3 to 4 years before being bottled and, like vintage port, improve with bottle aging. **Vintage character ports**—the lightest and fruitiest and ready to drink when bottled—are essentially high-quality ruby ports, blended from several vintages and wood aged. In countries other than Portugal, "port" is a generic name for wines created in the image of the Portuguese originals. Inexpensive "ports" will generally be labeled simply "ruby" or "tawny port." There are some non-Portuguese vintage ports that are made either from native Portuguese varieties or, often, ZINFANDEL or CABERNET SAUVIGNON.

> *Never have a small glass of port. . . . It just goes wambling around looking for damage to do. Have a large glass. It settles down and does you good.*
> LORD GODDARD, BRITISH SCHOLAR

**porter** A heavy, dark brown, strong-flavored beer first brewed in London. The dark color and deep flavor come from the addition of highly roasted MALT. Originally brewed in a bitter style, some of today's porters are slightly sweet. They're typically higher in alcohol than regular LAGERS. *See also* BEER.

**Port Sangaree** *see* SANGAREE

**poteen; potcheen** [poh-TEEN] Banned in Ireland since 1661, poteen is a clear, potent, illegally distilled IRISH WHISKEY, akin to American MOONSHINE. It can be made of grain, but is more commonly derived from potatoes. The name comes from the Gaelic *poitín,* "small pot," referring to the fact that the pot still (*see* DISTILLATION) is used for making this liquor. Bunratty Mead & Liqueur Company produces a 90-PROOF rendition exported to the United States.

**Pousse-Café; pousse café** [poos ka-FAY] 1. In the United States, *Pousse-Café* refers to an elaborate, multicolored after-dinner drink made by layering 2 to 7 or more LIQUEURS on top of one another without disturbing the layer below. This spectacular drink is like a miniature liquid sculpture with rainbow layers of brilliant color. As with so many spirited creations, the Pousse-Café debuted in New Orleans in the mid-nineteenth century. By the early 1900s, it had become the rage throughout America. The eponymous POUSSE-CAFÉ GLASS has straight sides so as to better balance the liqueurs. *See also* Floating and Layering Techniques, page 30. Pousse-Café (and layered SHOOTER) recipes in this book: ANGEL'S DELIGHT; ANGEL'S KISS; ANGEL'S TIT; B-52; CHOCOLATE-COVERED CHERRY; MEXICAN FLAG; OATMEAL COOKIE; PEPPERMINT PATTY; RUSSIAN QUAALUDE; SAVOY HOTEL; STARS AND STRIPES; TERMINATOR. 2. In France, *pousse café,* which literally means "push (down or back) the coffee," refers to any postprandial libation, from liqueurs to brandies.

**Pousse-Café glass** *see* Glassware, page 9

*Even though a number of people have tried, no one has yet found a way to drink for a living.*

JEAN KERR, AMERICAN WRITER, PLAYWRIGHT

## Prairie Fire

2 to 4 drops Tabasco sauce
1 1/2 oz. (3 Tbsp.) tequila

Pour Tabasco into chilled glass, followed by tequila.

**Praline** [prah-LEEN] A specialty of New Orleans, this pecan-flavored LIQUEUR is reminiscent of the famed praline candy. *See also* NUT-FLAVORED SPIRITS.

## Preakness Cocktail

1 1/2 oz. (3 Tbsp.) blended whiskey
1/2 oz. (1 Tbsp.) sweet vermouth
1/2 tsp. Bénédictine
1 to 2 dashes (about 1/16 to 1/8 tsp.) Angostura bitters
lemon twist

Shake liquid ingredients with ice. Strain into chilled glass; drop in lemon twist.

**Presbyterian** A bourbon HIGHBALL that uses both club soda and ginger ale.

2 oz. (1/4 cup) bourbon
cold club soda
cold ginger ale
lemon twist

Put 2 to 3 ice cubes in chilled glass. Add bourbon; top with equal parts club soda and ginger ale, stirring gently. Drop in lemon twist.

## Presidente #1

1½ oz. (3 Tbsp.) light rum
½ oz. (1 Tbsp.) dry vermouth
1 tsp. Triple Sec
1 to 2 dashes (about ¹⁄₁₆ to ⅛ tsp.) grenadine
lemon twist

Shake liquid ingredients with cracked ice. Strain into chilled glass; drop in lemon twist.

## Presidente #2

1½ oz. (3 Tbsp.) light rum
¾ oz. (1½ Tbsp.) sweet vermouth
1½ tsp. dry vermouth
1 dash (about ¹⁄₁₆ tsp.) grenadine
maraschino cherry

Shake liquid ingredients with cracked ice. Strain into chilled glass; garnish with cherry.

## Presto Cocktail

1½ oz. (3 Tbsp.) brandy
½ oz. (1 Tbsp.) sweet vermouth
½ oz. (1 Tbsp.) fresh orange juice
¼ tsp. Pernod or other anise-flavored liqueur

Shake ingredients with ice; strain into chilled glass.

## Prince Edward

1½ oz. (3 Tbsp.) Scotch
½ oz. (1 Tbsp.) Lillet blanc
1 tsp. Drambuie
orange slice

Shake liquid ingredients with ice. Strain into chilled glass over ice cubes; garnish with orange slice.

▶ **Variation** Substitute dry vermouth for the Lillet blanc.

## Prince of Wales

1 oz. (2 Tbsp.) brandy
1 oz. (2 Tbsp.) Madeira
1 tsp. Cointreau
2 to 4 dashes (about $1/8$ to $1/4$ tsp.) Angostura bitters
cold dry champagne
orange slice

Shake all ingredients except champagne and orange slice with cracked ice; strain into chilled glass. Top with champagne, stirring gently; garnish with orange slice.

★ **Prince's Grin** *see* PRINCE'S SMILE

## Prince's Smile

2 oz. ($1/4$ cup) gin
1 oz. (2 Tbsp.) apple brandy
1 oz. (2 Tbsp.) apricot brandy
$1/2$ tsp. fresh lemon juice

Shake ingredients with ice; strain into chilled glass.

★ **Prince's Grin** Substitute apple juice for the apple brandy and apricot nectar for the apricot brandy.

## Princeton Cocktail

$1^1/2$ oz. (3 Tbsp.) gin
$1^1/2$ oz. (3 Tbsp.) dry vermouth
2 tsp. fresh lime juice

Shake ingredients with ice; strain into chilled glass.

## Produced and Bottled By *see* WINE LABEL TERMS

---

*A prohibitionist is the sort of man one wouldn't care to drink with—even if he drank.*

H. L. MENCKEN, AMERICAN JOURNALIST, AUTHOR

---

**Prohibition** A dark and dry period from 1920 to 1933 (count 'em—13 years!) during which the Eighteenth Amendment prohibited the manufacture and sale of alcoholic beverages in the United States. To the joy of drinkers and chagrin of prohibitionists, this implausible law ended on December 5, 1933, when

Utah ratified the Twenty-first Amendment. Though eight states remained "dry," it's said that the happy sound of clinking glasses could be heard throughout the rest of the United States as celebrants began to party hearty. Anatomist and teacher Florence Sabin wittily summed up Prohibition with these words: "The prohibition law, written for weaklings and derelicts, has divided the nation, like Gaul, into three parts—wets, drys, and hypocrites."

**proof** A term for the strength of alcoholic beverages. In the United States, the proof listed on a bottle is always twice the amount of the ALCOHOL. Therefore, liquor labeled "80 Proof" contains 40 percent alcohol.

**prunelle** [proo-NEHL] 1. A brownish French LIQUEUR made from the fruit of the blackthorn tree, the sloe plum, which the French call *prunelle.* 2. Also the name of an EAU-DE-VIE made from the sloe.

**puff** Any combination of equal parts spirits and milk, topped off with soda water and served in an OLD-FASHIONED GLASS over ice cubes.

**pulque** [POOL-kay; POOL-keh] Harking back to the Aztecs and made in Mexico, pulque is a thick, milky-white, mildly alcoholic beverage FERMENTED from the juice of various species of agave (also known as the century plant). To make it more palatable, pulque is often flavored with any of various ingredients, including chiles, fruits, herbs, nuts, spices, and sugar. *See also* MEZCAL; TEQUILA.

*Sometimes too much to drink is barely enough.*
MARK TWAIN, AMERICAN AUTHOR, HUMORIST

**punch** Made in large quantities and generally served from a large punch bowl, punch is a cold mixture of various ingredients, including liquor, liqueur, wine, fruit juices, milk, or cream (as in EGGNOG) and carbonated beverages, often garnished with fresh fruit. CUPS are punches made in a pitcher and poured into glasses

or cups. *See also* ARTILLERY PUNCH; BOMBAY PUNCH; CHAM-
PAGNE PUNCH; FISH HOUSE PUNCH; MILK PUNCH; PISCO
PUNCH; PLANTER'S PUNCH; RUM PUNCH; SANGRÍA; SHARKY
PUNCH; WASSAIL BOWL.

**punt** the indentation in the bottom of a wine or champagne bottle. The punt's design serves two basic purposes—catching sediment and reinforcing the bottle. It also makes a convenient hand-
hold for pouring the wine.

**Punt è Mes** [poont ay MAYSS] A reddish-brown VERMOUTH-
style Italian APÉRITIF with a bittersweet herbal-orange flavor and
a syrupy texture. Punt è Mes is typically served over ice with a
spritz of soda water.

### Punt è Mes Negroni *see* NEGRONI

### Purple Hooter #1
$^3/_4$ oz. ($1^1/_2$ Tbsp.) vodka
$^3/_4$ oz. ($1^1/_2$ Tbsp.) Chambord
$^1/_2$ oz. (1 Tbsp.) cranberry juice

Shake ingredients with ice; strain into chilled glass.

### Purple Hooter #2
$^1/_2$ oz. (1 Tbsp.) vodka
$^1/_2$ oz. (1 Tbsp.) Chambord
$^1/_2$ oz. (1 Tbsp.) Triple Sec
$^1/_2$ oz. (1 Tbsp.) fresh lime juice

Shake ingredients with ice; strain into chilled glass.

### Purple Passion
$1^1/_2$ oz. (3 Tbsp.) vodka
3 oz. ($^3/_8$ cup) cold purple grape juice
3 oz. ($^3/_8$ cup) cold, unsweetened grapefruit juice

Stir ingredients together in chilled glass; add ice cubes.

★ **Purple Passion***ada* Substitute $^1/_4$ cup ginger ale for the vodka.

★ **Purple Passion***ada* *see* PURPLE PASSION

**pussyfoot** In cocktailese, a pussyfoot is a nonalcoholic cocktail,
such as a SHIRLEY TEMPLE.

*𝒟rink because you are happy,*
*but never because you are miserable.*

G. K. CHESTERTON, ENGLISH POET, ESSAYIST

## Quaker's Cocktail

3/4 oz. (1 1/2 Tbsp.) brandy
3/4 oz. (1 1/2 Tbsp.) light rum
2 tsp. fresh lemon juice
2 tsp. raspberry syrup
lemon twist

Shake liquid ingredients with ice. Strain into chilled glass; drop in lemon twist.

## Quarter Deck (Quarterdeck) Cocktail

1 1/2 oz. (3 Tbsp.) golden rum
1/2 oz. (1 Tbsp.) cream sherry
2 tsp. fresh lime juice

Stir ingredients with ice; strain into chilled glass.

## Quebec; Québec [kweh-BEHK; kay-BEHK]

1 1/2 oz. (3 Tbsp.) Canadian whisky
1/2 oz. (1 Tbsp.) dry vermouth
1 1/2 tsp. Amer Picon
1 1/2 tsp. maraschino liqueur

Shake ingredients with ice; strain into chilled glass.

## Queen Elizabeth; Queen Elizabeth Martini

1 1/2 oz. (3 Tbsp.) gin
1 oz. (2 Tbsp.) dry vermouth
1 1/2 tsp. Bénédictine

Stir ingredients with ice; strain into chilled glass.

## Queen Elizabeth Wine

1 1/2 oz. (3 Tbsp.) Bénédictine
3/4 oz. (1 1/2 Tbsp.) dry vermouth
3/4 oz. (1 1/2 Tbsp.) fresh lemon juice
lemon twist

Stir liquid ingredients with ice. Strain into chilled glass; drop in lemon twist.

## Queen's Park Swizzle

<sup>1</sup>/<sub>2</sub> lime
2 oz. (<sup>1</sup>/<sub>4</sub> cup) dark rum
2 dashes (about <sup>1</sup>/<sub>8</sub> tsp.) Angostura bitters
1 tsp. powdered sugar
mint sprig

Squeeze juice from lime into chilled glass filled with crushed ice; drop in lime shell. Add rum, bitters, and sugar. Rub a swizzle stick rapidly back and forth between your palms (or stir rapidly with a long spoon) until ingredients are mixed. Garnish with mint sprig.

**quetsch** [KETCH] A clear French EAU-DE-VIE with a spicy, sweet-tart flavor that comes from the tiny purple-blue plum (*quetsch*) from which it's made.

**quinine** [KWI-nine] An alkaloid that comes from the bark of the cinchona tree, an evergreen native to the mountainous areas of Central and South America. Quinine is the base flavor in most BITTERS and contributes the bitter essence to TONIC WATER. It's also the primary alkaloid used to treat malaria, which isn't to say that if you drink a lot of GIN AND TONICS you'll be cured of it.

**Racquet Club** *see* MARTINI

**raki; rakee** [RA-kee] Distilled from grains, grapes, or plums, raki is an anise-flavored BRANDY made in Turkey and the Balkans. *See also* ANISE-FLAVORED SPIRITS.

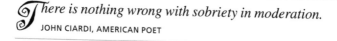

*There is nothing wrong with sobriety in moderation.*
JOHN CIARDI, AMERICAN POET

**Ramos Fizz** [RAY-mohss] A sinfully delicious concoction named for its inventor, Henry Ramos, who created it in New Orleans in the late nineteenth century. This recipe is courtesy of our friend and consummate host the late Fran Fraetis. It's definitely not for calorie watchers . . . and it's definitely delicious! *See also* GIN FIZZ.

2 oz. (¼ cup) gin
2 oz. (¼ cup) cream
½ oz. (1 Tbsp.) fresh lemon juice
½ oz. (1 Tbsp.) fresh lime juice
2 drops orange flower water
1 tsp. powdered sugar
½ cup cracked ice
cold club soda
orange slice

Combine all ingredients except club soda and orange slice in a blender. Cover and process at medium speed until smooth, 15 to 20 seconds. Pour into chilled glass. Top with soda; garnish with orange slice.

**raspberry-flavored spirits** *see* BERRY-FLAVORED SPIRITS; CHAMBORD; CORDIAL CAMPARI; FRAMBOISE

**ratafia** [rat-uh-FEE-uh] 1. A wine-based LIQUEUR fortified with BRANDY or other spirits and variously flavored with fruit kernels (such as peach pits), fruit, and almonds. 2. Once a general term for liqueur.

## Rattlesnake

1½ oz. (3 Tbsp.) bourbon or rye whiskey
1 tsp. fresh lemon juice
½ tsp. powdered sugar
¼ tsp. Pernod or other anise-flavored liqueur
1 egg white
lemon slice

Vigorously shake all ingredients except lemon slice with ice. Strain into chilled glass over ice cubes; garnish with lemon slice.

**raya** *see* SHERRY

## Red Apple

1 oz. (2 Tbsp.) vodka
1 oz. (2 Tbsp.) apple juice
½ oz. (1 Tbsp.) fresh lemon juice
1 tsp. grenadine

Shake ingredients with ice; strain into chilled glass over ice cubes.

*What contemptible scoundrel stole the cork from my lunch?*

W. C. FIELDS, AMERICAN ACTOR

## Red Cloud

1½ oz. (3 Tbsp.) gin
½ oz. (1 Tbsp.) apricot liqueur
½ oz. (1 Tbsp.) fresh lemon juice
1 tsp. grenadine

Shake ingredients with ice; strain into chilled glass.

## Red Lion

1½ oz. (3 Tbsp.) Grand Marnier
1 oz. (2 Tbsp.) gin
¾ oz. (1½ Tbsp.) fresh orange juice
¾ oz. (1½ Tbsp.) fresh lemon juice
½ orange slice

Shake liquid ingredients with ice. Strain into chilled glass; garnish with orange slice.

**Red Snapper** A 1930s name for the BLOODY MARY.

## Red Snapper Shooter

¾ oz. (1½ Tbsp.) Crown Royal Canadian whisky
¾ oz. (1½ Tbsp.) cranberry juice
½ oz. (1 Tbsp.) amaretto

Shake ingredients with ice; strain into chilled glass.

## Reform Cocktail

1½ oz. (3 Tbsp.) dry sherry
¾ oz. (1½ Tbsp.) dry vermouth
1 dash (about 1/16 tsp.) orange bitters
maraschino cherry

Stir liquid ingredients with ice. Strain into chilled glass; garnish with cherry.

## Remsen Cooler

2 oz. (¼ cup) Scotch
½ tsp. powdered sugar
cold club soda
lemon twist

Combine Scotch and sugar in chilled glass; stir until sugar dissolves. Add 3 to 4 ice cubes; top with club soda, stirring gently. Drop in lemon twist.

➤ **Gin Remsen Cooler** Substitute gin for the Scotch and ginger ale for the club soda.

### Renaissance Cocktail [rehn-ih-SAHNS]

1½ oz. (3 Tbsp.) gin
½ oz. (1 Tbsp.) dry sherry
½ oz. (1 Tbsp.) cream
freshly grated nutmeg

Shake liquid ingredients with ice. Strain into chilled glass over ice cubes; sprinkle with nutmeg.

### Rendezvous [RAHN-day-voo]

1½ oz. (3 Tbsp.) gin
½ oz. (1 Tbsp.) kirsch
½ oz. (1 Tbsp.) Campari
lemon twist

Shake liquid ingredients with ice. Strain into chilled glass; drop in lemon twist.

### Resolute Cocktail

1½ oz. (3 Tbsp.) gin
¾ oz. (1½ Tbsp.) apricot brandy
½ oz. (1 Tbsp.) fresh lemon juice

Shake ingredients with ice; strain into chilled glass.

*Inebriation is the great equalizer.*
PAUL KELLY, AMERICAN LAWYER

**retsina** [reht-SEE-nah] Made for more than 3,000 years, this traditional Greek wine is treated with pine-tree resin. This process gives the wine a distinctively turpentine-like flavor which, according to most non-Greeks, is an acquired taste. In Greece the word *retsina* (Greek for "resin") is synonymous with wine. Retsinas can be either white (labeled *Retsina*) or ROSÉ (labeled *Kokineli*); both styles should be served very cold.

## Rhett Butler

1½ oz. (3 Tbsp.) Southern Comfort
½ oz. (1 Tbsp.) fresh lime juice
1 tsp. fresh lemon juice
1 tsp. Triple Sec
½ tsp. powdered sugar

Shake ingredients with cracked ice; strain into chilled glass over ice cubes.

**Ricard** [ree-KARD] A French anise-flavored APÉRITIF made from anise (bulb and seeds) and myriad herbs.

**Rickey** Legend has it that this drink was created in the late 1800s at Washington, D.C.'s Shoemaker's Restaurant, purportedly for congressional lobbyist Joe Rickey, a renowned tippler. The rickey's distinguishing characteristic is that it contains no sweetener. Adding sugar converts the drink to a TOM COLLINS; using GINGER ALE as the mixer turns it into a BUCK. *See also* LIME RICKEY.

### Gin Rickey

2 oz. (¼ cup) gin
½ oz. (1 Tbsp.) fresh lime juice
cold club soda
lime wedge

Pour gin and lime juice into chilled glass over ice cubes. Top with club soda, stirring gently. Garnish with lime wedge.

➤ **Variations** Substitute bourbon, brandy, rum, rye, Scotch, sloe gin, tequila, vodka, or other potable for the gin. The drink is then called by the liquor used, such as "Bourbon Rickey" and so on.

**Riesling** [REEZ-ling; REES-ling] Hailing from Germany and considered among the world's great white wines, Rieslings are delicate but complex and characterized by a spicy, fruity flavor sometimes reminiscent of peaches and apricots. These white wines have a flower-scented BOUQUET, a long FINISH, and can range from very sweet to DRY. It's sometimes difficult to know if the wine you're buying is truly made from this superior grape because the name "Riesling" is used in many ways. In California, for instance, wines made from the *true* Riesling grape are known as **Johannisberg Riesling,** but there are other wines made from less prominent varieties labeled "Gray Riesling," "Emerald Riesling," and simply "Riesling." In Australia the word "Riesling" can refer to any type of white wine, whereas **Rhine Riesling** is the real thing. **Weisser Riesling** is the name used for the true Riesling by South Africans and some Germans. California winemakers now produce high-quality, German-style Rieslings, which are lighter, more delicate, and slightly to medium-sweet. There are also good Riesling wines from Oregon, Washington, and New York as well as from Australia, France, and Italy.

**Rob Roy** A MANHATTAN made with Scotch, this drink is named after the Scottish Robin Hood (Rob Roy), known to his mum as Robert Macgregor and featured in Sir Walter Scott's 1818 novel *Rob Roy.*

2 oz. (¼ cup) Scotch
1 oz. (2 Tbsp.) sweet vermouth
1 to 2 dashes (about ¹⁄₁₆ to ⅛ tsp.) Angostura bitters
maraschino cherry

Stir liquid ingredients with ice; strain into chilled cocktail glass. Or pour first 3 ingredients into an old-fashioned glass with ice; stir well. Garnish with cherry.

➤ **Dry Rob Roy** Substitute dry vermouth for the sweet vermouth; drop in lemon twist.

➤ **Perfect Rob Roy** Substitute 1 Tbsp. dry vermouth for 1 Tbsp. of the sweet vermouth.

*I think a man ought to get drunk at least twice a year just on principle, so he won't let himself get snotty about it.*

RAYMOND CHANDLER, AMERICAN AUTHOR

## Robson Cocktail

1 oz. (2 Tbsp.) Jamaican rum
2 tsp. fresh orange juice
2 tsp. fresh lemon juice
2 tsp. grenadine

Shake ingredients with ice; strain into chilled cocktail glass or an old-fashioned glass over ice cubes.

**rock and rye** An American RYE WHISKEY–based LIQUEUR flavored with a medley of fruit, which gives it citrusy overtones. Rock and rye is distinguished by a chunk of rock candy in each bottle. *See also* CITRUS-FLAVORED SPIRITS.

**Rock and Rye Cooler** Using bitter-lemon soda—available in most liquor stores and supermarkets—will give this drink more snap.

1½ oz. (3 Tbsp.) vodka
1 oz. (2 Tbsp.) rock and rye
½ oz. (1 Tbsp.) fresh lime juice
cold lemon soda
lime slice

Shake first 3 ingredients with ice. Strain into chilled glass filled with ice cubes. Top with soda, stirring gently; garnish with lime slice.

**rock candy swizzle stick** A SWIZZLE STICK formed by chunky sugar crystals sometimes used to stir sweet drinks. Rock candy is made by allowing a concentrated SUGAR SYRUP to evaporate slowly over several days, during which time the syrup dries and crystallizes. To make stir sticks, the syrup is dried around strings or small sticks. Rock candy swizzle sticks can be found in most liquor stores.

**rocks** *see* ON THE ROCKS

**rocks glass** *see* Glassware, page 10

## Rocky Green Dragon

1 oz. (2 Tbsp.) gin
½ oz. (1 Tbsp.) green Chartreuse
½ oz. (1 Tbsp.) cognac

Shake ingredients with cracked ice; strain into chilled glass.

## Rolls Royce *see* MARTINI

## Rolls Royce Parisian

1 oz. (2 Tbsp.) Cointreau
1 oz. (2 Tbsp.) fresh orange juice
³/₄ oz. (1¹/₂ Tbsp.) cognac

Shake ingredients with ice; strain into chilled glass.

## Root Beer Shooter

¹/₂ oz. (1 Tbsp.) Galliano
¹/₂ oz. (1 Tbsp.) Kahlúa
³/₄ oz. (1¹/₂ Tbsp.) cold cola

Pour all ingredients into chilled glass.

---

*A bottle of wine begs to be shared;
I have never met a miserly wine lover.*

CLIFTON FADIMAN, AMERICAN AUTHOR

---

## Rose Cocktail, English

1 oz. (2 Tbsp.) gin
¹/₂ oz. (1 Tbsp.) dry vermouth
¹/₂ oz. (1 Tbsp.) apricot brandy
1¹/₂ tsp. fresh lemon juice
¹/₂ tsp. grenadine

Frost rim of chilled glass by moistening with lemon juice or apricot brandy, then dipping rim into granulated sugar. Stir ingredients with ice; strain into glass.

## Rose Cocktail, French

1 oz. (2 Tbsp.) gin
¹/₂ oz. (1 Tbsp.) dry vermouth
¹/₂ oz. (1 Tbsp.) kirsch
1 dash (about ¹/₁₆ tsp.) grenadine

Stir ingredients with ice; strain into chilled glass.

## Rose Hall

1 1/2 oz. (3 Tbsp.) Jamaican rum
1 oz. (2 Tbsp.) fresh orange juice
1/2 oz. (1 Tbsp.) crème de banane
1 tsp. fresh lime juice
lime slice

Shake liquid ingredients with ice. Strain into chilled glass; garnish with lime slice.

## Roselyn Cocktail

1 1/2 oz. (3 Tbsp.) gin
3/4 oz. (1 1/2 Tbsp.) dry vermouth
1/4 tsp. grenadine
lemon twist

Stir liquid ingredients with ice. Strain into chilled glass; drop in lemon twist.

**Rose's lime juice** A sweetened, processed lime-flavored syrup.

**rosewater** A distillation of rose petals with an intensely perfumy flavor and fragrance. Available in liquor stores and many supermarkets.

**rosé wine** [roh-ZAY] French for "pink" or "rose colored," the word *rosé* is used in the wine world to describe wines of this color. As a rule, rosé wines are made from red grapes. However, contrary to the normal process of making red wine, the grape skins are left in contact with the wine for just 2 to 3 days and thereby contribute only a minute amount of color. This brief skin contact is also the reason rosés don't have as much BODY and CHARACTER as most red wines. They're also generally slightly sweet. In the United States, the term BLUSH WINE has all but replaced that of "rosé."

## Rosita [roh-SEE-tah]

1 oz. (2 Tbsp.) tequila
3/4 oz. (1 1/2 Tbsp.) Campari
1/2 oz. (1 Tbsp.) dry vermouth
1/2 oz. (1 Tbsp.) sweet vermouth
lemon twist

Fill chilled glass halfway with cracked ice. Add first 4 ingredients, stirring well. Add more cracked ice, if necessary; drop in lemon twist.

### Royal Gin Fizz *see* GIN FIZZ

### Royal Smile Cocktail

1 1/2 oz. (3 Tbsp.) apple brandy
3/4 oz. (1 1/2 Tbsp.) gin
2 tsp. fresh lemon juice
1 tsp. grenadine

Stir ingredients with ice; strain into chilled glass.

### ★ Roy Rogers

2 oz. (1/4 cup) fresh orange juice
1/2 oz. (1 Tbsp.) grenadine
6 oz. (3/4 cup) cold ginger ale
maraschino cherry

Pour orange juice and grenadine into glass filled with ice cubes. Top with ginger ale, stirring gently; garnish with cherry.

### Ruby Fizz

2 oz. (1/4 cup) sloe gin
1/2 oz. (1 Tbsp.) fresh lemon juice
1 tsp. grenadine
1 tsp. powdered sugar
1 egg white
cold club soda

Vigorously shake all ingredients except club soda with cracked ice; strain into chilled glass. Add 3 ice cubes; top with soda, stirring gently.

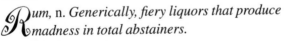

*ℛum, n. Generically, fiery liquors that produce madness in total abstainers.*

AMBROSE BIERCE, AMERICAN SATIRIST

**rum** Produced from sugarcane, rum is one of the oldest DISTIL-LATES made, dating back thousands of years. However, rum as we know it today was born in the West Indies, exactly on which island being open to conjecture. In 1493, Christopher Columbus played a role in rum's history by bringing sugarcane plantings on his second voyage to this region. By the seventeenth century, sugarcane had become an essential crop, with rum a growing industry. Toward the end of the 1700s, molasses was being shipped to New England, where it was used to make rum, which became America's most popular spirit at the time.

Rum is produced throughout the Caribbean as well as in Argentina, Australia, Brazil, Hawaii, Indonesia, Madagascar, Peru, the Philippines, and the continental United States. In the most basic terms, production begins with extracting the juice from sugarcane, then boiling it until reduced to a thick syrup. After being clarified, the syrup is separated into crystallized sugar and molasses. The molasses is mixed with water and yeast, FERMENTED, then distilled (*see* DISTILLATION) to less than 190 PROOF. Distillation processes vary, but most rums are produced with continuous stills; dark rums sometimes employ pot stills. Generally, only the middle portion of a distillation run is used because it produces a higher-quality product. Additives (SHERRY and COGNAC are the most common) can comprise no more than 1.5 percent of the final volume. Rum is oak AGED for 1 to 10 years, depending on the style, then bottled at anywhere from 80 to 151 proof. There are four basic styles of rum: light bodied, medium bodied, dark, and spiced or aromatic.

**Light rum** (also called *white* or *silver*) is DRY and colorless with a faintly sweet molasses flavor. It's typically aged for 6 to 12 months in uncharred oak barrels. Light-bodied rums are produced in Puerto Rico, the Dominican Republic, Haiti, Cuba, the Virgin Islands, Mexico, and Venezuela.

**Medium-bodied rums** (also called *gold* or *amber*) are richer flavored, deeper colored (from the addition of caramel and, occasionally, through longer aging), and mellower than light-bodied rums. They are sometimes distilled in pot stills and are also aged for about 3 years; those designated as **añejo rums** are aged for 4 to 10 years. Some are aged in charred barrels, which contributes color. Medium-bodied rums are produced by most of the same countries that produce their light-bodied counterparts.

**Dark rums** are typically aged for 5 to 7 years (and some for decades) and produced in pot stills. During the production of dark rum, "dunder"—the nonalcoholic residue (yeast, acids, and other congeners) left after distillation—is added to a new batch of water and molasses about to be fermented. This technique gives dark rums a fuller BODY, as well as richer flavors, AROMAS, and textures. Some long-aged dark rums have been favorably compared to fine COGNAC. **Jamaican rum** is simply a term for dark rums from Jamaica. **Demerara rum,** a definitive style of dark rum produced in Guyana, is medium bodied, very dark in color, aromatic, and generally bottled at extremely high (151) proofs. The primary producers of dark rum are Barbados, Guyana, Jamaica, Martinique, and Trinidad.

**Spiced** or **aromatic rums** have an exotically aromatic quality gained through the addition of spices or other tropical flavorings. *Batavia Arak,* made in Java, is a specialty rum that obtains its unique characteristics from the addition of wild yeast and dried rice cakes. **Flavored rums,** typically made from light-bodied rums, are infused (*see* INFUSION) with the essence of ingredients such as fruit or coconut. Although most rum is bottled at anywhere from 80 to 151 proof, some spiced and fruit-flavored rums are bottled at less than 80 proof.

Popular rum brands from Puerto Rico include Bacardi (the world's largest producer), Captain Morgan, Ron Del Barrilito, Ron Matusalem, and Ron Rico. From Jamaica come Appleton Estate, Myers's, and Strummer's. Other popular brands include Mount Gay and Cockspur from Barbados, Barbancourt from Haiti, and Pampero from Venezuela.

**Rum and Coke** *see* CUBA LIBRE

**Rum Cobbler** *see* COBBLER

**Rum Collins** *see* TOM COLLINS

**Rum Crusta** *see* CRUSTA

**Rum Daisy** *see* DAISY

### Rum Dubonnet

1¹/₂ oz. (3 Tbsp.) light rum
¹/₂ oz. (1 Tbsp.) Dubonnet rouge
1 tsp. fresh lime or lemon juice
lime or lemon twist

Shake liquid ingredients with ice. Strain into chilled glass; drop in citrus twist.

### Rum Fix *see* FIX

### Rum Highball *see* HIGHBALL

### Rum Milk Punch *see* MILK PUNCH

### Rumple Minze [ROOM-pl MIN-tse] A peppermint SCHNAPPS from Germany (where they spell it *schnaps*).

### Rum Punch

2¹/₂ oz. (5 Tbsp.) dark rum
1 oz. (2 Tbsp.) fresh lime juice
2 Tbsp. brown sugar
1 tsp. grenadine
¹/₂ tsp. Triple Sec
¹/₂ cup cracked ice
orange slice
maraschino cherry

Combine all ingredients except fruit in a blender. Cover and process at medium speed until smooth, about 15 seconds. Pour into chilled glass over ice cubes; garnish with orange slice and cherry.

### Rum Rickey *see* RICKEY

### Rum Shrub *see* SHRUB

### Rum Sling *see* SLING

### Rum Smash *see* SMASH

### Rum Sour *see* SOUR

### Rum Stinger *see* STINGER

### Rum Swizzle *see* SWIZZLE

### Rumtini *see* MARTINI

**Russian Bear** Kin to the WHITE RUSSIAN, only the "Bear" uses crème de cacao rather than KAHLÚA.

2 oz. ($^1/_4$ cup) vodka
1 oz. (2 Tbsp.) white crème de cacao
$^1/_2$ oz. (1 Tbsp.) cream

Shake ingredients with ice; strain into chilled glass.

### Russian Cocktail

1 oz. (2 Tbsp.) gin
1 oz. (2 Tbsp.) vodka
1 oz. (2 Tbsp.) white crème de cacao

Shake ingredients with ice; strain into chilled glass.

### Russian Coffee

1 oz. (2 Tbsp.) vodka
1 oz. (2 Tbsp.) Kahlúa or Tia Maria
1 oz. (2 Tbsp.) cream
$^1/_2$ cup crushed ice

Combine all ingredients in a blender. Cover and process at medium speed until smooth, about 15 seconds. Pour into chilled glass.

**Russian Quaalude** [KWAY-lood] The presentation of this drink has many forms—take your choice. *See* Floating and Layering Techniques, page 30.

$^3/_4$ oz. (1 $^1/_2$ Tbsp.) Frangelico
$^3/_4$ oz. (1 $^1/_2$ Tbsp.) Irish cream liqueur
$^3/_4$ oz. (1 $^1/_2$ Tbsp.) vodka

Shake ingredients with ice; strain into chilled glass. Or fill glass with ice cubes; pour in ingredients, stirring lightly. Or pour Frangelico into glass without ice; layer remaining ingredients in order given, slowly pouring each one over the back (rounded) side of a spoon so that it floats on top of the one below. Don't mix.

### Russian Rose

2 oz. ($^1/_4$ cup) vodka
$^3/_4$ oz. (1 $^1/_2$ Tbsp.) grenadine
2 dashes (about $^1/_8$ tsp.) orange bitters

Shake ingredients with ice; strain into chilled glass.

**russian stout** *see* STOUT

**Rusty Nail** Referred to by some as *Nail Drive.*

    1½ oz. (3 Tbsp.) Scotch
    1 oz. (2 Tbsp.) Drambuie

Stir ingredients together in chilled glass filled with ice cubes.

**Rye Rickey** *see* RICKEY

**Rye Sling** *see* SLING

**rye whiskey** Although this great American product is similar in taste to a rich BOURBON, rye whiskey is often described as having an assertively spicy flavor. Wheat and barley are frequently used in making rye whiskey, but United States law requires that it be made with a minimum of 51 percent rye. (In Canada "rye" whiskies are under no such restrictions and can be made with corn, barley, and wheat as well.) Additionally, like other straight whiskeys (*see* WHISKEY), American ryes must not exceed 160 PROOF, must be AGED in oak barrels for a minimum of 2 years, and may only be diluted with water to no less than 80 proof. Three popular brands of American rye are Old Overholt 4-Year-Old Straight Rye, Wild Turkey Straight Rye, and Mount Vernon. *See also* WHISK(E)Y-BASED LIQUEURS.

### Rye (Whiskey) Cocktail

    2 oz. (¼ cup) rye whiskey
    1 tsp. powdered sugar
    1 to 2 dashes (about ¹⁄₁₆ to ⅛ tsp.) Angostura bitters
    maraschino cherry

Shake liquid ingredients with ice. Strain into chilled glass; garnish with cherry.

---

*If you drink, don't drive. Don't even putt.*
DEAN MARTIN, AMERICAN SINGER, ACTOR

---

**Sabra** [SAH-bruh] Made in Israel, this russet-colored, intensely sweet LIQUEUR has a chocolate-orange flavor that comes from

Jaffa oranges and Swiss chocolate. *See also* CHOCOLATE-FLAVORED SPIRITS.

**Safari Exotic Liqueur** A brilliant amber-colored Dutch LIQUEUR made with tropical fruit, which gives it a sweet mango-orange flavor.

⭑ **Safe Sex on the Beach** *see* SEX ON THE BEACH

**sake** [SAH-kee] Although often called "Japanese rice wine," sake is considered a beer by some because unlike wine, which is made from fruit, it's made from grain. In the United States, the B.A.T.F. (Bureau of Alcohol, Tobacco, and Firearms) categorizes sake as "wine from other agricultural products." In the most basic terms, sake is made from specially selected steamed rice that's fermented (*see* FERMENTATION), filtered, heated, and matured in casks. Sake's alcohol level is 12 to 16 percent—more than beer, less than most grain-based liquors, and in the general range of most wines. Sake, which is colorless (or very pale yellow) and slightly sweet, is traditionally served warm in small porcelain cups called *sakazuki*. Another popular Japanese rice wine is *Mirin*.

**Saketini** [sah-kee-TEE-nee] *see* MARTINI

**Salty Dog**

1½ oz. (3 Tbsp.) gin or vodka
6 oz. (¾ cup) unsweetened grapefruit juice

Frost rim of chilled glass by moistening with grapefruit juice, then dipping rim into salt. Pour ingredients into glass filled with ice cubes; stir well.

**Sambuca** [sam-BOO-kuh] Made in Italy, this colorless, anise-flavored LIQUEUR is drier (*see* DRY) than most potables of its kind. It's based on the elderberry, the fruit of the elder (genus *Sambucus*), from which it gets its name. Sambuca is frequently served with 3 to 4 coffee beans floating on the surface. The liqueur is ignited, which "roasts" the beans and infuses the liqueur with flavor. **Sambuca Negra** is a dark brown, coffee-flavored version. *See also* ANISE-FLAVORED SPIRITS.

## Sanctuary

1 $^1/_2$ oz. (3 Tbsp.) Dubonnet rouge
$^3/_4$ oz. (1 $^1/_2$ Tbsp.) Amer Picon
$^3/_4$ oz. (1 $^1/_2$ Tbsp.) Cointreau or Triple Sec
lemon twist

Shake liquid ingredients with ice. Strain into chilled glass; drop in lemon twist.

## San Francisco Cocktail

$^3/_4$ oz. (1 $^1/_2$ Tbsp.) sloe gin
$^3/_4$ oz. (1 $^1/_2$ Tbsp.) dry vermouth
$^3/_4$ oz. (1 $^1/_2$ Tbsp.) sweet vermouth
1 dash (about $^1/_{16}$ tsp.) Angostura bitters
1 dash (about $^1/_{16}$ tsp.) orange bitters
maraschino cherry

Shake liquid ingredients with ice. Strain into chilled glass; drop in cherry.

**Sangaree** [san-gah-REE] An eighteenth-century American drink influenced by the Spanish SANGRÍA. The original sangarees were simple concoctions of sweetened FORTIFIED WINES (like port or sherry) served over ice. Modern-day versions often combine two or more spirits and are sometimes served hot (*see also* Hot Drinks, page 29). One thing all sangarees have in common is a generous dusting of nutmeg.

### Brandy Sangaree

2 oz. ($^1/_4$ cup) brandy
$^1/_2$ tsp. powdered sugar
cold club soda
$^1/_2$ oz. (1 Tbsp.) ruby port
freshly grated nutmeg

Combine brandy and sugar in chilled glass; stir until sugar dissolves. Add 3 to 4 ice cubes. Top with club soda, stirring gently. Float port on top by slowly pouring it over the back (rounded) side of a spoon; don't mix. Sprinkle with nutmeg.

➤ **Variations** Substitute gin, sherry, whiskey, or other potable for the brandy. The liquor used gives the drink its name, such as "Gin Sangaree" and so on.

**Sangría** [san-GREE-uh] The name comes from the Spanish word *sangre,* "blood," after the blood-red color of the classic red-wine *sangría.* The white-wine version is called *Sangría Blanca,* "white sangría."

MAKES ABOUT TEN 8-OUNCE SERVINGS

2 (750 ml) bottles dry red wine (Cabernet Sauvignon, Burgundy, etc.)
6 oz. (³/₄ cup) Triple Sec or Cointreau
6 oz. (³/₄ cup) fresh orange juice
3 oz. (³/₈ cup) fresh lemon or lime juice
3 oz. (³/₈ cup) brandy, optional
about ¹/₂ cup sugar
16 oz. (1 pint; 2 cups) cold club soda or citrus-flavored mineral water
1 orange, sliced
1 lemon, sliced

Pour first 4 (5 if using the brandy) ingredients into a punch bowl. Sweeten to taste with sugar, stirring well to dissolve. Cover and refrigerate for at least 2 hours. Just before serving, stir in club soda or mineral water. Add a block of ice (see Punch Bowl Ice, page 17) and fruit slices. Serve over ice cubes in large, chilled wineglasses.

➤ **Champagne Sangría** Substitute cold dry champagne for the red wine. Don't add champagne until just before serving. In addition to the orange and lemon slices, add about 15 green grapes.

➤ **Sangría Blanca** Substitute dry white wine (Chardonnay, Sauvignon Blanc, etc.) for the red wine, and peach slices for the sliced citrus. Float several sprigs of mint on the surface.

*Zen martini: A martini with no vermouth at all.
And no gin, either.*
P. J. O'ROURKE, AMERICAN WIT, AUTHOR

**Sangrita** [san-GREE-tuh] Although sometimes confused with SANGRÍA, sangrita—with its tomato–orange juice base and kick of hot peppers—is markedly different. Served as a chaser to a shot of tequila, it's guaranteed to light your burners. For those who haven't tried it, green Tabasco sauce is made from jalapeño peppers. This concoction is *supposed* to be hot, so don't stint on the Tabasco.

**MAKES ABOUT 1²/₃ CUPS, OR ABOUT SEVEN 2-OUNCE SERVINGS**

8 oz. (1 cup) tomato juice
4 oz. (¹/₂ cup) fresh orange juice
1¹/₂ oz. (3 Tbsp.) fresh lime juice
2 tsp. green Tabasco sauce
1 tsp. Worcestershire sauce
¹/₄ tsp. white pepper
¹/₄ tsp. celery salt
salt
1¹/₂ oz. (1 Tbsp.) tequila *per serving*

Combine first 7 ingredients in a pitcher, stirring to mix well. Taste and add salt if necessary. Cover and refrigerate at least 2 hours; can be refrigerated for up to 5 days. To serve, pour tequila into shot glass and about 2 oz. (¹/₄ cup) sangrita into another shot or very small glass. Toss back the tequila and chase it with the sangrita.

**San Juan** [san WAHN] To be perfectly legit, Puerto Rican rum should be used—but who'll know if no one's looking?

1¹/₂ oz. (3 Tbsp.) light rum
1 oz. (2 Tbsp.) cold unsweetened grapefruit juice
2 tsp. fresh lime juice
1 tsp. cream of coconut
¹/₂ cup crushed ice
2 tsp. 151-proof rum

Combine all ingredients except 151-proof rum in a blender. Cover and process at medium speed until smooth, about 15 seconds; pour into chilled glass. Float rum on top by slowly pouring it over the back (rounded) side of a spoon; don't mix.

★ **San Juanita** Omit rum; increase grapefruit juice to 2 oz. (¹/₄ cup) and lime juice and cream of coconut to 1 Tbsp. each.

★ **San Juanita** *see* SAN JUAN

## San Sebastian

1 oz. (2 Tbsp.) gin
$^1/_2$ oz. (1 Tbsp.) unsweetened grapefruit juice
$^1/_2$ oz. (1 Tbsp.) fresh lemon juice
1$^1/_2$ tsp. 151-proof rum
1$^1/_2$ tsp. Triple Sec

Shake ingredients with ice; strain into chilled glass.

## Santiago Cocktail [san-tee-AH-goh]

1$^1/_2$ oz. (3 Tbsp.) light rum
$^1/_2$ oz. (1 Tbsp.) fresh lime juice
$^1/_2$ tsp. powdered sugar
$^1/_4$ tsp. grenadine

Shake ingredients with ice; strain into chilled glass.

*I* always *wake up at the crack of ice.*
JOE E. LEWIS, AMERICAN ENTERTAINER

## Saratoga Cocktail [sehr-uh-TOH-guh]

2 oz. ($^1/_4$ cup) brandy
2 tsp. unsweetened pineapple juice
1 tsp. fresh lemon juice
$^1/_4$ tsp. maraschino liqueur
1 dash (about $^1/_{16}$ tsp.) Angostura bitters

Shake ingredients with ice; strain into chilled glass.

**saucer glass** *see* Glassware, page 10

## Saucy Sue

2 oz. ($^1/_4$ cup) apple brandy
$^1/_2$ tsp. apricot brandy
$^1/_8$ tsp. Pernod or other anise-flavored liqueur
orange twist, optional

Stir liquid ingredients with ice. Strain into chilled glass; garnish with orange twist, if desired.

**Sauternes; sauterne** [soh-TEHRN] 1. Sauternes, one of the most celebrated wines in the world, comes from the eponymous APPELLATION in the Graves district of BORDEAUX. These rich, sweet wines are made primarily from Sémillon grapes, generally with small additions of SAUVIGNON BLANC and Muscadelle. The best Sauternes come from vines that have been hand picked (some as many as 12 separate times) to ensure that the grapes are culled at the perfect degree of ripeness. In good years, the right climatic conditions infect the grapes with *Botrytis cinerea,* a mold that causes the grapes to shrivel, leaving sugar-laden fruit full of rich, concentrated flavors. The resulting wines have a complex honeyed AROMA and flavor. French winemakers only produce sweet Sauternes in years when the grapes are perfectly ripened and *botrytis* infected—otherwise they turn their grapes into fully DRY wines. The eminent Château d'Yquem, the most famous of the châteaux in Sauternes, undisputedly makes the best wines in the area. 2. **Sauterne** is a generic name used in the United States for some inexpensive white wines made from various mediocre grapes and ranging from dry to semi-sweet.

**Sauvignon Blanc** [SOH-vihn-yoh*n* BLAH*N*; SOH-vee-nyaw*n* BLAH*N*GK] Wine produced from a white-wine grape widely cultivated in France and California. Sauvignon Blancs—now California's second best-selling VARIETAL WINES after CHAR-DONNAY—are made in a variety of styles, from crisp and un-oaked, to the rounder, softer Sémillon blends. Typically, Sauvignon Blancs have noticeable acidity and a grassy, herbaceous AROMA and flavor; they should generally be drunk young. In California Robert Mondavi created renewed interest in Sauvignon Blanc when he introduced an oaky-styled version he called *Fumé Blanc.*

**Savoy Hotel** *See* Floating and Layering Techniques, page 30.

½ oz. (1 Tbsp.) brandy
½ oz. (1 Tbsp.) Bénédictine
½ oz. (1 Tbsp.) dark crème de cacao

Add ingredients in order given, slowly pouring each one over the back (rounded) side of a spoon so that it floats on top of the one below. Don't mix.

*any people go into a bar optimistically . . . and come out misty optically.*

## Saxon Cocktail

2 oz. (¹/₄ cup) light rum
2¹/₂ tsp. fresh lime juice
2 dashes (about ¹/₈ tsp.) grenadine
orange twist

Shake liquid ingredients with ice; strain into chilled glass. Drop in twist.

**Sazerac** [SAZ-uh-rak] The name of this potent cocktail comes from the fact that it was originally served at New Orleans' Sazerac Coffee House; there's also a theory that the originals were made with Sazerac-du-Forge, a French BRANDY. HERBSAINT—another New Orleans original—is a classic ingredient, but other anise-flavored LIQUEURS may be substituted. For those in a real rush, there's a premixed "Sazerac Cocktail" available in some liquor stores. However you prepare Sazeracs, start with a glass that's been chilled in the freezer for at least an hour.

 ¹/₄ tsp. Herbsaint, Pernod, or other anise-flavored liqueur
¹/₂ tsp. sugar
1 tsp. water
2 dashes (about ¹/₈ tsp.) Péychaud's bitters
2 oz. (¹/₄ cup) bourbon or rye whiskey
lemon twist

Put Herbsaint into icy-cold glass; turn glass so liqueur coats the inside. Add sugar, water, and bitters, stirring to dissolve sugar. Fill glass with ice cubes; add bourbon, stirring well. Drop in lemon twist.

## Scarlett O'Hara

 2 oz. (¹/₄ cup) Southern Comfort
2 oz. (¹/₄ cup) cranberry juice
¹/₂ oz. (1 Tbsp.) fresh lime juice

Shake ingredients with ice; strain into chilled glass.

**Schiedam** *see* GIN

**Schnapps** [SHNAHPS] From the German *Schnaps,* meaning "mouthful," the word refers to any of various flavorful alcoholic beverages made from grains or potatoes. Although sweet **peppermint schnapps** is undoubtedly the most widely known version, this potable may be flavored with herbs and seeds (including aniseed, caraway seed, dill, and fennel) and can range from sweet to DRY. Denmark produces the majority of schnapps, with Germany coming in second.

**schooner** [SKOO-ner] In the world of glassware, a schooner is a tall glass that holds about 16 ounces and is typically used for BEER.

**Scorpion** [SKOR-pee-uhn]

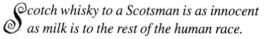

2 oz. (¼ cup) light or gold rum
2 oz. (¼ cup) fresh orange juice
1½ oz. (3 Tbsp.) fresh lemon juice
1 oz. (2 Tbsp.) brandy
½ oz. (1 Tbsp.) orgeat syrup
½ cup crushed ice
orange slice

Combine all ingredients except orange slice in a blender. Cover and process at medium speed until smooth, about 15 seconds. Pour into chilled glass; garnish with orange slice.

> *Scotch whisky to a Scotsman is as innocent as milk is to the rest of the human race.*
>
> MARK TWAIN, AMERICAN AUTHOR

**Scotch; Scotch whisky** A whisky that must be distilled and AGED for 3 years in Scotland but may be bottled in other countries. The majority of Scotches are aged for 5 to 10 years, some much longer. There are two main types of Scotch whisky (yes, like Canadian whisky, spelled without the *e*)—malt and grain. **Malt whisky,** produced in an old-fashioned pot still (*see* DISTILLATION), is made from malted barley—grain that's been germinated or sprouted, which converts its starch to sugar. The malted barley is dried over peat fires, which contributes the characteristic smoky flavor so loved by Scotch drinkers. Malt whiskies are aged for up to 15 years. **Grain whisky,** distilled in a continuous still, is made with malted barley mixed with various unmalted grains—primarily corn, but also barley and wheat. It's aged for 6 to 8 years and used primarily for blending.

**Blended Scotch** is a combination of up to 50 different malt whiskies plus grain whisky. These Scotches are blended to achieve consistency and have a more uniform AROMA and flavor than single malts. Although single-malt Scotch has gained recognition over the last decade, blended Scotch still makes up about 95 percent of the market. Popular blends are Ballantine, Chivas Regal, Cutty Sark, Dewar's, Famous Grouse, Johnny Walker, J&B (Justerini & Brooks), and Teacher's.

**Single-malt (unblended) Scotch** is produced and bottled by a single distillery without being blended with other Scotch whiskies. It varies significantly from distiller to distiller (and there are roughly 100 malt distilleries in Scotland) depending on distillation techniques, aging practices, differences in the local water used for dilution, and myriad other environmental factors. The terms **Highlands Scotch** and **Lowlands Scotch** are single-malt descriptors referring simply to geographical locations but not necessarily describing particular flavor characteristics. To determine the boundary between the High- and Lowlands, draw a line across Scotland from Greenrock to Dundee, which would be the border between the Highlands (north of the line) and the Lowlands (south of the line). Popular single-malt Scotches include The Balvenie, Bowmore, Glenlivet, Glenfiddich, Highland Park, Knockando, and Macallan. *See also* WHISK(E)Y-BASED LIQUEURS.

**Scotch ale** *see* ALE

**Scotch Cobbler** *see* COBBLER

## Scotch Cooler

2 oz. ($^1/_4$ cup) Scotch
$^1/_4$ tsp. crème de menthe
cold club soda

Pour Scotch and crème de menthe into chilled glass filled with ice cubes. Top with club soda, stirring gently.

**Scotch Holiday Sour** *see* SOUR

**Scotch Manhattan** *see* ROB ROY

**Scotch Milk Punch** *see* MILK PUNCH

## Scotch Mist

$1^1/_2$ to 2 oz. (3 to 4 Tbsp.) Scotch
lemon twist

Pack chilled glass with crushed ice. Pour in Scotch; drop in lemon twist.

---

*An umbrella is of no avail against a Scotch mist.*
JAMES RUSSELL LOWELL, AMERICAN POET, EDITOR

---

**Scotch Rickey** *see* RICKEY

**Scotch Sling** *see* SLING

**Scotch Smash** *see* SMASH

**Scotch Sour** *see* SOUR

**Scotch Stinger** *see* STINGER

**Scotch Swizzle** *see* SWIZZLE

**Screaming Orgasm** *see* ORGASM

**Screwdriver** Legend has it that this drink got its name in the 1950s from American oil-rig workers stationed in the Middle East, who purportedly opened and stirred cans of this concoction with their screwdrivers. A HARVEY WALLBANGER is a Screwdriver with a FLOAT of GALLIANO.

1 ¹/₂ to 2 oz. (3 to 4 Tbsp.) vodka
4 to 6 oz. (¹/₂ to ³/₄ cup) cold fresh orange juice
orange slice

Pour vodka and orange juice into chilled glass filled with ice cubes; stir well. Garnish with orange slice.

➤ **Cordless Screwdriver** Chill vodka; pour into chilled shot glass. Accompany with an orange wedge dipped in sugar. Shoot the vodka, then bite down on and suck the orange.

➤ **Creamy Screwdriver** Add 1 egg yolk, 1 tsp. sugar, and ¹/₂ cup crushed ice. Combine all ingredients except orange slice in blender; cover and process until smooth, about 15 seconds. Pour into chilled glass over ice cubes; garnish with orange slice.

*When I was younger, I made it a rule never to take strong drink before lunch. It is now my rule never to do so before breakfast.*

WINSTON CHURCHILL, BRITISH POLITICIAN, WRITER

**screwpull** *see* Bar Equipment (Corkscrews), page 4

## Sea Breeze

4 oz. (¹/₂ cup) unsweetened grapefruit juice
3 oz. (³/₈ cup) cranberry juice
1 ¹/₂ oz. (3 Tbsp.) vodka
lime wedge, optional

Pour liquid ingredients into chilled glass two-thirds full of ice cubes; mix well. Garnish with lime wedge, if desired.

★ **Mild Sea Breeze** Omit vodka; increase cranberry juice to ¹/₂ cup and grapefruit juice to ²/₃ cup.

**sec** [SEHK] French for DRY, which in the wine world means "not sweet." When used in relation to STILL (nonsparkling) WINES, *sec* describes a wine with little if any residual sugar. In SPARKLING WINES like CHAMPAGNE, however, *sec* refers to a relatively sweet wine, whereas *demi-sec* means one that's even sweeter.

**Sekt** [ZEHKT] A German term for SPARKLING WINE. *See also* CHAMPAGNE.

**seltzer water** *see* CLUB SODA

### September Morn

1¹/₂ oz. (3 Tbsp.) light rum
2 tsp. fresh lime juice
³/₄ tsp. grenadine
¹/₂ egg white (about 1 Tbsp.) (*See* page 14, How to Divide Egg Whites in Half)

If desired, moisten chilled glass rim with a little grenadine, then dip rim into granulated sugar. Shake ingredients with ice; strain into glass.

*efinition of whiskey:
Bottled trouble.*

### 7 & 7

1¹/₂ oz. (3 Tbsp.) Seagram 7 Crown blended whiskey
4 oz. (¹/₂ cup) 7-Up
lime slice, optional

Pour whiskey into chilled glass filled with ice cubes. Add 7-Up, stirring gently; garnish with lime slice, if desired.

### Seventh Heaven

1¹/₂ oz. (3 Tbsp.) gin
¹/₂ oz. (1 Tbsp.) maraschino liqueur
¹/₂ oz. (1 Tbsp.) unsweetened grapefruit juice
mint sprig

Shake liquid ingredients with ice. Strain into chilled glass; garnish with mint sprig.

### Sevilla [seh-VEE-yuh]

1 oz. (2 Tbsp.) dark rum
1 oz. (2 Tbsp.) sweet vermouth
orange twist

Shake liquid ingredients with ice. Strain into chilled glass; drop in orange twist.

## Sevilla Flip

1 1/2 oz. (3 Tbsp.) light rum
1 1/2 oz. (3 Tbsp.) ruby port
1 egg
1/2 tsp. sugar
freshly grated nutmeg

Vigorously shake first 4 ingredients with cracked ice. Strain into chilled glass; sprinkle with nutmeg.

## Seville [seh-VILL]

1 1/2 oz. (3 Tbsp.) gin
1/2 oz. (1 Tbsp.) sherry
1/2 oz. (1 Tbsp.) fresh orange juice
1/2 oz. (1 Tbsp.) fresh lemon juice
2 tsp. powdered sugar

Shake ingredients with ice; strain into chilled glass.

**Sex on the Beach #1** Another drink with several different versions, including a SHOOTER. But then everyone wants to get into the act with this kind of name.

3 oz. (3/8 cup) cranberry juice
3 oz. (3/8 cup) fresh orange juice or unsweetened
grapefruit juice
1 oz. (2 Tbsp.) vodka
1 oz. (2 Tbsp.) peach schnapps
maraschino cherry

Pour all ingredients except cherry into chilled glass over ice cubes; stir well. Garnish with cherry.

★ **Safe Sex on the Beach** Omit vodka and schnapps; add 2 oz. (1/4 cup) peach nectar.

## Sex on the Beach #2

1 oz. (2 Tbsp.) vodka
1 oz. (2 Tbsp.) unsweetened pineapple juice
1/2 oz. (1 Tbsp.) Chambord
1/2 oz. (1 Tbsp.) melon liqueur
2 tsp. cranberry juice

Shake first 4 ingredients with ice; strain into chilled glass, either straight up or over ice cubes. Float cranberry juice on top by slowly pouring it over the back (rounded) side of a spoon; don't mix.

### Sex on the Beach Shooter

³/₄ oz. (1 ¹/₂ Tbsp.) vodka
³/₄ oz. (1 ¹/₂ Tbsp.) peach schnapps
¹/₂ oz. (1 Tbsp.) fresh orange juice

Shake ingredients with ice; strain into chilled glass.

### Shady Lady

4 oz. (¹/₂ cup) unsweetened grapefruit juice
1 oz. (2 Tbsp.) tequila
1 oz. (2 Tbsp.) melon liqueur

Pour ingredients into chilled glass filled with ice cubes.

### Shamrock *see* EVERYBODY'S IRISH

---

*I have taken more out of alcohol than alcohol has taken out of me.*

WINSTON CHURCHILL, BRITISH POLITICIAN, WRITER

---

### Shandy; Shandygaff

Dating back to at least the late nineteenth century, this British concoction is not only refreshing, but delivers half the alcohol as straight beer or ale. Shandygaff, the original form of the word, is thought to come from the London vernacular for a pint of beer, "shant of gatter" (*shanty* being a public house, *gatter* an idiom for water).

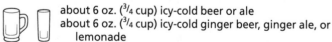

about 6 oz. (³/₄ cup) icy-cold beer or ale
about 6 oz. (³/₄ cup) icy-cold ginger beer, ginger ale, or lemonade

Pour equal amounts of beer and ginger beer into chilled glass; stir gently.

### Shanghai Cocktail [SHANG-hi; shang-HI]

1 ¹/₂ oz. (3 Tbsp.) dark rum
³/₄ oz. (1 ¹/₂ Tbsp.) fresh lemon juice
¹/₂ oz. (1 Tbsp.) anisette
¹/₄ to ¹/₂ tsp. grenadine

Shake ingredients with ice; strain into chilled glass.

**Shark's Tooth #1** The original Trader Vic's recipe.

1 oz. (2 Tbsp.) 151-proof rum
$^1/_2$ oz. (1 Tbsp.) fresh lime juice
$^1/_2$ oz. (1 Tbsp.) fresh lemon juice
1 dash (about $^1/_{16}$ tsp.) grenadine
1 dash (about $^1/_{16}$ tsp.) rock candy syrup
cold club soda
lime wedge

Shake all ingredients except club soda and lime wedge with ice; strain into chilled glass. Top with soda, stirring gently; garnish with lime wedge.

**Shark's Tooth #2**

1$^1/_2$ oz. (3 Tbsp.) golden or dark rum
1 tsp. sweet vermouth
1 tsp. sloe gin
1 tsp. passion-fruit syrup
1 tsp. fresh lemon juice
2 dashes (about $^1/_8$ tsp.) Angostura bitters

Shake ingredients with ice; strain into chilled glass.

*I have to think hard to name an interesting man who does not drink.*

RICHARD BURTON, WELSH ACTOR

**Sharky Punch**

1$^1/_2$ oz. (3 Tbsp.) Calvados or other apple brandy
$^1/_2$ oz. (1 Tbsp.) rye whiskey
$^1/_2$ tsp. sugar
cold club soda

Shake all ingredients except club soda with cracked ice. Strain into chilled glass filled halfway with cracked ice. Top with soda, stirring gently.

**sherry** True sherry is a FORTIFIED WINE made in a designated area located in the vicinity of the town of Jerez de la Frontera in southern Spain's Andalusia region. Sherry, along with PORT and MADEIRA, is considered one of the world's great fortified wines. Sherry ranges broadly in color, flavor, and sweetness, but there are fundamentally only two types—fino and oloroso. They are differentiated by alcohol level and a peculiar yeast called *flor*.

**Fino sherry,** a pale, delicate, and very DRY wine, is considered by many to be the world's finest. Its sharp, tangy characteristic is the result of the flor, which also forms a thick layer on the wine's surface, thereby insulating it from oxidization and helping it retain its pale color. Flor won't develop in wines with over $15\frac{1}{2}$ percent alcohol, thereby making fino-style wines less alcoholic. Finos are excellent when young, but may lose some of their vitality when AGED. **Fino amontillado** sherry is amber colored and has a slightly nutty flavor, the result of the fino losing its flor after about 6 years. **Amontillado** is darker in color and softer flavored than a fino amontillado because of longer aging. **Manzanilla** is the lightest, most delicate, and most pungent of the fino-style sherries; **manzanilla pasada** has a nutty flavor and darker color. **Pale cream sherry** is a sweetened fino.

**Oloroso sherry** is fortified up to 18 percent alcohol and is typically DRY. Because of its higher alcohol content, oloroso is not protected by a layer of flor and is therefore exposed to oxidation, which turns its color from gold to brown and contributes rich, nutty-raisiny characteristics to both AROMA and flavor. Olorosos are generally aged longer than other sherries, which makes them more expensive. **Rayas** are lower-grade olorosos; **cream sherries** are heavily sweetened low-grade olorosos. **Amoroso** (also called *East India*) is a sweetened oloroso, as is the very dark, extremely sweet **brown sherry. Golden sherry** is a name sometimes used for very light olorosos.

A true sherry's quality is consistent year after year because the Spanish use the *solera* system of topping off older wines with new ones. The solera system consists of tiers of sherry casks, containing the oldest to the most recently made wines. Typically, one quarter to one third of the oldest wine is drawn off for bottling then replaced by wine from the next oldest tier and so on up through the system. With this process, the older wines infuse the younger ones with CHARACTER, while the younger wines contribute nutrients to the mix (which, in fino-style wines, furnishes the flor with nourishment).

Sherry-style wines are now also made in the United States, and other parts of the world, including Australia and South Africa. Some producers use flor inoculations and the solera system to approximate the Spanish sherries. However, many so-called sherries are inexpensive potables that in no way resemble the Spanish originals. Sherries can be drunk before or after dinner. Dry sherries are usually served chilled, sweet sherries at room temperature.

*Alcohol removes warts.
Not from me—from whomever I'm with.*

JACKIE GLEASON, AMERICAN TV ICON, COMEDIAN, ACTOR

### Sherry Cobbler *see* COBBLER

### Sherry Cocktail

2¹/₂ oz. (¹/₅ Tbsp.) cream sherry
1 to 2 dashes (about ¹/₁₆ to ¹/₈ tsp.) Angostura bitters
orange twist

Stir liquid ingredients with ice. Strain into chilled glass; garnish with orange twist.

### Sherry Eggnog *see* EGGNOG

### sherry glass *see* Glassware, page 10

### Sherry Sangaree *see* SANGAREE

★ **Shirley Temple** One of the original nonalcoholic "cocktails," named for the famous child actor of the 1930s who in later life (as Shirley Temple Black) gained a different kind of fame as a United States diplomat.

about 6 oz. (³/₄ cup) cold ginger ale
1 to 2 tsp. grenadine
orange slice
maraschino cherry

Gently stir together ginger ale and grenadine in chilled glass; add ice cubes, if desired. Garnish with orange slice and cherry.

**shooter** A one-gulp libation that, until the late 1970s, referred to a simple SHOT of straight spirits (WHISKEY, VODKA, etc.) served in a SHOT GLASS. Today's shooters—with names like B-52 and KAMIKAZE—are no longer simple, but have metamorphosed into concoctions of two or more spirits, sometimes layered, sometimes shaken. Most shooters are served NEAT. People who actually like the taste of a good cocktail tend to shake their heads in disbelief at the current shooter craze, for knocking the drink back in one gulp leaves little impression in the mouth. There is one sensation that shooter show-offs *do* report, however, and that's the mind-numbing fog that quickly sets in after two or three in quick succession. *See also* AFTER 5; BRAIN HEMORRHAGE; BUTTERY NIPPLE; CEMENT MIXER; CHIP SHOT SHOOTER; CHOCOLATE-COVERED CHERRY; CORDLESS SCREWDRIVER; GIRL SCOUT COOKIE; GREEN LIZARD; HARBOR LIGHTS; IRA; JELL-O SHOT; JELLY BEAN; KEY LIME PIE; LEMON DROP SHOOTER; LIQUID COCAINE; MELON BALL SHOOTER; MEXICAN FLAG; MIND ERASER; OATMEAL COOKIE; ORGASM; PEPPERMINT PATTY; PRAIRIE FIRE; PURPLE HOOTER; RED SNAPPER SHOOTER; ROOT BEER SHOOTER; RUSSIAN QUAALUDE; SEX ON THE BEACH SHOOTER; SILK PANTIES; SURFER ON ACID; TOOTSIE ROLL; WOO-WOO.

**short drinks** A term for drinks up to 3½ ounces. *See also* TALL DRINKS.

**shot; shot glass** A **shot** is a small amount of alcohol, generally ranging from 1 to 2 ounces. The word "jigger" is a synonym for shot. A **shot glass** is a tiny drinking glass–shaped vessel in which a shot is measured and/or served. Order "a shot of WHISKEY" and you'll get a shot glass of liquor. *See also* Glassware, page 10.

### Shriner Cocktail

1½ oz. (3 Tbsp.) brandy
1½ oz. (3 Tbsp.) sloe gin
½ tsp. sugar syrup
2 dashes (⅛ tsp.) Angostura bitters
lemon twist

Stir liquid ingredients with ice. Strain into chilled glass; garnish with lemon twist.

**Shrub** With its origins in merry old England, a shrub is made by macerating fruit in liquor for 1 to 6 weeks. Nonalcoholic shrubs are made with fruit juice, vinegar, and sugar, and are usually consumed right after mixing. With or without liquor, shrubs are served over ice and can be mixed with soda water if desired.

MAKES ABOUT SIXTEEN 6-OUNCE SERVINGS

64 oz. (2 quarts; 8 cups) brandy or rum
juice and zest (colored portion of peel) of 2 lemons and
   2 oranges
4 cups sugar
32 oz. (1 quart; 4 cups) water
cold club soda, optional
orange slice, optional

Stir liquor with citrus juice and zest in a large glass container. Seal tightly; set in a cool, dark place for 1 week. Bring sugar and water to a boil, stirring until sugar is dissolved; cool to room temperature. Strain liquor and add sugar water, stirring well. Seal tightly in clean bottles and store in a cool, dark place for at least 1 week before serving. Serve over ice cubes, topped with a splash of cold club soda, if desired, and garnished with an orange slice.

**Sidecar** There are several stories as to who created this cocktail, not to mention for whom it was named. It seems to have first appeared in the early 1900s, and many attribute its origins to Harry's Bar in Paris. All agree that it was created for a gent whose preferred mode of transportation was a motorcycle sidecar.

2 oz. ($^{1}/_{4}$ cup) brandy
$^{1}/_{2}$ to $^{3}/_{4}$ oz. (1 to 1$^{1}/_{2}$ Tbsp.) Cointreau or Triple Sec
$^{1}/_{2}$ oz. (1 Tbsp.) fresh lemon juice
lemon twist, optional

Shake liquid ingredients with cracked ice. Strain into chilled glass; drop in lemon twist, if desired.

➤ **Boston Sidecar** Reduce brandy to 1 oz. (2 Tbsp.), add 1 oz. light rum, and substitute lime juice for the lemon juice.

➤ **Gin (Chelsea) Sidecar** Substitute gin for the brandy.

➤ **Polish Sidecar** Reduce brandy to 1$^{1}/_{2}$ oz. (3 Tbsp.), add $^{3}/_{4}$ oz. (1$^{1}/_{2}$ Tbsp.) blackberry brandy, and drop in 2 to 3 fresh blackberries.

## Silk Panties

³/₄ oz. (1¹/₂ Tbsp.) vodka
³/₄ oz. (1¹/₂ Tbsp.) peach schnapps

Shake ingredients with ice; strain into chilled old-fashioned glass over ice cubes or into a shot glass.

## Silver Bullet

1 oz. (2 Tbsp.) gin
1 oz. (2 Tbsp.) kümmel
¹/₂ oz. (1 Tbsp.) fresh lemon juice

Shake ingredients with ice; strain into chilled glass.

## Silver Cocktail

1 oz. (2 Tbsp.) gin
1 oz. (2 Tbsp.) dry vermouth
¹/₂ tsp. maraschino liqueur
2 dashes (about ¹/₈ tsp.) orange bitters
lemon twist

Shake liquid ingredients with ice. Strain into chilled glass; drop in lemon twist.

## Silver Fizz *see* GIN FIZZ

---

*Sign over a Chicago bar:*
IF YOU DRINK TO FORGET, PAY IN ADVANCE.

---

## Silver Streak

1¹/₂ oz. (3 Tbsp.) gin
1 oz. (2 Tbsp.) kümmel

Shake ingredients with ice; strain into chilled glass.

## simple syrup *see* SUGAR SYRUP

**Singapore Sling** This international classic was created by bartender Ngiam Tong Boon at Singapore's Raffles Hotel in 1915. *See also* SLING.

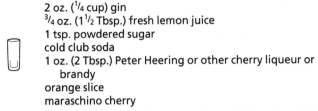

2 oz. (¹/₄ cup) gin
³/₄ oz. (1¹/₂ Tbsp.) fresh lemon juice
1 tsp. powdered sugar
cold club soda
1 oz. (2 Tbsp.) Peter Heering or other cherry liqueur or
    brandy
orange slice
maraschino cherry

Shake first 3 ingredients with ice; strain into chilled glass filled with ice cubes. Top with club soda, stirring gently. Float Peter Heering on top by slowly pouring it over the back (rounded) side of a spoon; don't mix. Garnish with orange slice and cherry.

### single-barrel whiskey *see* BOURBON

### single-malt whisk(e)y
Whiskey made only from malted (*see* MALT) barley and from a "single" distillery. Such whiskeys are typically richer in flavor and usually more expensive than BLENDED WHISK[E]YS. There are myriad single-malt SCOTCHES as well as some single-malt IRISH WHISKEYS available.

### Sink or Swim

1¹/₂ oz. (3 Tbsp.) brandy
2 tsp. sweet vermouth
2 dashes (about ¹/₈ tsp.) Angostura bitters
lime slice

Shake liquid ingredients with ice. Strain into chilled glass; garnish with lime slice.

### sirop d'amandes [see-ROA dah-MAHNDS] *see* ORGEAT
SYRUP; SYRUPS, FLAVORED

### sirop de cassis [see-ROA day kah-SEES] The French name for
black-currant syrup. *See also* SYRUPS, FLAVORED.

*It is an odd but universally held opinion that anyone who doesn't drink must be an alcoholic.*

P. J. O'ROURKE, AMERICAN WIT, AUTHOR

**sirop de citron** [see-ROA day see-TRAW*N*] A sweet syrup with a zesty lemon flavor. *See also* SYRUPS, FLAVORED.

**sirop de groseilles** [see-ROA day groh-ZAY] A sweetened syrup flavored with red currants. *See also* SYRUPS, FLAVORED.

### Sir Walter (Raleigh) Cocktail

1 1/2 oz. (3 Tbsp.) brandy
3/4 oz. (1 1/2 Tbsp.) light rum
1 tsp. Triple Sec
1 tsp. grenadine
1 tsp. fresh lime juice

Shake ingredients with ice; strain into chilled glass.

**Sling** In general, a sling is a RICKEY made with water instead of club soda. *See also* SINGAPORE SLING.

#### Gin Sling

2 oz. (1/4 cup) gin
1/2 oz. (1 Tbsp.) fresh lemon or lime juice
1 1/2 tsp. sugar syrup
cold water
lemon or lime wedge

Pour gin, lemon or lime juice, and sugar syrup into chilled glass filled with ice cubes. Top with water, stirring well. Garnish with lemon or lime wedge.

➤ **Variations** Substitute bourbon, brandy, rum, rye, Scotch, sloe gin, tequila, vodka, or other potable for the gin. The drink is then called by the liquor used, such as "Scotch Sling" and so on.

### Slippery Nipple

1 oz. (2 Tbsp.) Sambuca
1 oz. (2 Tbsp.) Irish cream liqueur

Shake ingredients with ice; strain into chilled glass.

**slivovitz** [SLIHV-uh-vihts; SLIHV-uh-wihts] A DRY, colorless, slightly bitter plum BRANDY.

*𝒷randy,* n. *A cordial composed of one part thunder-and-lightning, one part remorse, two parts bloody murder, one part death-hell-and-the-grave, and four parts clarified Satan.*

AMBROSE BIERCE, AMERICAN SATIRIST

### Sloe Comfortable Screw *See also* SLOE SCREW.

1¹/₂ oz. (3 Tbsp.) vodka
¹/₂ oz. (1 Tbsp.) sloe gin
¹/₂ oz. (1 Tbsp.) Southern Comfort
about 4 ounces (¹/₂ cup) cold fresh orange juice

Fill chilled glass with ice cubes. Add first 3 ingredients; top with orange juice, stirring well.

**sloe gin** Not a "real" GIN, but a sweet, red, wood-aged LIQUEUR based on gin. Its name comes from the fact that it is flavored with the fruit of the blackthorn tree, the sloe plum.

### Sloe Gin Cocktail

2 oz. (¹/₄ cup) sloe gin
¹/₂ tsp. dry vermouth
1 dash (about ¹/₁₆ tsp.) orange bitters

Stir ingredients with ice; strain into chilled glass.

### Sloe Gin Fizz *see* GIN FIZZ

### Sloe Gin Rickey *see* GIN RICKEY

### Sloe Gin Sling *see* SLING

**Sloe Screw** The provocative name comes from the fact that this drink is like a SCREWDRIVER made with SLOE GIN. Although the traditional way to prepare it is to stir the two ingredients together, it's much showier to float the orange juice on top of the sloe gin and let the imbiber stir his/her own. Add SOUTHERN COMFORT and VODKA, and you have a SLOE COMFORTABLE SCREW.

1¹/₂ oz. (3 Tbsp.) sloe gin
about 4 ounces (¹/₂ cup) fresh orange juice

Pour ingredients into chilled glass filled with ice cubes; stir well. Or pour sloe gin into chilled glass filled with ice cubes, then float orange juice on top by slowly pouring it over the back (rounded) side of a spoon; don't mix.

### Sloe Tequila

1 oz. (2 Tbsp.) tequila
$^1/_2$ oz. (1 Tbsp.) sloe gin
$^1/_2$ oz. (1 Tbsp.) fresh lime juice
$^1/_2$ cup crushed ice
long strip of cucumber peel

Combine all ingredients except cucumber peel in a blender. Cover and process at medium speed until smooth, about 15 seconds; pour into chilled glass. Add ice cubes; garnish with cucumber peel.

### Sloe Vermouth

1 oz. (2 Tbsp.) sloe gin
1 oz. (2 Tbsp.) dry vermouth
2 tsp. fresh lemon juice

Shake ingredients with ice; strain into chilled glass.

### Sloppy Joe's Cocktail #1

$^3/_4$ oz. (1$^1/_2$ Tbsp.) light rum
$^3/_4$ oz. (1$^1/_2$ Tbsp.) dry vermouth
$^1/_2$ oz. (1 Tbsp.) fresh lime juice
$^1/_4$ tsp. grenadine
$^1/_4$ tsp. Triple Sec

Shake ingredients with ice; strain into chilled glass.

### Sloppy Joe's Cocktail #2

$^3/_4$ oz. (1$^1/_2$ Tbsp.) brandy
$^3/_4$ oz. (1$^1/_2$ Tbsp.) ruby port
$^3/_4$ oz. (1$^1/_2$ Tbsp.) pineapple juice
$^1/_4$ tsp. grenadine
$^1/_4$ tsp. Triple Sec

Shake ingredients with ice; strain into chilled glass.

**small-batch whiskey** *see* BOURBON

★ **Smart Head** *see* EGGHEAD

> *y the time a bartender knows what drink a man will have before he orders, there is little else about him worth knowing.*

DON MARQUIS, AMERICAN HUMORIST, JOURNALIST

**smash** Said to have been named after the finely crushed ice over which this drink is served, a smash is basically a short JULEP.

### Brandy Smash

6 medium fresh mint leaves
1 tsp. sugar
½ oz. (1 Tbsp.) cold club soda
2 oz. (¼ cup) brandy
orange slice
maraschino cherry
mint sprig

Muddle mint leaves, sugar, and club soda in chilled glass until leaves are crushed and sugar is dissolved. Fill glass with crushed ice. Pour in brandy; stir thoroughly. Add more crushed ice to within ½ inch of rim; garnish with orange slice, cherry, and mint sprig; serve with straw.

➤ **Variations** Substitute cider, gin, rum, or Scotch for the brandy. The drink is then called by the liquor used, such as "Scotch Smash" and so on.

**★ Sneaky Colada** *see* PIÑA COLADA

**snifter** *see* Glassware, page 10

**snort** A snort, alcoholically speaking, is simply a drink, often taken in one gulp like a SHOT. A "snorter" is an extra-large version of the same.

### Snowball

1½ oz. (3 Tbsp.) gin
½ oz. (1 Tbsp.) Pernod or other anise-flavored liqueur
½ oz. (1 Tbsp.) cream

Shake ingredients with ice; strain into chilled glass.

⭐ **Sober Clam Digger** *see* CLAM DIGGER

**soda water** *see* CLUB SODA

⭐ **Soft Cider Cup** *see* CIDER CUP

**soft drink** A generic term for a beverage that doesn't contain alcohol. The majority of soft drinks are carbonated, although effervescence is not a requisite.

**Sombrero** [sawm-BREH-roh]

2 oz. (¹/₄ cup) coffee-flavored brandy, Kahlúa, or Tia Maria
1 oz. (2 Tbsp.) cream

Pour brandy into chilled glass filled with ice cubes. Float cream on top by slowly pouring it over the back (rounded) side of a spoon; don't mix.

*Some men are like musical glasses—to produce their finest tones you must keep them wet.*

SAMUEL TAYLOR COLERIDGE, ENGLISH POET, CRITIC

**Sour** One of the classic cocktails, the sour dates back to at least the mid-nineteenth century. Its moniker comes from—you guessed it—its flavor, contributed by fresh lemon juice, to which liquor and a soupçon of sugar are added. Although the Whiskey Sour is the original, there are myriad renditions using other liquors, eggs, and LIQUEURS. The one thing all sours have in common is that they're always shaken and traditionally served in their namesake SOUR GLASS, but they may also be served in an OLD-FASHIONED or HIGHBALL GLASS, either STRAIGHT UP or ON THE ROCKS. *See also* AGED WHISKEY SOURS; EGG SOUR.

**Whiskey Sour**

2 oz. (¹/₄ cup) blended whiskey
³/₄ to 1 oz. (1¹/₂ to 2 Tbsp.) fresh lemon juice
1 tsp. powdered sugar
half slice orange or lemon
maraschino cherry

Shake liquid ingredients with ice. Strain into chilled glass; garnish with orange or lemon slice and cherry.

➤ **Variations** Substitute brandy, gin, rum, tequila, or vodka for the whiskey. The drink is then called by the liquor used, such as "Brandy Sour" and so on.

➤ **Boston Sour** Add 1 egg white to ingredients; shake vigorously.

➤ **Double Standard Sour** Reduce whiskey to ³/₄ oz. (1¹/₂ Tbsp.) and add ³/₄ oz. gin plus ¹/₂ tsp. grenadine.

➤ **Fireman's Sour** Substitute light rum for the whiskey and 1 oz. (2 Tbsp.) fresh lime juice for the lemon juice; add 1 to 2 tsp. grenadine.

➤ **Frisco Sour** Add 2 tsp. Bénédictine; use half lemon juice and half lime juice.

➤ **New York Sour** Make whiskey sour as usual; pour into glass. Float ¹/₂ to 1 oz. (1 to 2 Tbsp.) dry red wine (Cabernet Sauvignon, Burgundy, etc.) on top.

➤ **Scotch Holiday Sour** Use Scotch whisky and add 1 oz. (2 Tbsp.) cherry brandy and ¹/₂ oz. (1 Tbsp.) sweet vermouth; garnish with lemon slice.

**sour glass** *see* Glassware, page 10

**sour mash** *see* BOURBON; MASH

## Southern Bride

1¹/₂ oz. (3 Tbsp.) gin
1 oz. (2 Tbsp.) unsweetened grapefruit juice
¹/₄ tsp. maraschino liqueur

Shake ingredients with ice; strain into chilled glass.

**Southern Comfort** The oldest American LIQUEUR, Southern Comfort is BOURBON based and amber colored, and has a sweet, smooth flavor reminiscent of oranges and peaches. *See also* PEACH-FLAVORED SPIRITS; WHISK(E)Y-BASED LIQUEURS.

## Southern Gin Cocktail

2 oz. ($^1/_4$ cup) gin
$^1/_2$ tsp. Triple Sec
2 dashes (about $^1/_8$ tsp.) orange bitters
lemon twist

Shake liquid ingredients with ice. Strain into chilled glass; drop in lemon twist.

## Soviet

$1^1/_2$ oz. (3 Tbsp.) vodka
$^1/_2$ oz. (1 Tbsp.) dry vermouth
$^1/_2$ oz. (1 Tbsp.) Amontillado sherry
lemon twist

Shake liquid ingredients with ice. Strain into chilled glass; drop in lemon twist.

## Spanish Town Cocktail

2 oz. ($^1/_4$ cup) light rum
$^1/_2$ tsp. Triple Sec

Shake ingredients with ice; strain into chilled glass.

**sparkling water** Any water that's effervescent, either through natural or manmade carbonation. *See also* club soda.

**sparkling wine** *see* wine

## Special Rough Cocktail

$1^1/_2$ oz. (3 Tbsp.) apple brandy
$1^1/_2$ oz. (3 Tbsp.) brandy
$^1/_2$ tsp. Pernod or other anise-flavored liqueur

Stir ingredients with ice; strain into chilled glass.

*My first wife drove me to drink. I shall always be grateful to her for that.*

W. C. FIELDS, AMERICAN ACTOR

**spirit(s)** A general term for alcoholic beverages. *See also* alcohol; liquor.

**Spritzer** A spritzer can be served in almost any drinking vessel, from a WINEGLASS to a COLLINS GLASS. The size you use dictates the amount of wine (or other spirit) you will put in it, but the basic proportion is about half wine, half club soda. Starting with chilled wine will mean less dilution by melting ice cubes.

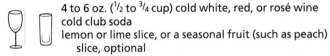

4 to 6 oz. ($^{1}/_{2}$ to $^{3}/_{4}$ cup) cold white, red, or rosé wine
cold club soda
lemon or lime slice, or a seasonal fruit (such as peach) slice, optional

Pour wine into chilled glass filled with ice cubes. Add club soda, stirring gently. If desired, garnish with fruit.

**Spumante;** *pl.* **Spumanti** [spoo-MAHN-tay; spoo-MAHN-tee] 1. The Italian word for "sparkling." 2. A generic term for Italian SPARKLING WINES. *See also* ASTI SPUMANTE; CHAMPAGNE.

**Star Cocktail**

1$^{1}/_{2}$ oz. (3 Tbsp.) apple brandy
1$^{1}/_{2}$ oz. (3 Tbsp.) sweet vermouth
2 dashes (about $^{1}/_{8}$ tsp.) Angostura bitters
lemon twist

Stir liquid ingredients with ice. Strain into chilled glass; drop in lemon twist.

**Star Daisy** *see* DAISY

**Stars and Stripes** *See* Floating and Layering Techniques, page 30.

$^{1}/_{2}$ oz. (1 Tbsp.) grenadine or maraschino liqueur
$^{1}/_{2}$ oz. (1 Tbsp.) cream
$^{1}/_{2}$ oz. (1 Tbsp.) blue curaçao

Pour first ingredient into chilled glass. One by one, add remaining ingredients in order given, slowly pouring each one over the back (rounded) side of a spoon so that each one floats on top of the one below. Don't mix.

**Steinhäger** A special German GIN made from a MASH of crushed juniper berries, then redistilled in a pot still (*see* DISTILLATION). Steinhäger is named for the Westphalian town where it's made.

*A bartender throws this drunk out of his bar. Minutes later, the guy's back, demanding a whiskey, only to be thrown out again. This happens four more times before the drunk, shaking his head, says, "For Pete's sake, d'ya work in every joint on this block?"*

**still** *see* DISTILLATION

**still wine** *see* WINE

**Stinger** Although Stingers can be made with any kind of liquor, the classic version employs brandy.

> 1 ½ oz. (3 Tbsp.) brandy
> ¾ oz. (1 ½ Tbsp.) white crème de menthe

Shake ingredients with ice; strain into chilled cocktail or old-fashioned glass, either straight up or over crushed ice.

➤ **Variations** Substitute bourbon, rum, Galliano, Scotch, tequila, vodka, or other potable for the brandy. The drink is then called by the liquor used, such as "Tequila Stinger" and so on.

➤ **Green Russian** Substitute vodka for the brandy and green crème de menthe for the white.

➤ **Turkey Shoot** Substitute Wild Turkey bourbon for the brandy. If desired, serve in a brandy snifter.

**Stirrup Cup**

> 1 ½ oz. (3 Tbsp.) brandy
> 1 ½ oz. (3 Tbsp.) cherry brandy
> ¾ oz. (1 ½ Tbsp.) fresh lemon juice
> 1 tsp. powdered sugar

Shake ingredients with ice; strain into chilled glass over ice cubes.

**Stone Fence**

> 2 oz. (¼ cup) Scotch
> 2 dashes (about ⅛ tsp.) Angostura bitters
> cold club soda or apple cider

Pour Scotch and bitters into chilled glass filled with ice cubes. Top with club soda or cider, stirring gently.

**Stonsdorfer bitters** *See* BITTERS

*ost people hate the taste of beer—to begin with. It is, however, a prejudice that many people have been able to overcome.*

WINSTON CHURCHILL, BRITISH POLITICIAN, AUTHOR

**stout** A strong, dark (almost black) ALE that originated in the British Isles. **Dry stout** or **Irish stout** has a hoppier (*see* HOPS) character and is less malty (*see* MALT). American versions are often made with a combination of pale malt and dark-roasted *unmalted* barley, while European stouts are generally made totally with malted barley. Ireland's **Guinness** is the most famous of the DRY stouts. **Sweet stout,** an English version, is less bitter and often lower in alcohol. Because some sweet stouts have a slightly lactic flavor they're sometimes referred to as **milk stouts. Oatmeal stout** is a style of sweet stout that uses oatmeal, which adds a silky-smooth mouth-feel. **Russian stout** or **Imperial stout** was originally a very strong-flavored, high-alcohol brew produced in Britain from the late 1700s until the early 1900s for export to Russia. Modern versions—also strongly flavored and high in alcohol—are unpasteurized, cask AGED for 2 months, and bottle aged for a year. *See also* BEER.

**Straight Law**

1 ½ oz. (3 Tbsp.) dry sherry
¾ oz. (1 ½ Tbsp.) gin
lemon twist

Shake liquid ingredients with ice. Strain into chilled glass; drop in lemon twist.

**straight up; straight** A term for a drink served sans ice, as opposed to one served over ice (ON THE ROCKS). It can either refer to straight liquor poured into a chilled glass, or to a drink first mixed with ice, then strained into a chilled glass (as with a MAR-TINI). This term is sometimes simplified to "up."

**strainer** *see* Bar Equipment, page 7

**strawberry-flavored spirits** *see* FRAISE DES BOIS

**Strega** [STRAY-gah] Italian for "witch," this refreshing, herb-flavored LIQUEUR is bewitching, indeed. Strega, also called *Liquore Strega,* is made from over 70 herbs and has a brilliant, shimmering yellow-green color. *See also* HERB-FLAVORED SPIRITS.

**Strega Flip**

1 oz. (2 Tbsp.) Strega
1 oz. (2 Tbsp.) brandy
2 tsp. fresh orange juice
1 tsp. fresh lemon juice
1 tsp. powdered sugar
1 egg
freshly grated nutmeg

Vigorously shake all ingredients except nutmeg with ice. Strain into chilled glass; sprinkle with nutmeg.

**stuffed** Bartender lingo for filling a glass as full as possible with ice. Stuffed is the opposite of NEAT.

**sugar syrup** Also called *simple syrup* (particularly among bartenders) and *gomme syrup,* sugar syrup is a cooked solution of sugar and water. For recipe, *see* Ingredients, page 19.

**Suissesse** [sweess-EHSS]

1$\frac{1}{2}$ oz. (3 Tbsp.) Pernod or other anise-flavored liqueur
$\frac{1}{2}$ oz. (1 Tbsp.) anisette
$\frac{1}{2}$ egg white (about 1 Tbsp.) (*See* page 14, How to Divide Egg Whites in Half)
$\frac{1}{4}$ tsp. cream, optional

Vigorously shake ingredients with ice; strain into chilled glass.

**Surfer on Acid**

$\frac{3}{4}$ oz. (1$\frac{1}{2}$ Tbsp.) Malibu
$\frac{3}{4}$ oz. (1$\frac{1}{2}$ Tbsp.) Jägermeister
$\frac{1}{2}$ oz. (1 Tbsp.) unsweetened pineapple juice

Shake ingredients with ice; strain into chilled glass.

**suze** [SEUZ] A bright yellow, extremely bitter, and astringent French APÉRITIF based on gentian root.

**Swedish Punsch** A RUM-based LIQUEUR with a spicy-sweet flavor. It's either taken as an after-dinner drink or mixed with hot water and served as a punch.

**sweet & sour mix** *see* Ingredients, page 19

---

*The three-martini lunch is the epitome of American efficiency. Where else can you get an earful, a bellyful, and a snootful at the same time?*

GERALD R. FORD, 38TH UNITED STATES PRESIDENT

---

**Sweet Martini** *see* MARTINI

**swill** *n.* In the world of alcohol the word "swill" refers to BOOZE of appalling quality. **swill** *v.* To grossly guzzle a drink.

**Swizzle** *n.* Originating in the Caribbean and dating back to at least the early 1800s, swizzles began as tall rum drinks poured over crushed ice and "swizzled" with a long, sturdy twig. The swizzling was accomplished by placing the twig between one's palms and rapidly rubbing them together, thereby gyrating the twig and producing a frosty libation, with the liquor diluted by the melting ice. Today's swizzle is more likely to be stirred with a long spoon, and it can be made with almost any type of spirit. The drink is named after whatever liquor is in it, as in "Gin Swizzle" or "Rum Swizzle." *See also* APPLE SWIZZLE; INDEPENDENCE SWIZZLE; QUEEN'S PARK SWIZZLE. **swizzle** *v.* 1. To agitate a beverage with a SWIZZLE STICK, thereby mixing the ingredients. 2. To knock back a drink in gulps.

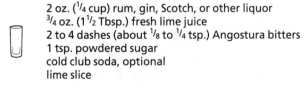

2 oz. (¹/₄ cup) rum, gin, Scotch, or other liquor
³/₄ oz. (1¹/₂ Tbsp.) fresh lime juice
2 to 4 dashes (about ¹/₈ to ¹/₄ tsp.) Angostura bitters
1 tsp. powdered sugar
cold club soda, optional
lime slice

Pour first 4 ingredients into chilled glass filled with crushed ice. Rub a swizzle stick rapidly back and forth between your palms (or stir rapidly with a long spoon) until ingredients are mixed. Top with club soda, if desired, stirring gently; garnish with lime slice.

*There are only two times when I drink:*
*When I'm with someone and when I'm alone.*
DEE NIAL

**swizzle stick** A rod for stirring cocktails in the glass. Swizzle sticks are made of various materials (glass, twisted cellophane, wood, etc.) and come in several lengths. They're also called *cocktail sticks. See also* ROCK CANDY SWIZZLE STICK.

**syrups, flavored** Flavored syrups—GRENADINE being the most widely known—are used in mixed drinks for flavor and sweetness. Made with concentrated fruit juices and other flavorings, they come in myriad flavors including almond, apricot, banana, blueberry, caramel, coconut, coffee, cranberry, grenadine, hazelnut, lemon, lime, mango, maple, mint, orange, papaya, passion fruit, raspberry, strawberry, and vanilla. Moderation is the byword when using these syrups in drinks, as their flavors are very concentrated. *See also* FALERNUM; ORGEAT SYRUP, SIROP DE CASSIS; SIROP DE CITRON; SIROP DE GROSEILLES; SUGAR SYRUP.

### Tahiti Club

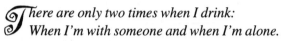

2 oz. (¼ cup) light rum
½ oz. (1 Tbsp.) fresh lime juice
½ oz. (1 Tbsp.) fresh lemon juice
½ oz. (1 Tbsp.) unsweetened pineapple juice
½ tsp. maraschino liqueur
lime or lemon slice

Shake liquid ingredients with ice. Strain into chilled glass over ice cubes; garnish with lime or lemon slice.

### Tailspin

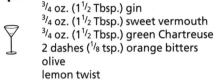

³/₄ oz. (1¹/₂ Tbsp.) gin
³/₄ oz. (1¹/₂ Tbsp.) sweet vermouth
³/₄ oz. (1¹/₂ Tbsp.) green Chartreuse
2 dashes (¹/₈ tsp.) orange bitters
olive
lemon twist

Shake liquid ingredients with ice. Strain into chilled glass half filled with crushed ice; drop in olive and lemon twist.

**tall drinks** A term for drinks containing 6 or more ounces. The term "tall" is also used when asking for a drink that is customarily served in a short (OLD-FASHIONED) glass to be served in a larger one, such as a COLLINS GLASS or a HIGHBALL GLASS. Also known as a LONG DRINK. *See also* SHORT DRINKS.

★ **T and B** Short for *Tonic and Bitters*—our favorite nonalcoholic refresher!

4 to 6 dashes (about ¹/₄ to ³/₈ tsp.) Angostura bitters
¹/₄ lime
cold tonic water

Fill chilled glass with ice cubes. Add bitters and squeeze out the lime juice, dropping the shell into the glass. Top with tonic water, stirring gently.

### Tango Cocktail

1 oz. (2 Tbsp.) gin
¹/₂ oz. (1 Tbsp.) dry vermouth
¹/₂ oz. (1 Tbsp.) sweet vermouth
¹/₂ oz. (1 Tbsp.) fresh orange juice
¹/₂ tsp. Triple Sec

Shake ingredients with ice; strain into chilled glass.

**tannin** An astringent substance (tannic acid) found in a wide variety of plants and tree barks. Tannin in wine, for example, comes from grape seeds, skins, and stems as well as from oak barrels, particularly new ones. The word comes from the French *tan,* "crushed oak bark."

**teetotaler** [tee-TOHT-ler] Someone who wouldn't buy this book because they don't drink anything alcoholic.

*All of the great villainies of history, from the murder of Abel to the Treaty of Versailles, have been perpetuated by sober men, and chiefly by teetotallers.*

H. L. MENCKEN, AMERICAN JOURNALIST, AUTHOR

## Temptation Cocktail

1 1/2 oz. (3 Tbsp.) whiskey
1/4 tsp. Pernod or other anise-flavored liqueur
1/4 tsp. Dubonnet rouge
1/4 tsp. Cointreau
orange twist
lemon twist

Shake liquid ingredients with ice. Strain into chilled glass; drop in citrus twists.

## Tempter Cocktail

1 1/2 oz. (3 Tbsp.) ruby port
1 1/2 (3 Tbsp.) apricot brandy

Shake ingredients with ice; strain into chilled glass over ice cubes.

## Tennessee

2 oz. (1/4 cup) rye whiskey
3/4 oz. (1 1/2 Tbsp.) maraschino liqueur
1/2 oz. (1 Tbsp.) fresh lemon juice

Shake ingredients with ice; strain into chilled glass over ice cubes.

**Tennessee whiskey** A straight WHISKEY that is, for the most part, very similar to BOURBON, which is why it's sometimes called "Tennessee bourbon." It must be made from a MASH containing at least 51 percent of a single grain (usually, but not always, corn), must not exceed 160 PROOF (80 percent alcohol), must be AGED in oak barrels for 2 years, and may only be diluted with water to no less than 80 proof. The biggest difference between bourbon and Tennessee whiskey is that the latter is slowly filtered through large vats of sugar-maple charcoal, which gives it a definitively sweet characteristic. Jack Daniel's and George

Dickel are the major producers of Tennessee whiskey. *See also* WHISK(E)Y-BASED LIQUEURS.

**tequila** [teh-KEE-luh] Tequila is made in and around the small town of Tequila, in Mexico's Jalisco province. Mexico has decreed that, in order to be classified as tequila, DISTILLED SPIRITS must be produced from blue agave plants grown in a precisely delineated area in the five Mexican states of Guanajuato, Jalisco, Michoacan, Nayarit, and Tamaulipas. Tequila must comprise at least 51 percent blue agave; the most common ingredient utilized for the remaining 49 percent is sugarcane, although other raw products may be used. Tequilas labeled "100% Blue Agave" are generally the best. The blue agave, which is genetically closer to a lily than a cactus, can take 8 to 12 years to mature. At that point the plants are cut off at the root and trimmed to remove the outer leaves, exposing the heart (called *piña,* "pineapple," by the Mexicans after the fruit it resembles), which weighs 50 to 150 pounds and contains a sweet juice called *aguamiel,* "honey water." These huge agave hearts are transported to the distillery, where they are steamed or roasted to extract their sugars. After the cooked agave is shredded, it's FERMENTED for several days before being DISTILLED twice in pot stills (a process similar to that for COGNAC) to about 150 PROOF. Tequila is generally bottled at 80 proof, although some of the AGED versions are bottled at high alcohol levels.

By Mexican law, there are four categories of tequila: *blanco, joven abocado, reposado,* and *añejo.* Tequila **blanco,** also known as *white, silver,* or *plata,* is bottled soon after distillation. Its flavor is smooth and fresh with an herbaceous, peppery quality. Tequila **joven abocado,** also called *gold,* is a tequila blanco with flavoring and coloring added, typically through the addition of caramel. Legally it does not have to be aged. Tequila **reposado,** which may also have flavoring and coloring added, must be aged a minimum of 2 months, and can be aged for up to a year. Wood aging (usually in oak, sometimes redwood) endows reposados with hints of vanilla and spice and produces a mellower CHARACTER than that of tequila blanco. Some reposados also use the word "gold" on their label, which has promoted the impression that all golds have been aged, although there's no legal requirement as such. Tequila **añejo** is aged for at least 1 year and often 2 to 3 years. The best añejos (which some liken to fine cognacs) have a smooth, elegant, complex flavor, the result of a perfect marriage between wood aging and the intrinsically sweet agave. Popular brands of tequila include Herradura, José Cuervo, Patrón, Pepe Lopez, Porfidio, Sauza, El Tesoro de Don Felipe, Torada, and El Viejito. *See also* MEZCAL and PULQUE.

---

*Lead me not into temptation; I can find the way myself.*
RITA MAE BROWN, AMERICAN AUTHOR

---

## Tequila Ghost

2 oz. (¹/₄ cup) tequila
1 oz. (2 Tbsp.) Pernod or other anise-flavored liqueur
¹/₂ oz. (1 Tbsp.) fresh lemon juice

Shake ingredients with ice; strain into chilled glass over ice cubes.

## Tequila Maria *see* BLOODY MARIA

## Tequila Mockingbird

2 oz. (¹/₄ cup) tequila
1 oz. (2 Tbsp.) white crème de menthe
¹/₂ oz. (1 Tbsp.) fresh lime juice
lime slice

Shake liquid ingredients with ice. Strain into chilled glass; garnish with lime slice.

## Tequila Rickey *see* RICKEY

## Tequila Sling *see* SLING

## Tequila Sour *see* SOUR

## Tequila Stinger *see* STINGER

**Tequila Sunrise** Because the grenadine is heavier than the other ingredients in this drink, it sinks to the bottom, creating a red "sunrise" effect, contrasting with the yellow-gold orange juice.

1 1/2 oz. (3 Tbsp.) tequila
about 6 oz. (3/4 cup) fresh orange juice
1/2 to 1 oz. (1 to 2 Tbsp.) grenadine
orange slice

Place 3 to 4 ice cubes in chilled glass; add tequila. Pour in orange juice to within 1 1/2 inches of glass rim; stir well. Add grenadine, letting it settle to the bottom of the glass (do not stir). Garnish with orange slice.

★ **Grenada Sunset** Omit tequila; add 4 dashes (about 1/4 tsp.) orange bitters.

## Tequini *see* MARTINI

## Terminator *See* Floating and Layering Techniques, page 30.

1/2 oz. (1 Tbsp.) Kahlúa or Tia Maria
1/2 oz. (1 Tbsp.) Irish cream liqueur
1/2 oz. (1 Tbsp.) Sambuca
1/2 oz. (1 Tbsp.) Grand Marnier or Triple Sec
1/2 oz. (1 Tbsp.) vodka

Pour first ingredient into glass. One by one, add remaining ingredients in order given, slowly pouring each one over the back (rounded) side of a spoon so that each one floats on top of the one below. Do not mix.

## Thanksgiving Special

1 oz. (2 Tbsp.) gin
1 oz. (2 Tbsp.) dry vermouth
1 oz. (2 Tbsp.) apricot brandy
1/4 tsp. fresh lemon juice
maraschino cherry

Shake liquid ingredients with ice. Strain into chilled glass; garnish with cherry.

## Third Degree Cocktail *see* MARTINI

## Third Rail Cocktail

3/4 oz. (1 1/2 Tbsp.) light rum
3/4 oz. (1 1/2 Tbsp.) brandy
3/4 oz. (1 1/2 Tbsp.) apple brandy
1/4 tsp. Pernod or other anise-flavored liqueur

Shake ingredients with ice; strain into chilled glass.

### Thistle Cocktail

1 1/2 oz. (3 Tbsp.) Scotch
1 1/2 oz. (3 Tbsp.) sweet vermouth
2 dashes (about 1/8 tsp.) Angostura bitters

Stir ingredients with ice; strain into chilled glass.

### Three Miller Cocktail

1 1/2 oz. (3 Tbsp.) light rum
3/4 oz. (1 1/2 Tbsp.) brandy
1 tsp. grenadine
1/4 tsp. fresh lemon juice
lemon twist, optional

Shake liquid ingredients with ice. Strain into chilled glass; drop in lemon twist, if desired.

**three sheets to (in) the wind** An expression commonly used for someone who's drunk: "He's three sheets to the wind." It comes from a sailor's expression relating to securing the three corners of a sail to a boat with ropes, referred to as "sheets." If all three sheets were unsecured, the sail would flutter and flap "in the wind," causing the vessel to sway uncontrollably.

*I decided to stop drinking with creeps. I decided to drink only with friends. I've lost 30 pounds.*

ERNEST HEMINGWAY, AMERICAN AUTHOR

### Three Stripes Cocktail

1 oz. (2 Tbsp.) gin
1/2 oz. (1 Tbsp.) dry vermouth
1/2 oz. (1 Tbsp.) fresh orange juice

Shake ingredients with ice; strain into chilled glass.

### Thunder Cocktail

2 1/2 oz. (5 Tbsp.) brandy
1 egg yolk
1/2 tsp. sugar
Pinch of cayenne pepper

Vigorously shake ingredients with cracked ice; strain into chilled glass.

**Tia Maria** Made in Jamaica, this RUM-based, coffee-flavored LIQUEUR is purportedly made from a formula that dates back to the mid-seventeenth century. It's said that when the British seized Jamaica (then belonging to Spain) in 1655, the formula for this now famous liqueur was saved by a Jamaican family's housekeeper, Tia Maria. Drier and lighter than KAHLÚA, Tia Maria is made from Blue Mountain coffee. *See also* COFFEE-FLAVORED SPIRITS.

### Tiger's Milk

4 oz. ($^1/_2$ cup) half & half
1 oz. (2 Tbsp.) golden or dark rum
1 oz. (2 Tbsp.) brandy
1 tsp. sugar
freshly grated nutmeg

Shake all the ingredients except nutmeg with ice. Strain into chilled glass; sprinkle with nutmeg.

### Tiger Tail

6 oz. ($^3/_4$ cup) fresh orange juice
1$^1/_2$ oz. (3 Tbsp.) Pernod or other anise-flavored liqueur
lime slice

Pour liquid ingredients into chilled glass filled with ice cubes; stir well. Garnish with lime slice.

**Tiramisu** [tih-ruh-mee-SOO] A dark brown Italian LIQUEUR with a pronounced coffee-almond flavor. Its namesake is the ethereal Italian dessert that layers spongecake brushed with a coffee-Marsala mixture with mascarpone cheese and chocolate. The Italian word *tiramisù* translates to "carry me up," presumably to heaven. *See also* COFFEE-FLAVORED SPIRITS.

### TNT

1$^1/_2$ oz. (3 Tbsp.) rye whiskey
1$^1/_2$ oz. (3 Tbsp.) Pernod or other anise-flavored liqueur
Shake ingredients with ice; strain into chilled glass.

**toast** *see* The Art of Toasting, page 36

## Toasted Almond

1½ oz. (3 Tbsp.) Kahlúa or other coffee liqueur
1½ oz. (3 Tbsp.) half & half
1 oz. (2 Tbsp.) amaretto

Shake ingredients with ice; strain into chilled glass over ice cubes.

**toddy;** *pl.* **toddies** Although toddy has different meanings around the world, in the United States and Britain it refers to a hot water–based drink, generally spiced and liberally laced with liquor. The word "toddy" is a derivation of *tari,* the sweet sap of several Asian palm trees, which was used to make fermented beverages, alcoholic and otherwise. *See also* HOT BRICK TODDY; HOT TODDY.

## Tom and Jerry *See also* Hot Drinks, page 29.

1 egg
1 oz. (2 Tbsp.) dark rum
1 oz. (2 Tbsp.) brandy
1 tsp. sugar
about 6 oz. (³/₄ cup) boiling water or hot milk
freshly grated nutmeg

Separate egg and combine yolk with rum and brandy in small bowl; whisk with a fork until frothy. In another bowl, beat egg white until soft peaks form. Add sugar and beat until stiff; fold into egg-liquor mixture. Pour mixture into warm mug; top with hot water or milk, stirring gently. Sprinkle with nutmeg.

> *When things get too unpleasant, I burn the day's newspaper, pull down the curtains, get out the jugs, and put in a civilized evening.*
>
> H. L. MENCKEN, AMERICAN JOURNALIST, AUTHOR

**Tom Collins** This most popular member of the COLLINS family dates back to about the mid-nineteenth century, although there is some question whether it originated in England, America, or Australia. According to some pundits, the name comes from the fact that this drink was originally made with Old Tom, a sweetened gin now made only in limited quantities. Others claim that it was named after the bartender who created it, though none can pinpoint when and where. Whatever its origin, the modern Tom Collins is made with DRY gin. In days of old, a counterpart—John Collins—was made with GENEVER gin but now uses WHISKEY. A FRENCH 75 is a Collins made with COGNAC and CHAMPAGNE.

> 2 oz. (¼ cup) gin
> 1 oz. (2 Tbsp.) fresh lemon juice
> 1 tsp. powdered sugar
> cold club soda
> lemon slice
> maraschino cherry

Combine first 3 ingredients in chilled glass; stir well. Add 3 to 4 ice cubes; top with club soda, stirring gently. Garnish with lemon slice and cherry.

➤ **Variations** Substitute bourbon, brandy, rum, rye, Scotch, tequila, vodka, or other potable for the gin. The drink is then called by the liquor used, such as "VODKA Collins" and so on.

### Tonic and Bitters *see* T and B

**tonic water** A processed water charged with carbon dioxide and flavored with fruit extracts, sugar (or artificial sweetener), and a soupçon of QUININE, which is why it's also sometimes called "quinine water." Tonic water is a favorite mixer, as in the popular GIN AND TONIC.

### Tootsie Roll

> ½ oz. (1 Tbsp.) vodka
> ½ oz. (1 Tbsp.) crème de cacao
> ½ oz. (1 Tbsp.) cold fresh orange juice

Pour all ingredients into chilled glass.

**top, to; top off** In the bartending world, the term "top" is synonymous with "fill." Otherwise, to "top with soda water" means to "fill it to the top."

**Toreador** [TOR-ee-uh-dor] For the lightest dusting of cocoa, place the powder in a fine strainer and gently shake it over the drink.

1 ½ oz. (3 Tbsp.) tequila
½ oz. (1 Tbsp.) white crème de cacao
dollop of whipped cream
unsweetened cocoa powder

Shake tequila and crème de cacao with ice; strain into chilled glass. Top with whipped cream; dust lightly with cocoa.

**Torridora Cocktail** [TORR-ee-doh-rah]

1 ½ oz. (3 Tbsp.) light rum
½ oz. (1 Tbsp.) coffee-flavored brandy, Kahlúa, or Tia Maria
1 ½ tsp. cream
1 tsp. 151-proof rum

Shake first 3 ingredients with ice; strain into chilled glass. Float 151-proof rum on top by slowly pouring it over the back (rounded) side of a spoon; don't mix.

**tot** A British term for a small amount, generally of liquor, as in "I'll just have a wee tot." Synonymous with the noun NIP.

**Tovarich Cocktail** [tuh-VAHR-ich]

1 ½ oz. (3 Tbsp.) vodka
1 oz. (2 Tbsp.) kümmel
½ oz. (1 Tbsp.) fresh lime juice

Shake ingredients with ice; strain into chilled glass.

**Trappist beer** Dating back to the Middle Ages, Trappist beers refer to any of the ALES produced by the six brewing abbeys still in existence (Schaapskooi in the Netherlands; Chimay, Orval, Rochefort, Saint Sixtus, and Westmalle in Belgium). They're generally dark amber to brown in color, strongly flavored, and range in alcohol content from about 6 to 12 percent. *See also* BEER.

**Trilby Cocktail**

2 oz. (¼ cup) bourbon
1 oz. (2 Tbsp.) sweet vermouth
4 dashes (about ¼ tsp.) orange bitters

Stir ingredients with ice; strain into chilled glass.

**Triple Sec** An elegant form of CURAÇAO, this orange LIQUEUR is flavored with the peels of both sweet and bitter oranges. Although the name means "triple DRY," this smooth, fruity liqueur is sweet, though not cloying. *See also* CITRUS-FLAVORED SPIRITS; ORANGE-FLAVORED SPIRITS.

> *Everyone should believe in something. I believe I'll have another drink.*
>
> ATTRIBUTED TO BOTH GROUCHO MARX AND W. C. FIELDS,
> AMERICAN COMEDIANS

**Trois Rivières** [TRWAH ree-VYEHR] French for "three rivers."

1 ¹/₂ oz. (3 Tbsp.) Canadian whisky
¹/₂ oz. (1 Tbsp.) Dubonnet rouge
1 ¹/₂ tsp. Cointreau or Triple Sec
orange twist

Shake liquid ingredients with ice. Strain into chilled glass; drop in orange twist.

**Truffles** A rich, creamy LIQUEUR with a milk-chocolate flavor. *See also* CHOCOLATE-FLAVORED SPIRITS.

**Tuaca** [too-AH-kah] From the Tuscan region of Italy, this BRANDY-based LIQUEUR is the color of pale honey and flavored with citrus fruits and spices; its taste is reminiscent of butterscotch.

**Tulip Cocktail**

³/₄ oz. (1 ¹/₂ Tbsp.) apple brandy
³/₄ oz. (1 ¹/₂ Tbsp.) sweet vermouth
2 tsp. apricot brandy
1 ¹/₂ tsp. fresh lemon juice

Shake ingredients with cracked ice; strain into chilled glass.

**tulip glass** *see* Glassware, page 10

## Turf Cocktail

1 oz. (2 Tbsp.) gin
1 oz. (2 Tbsp.) dry vermouth
$^{1}/_{2}$ tsp. Pernod or other anise-flavored liqueur
$^{1}/_{2}$ tsp. fresh lemon juice
2 dashes (about $^{1}/_{8}$ tsp.) Angostura bitters

Shake ingredients with ice; strain into chilled cocktail glass or over ice cubes in an old-fashioned glass.

## Turkey Shoot *see* STINGER

## Tuxedo Cocktail

1$^{1}/_{2}$ oz. (3 Tbsp.) gin
1$^{1}/_{2}$ oz. (3 Tbsp.) dry vermouth
$^{1}/_{4}$ tsp. maraschino liqueur
$^{1}/_{4}$ tsp. Pernod or other anise-flavored liqueur
2 dashes (about $^{1}/_{8}$ tsp.) orange bitters
maraschino cherry

Stir liquid ingredients with ice. Strain into chilled glass; garnish with cherry.

## Twin Hills

2 oz. ($^{1}/_{4}$ cup) rye whiskey
$^{1}/_{2}$ oz. (1 Tbsp.) Bénédictine
2 tsp. fresh lemon juice
2 tsp. fresh lime juice
1$^{1}/_{2}$ tsp. sugar syrup
half lemon slice
half lime slice

Shake all the ingredients except fruit with ice. Strain into chilled glass; garnish with citrus slices.

## Twin Six Cocktail

1$^{1}/_{2}$ oz. (3 Tbsp.) gin
$^{1}/_{2}$ oz. (1 Tbsp.) sweet vermouth
$^{1}/_{2}$ oz. (1 Tbsp.) fresh orange juice
$^{1}/_{8}$ tsp. grenadine
1 egg white

Vigorously shake ingredients with cracked ice; strain into chilled glass.

**twist** In the world of cocktails, the word "twist" is used in two ways: The noun form describes a small piece of citrus peel (*see* Garnishing with citrus twists, page 15); the verb form describes the action of twisting the peel over a drink so that it exudes a spray of its essential oils.

**Ulanda** [yoo-LAN-duh; yoo-LAHN-duh]

1 1/2 oz. (3 Tbsp.) gin
3/4 oz. (1 1/2 Tbsp.) Triple Sec
1/4 tsp. Pernod or other anise-flavored liqueur

Shake ingredients with ice; strain into chilled glass.

**Underberg bitters** [OON-der-behrk] *See* BITTERS

**Unicum bitters** [OO-nih-kum] *See* BITTERS

**Union Jack Cocktail**

1 1/2 oz. (3 Tbsp.) gin
1/2 oz. (1 Tbsp.) crème Yvette

Shake ingredients with ice; strain into chilled glass.

**up** *See* STRAIGHT UP

---

*Life itself is the proper binge.*
JULIA CHILD, AMERICAN TV ICON, AUTHOR

---

**Valencia** [vuh-LEHN-she-uh]

2 oz. (1/4 cup) apricot brandy
1 oz. (2 Tbsp.) fresh orange juice
2 to 4 dashes (about 1/8 to 1/4 tsp.) orange bitters

Shake ingredients with ice; strain into chilled glass.

**Vanderbilt**

2 oz. (1/4 cup) brandy
1 oz. (2 Tbsp.) cherry brandy
1 tsp. sugar syrup
2 to 4 dashes (about 1/8 to 1/4 tsp.) Angostura bitters

Stir ingredients with ice; strain into chilled glass.

**Van der Hum** Made in South Africa, this BRANDY-based LIQUEUR has a tangerine flavor. In Dutch, the name roughly translates to "what's his name." *See also* CITRUS-FLAVORED SPIRITS.

**Vandermint** A dark brown Dutch LIQUEUR with a chocolate-mint flavor. *See also* CHOCOLATE-FLAVORED SPIRITS; MINT-FLAVORED SPIRITS.

**vanilla-flavored spirits** *see* CRÈME DE VANILLE; CUARENTA Y TRES

**varietal wine; varietal** [vuh-RI-ih-tuhl] A wine labeled with the name of the dominant grape variety from which it's made, such as CABERNET SAUVIGNON, CHARDONNAY, MERLOT, and so on. This practice takes place primarily in North and South America, Australia, New Zealand, and parts of Europe. Most areas have rules about what can be called a varietal wine—in the United States, for example, at least 75 percent of the wine must come from the grape variety named on the label, while in Australia the requirement is 80 percent. In Europe, rather than use varietal names, the practice has been to label better wines according to origin, such as region, district, or village.

**Velvet Hammer #1** The "Hammer" is kin to the ALEXANDER. The following two versions are the most popular, with the vodka version less sweet.

> 1 ½ oz. (3 Tbsp.) vodka
> 1 oz. (2 Tbsp.) white crème de cacao
> 1 oz. (2 Tbsp.) half & half or cream

Shake ingredients with ice; strain into chilled glass.

**Velvet Hammer #2**

> 1 oz. (2 Tbsp.) Cointreau
> 1 oz. (2 Tbsp.) white crème de cacao
> 1 oz. (2 Tbsp.) half & half or cream
> ½ oz. (1 Tbsp.) brandy

Shake ingredients with ice; strain into chilled glass.

**vermouth** [ver-MOOTH] A FORTIFIED WINE flavored with complex formulas of countless botanicals, including herbs, spices, flowers, and seeds—the exact recipe depending on the producer. The word "vermouth" comes from the German *Wermut* or *Vermut,* "wormwood," which before it was declared poisonous was once the principal flavoring ingredient. Vermouth was used for medicinal purposes eons ago, with some historians dating it back to the time of Hippocrates. There are two primary styles of vermouth—sweet (red) and DRY (white); all vermouths are made from white wines. **Sweet vermouth** (introduced in 1786 by Italian Antonio Benedetto Carpano) is reddish brown in color (from the addition of caramel) and has a slightly sweet flavor. This Italian-style vermouth is served as an APÉRITIF and used in cocktails with a sweet edge like MANHATTANS. **Dry vermouth** was created by Frenchman Joseph Noilly in 1800, which is why it's commonly referred to as *French vermouth.* Today, however, it's also produced in other countries, including Italy and the United States. Dry vermouth is served as an apéritif and used in dry cocktails like MARTINIS. Drinks made with half sweet and half dry vermouth are referred to as PERFECT, as in a perfect manhattan. In general, the flavor of vermouth gradually begins to dissipate as soon as the bottle is opened. It can be stored for at least 3 months in the refrigerator, with some companies claiming a 6-month flavor life. Some of the better-known brands of vermouth are Cinzano, Martini & Rossi, and Noilly Prat.

### Vermouth Cassis

2 oz. (¼ cup) dry vermouth
1 oz. (2 Tbsp.) crème de cassis
cold club soda
lemon twist

Pour vermouth and cassis into chilled glass filled with ice cubes. Top with club soda, stirring gently; garnish with lemon twist.

### Vermouth Cocktail

This PERFECT version is the classic recipe; however, 2 ounces of either dry or sweet vermouth may also be used.

1 oz. (2 Tbsp.) dry vermouth
1 oz. (2 Tbsp.) sweet vermouth
2 dashes (about ⅛ tsp.) orange bitters
maraschino cherry

Stir liquid ingredients with ice. Strain into chilled glass; garnish with cherry.

---

*⟨ like a good martini, one or two at the most. After one I'm under the table, after two, I'm under the host.*

DOROTHY PARKER, AMERICAN WRITER

---

**Vesper, The** The infamous James Bond Martini from *Casino Royale,* named after Vesper Lynd, the book's heroine. It's a *serious* drink, but Bond explains why: "I never have more than one drink before dinner. But I do like that one to be large and very strong and very cold and very well-made. I hate small portions of anything, particularly when they taste bad." No arguments here! *See also* MARTINI.

3 oz. (³/₈ cup) gin
1 oz. (2 Tbsp.) vodka (*Bond prefers Russian*)
¹/₂ oz. (1 Tbsp.) Lillet blanc
large slice of lemon peel

Shake liquid ingredients with ice. Strain into chilled glass; drop in lemon peel.

### Via Veneto

2 oz. (¹/₄ cup) brandy
¹/₂ oz. (1 Tbsp.) Sambuca
¹/₂ oz. (1 Tbsp.) fresh lemon juice
1¹/₂ tsp. sugar syrup
¹/₂ egg white (about 1 Tbsp.) (*See* page 14, How to
   Divide Egg Whites in Half)

Vigorously shake ingredients with ice; strain into chilled glass.

### Victor

1¹/₂ oz. (3 Tbsp.) gin
¹/₂ oz. (1 Tbsp.) brandy
¹/₂ oz. (1 Tbsp.) sweet vermouth

Shake ingredients with ice; strain into chilled glass.

**Vin Chaud** [va*n* SHOH] *see* MULLED WINE

**vienna beer** An amber-red, LAGER-style beer originally produced in Vienna, Austria. The color is derived from kilned MALT, which has a reddish color. Vienna beers have a malty, lightly hopped (*see* HOPS) flavor. *See also* BEER.

**viniculture; viniculturist** [VIHN-ih-kuhl-cher] The study or science of making wines. *See also* ENOLOGY; VITICULTURE.

**vinification** [vihn-ih-fih-KAY-shuhn] The process of making wines.

**vinify; vinified** [VIHN-uh-fi] To produce wine from grapes or other fruit.

**vintage** [VIHN-tihj] A wine-world term that describes both the year of the actual grape harvest and the wine made from those grapes. In the United States, the label may list the **vintage year** if 95 percent of the wine comes from grapes harvested that year. If a blend of grapes from 2 or more years is used, the wine is **non-vintage** (NV), but that doesn't mean it's not as good as a vintage wine. Consumers should consider a vintage year only as a general guideline. An excellent year for a growing region translates to grapes of generally superior quality, which means there are more choices for fine wines of that vintage. In the end, however, each wine must be judged on its own merit.

**Virgin** Cocktail lingo for any drink served sans liquor; one of the most common of these is Virgin Mary—a BLOODY MARY without the VODKA.

☆ **Virgin Mary** *see* BLOODY MARY

**viticulture; viticulturist** [VIHT-ih-kuhl-cher] The cultivation of grapevines, or the study or science of grapes and their culture. *See also* ENOLOGY; VINICULTURE.

**vodka** A NEUTRAL SPIRIT (made from grain, fruits, or vegetables) that is distilled to at least 190 PROOF, bottled at a minimum of 80 proof, and devoid of distinctive CHARACTER, AROMA, taste, or color. Vodka is thought to date back to the twelfth century, although there's some debate over its origin—Russia or Poland. Early versions, however, were nothing like today's highly refined vodka, which evolved in the 1830s after the introduction of the continuous still and the discovery of charcoal filtering. The name "vodka" comes from the Russian *zhizennia voda,* "water of life."

Vodkas can be made from everything from potatoes to beets, although those made from grain (primarily barley and wheat, sometimes rye or corn) are considered the best. Vodka's purity is the result of DISTILLATION at high proof levels, then filtration through activated charcoal to remove most of the remaining impurities (congeners) that would contribute distinctive characteristics. Some vodkas are triple-filtered for ultimate purity. Even so, connoisseurs note distinct flavor differences when vodkas are tasted at room temperature sans mixers. **Flavored vodkas,** long common in Russia and Poland, are becoming increasingly popular in the United States. They're generally lower in alcohol (between 60 and 80 proof) and can be flavored with any of various ingredients, including coffee beans, herbs, fruit, and even chile peppers. Some flavored vodkas are slightly sweetened. Popular unflavored brands in the marketplace today include Absolut, Belvedere, Denaka, Finlandia, Gilbey's, Glacier, Gordon's, Ketel One, Luksusowa, Skyy, Smirnoff (and Smirnoff Black Label), Stolichnaya (and Stolichnaya Gold), and Tanqueray Sterling. Many of the same producers also market flavored vodkas, but Absolut, Finlandia, and Stolichnaya have the most selections. *See also* INFUSED VODKA.

**Vodka and Tonic** *see* GIN AND TONIC

**Vodka Collins** *see* TOM COLLINS

**Vodka Rickey** *see* RICKEY

> *. . . vodka (no color, no taste, no smell) . . . is the ideal intoxicant for the drinker who wants no reminder of how hurt Mother would be if she knew what he was doing.*
>
> A. J. LIEBLING, AMERICAN JOURNALIST

**Vodka Sling** *see* SLING

**Vodka Sour** *see* SOUR

**Vodka Stinger** *see* STINGER

### Volga Boatman

1½ oz. (3 Tbsp.) vodka
1 oz. (2 Tbsp.) cherry brandy
1 oz. (2 Tbsp.) fresh orange juice
maraschino cherry

Shake liquid ingredients with ice. Strain into chilled glass; garnish with cherry.

**Vov Zabajone** [VOHV dzah-bah-YOHN] An Italian eggnog LIQUEUR with the flavor of Italy's famous zabaglione, that ethereal foamy custard made with egg yolks, MARSALA, and sugar. *See also* EGGNOG-FLAVORED SPIRITS.

### Waikiki Beachcomber [wi-kih-KEE]

¾ oz. (1½ Tbsp.) gin
¾ oz. (1½ Tbsp.) Cointreau or Triple Sec
¾ oz. (1½ Tbsp.) unsweetened pineapple juice

Shake ingredients with ice; strain into chilled glass.

**waiter's friend** *see* Bar Equipment (Corkscrews), page 4

### Ward Eight

2 oz. (¼ cup) rye whiskey
¾ oz. (1½ Tbsp.) fresh lemon juice
1 tsp. grenadine
1 tsp. powdered sugar
1 orange slice
1 lemon slice
1 maraschino cherry

Shake first 4 ingredients with ice; strain into chilled glass filled halfway with cracked ice. Garnish with fruit.

**Warsaw**

1 ½ oz. (3 Tbsp.) vodka
½ oz. (1 Tbsp.) dry vermouth
2 tsp. blackberry brandy
1 tsp. fresh lemon juice
lemon twist

Shake liquid ingredients with ice; strain into chilled glass. Drop in lemon twist.

**Washington**

1 ½ oz. (3 Tbsp.) dry vermouth
½ oz. (1 Tbsp.) brandy
¼ tsp. powdered sugar
2 dashes (about ⅛ tsp.) Angostura bitters

Shake ingredients with ice; strain into chilled glass.

**wassail; Wassail Bowl** [WAH-suhl] *n.* 1. A toast to someone's well-being, originating from the old English custom of saluting the health of guests at a celebration by passing a bowl of spiced ALE from which each person would drink and then say, *Wass hael,* Saxon for "Be whole" or "Be healthy." 2. The beverage used in such toasting, typically a spiced ale or wine; also called a *Wassail Bowl.* 3. An occasion characterized by festive drinking. A **wassailer** is one who does the toasting or drinking. **wassail; wassailing** *v.* 1. To toast; drink to the health of. 2. To drink wassail. *See also* Hot Drinks, page 29.

MAKES ABOUT TWELVE 6-OUNCE SERVINGS

12 tiny tart apples
4 (12 oz.) bottles of ale
¾ cup packed brown sugar
juice and peel of 1 large orange
juice and peel of 1 large lemon
1 tsp. *each* ground nutmeg, allspice, and cinnamon
½ tsp. *each* ground ginger and cloves
16 oz. (1 pint; 2 cups) sweet sherry
8 oz. (1 cup) brandy

Place apples on ungreased baking sheet; bake in preheated 350°F oven for 30 minutes. Remove from oven and set aside. Put 2 bottles ale in large pot (not aluminum) along with sugar, orange juice and peel, lemon juice and peel, and spices; bring to boil over medium heat, stirring occasionally. Reduce heat to low; simmer for 20 minutes. Add remaining 2 bottles ale, sherry, and brandy; heat just until steaming (don't boil). Pour into large, heatproof bowl; add baked apples. Ladle into mugs or heatproof punch cups, adding an apple to each serving. Leftover wassail can be tightly covered and stored in a cool place for at least 6 months.

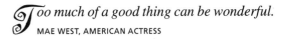

*oo much of a good thing can be wonderful.*
MAE WEST, AMERICAN ACTRESS

### Watermelon #1

3 oz. ($^3/_8$ cup) fresh orange juice
1 oz. (2 Tbsp.) Southern Comfort
$^1/_2$ oz. (1 Tbsp.) amaretto
2 dashes (about $^1/_8$ tsp.) grenadine

Shake ingredients with ice; strain into chilled glass over ice cubes.

### Watermelon #2

2 oz. ($^1/_4$ cup) cranberry juice
1 oz. (2 Tbsp.) vodka
1 oz. (2 Tbsp.) Midori or other melon liqueur
$^1/_4$ tsp. grenadine

Shake ingredients with ice; strain into chilled glass over ice cubes.

### Wedding Belle

1 oz. (2 Tbsp.) gin
1 oz. (2 Tbsp.) Dubonnet rouge
1 oz. (2 Tbsp.) fresh orange juice
$^1/_2$ oz. (1 Tbsp.) cherry brandy

Shake ingredients with cracked ice; strain into chilled glass.

## Wembly Cocktail

1 ½ oz. (3 Tbsp.) gin
¾ oz. (1 ½ Tbsp.) dry vermouth
1 ½ tsp. apple brandy
½ tsp. apricot brandy

Stir ingredients with ice; strain into chilled glass.

**wheat beer** A beer made primarily from malted wheat and characterized by its pale color and subtle, LAGER-like flavor. Technically it should be classified as an ALE, since it's a top-fermented brew. *See also* BEER.

## Whip Cocktail

1 ½ oz. (3 Tbsp.) brandy
1 oz. (2 Tbsp.) dry vermouth
1 oz. (2 Tbsp.) sweet vermouth
½ tsp. Triple Sec
¼ tsp. Pernod or other anise-flavored liqueur

Stir ingredients with ice; strain into chilled glass.

---

*There's no such thing as bad whiskey. Some whiskeys just happen to be better than others. But a man shouldn't fool with booze until he's fifty, and then he's a damn fool if he doesn't.*

WILLIAM FAULKNER, AMERICAN NOVELIST

---

**whiskey; whisky** [HWIHSK-ee; WIHSK-ee] An alcoholic DIS-TILLATE that takes its name from the Celtic (Gaelic) *uisqebaugh* (pronounced oos-kee-BAW or whis-kee-BAW), which means "water of life." Whiskey is made from the fermented MASH of cereal grains, such as barley, corn, oats, rye, and wheat, and is generally produced in countries that grow these grains. The most significant producers are Canada, Ireland, Scotland, and the United States. Traditionally, whiskies made in Scotland and Canada are spelled *whisky*, without the *e*. A number of factors influence the flavor and quality of whiskey: the type of grain and how it's treated, the types of yeast used, the method of DISTILLATION,

AGING factors (including the wood and size of the barrel and the length of aging time), and the water source.

**Straight whiskey** must be made from at least 51 percent of a grain, must not exceed 160 PROOF (80 percent alcohol), must be aged in oak barrels for 2 years, and may only be diluted by the addition of water to no less than 80 proof. Straight whiskeys may be combined as long as they all come from the same distillery and were made during the same distilling period. Examples of straight whiskeys are BOURBON, TENNESSEE, and RYE. Straight whiskeys from different distilleries or divergent distilling periods may be blended, but then they must be labeled "blended bourbon whiskey," "blended rye whiskey," and so on.

**Blended whiskey** is a combination of two or more (at least 20 percent), 100-proof straight whiskeys blended with NEUTRAL SPIRITS, grain spirits, or light whiskeys. Some of the better-known blends are Barton Reserve, Imperial, and Seagram's 7 Crown.

**Light whiskey** has been distilled to a higher-than-normal alcohol level (typically over 160 PROOF, or 80 percent alcohol), then diluted with more water than usual. It's stored in charred-oak containers, which contributes a distinctive CHARACTER that, though less assertive than that of straight whiskey, is nonetheless flavorful. Such whiskey is generally used for blending. *See also* CANADIAN WHISKY; IRISH WHISKEY; SCOTCH WHISKY; WHISK(E)Y-BASED LIQUEURS.

**whisk(e)y-based liqueurs** *see* DRAMBUIE; GLAYVA; IRISH MIST; SOUTHERN COMFORT; WILD TURKEY LIQUEUR

## Whiskey Cocktail

2 oz. ($^1/_4$ cup) rye whiskey
$^1/_2$ tsp. sugar syrup
2 dashes (about $^1/_8$ tsp.) Angostura bitters
orange slice
maraschino cherry

Stir first 3 ingredients with ice. Strain into chilled glass; garnish with fruit.

## Whiskey Collins *see* TOM COLLINS

**whiskey glass** *see* Glassware, page 10

*It may be true that whiskey kills germs,
but how can you get them to drink it?*

**Whiskey Sangaree** *see* SANGAREE

**Whiskey Sour** *see* AGED WHISKEY SOURS; SOUR

**whiskey sour glass** *see* Glassware, page 10

**White Chocolate Martini** *see* CHOCOLATE MARTINI

## White Lady

1 1/2 oz. (3 Tbsp.) gin
3/4 oz. (1 1/2 Tbsp.) Cointreau
3/4 oz. (1 1/2 Tbsp.) fresh lemon juice

Shake ingredients with ice; strain into chilled glass.

## White Lily

3/4 oz. (1 1/2 Tbsp.) gin
3/4 oz. (1 1/2 Tbsp.) light rum
3/4 oz. (1 1/2 Tbsp.) Cointreau or Triple Sec
1/4 tsp. Pernod or other anise-flavored liqueur

Shake ingredients with ice; strain into chilled glass.

## White Lion

1 1/2 oz. (3 Tbsp.) light rum
3/4 oz. (1 1/2 Tbsp.) fresh lemon juice
1/2 tsp. grenadine
2 dashes (about 1/8 tsp.) Angostura bitters
1 tsp. powdered sugar

Shake ingredients with ice; strain into chilled glass.

## White Rose

1 1/2 oz. (3 Tbsp.) gin
1/2 oz. (1 Tbsp.) fresh orange juice
1/2 oz. (1 Tbsp.) fresh lime juice
1 tsp. sugar syrup
1/2 egg white (about 1 Tbsp.) (See page 14, How to
    Divide Egg Whites in Half)

Shake ingredients with ice; strain into chilled glass.

**White Russian** *see* BLACK RUSSIAN

**White Spider** Although crème de menthe was once the norm in this drink, many bartenders have replaced it with the popular peppermint schnapps.

1 1/2 oz. (3 Tbsp.) vodka
1 oz. (2 Tbsp.) peppermint schnapps or white crème de menthe

Shake ingredients with ice; strain into chilled glass.

## White Way Cocktail

1 1/2 oz. (3 Tbsp.) gin
3/4 oz. (1 1/2 Tbsp.) white crème de menthe

Shake ingredients with cracked ice; strain into chilled glass.

## Why Not?

1 oz. (2 Tbsp.) gin
3/4 oz. (1 1/2 Tbsp.) apricot brandy
1/2 oz. (1 Tbsp.) dry vermouth
1/8 tsp. fresh lemon juice

Shake ingredients with cracked ice; strain into chilled glass.

## Widow's Kiss

1 oz. (2 Tbsp.) apple brandy
1/2 oz. (1 Tbsp.) Bénédictine
1/2 oz. (1 Tbsp.) yellow Chartreuse
1 to 2 dashes (about 1/16 to 1/8 tsp.) Angostura bitters

Shake ingredients with ice; strain into chilled glass.

**Wild Turkey Liqueur** Golden yellow in color, this liqueur is based on Wild Turkey BOURBON and is flavored with honey and spices. It's thick, very sweet, and distinctly bourbon flavored. *See also* WHISK(E)Y-BASED LIQUEURS.

## Will Rogers

1 1/2 oz. (3 Tbsp.) gin
1/2 oz. (1 Tbsp.) dry vermouth
1/2 oz. (1 Tbsp.) fresh orange juice
1 1/2 tsp. Triple Sec

Shake ingredients with ice; strain into chilled glass.

*Food without wine is a corpse; wine without food is a ghost; united and well matched they are as body and soul, living partners.*

ANDRÉ SIMON, FRENCH GASTRONOME, WRITER

**wine** In general, the word "wine" refers to the naturally FER-MENTED juice of grapes, although the term can broadly include alcoholic beverages created from other fruits and even vegetables and grains. Wine's rich history, with roots reaching back almost 12,000 years, has evolved along with that of man. As various cultures expanded into new parts of the world, so did the grapevine and the art of winemaking. Today, there are vineyards throughout the world, with good wine being produced in such far-ranging locations as the United States, Europe, South Africa, Australia, and South America. Wine is broadly classified as follows: 1. **Sparkling wines**—effervescent wines that contain carbon dioxide gas (either natural or manmade), such as champagne and Asti Spumante. 2. **Still wines**—those that are nonsparkling (uncarbonated), red, white, or rosé and DRY or sweet. 3. **Fortified wines**—those augmented with brandy or other spirits, such as sherry and port. And 4. **Aromatic wines**—those flavored with herbs and spices, such as vermouth. See also APPELLATION; ASTI SPUMANTE; BLUSH WINE; BODY; BORDEAUX; BOUQUET; BRANDY; BURGUNDY; CABERNET SAUVIGNON; CHABLIS; CHAMPAGNE; CHARACTER; CHARDONNAY; CHIANTI; CLARET; COGNAC; DECANT; FERMENTATION; FINING; MADEIRA; MARSALA; MERITAGE; MERLOT; MULLED WINE; PORT; RETSINA; RIESLING; ROSÉ; SAKE; SAUTERNES; SAUVIGNON BLANC; SEC; SHERRY; VARIETAL WINE; VERMOUTH; VINIFICATION; VINTAGE; VITICULTURE; WINE LABEL TERMS; ZINFANDEL; Tricks of the Trade (Opening Wine and Champagne Bottles), page 25.

*A wine drinker, being at table, was offered grapes at dessert. "Thank you," he said, pushing the dish away from him, "but I am not in the habit of taking my wine in pills."*

JEAN-ANTHELME BRILLAT-SAVARIN, FRENCH POLITICIAN, GASTRONOME, WRITER

**wine bottle sizes** *see* Sizes of Wine and Spirit Bottles, page 22

**wineglasses** *see* Glassware, page 10

**wine label terms** Here's an explanation of some of those seemingly "generic" wine label terms: **Estate bottled** tells you that 100 percent of the grapes from which the wine was made were grown in the winery's own vineyards, or from vineyards (in the same APPELLATION) controlled by the winery through a long-term lease. Furthermore, such wines must be vinified and bottled at that winery. **Château bottled** has a comparable meaning. Both terms describe a wine of superior quality and CHARACTER. Comparable European phrases are: in France—*Mis en Bouteille au Domaine, Mis au Domaine, Mis en Bouteille a la Propriété,* and *Mis en Bouteille du Château;* in Italy—*Imbottigliato All'origine;* and in Germany—*Erzeugerabfüllung.*

   **Grown, Produced, and Bottled By** is comparable to the "estate bottled" designation and refers to the fact that the grapes were grown at the winery vineyards (or at vineyards controlled by the winery) and that the wine was vinified and bottled at the winery. **Produced and Bottled By** indicates that the winery crushed, fermented, and bottled a minimum of 75 percent of the wine in that particular bottling. The phrase, however, does not mean that the winery grew the grapes. **Made and Bottled By** means that a minimum of 10 percent of the wine was FERMENTED at the winery—the other 90 percent could have come from other sources. This designation does not generally indicate the quality implied by the phrase "Produced and Bottled By." **Bottled by** alone on a label indicates simply that the only role the winery most likely played in the wine's production was to purchase and bottle wine that was made somewhere else.

**Wine Spritzer** *see* SPRITZER

**wing opener** *see* Bar Equipment (Corkscrews), page 4

**Woodstock**

> 1 ½ oz. (3 Tbsp.) gin
> 1 oz. (2 Tbsp.) fresh lemon juice
> 2 tsp. maple syrup
> 2 dashes (about ⅛ tsp.) orange bitters

Shake ingredients with ice; strain into chilled glass.

### Woodward

1 ¹/₂ oz. (3 Tbsp.) Scotch
¹/₂ oz. (1 Tbsp.) dry vermouth
¹/₂ oz. (1 Tbsp.) unsweetened grapefruit juice

Shake ingredients with ice; strain into chilled glass.

*I don't drink; I don't like it—it makes me feel good.*
OSCAR LEVANT, AMERICAN COMPOSER, PIANIST

### Woo-Woo

³/₄ oz. (1 ¹/₂ Tbsp.) vodka
³/₄ oz. (1 ¹/₂ Tbsp.) peach schnapps
¹/₂ oz. (1 Tbsp.) cranberry juice

Shake ingredients with ice; strain into chilled glass.

➤ **Variation:** Increase cranberry juice to 2 oz. (¹/₄ cup). Shake ingredients with ice; strain into chilled highball glass over ice cubes.

**wort** *see* MASH

### Xanthia Cocktail [ZAN-thee-uh]

³/₄ oz. (1 ¹/₂ Tbsp.) gin
³/₄ oz. (1 ¹/₂ Tbsp.) cherry brandy
³/₄ oz. (1 ¹/₂ Tbsp.) yellow Chartreuse

Stir ingredients with ice; strain into chilled glass.

### Xeres Cocktail [heh-RREHS] Xeres is the former name of Jerez
(Jerez de la Frontera), a city northeast of Cádiz in southern Spain's Andalusia region. This drink's named for its use of sherry, which comes from this region.

2 ¹/₂ oz. (5 Tbsp.) dry sherry
1 to 2 dashes (about ¹/₁₆ to ¹/₈ tsp.) orange bitters
1 to 2 dashes (about ¹/₁₆ to ¹/₈ tsp.) peach bitters

Shake ingredients with ice; strain into chilled glass.

## XYZ Cocktail

1 1/2 oz. (3 Tbsp.) dark rum
3/4 oz. (1 1/2 Tbsp.) Triple Sec
1/2 oz. (1 Tbsp.) fresh lemon juice

Shake ingredients with ice; strain into chilled glass.

## Yale Cocktail

1 1/2 oz. (3 Tbsp.) gin
1/2 oz. (1 Tbsp.) dry vermouth
1/4 tsp. maraschino liqueur
2 to 4 dashes (about 1/8 to 1/4 tsp.) orange bitters

Shake ingredients with cracked ice; strain into chilled glass.

➤**Variation** Substitute blue curaçao for the maraschino liqueur.

## yard of flannel *see* FLIP

---

*y grandmother is eighty-two and still doesn't need glasses . . . drinks right out of the bottle.*

HENNY YOUNGMAN, AMERICAN COMEDIAN

---

## Yellow Bird

2 oz. (1/4 cup) golden rum
1/2 oz. (1 Tbsp.) Galliano
1/2 oz. (1 Tbsp.) Triple Sec
1/2 oz. (1 Tbsp.) fresh lime juice

Shake ingredients with ice; strain into chilled glass over ice cubes.

## Yellow Fingers

1 1/2 oz. (3 Tbsp.) gin
3/4 oz. (1 1/2 Tbsp.) blackberry brandy
1/2 oz. (1 Tbsp.) crème de banane
1/2 oz. (1 Tbsp.) cream

Shake ingredients with ice; strain into chilled glass.

## Yellow Parrot Cocktail

³/₄ oz. (1¹/₂ Tbsp.) yellow Chartreuse
³/₄ oz. (1¹/₂ Tbsp.) Pernod or other anise-flavored liqueur
³/₄ oz. (1¹/₂ Tbsp.) apricot brandy

Shake ingredients with ice; strain into chilled glass.

---

*You Americans have the loveliest wines in the world, you know, but you don't realize it. You call them "domestic" and that's enough to start trouble anywhere.*

H. G. WELLS, BRITISH WRITER

---

**Zinfandel** [ZIHN-fuhn-dehl] Considered California's red-wine grape because it's not widely grown anywhere else, Zinfandel is now that state's most extensively planted red grape. Versatile Zinfandel can be variously vinified to create several different styles of wine. The most popular are wonderfully flavorful red wines, which can range in BODY from light to robust, and have berrylike, spicy flavors and plenty of TANNIN and ALCOHOL. These reds have enough depth, complexity, and longevity to be compared to CABERNET SAUVIGNONS. Another style is **white zinfandel,** a fruity, slightly sweet BLUSH WINE that ranges in color from light to dark pink. The Zinfandel grape is also used as a base for certain SPARKLING WINES, late-harvest wines, and even some PORT-style wines.

**Zombie** You'll understand how this drink got its name if you have more than one—too many of them and you'll definitely feel like the walking dead the next day. The Zombie is reputed to have been created in the mid-1930s at Hollywood's famous Don the Beachcomber restaurant.

1¹/₂ oz. (3 Tbsp.) light rum
1 oz. (2 Tbsp.) passion-fruit syrup
1 oz. (2 Tbsp.) unsweetened pineapple juice
1 oz. (2 Tbsp.) fresh orange juice
³/₄ oz. (1¹/₂ Tbsp.) dark rum
¹/₂ oz. (1 Tbsp.) apricot brandy
¹/₂ oz. (1 Tbsp.) fresh lime juice
1 tsp. powdered sugar

¹/₂ cup crushed ice
2 tsp. 151-proof rum
pineapple spear
orange slice
maraschino cherry
mint sprig

Combine first 9 ingredients in a blender. Cover and process at medium speed until smooth, about 15 seconds; pour into chilled glass. Float 151-proof rum on top by slowly pouring it over the back (rounded) side of a spoon; don't mix. Garnish with fruit and mint.

*The fact that you don't drink at all is the greatest argument for drunkenness I know.*

HUMPHREY BOGART, AMERICAN ACTOR (SAID TO A CONNIVING, TEETOTALING MOVIE PRODUCER IN THE FILM *THE BAREFOOT CONTESSA*)

# Bibliography

Baylay, Stephen. *Gin.* England: Balding & Mansell, 1994.

Bishop, George. *The Booze Reader: A Soggy Saga of a Man in His Cups.* Los Angeles: Sherbourne Press, Inc., 1965.

Brander, Michael. *Brander's Guide to Scotch Whisky.* New York: Lyons & Burford, Publishers, 1996.

Conrad III, Barnaby. *Absinthe: History in a Bottle.* San Francisco: Chronicle Books, 1995.
———. *The Martini.* San Francisco: Chronicle Books, 1995.

DeVoto, Bernard. *The Hour.* Cambridge, MA: Riverside Press, 1948.

Doxat, John. *Stirred Not Shaken: The Dry Martini.* London: Hutchinson Benham, Ltd., 1976.

Faith, Nicholas. *Cognac.* Boston: David R. Godine, 1987.

Forget, Carl. *The Association of Brewers' Dictionary of Beer and Brewing.* Boulder, CO: Brewers Publications, 1988.

Grimes, William. *Straight Up or On the Rocks: A Cultural History of American Drink.* New York: Simon & Schuster, 1993.

Grossman, Harold J. *Grossman's Guide to Wines, Beers, and Spirits, 6th ed.* New York: Charles Scribner's Sons, 1983.

Hallgarten, Peter. *Spirits and Liqueurs.* London: Faber & Faber, 1983.

Hastings, Derek. *Spirits & Liqueurs of the World.* London: Footnote Productions, Ltd., 1984.

Herbst, Sharon Tyler. *The Food Lover's Tiptionary.* New York: Hearst Books, 1994.
———. *Never Eat More Than You Can Lift.* New York: Broadway Books, 1997.
———. *The New Food Lover's Companion.* Hauppauge, NY: Barron's Educational Series, Inc., 1995.

Herbst, Ron, and Sharon Tyler Herbst. *The Wine Lover's Companion.* Hauppauge, NY: Barron's Educational Series, Inc., 1995.

Hutson, Lucinda. *Tequila!* Berkeley, CA: Ten Speed Press, 1995.

Jackson, Michael. *Bar & Cocktail Companion.* Philadelphia: Running Press, 1995.
———. *Michael Jackson's Complete Guide to Single Malt Scotch.* Philadelphia: Running Press, 1994.
———. *The World Guide to Whisky.* London: Dorling Kindersley, 1987.

Jeffers, H. Paul. *High Spirits: A Celebration of Scotch, Bourbon, Cognacs, and More . . .* New York: Lyons & Burford, Publishers, 1997.

Lanza, Joseph. *The Cocktail: The Influence of Spirits on the American Psyche.* New York: Picador USA, 1995.

Lord, Tony. *The World Guide to Spirits, Apéritifs and Cocktails.* New York: Sovereign Books, 1979.

Mariani, John F. *The Dictionary of American Food and Drink.* New York: Hearst Books, 1994.

Miller, Anistatia R., and Jared M. Brown. *Shaken Not Stirred: A Celebration of the Martini.* New York: HarperCollins, 1997.

Pacult, F. Paul. *Kindred Spirits: The Spirit Journal Guide to the World's Distilled Spirits and Fortified Wines.* New York: Hyperion, 1997.

Regan, Gary, and Mardee Haidin. *The Martini Companion: A Connoisseur's Guide.* Philadelphia: Running Press, 1997.

————. *The Book of Bourbon and Other Fine American Whiskies.* Vermont: Chapters Publishing, Ltd., 1995.

Salle, Jacques. *The Larousse Book of Cocktails.* New York: Henry Holt & Co., 1985.

Visakay, Stephen. *Vintage Bar Ware: Identification and Value Guide.* Kentucky: Collector Books, 1997.

Watney, John. *Mother's Ruin: A History of Gin.* London: Peter Owen, Ltd., 1976.

White, Francesca. *Cheers! A Spirited Guide to Liquors and Liqueurs.* London: Paddington Press, 1977.

# Drinks by Alcoholic Ingredients
## (Liquor or Liquor Flavor)

*Drinks contain at least ¹/₂ ounce of the liquor under which they're listed.*

**ALMOND LIQUEURS**
*see* Amaretto; Crème de
Noyaux

**AMARETTO**
*see also* Crème de
Noyaux
Alabama Slammer
Bocci Ball
Café Amaretto
Ferrari
French Connection
Godchild
Godfather
Godmother
Hawaiian Punch
Italian Coffee
Nutty Colada
Orgasm
Pink Almond
Red Snapper Shooter
Toasted Almond
Watermelon #1

**AMER PICON**
Amer Picon Cocktail
Picon Cocktail
Picon Fizz
Sanctuary

**ANISE-FLAVORED
LIQUEURS**
*see* Anisette; Pernod;
Sambuca

**ANISETTE**
*see also* Pernod
All-White Frappé
Blanche
Duchess
Jelly Bean

London Fog
Millionaire
Shanghai Cocktail

**APPLE BRANDY**
*see also* Cider
A.J.
Angel Face
Apple Blow Fizz
Apple Brandy Cocktail
Apple Brandy Highball
Apple Buck
Applecar
Apple Daiquiri
Apple Swizzle
Barton Special
Bolero
Canadian Apple
Cider Cup
Corpse Reviver #1
Deauville
Dempsey
Depth Bomb
Empire
Happy Apple
Harvard Cooler
Honeymoon
Jack-in-the-Box
Jack Rose
Jersey Lightning
Joulouville
Liberty Cocktail
Moonlight
Mulled Cider
Prince's Smile
Royal Smile Cocktail
Saucy Sue
Sharky Punch
Special Rough Cocktail
Star Cocktail

Star Daisy
Third Rail Cocktail
Tulip Cocktail
Widow's Kiss

**APRICOT
BRANDY/LIQUEUR**
Angel Face
Apricot Cocktail
Apricot Lady
Barnum
Boston Cocktail
Bronx Cheer
Claridge
Costa Del Sol
Devil's Tail
Empire
Favorite Cocktail
Fifth Avenue
Flamingo
Frankenjack Cocktail
Golden Daze
Golden Slipper
Hop Toad
Kyoto Cocktail #1
Leave-It-to-Me #1
Mañana
Midnight Cocktail
Paradise Cocktail
Pendennis Club
Prince's Smile
Red Cloud
Resolute Cocktail
Rose Cocktail, English
Tempter Cocktail
Thanksgiving Special
Valencia
Why Not?
Yellow Parrot Cocktail
Zombie

**AQUAVIT**
Midnight Sun

**BANANA LIQUEUR**
*see* Crème de Banane

**BEER AND ALE**
Beer Buster
Black Velvet
Bloody Brew
Boilermaker
Depth Charge
Shandy

**BÉNÉDICTINE**
Chrysanthemum
Gypsy
Honeymoon
Honolulu Cocktail #2
Monkey Gland
Preakness Cocktail
Queen Elizabeth Wine
Savoy Hotel
Twin Hills
Widow's Kiss

**BLACKBERRY
BRANDY/LIQUEUR**
Allegheny
Cádiz
Chi-Chi
Jelly Bean
Polish Sidecar
Polonaise
Poop Deck Cocktail
Yellow Fingers

**BLENDED WHISKEY**
Algonquin
Blue Blazer
Boston Sour
Cablegram
Coffee Eggnog
Delta
Dinah
Double Standard Sour
Fancy Whiskey
Hot Brick Toddy
Hot Toddy
Indian River
Japanese Fizz

King Cole Cocktail
Ladies' Cocktail
Lawhill Cocktail
Linstead
Los Angeles Cocktail
Manhasset
Old-Fashioned
Opening Cocktail
Oriental Cocktail
Palmer
Pink Almond
Preakness Cocktail
Whiskey Collins
Whiskey Sangaree
Whiskey Sour

**BOURBON**
Admiral
Aged Whiskey Sours
Allegheny
Anchors Aweigh
Black Hawk
Blizzard
Bourbon à la Crème
Bourbon Collins
Bourbon Crusta
Bourbon Daisy
Bourbon Milk Punch
Bourbon Rickey
Bourbon Sling
Bourbon Stinger
Chapel Hill
Commodore Cocktail
Dixie Whiskey
Eggnog
Godfather
Highball
Horse's Neck
Hot Buttered Bourbon
Huntress Cocktail
Imperial Fizz
Italian Stallion
Jocose Julep
Kentucky Cocktail
Kentucky Colonel
Milk Punch
Millionaire
Mint Julep
Nevins

New York Cocktail
Sazerac
Trilby Cocktail
Turkey Shoot

**BRANDY**
*see also* Apple Brandy;
    Apricot Brandy;
    Blackberry Brandy;
    Cherry Brandy; Co-
    gnac; Peach Brandy
Alabama
American Beauty
Andalusia
Angel's Kiss
Artillery Punch
Bermuda Highball
Between the Sheets
Blackjack
Blue Angel
Bombay Cocktail
Bombay Punch
Bosom Caresser
Brandied Madeira
Brandied Port
Brandy Alexander
Brandy Buck
Brandy Cassis
Brandy Cobbler
Brandy Collins
Brandy Crusta
Brandy Daisy
Brandy Eggnog
Brandy Fix
Brandy Gump
Brandy Manhattan
Brandy Milk Punch
Brandy Old-Fashioned
Brandy Rickey
Brandy Sangaree
Brandy Shrub
Brandy Sling
Brandy Smash
Brandy Sour
Bull's Milk
Café Amaretto
Café Royale
Carroll Cocktail
Champagne Cup

Prince of Wales
Sangría

**CHARTREUSE, GREEN**
Bijou Cocktail
Green Lizard
Jewel Cocktail
Lollipop
Rocky Green Dragon
Tailspin

**CHARTREUSE, YELLOW**
Alaska
Cloister
Golden Slipper
Widow's Kiss
Xanthia Cocktail
Yellow Parrot Cocktail

**CHERRY
BRANDY/LIQUEUR**
*see also* Kirsch; Peter
  Heering
Ankle Breaker
Blood and Sand
Bulldog Cocktail
Canadian Cherry
Cherry Blossom
Cherry Cobbler
Cherry Daiquiri
Cherry Rum
Dubonnet Fizz
Gilroy
Hudson Bay
Hunter's Cocktail
Huntress Cocktail
Ladyfinger
Merry Widow #1
Nightmare
Orange Oasis
Polynesian Cocktail
Scotch Holiday Sour
Singapore Sling
Stirrup Cup
Vanderbilt
Volga Boatman
Wedding Belle
Xanthia Cocktail

**CHOCOLATE LIQUEUR**
*see* Crème de Cacao

**CIDER**
*see also* Apple Brandy
Cider Cup
Cider Grog
Cider Smash
Happy Apple
Mulled Cider
Sinless Cider
Soft Cider Cup
Stone Fence

**COCONUT
LIQUEUR/SPIRITS**
Bahama Mama
Infused Vodka
  (coconut)
Surfer on Acid

**COFFEE LIQUEURS
(KAHLÚA; TIA MARIA)**
After 5
B-52
Black Magic
Black Russian
Brave Bull
Bushwhacker
Café Romano
Cara Sposa
Chocolate-Covered
  Cherry
Coffee Eggnog
Coffee Flip
Coffee Grasshopper
Freddy Fudpucker (vari-
  ation)
Gentle Bull
Jamaican Coffee
Kahlúa Toreador
Kingston Cocktail
Mexican Coffee
Mexican Grasshopper
Mind Eraser
Mocha Mint
Mudslide
Olé
Orgasm
Root Beer Shooter
Russian Coffee
Sombrero

Terminator
Toasted Almond
Torridora Cocktail

**COGNAC**
*see also* Brandy
Café Diablo
French 75
International Cocktail
Rocky Green
  Dragon
Rolls Royce Parisian

**COINTREAU**
*see also* Grand Marnier;
  Mandarine Napoléon;
  Triple Sec
Acapulco
Alabama
Beachcomber
Bermuda Bouquet
Between the Sheets
Blanche
Bombay Punch
Café Diablo
Champagne Cup
Claridge
Corpse Reviver #3
Cosmopolitan
Costa Del Sol
Curaçao Cooler
Deauville
Dream Cocktail
Egg Sour
Gloom Chaser
Hoopla
Lollipop
Maiden's Prayer
Margarita
Pacific Pacifier
Rolls Royce Parisian
Sanctuary
Sangría
Sidecar
Trois Rivières
Velvet Hammer #2
Waikiki Beachcomer
White Lady
White Lily

Allies
Angel Face
Angler's Cocktail
Aperitivo
Artillery
Artillery Punch
Aviation
Bacardi Special
Barnum
Barton Special
Beauty Spot
Belmont Cocktail
Bennett Cocktail
Bermuda Bouquet
Bermuda Rose
Bijou Cocktail
Billy Taylor
Biscayne
Blond Bombshell
Bloodhound
Blue Moon
Bonnie Prince
Boomerang
Boston Cocktail
Bronx Cocktail
Bronx Terrace Cocktail
Brown Cocktail
Bulldog Highball
Bullshot
B.V.D.
Cabaret
Caruso
Casino
Champagne Collins
Chatham
Cherry Cobbler
Claridge
Cloister
Clover Club
Colonial
Corpse Reviver #3
Costa Del Sol
Crimson
Damn the Weather
Danish Gin Fizz
Delmonico
Dempsey
Dixie
Double Standard Sour

Dreamsicle
Dubarry Cocktail
Dubonnet Cocktail
Earthquake
Egg Cream Special
Electric Lemonade
   (variation)
Emerald Isle Cocktail
Emerson
Empire
Fallen Angel
Fancy Gin
Farmer's Cocktail
Favorite Cocktail
Fifty-Fifty
Fine and Dandy
Flamingo
Florida
Flying Dutchmen
Fog Cutter
Foghorn
Frankenjack Cocktail
Froth Blower Cocktail
Genoa
Gilroy
Gimlet
Gin Aloha
Gin Buck
Gin and French
Gin and It
Gin and Sin
Gin and Tonic
Gin Cobbler
Gin Cocktail
Gin Crusta
Gin Daisy
Gin Fix
Gin Fizz
Gin Milk Punch
Gin Remsen Cooler
Gin Rickey
Gin Sangaree
Gin Sidecar
Gin Sling
Gin Smash
Gin Sour
Gin Swizzle
Golden Daze
Golden Fizz

Golf Cocktail
Grand Passion
Grand Royal Fizz
Granville
Grapefruit Cocktail
Great Secret
Greenback
Green Devil
Green Dragon
Gypsy Cocktail
Harlem
Hasty
Hawaiian Cocktail
Hoffman House
Homestead
Honolulu Cocktail #1
Honolulu Cocktail #2
Hudson Bay
Hula-Hula
Ideal
Imperial Cocktail
Inca
Income Tax Cocktail
Jamaica Glow
Jell-O Shot
Jewel Cocktail
Jockey Club
Joulouville
Journalist
Judge, Jr. Cocktail
Judgette Cocktail
Jupiter Cocktail
Kingston #1
Knickerbocker Cocktail
Knockout Cocktail
Kup's Indispensable
Kyoto Cocktail #1
Kyoto Cocktail #2
Ladyfinger
Leapfrog
Leap Year Cocktail
Leave-It-to-Me #1
Leave-It-to-Me #2
Lillet Cocktail
Little Devil
London Cocktail
Lone Tree Cocktail
Long Island Ice Tea
Loudspeaker

Irish Eyes (Are Smiling)
Irish Fix
Irish Kilt
Irish Shillelagh
Leprechaun
Paddy Cocktail
Shamrock

**JÄGERMEISTER**
Liquid Cocaine #1
Liquid Cocaine #2
Oatmeal Cookie (variation)
Surfer on Acid

**KAHLÚA**
*see* Coffee Liqueurs

**KIRSCH**
*see also* Cherry
  Brandy/Liqueur; Peter
  Heering
Blackjack
Cherry Blossom
Ladyfinger
Lollipop
Ostend Fizz
Pink Almond
Rendezvous
Rose Cocktail, French

**KÜMMEL**
Green Dragon
Kingston #2
Silver Bullet
Silver Streak
Tovarich Cocktail

**LILLET**
Bonnie Prince
Great Secret
Hoopla
Lillet Cocktail
Prince Edward
Vesper, The

**MADEIRA**
Bosom Caresser
Brandied Madeira
Nightmare
Prince of Wales

**MANDARINE
NAPOLÉON LIQUEUR**
Dreamsicle

**MARASCHINO
LIQUEUR**
Allen Cocktail
Angel's Tit
Bombay Punch
Champagne Punch
Honolulu Cocktail #2
Merry Widow #1
Seventh Heaven
Stars and Stripes
Tennessee

**MELON LIQUEUR**
Kyoto Cocktail #2
Melon Ball
Melon Ball Shooter
Melon Margarita
Sex on the Beach #2
Shady Lady
Watermelon #2

**METAXA**
Greek Buck

**MINT-FLAVORED
LIQUEURS**
*see* Crème de Menthe;
  Peppermint Schnapps

**ORANGE-FLAVORED
LIQUEURS**
*see* Cointreau; Grand
  Marnier; Mandarine
  Napoléon; Triple Sec

**PARFAIT AMOUR**
Blue Angel

**PEACH
BRANDY/LIQUEUR/
SCHNAPPS**
Brain Hemorrhage
Corkscrew
Frozen Fruit Daiquiri
Fish House Punch
Fuzzy Navel
Heatwave
Judgette Cocktail

Peach Buck
Peach Margarita
Peaches and Cream
Sex on the Beach #1
Sex on the Beach
  Shooter
Silk Panties
Woo-Woo

**PEPPERMINT
SCHNAPPS**
*see also* Crème de Menthe
After Five
Depth Charge
Girl Scout Cookie
Glad Eye(s)
Hot Pants
Peppermint Patty
White Spider

**PERNOD**
*see also* Anisette
Absinthe Special
Absinthe Suissesse
Dixie
Earthquake
Eye-Opener
Glad Eye(s)
Kiss Me Quick
Knockout Cocktail
Pernod Cocktail
Pernod Flip
Pernod Frappé
Snowball
Suissesse
Tequila Ghost
Tiger Tail
TNT
Yellow Parrot Cocktail

**PETER HEERING**
*see also* Cherry
  Brandy/Liqueur;
  Kirsch
Danish Gin Fizz
Singapore Sling

**PISCO**
Pisco Punch

Presidente #1
Presidente #2
Quaker's Cocktail
Quarter Deck Cocktail
Queen's Park Swizzle
Robson Cocktail
Rose Hall
Rum Cobbler
Rum Collins
Rum Crusta
Rum Daisy
Rum Dubonnet
Rum Fix
Rum Highball
Rum Milk Punch
Rum Punch
Rum Rickey
Rum Shrub
Rum Sling
Rum Smash
Rum Sour
Rum Stinger
Rum Swizzle
Rumtini
San Juan
Santiago Cocktail
Saxon Cocktail
Scorpion
September Morn
Sevilla
Sevilla Flip
Shanghai Cocktail
Shark's Tooth #1
Shark's Tooth #2
Sir Walter (Raleigh)
Sloppy Joe's Cocktail #1
Spanish Town
  Cocktail
Tahiti Club
Third Rail Cocktail
Three Miller Cocktail
Tiger's Milk
Tom and Jerry
Torridora Cocktail
White Lily
White Lion
XYZ Cocktail
Yellow Bird
Zombie

**RUMPLE MINZE**
Liquid Cocaine #1
Liquid Cocaine #2

**RYE WHISKEY**
Blinker
Byrrh Cocktail
Cowboy
Earthquake
Fox River
Highball
Horse's Neck
Hunter's Cocktail
Klondike Cooler
Manhattan
Milk Punch
New York Cocktail
Old Pal
Rattlesnake
Rye (Whiskey) Cocktail
Rye Collins
Rye Milk Punch
Rye Sling
Sazerac
Sharky Punch
Tennessee
TNT
Twin Hills
Ward Eight
Whiskey Cocktail

**SAKE**
Saketini

**SAMBUCA**
Aperitivo
Café Romano
Genoa
Slippery Nipple
Terminator
Via Veneto

**SCOTCH**
Affinity #1
Affinity #2
Barton Special
Blood and Sand
Bobby Burns
Flying Scotsman
Godfather
Highball

Highland Fling
Hole-in-One
Horse's Neck
Irish Kilt
Loch Lomond
Mamie Taylor
Miami Beach
Morning Glory
Morning Glory Fizz
Prince Edward
Remsen Cooler
Rob Roy
Rusty Nail
Scotch Cobbler
Scotch Collins (varia-
  tion)
Scotch Cooler
Scotch Holiday Sour
Scotch Manhattan
Scotch Milk Punch
Scotch Mist
Scotch Rickey
Scotch Sling
Scotch Smash
Scotch Sour
Scotch Stinger
Scotch Swizzle
Scotini
Stone Fence
Thistle Cocktail
Woodward

**SHERRY**
Adonis
Affinity #2
Andalusia
Bombay Punch
Brazil Cocktail
Cádiz
Creamy Orange
East Indian
Inca
Merry Widow #2
Polonaise
Quarter Deck Cocktail
Reform Cocktail
Renaissance Cocktail
Seville
Sherry Cobbler

Alfonso Special
Algonquin
Allegheny
Allies
American Beauty
Beauty Spot
Bermuda Highball
Bittersweet
Bloodhound
Bombay Cocktail
Boomerang
Brandied Madeira
Brazil Cocktail
Bronx Cocktail
Bronx Terrace
  Cocktail
Brown Cocktail
B.V.D.
Byrrh Cocktail
Caruso
Chrysanthemum
Claridge
Corkscrew
Country Club Cooler
Delmonico
Diablo
Diplomat
Dixie
Dry Manhattan
Dry Rob Roy
Dubarry Cocktail
Duchess
East Indian (Special)
El Presidente #1
Fantasio
Farmer's Cocktail
Favorite Cocktail
Ferrari
Fifty-Fifty
Frankenjack Cocktail
Gilroy
Gin and French
Golf Cocktail
Green Room
Hasty
Havana Club
Hoffman House
Hole-in-One
Ideal

Imperial Cocktail
Inca
Judgette Cocktail
Jupiter Cocktail
Kangaroo
Knickerbocker
  Cocktail
Knockout Cocktail
Kup's Indispensable
Kyoto Cocktail #1
Kyoto Cocktail #2
Lawhill Cocktail
Leave-It-to-Me #1
Lone Tree Cocktail
Martinez
Maurice
Merry Widow #3
Miami Beach
Montana
Morning Cocktail
Negroni
Pall Mall
Parisian
Perfect Cocktail
Perfect Manhattan
Perfect Rob Roy
Piccadilly Cocktail
Pink Panther
Plaza Cocktail
Pompano
Presidente #1
Prince Edward (varia-
  tion)
Princeton Cocktail
Quebec
Queen Elizabeth
Queen Elizabeth Wine
Reform Cocktail
Rose Cocktail,
  English
Rose Cocktail,
  French
Roselyn Cocktail
Rosita
San Francisco
  Cocktail
Shamrock
Silver Cocktail
Sloe Vermouth

Sloppy Joe's
  Cocktail #1
Soviet
Tango Cocktail
Thanksgiving Special
Three Stripes
  Cocktail
Turf Cocktail
Tuxedo Cocktail
Vermouth Cassis
Vermouth Cocktail
Warsaw
Washington
Wembly Cocktail
Whip Cocktail
Why Not?
Will Rogers
Woodward
Yale Cocktail

**VERMOUTH, SWEET**

Addington
Adonis
Affinity #1
Americano
Artillery
Beauty Spot
Bijou Cocktail
Bittersweet
Blackthorn
Blood and Sand
Bloodhound
Bobby Burns
Bombay Cocktail
Bronx Cocktail
Calisay Cocktail
Carroll Cocktail
Charles Cocktail
Cold Deck
Corpse Reviver #1
Damn the Weather
Delmonico
Diplomat
Duchess
Emerson
Farmer's Cocktail
Flying Scotsman
Fort Lauderdale
Froupe

Vodka Sour
Vodka Stinger
Volga Boatman
Warsaw
Watermelon #2
White Spider
Woo-Woo

**WHISKEY**
*see* Blended Whiskey;
  Bourbon; Canadian
  Whisky; Irish
  Whiskey; Scotch

**WINE, RED**
*see also* Port
Artillery Punch
Claret Cobbler
Jamaica Glow
Mulled Wine
New York Sour
Sangría
Spritzer

**WINE, WHITE**
*see also* Champagne
Kir
Pineapple
  Cooler
Sangría Blanca
Spritzer

# Drinks by Primary Nonalcoholic Ingredients

*Drinks contain at least ¹/₂ ounce of the ingredient under which they're listed; garnish ingredients (such as whipped cream) are not listed.*

Los Angeles (whole)
Love Cocktail (white)
Matinee (white)
Millionaire (white)
Million Dollar Cocktail
  (white)
Morning Glory Fizz
  (white)
Nightcap #2 (yolk)
Party Eggnog (whole)
Pernod Flip (whole)
Pink Lady (white)
Pink Panther (white)
Pink Rose (white)
Rattlesnake (white)
Royal Gin Fizz (whole)
September Morn (white)
Sevilla Flip (whole)
Silver Fizz (white)
Strega Flip (whole)
Suissesse (white)
Thunder Cocktail (yolk)
Tom and Jerry (whole)
Twin Six (white)
Via Veneto (white)
White Rose (white)

**FRUIT JUICE**

(*see* Cranberry, Grape,
  Guava, Lemon, Lime,
  Orange, Passion Fruit,
  Peach, Pineapple, and
  Tomato Juices)

**GRAPE JUICE**

Mimosa Light
Purple Passion

**GRENADINE**

Gloom Chaser
Mai Tai
Mexican Flag
Old Pal
Opening Cocktail
Passion Perfect
Picon Fizz
Roy Rogers
Russian Rose
Stars and Stripes
Tequila Sunrise

**GUAVA NECTAR**

Navy Grog
Ocho Rios

**LEMON JUICE**

Admiral
Aged Whiskey Sours
Alabama Slammer
Albemarle Fizz
All-White Frappé
Applecar
Apricot Cocktail
Artillery Punch
Aviation
Bishop, The
Blizzard
Blond Bombshell
Bloody Mary
Bombay Punch
Boston Cooler
Brandied Port
Brandy Cassis
Brandy Gump
Buck
Bullfrog
Cablegram
Champagne Collins
Champagne Punch
Champs Elysées
Chapala
Chapel Hill
Clover Club
Commodore Cocktail
Corpse Reviver #3
Crusta
Daisy
Dancing Leprechaun
Deauville
Dinah
Dubonnet Fizz
Egg Sour
Fallen Angel
Fine and Dandy
Fish House Punch
Fix
Fog Cutter
French 75
Gauguin
Gilroy

Gin and Sin
Gin Fizz
Gloom Chaser
Grand Royal Fizz
Green Dragon
Grog
Happy Apple
Harvard Cooler
Honeymoon
Hoopla
Imperial Fizz
Irish Kilt
Irish Shillelagh
Jack-in-the-Box
Joulouville
Kingston #1
Kretchma Cocktail
Leapfrog
Long Island Ice Tea
Loudspeaker
Maiden's Prayer
Mandeville
Manhasset
Mexicana
Midnight Cocktail
Moonlight
Morning Glory Fizz
New York Cocktail
Ninotchka
Pink Almond
Planter's Cocktail
Planter's Punch
Polo Cocktail
Queen Elizabeth Wine
Ramos Fizz
Red Apple
Red Cloud
Red Lion
Resolute Cocktail
Ruby Fizz
Sangría
San Sebastian
Scorpion
Serpent's Tooth
Seville
Shanghai Cocktail
Shark's Tooth #1
Sidecar
Silver Bullet

Jamaica Glow
Kingston #2
Limbo
Madras
Maiden's Prayer
Maurice
Melon Ball
Mimosa
Monkey Gland
Navy Grog
New Orleans Buck
Olympic
Opal Cocktail
Orange Blossom
Orange Buck
Orange Oasis
Paradise Cocktail
Pink Panther
Planter's Punch
Polo Cocktail
Presto Cocktail
Red Lion
Rolls Royce Parisian
Rose Hall
Roy Rogers
Sangría
Sangrita
Scorpion
Screwdriver
Seville
Sex on the Beach #1
Sex on the Beach
    Shooter
Sloe Comfortable Screw
Sloe Screw
Tango Cocktail
Tequila Sunrise

Three Stripes Cocktail
Tiger Tail
Tootsie Roll
Twin Six Cocktail
Valencia
Volga Boatman
Watermelon #1
Wedding Belle
White Rose
Will Rogers
Zombie

## PASSION-FRUIT JUICE/SYRUP
Gauguin
Grand Passion
Hurricane
Navy Grog
Passion Daiquiri
Passion Perfect
Zombie

## PEACH NECTAR
Bellini
Peach Cobbler
Peachy Creamy
Safe Sex on the Beach

## PINEAPPLE JUICE
Algonquin
Bahama Mama
Bay Breeze
Blue Hawaiian
Chi-Chi
Cuban Special
El Presidente #2
Frozen Matador
Gin Aloha

Goldfinger
Harlem
Havana Cocktail
Havana Special
Hawaiian Cocktail
Hawaiian Punch
Heatwave
Hurricane
Irish Fix
Jack-in-the-Box
Kentucky Cocktail
Linstead
Mary Pickford
Matador
Melon Ball
Melon Ball Shooter
Mexicana
Million Dollar Cocktail
Navy Grog
Park Avenue
Piña Colada
Pineapple Cooler
Pineapple Fizz
Sex on the Beach #2
Sloppy Joe's Cocktail #2
Surfer on Acid
Tahiti Club
Waikiki Beachcomber
Zombie

## TOMATO JUICE
Blond Bombshell
Bloody Brew
Bloody Bull
Bloody Mary
Clam Digger
Sangrita

# Drinks by Classic Categories

*Classic drinks styles from the Julep (which dates back to the 1800s) to the newest classification—the Shooter. See also Index 4 for Drinks by Special Categories (hot, flaming, and so on).*

Angel's Delight
Angel's Kiss
Angel's Tit
Savoy Hotel
Stars and Stripes
Terminator

**PUFF**
*see* A-to-Z listing for
   PUFF

**PUNCH**
*See also* Cup.
Artillery Punch
Bombay Punch
Champagne Punch
Claret Punch
Fish House Punch
Hawaiian Punch
Milk Punch
Pisco Punch
Planter's Punch
Rum Punch
Sangría
Sharky Punch
Wassai Bowl

**RICKEY**
Bourbon Rickey
Brandy Rickey
Ginger-Lime Rickey
Gin Rickey
Lime Rickey
Rum Rickey
Rye Rickey
Scotch Rickey
Sloe Gin Rickey
Tequila Rickey
Vodka Rickey

**SANGAREE**
Brandy Sangaree
Gin Sangaree
Port Sangaree
Sherry Sangaree
Whiskey Sangaree

**SHOOTER**
After 5
B-52 (*layered*)
Brain Hemorrhage
Buttery Nipple
Cement Mixer
Chip Shot Shooter
Chocolate-Covered
   Cherry (*layered*)
Cordless Screwdriver
Girl Scout Cookie
Green Lizard
Harbor Lights
IRA
Jell-O Shot
Jelly Bean
Kamikaze
Key Lime Pie
Lemon Drop
Liquid Cocaine #1 and
   #2
Melon Ball Shooter
Mexican Flag (*layered*)
Mind Eraser
Oatmeal Cookie (*lay-
   ered*)
Orgasm
Peppermint Patty (*lay-
   ered*)
Prairie Fire
Purple Hooter #1 and #2
Red Snapper Shooter
Root Beer Shooter
Russian Quaalude (*lay-
   ered*)
Sex on the Beach #1 and
   #2
Silk Panties
Surfer on Acid
Tootsie Roll
Woo-Woo

**SHRUB**
Brandy Shrub
Rum Shrub

**SLING**
Bourbon Sling
Brandy Sling
Gin Sling
Rum Sling
Rye Sling
Scotch Sling
Singapore Sling
Sloe Gin Sling
Tequila Sling
Vodka Sling

**SMASH**
Brandy Smash
Cider Smash
Gin Smash
Rum Smash
Scotch Smash

**SOUR**
Aged Whiskey Sours
Boston Sour
Brandy Sour
Double Standard Sour
Egg Sour
Fireman's Sour
Frisco Sour
Gin Sour
New York Sour
Rum Sour
Scotch Holiday Sour
Tequila Sour
Vodka Sour
Whiskey Sour

**SWIZZLE**
Apple Swizzle
Gin Swizzle
Independence Swizzle
Queen's Park Swizzle
Rum Swizzle
Scotch Swizzle

**TODDY**
Hot Brick Toddy
Hot Toddy

# Drinks by Special Categories

**AFTER-DINNER DRINKS**

Here are just a few of the hundreds of postprandial choices in this book.

Angel's Tip
B & B
Blackjack
Brandy
Brandy Alexander
Café Romano
Cognac
Dreamsicle
Golden Cadillac
Grappa
Grasshopper
Irish Eyes (Are Smiling)
Liqueur Frappé (*see* FRAPPÉ)
Liqueurs, any flavor
Mocha Mint
Nightcap #1
Nightcap #2
Peaches and Cream
Pink Gin
Pink Squirrel
Port
Savoy Hotel
Sombrero
Stinger
Velvet Hammer #1 and #2

**APÉRITIFS**

What one takes as an apéritif depends greatly on personal taste. Following are some popular choices.

Adonis
Americano
Amer Picon
Aperitivo
Bittersweet
Bronx Cocktail
B.V.D.
Campari
Champagne
Champagne Cocktail
Chrysanthemum
Dubonnet Cocktail
French 75
Kir
Kir Royale
Lillet
Manhattan
Martini
Negroni
Old-Fashioned
Pernod or other anise-flavored liqueur
Pink Gin
Ricard
Sherry Cocktail
Sidecar
Spritzer
Straight Law
Third Rail
Vermouth Cassis
Victor
White Lady

**BLENDER DRINKS**

Anna's Banana
Banana Daiquiri
Blizzard
Blond Bombshell
Blue Hawaiian
Bushwhacker
Cara Sposa

Coffee Eggnog
Creamsicle
Creamy London Fog
Creamy Screwdriver
Dreamsicle
Egghead
Frozen Berkley
Frozen Daiquiri
Frozen Fruit Daiquiri
Frozen Margarita
Gauguin
Golden Cadillac
Jocose Julep
Navy Grog
Ocho Rios
Peach or Strawberry Margarita
Pernod Flip
Piña Colada
Pisco Punch
Poco Rios
Ramos Fizz
Rum Punch
Russian Coffee
San Juan
Scorpion
Sloe Tequila
Smart Head
Zombie

**FLAMING DRINKS**

Blue Blazer
Café Diablo
Café Royale

**HOT DRINKS**

Blue Blazer
Café Amaretto
Café Diablo
Café Royale
Classic Hot Bishop

Gorilla Sweat
Hot Brick Toddy
Hot Bullshot (*see* BULL-
    SHOT)
Hot Buttered Rum
Hot Eggnog
Hot Milk Punch
Hot Spiced Wine
Hot Toddy
Irish Coffee
Italian Coffee
Jamaican Coffee
Mexican Coffee
Mulled Cider
Mulled Wine
Nightcap #1, #2
Tom and Jerry
Wassail

## LOW-ALCOHOL DRINKS

Hundreds of drinks—
    primarily those with
    mixers—can become
    low-alcohol potables
    by simple reducing the
    amount of spirit used.
    Following are some
    favorites.
Adonis
Amer Picon Cocktail
Bellini
Bittersweet
Cobblers
Coolers
East Indian
Fizzes
Kir
Kir Royale
Mimosa
Reform Cocktail
Rickeys
Shandy
Spritzers
Swizzles

Vermouth Cocktail
Xeres Cocktail

## NONALCOHOLIC DRINKS

Apple Juice Fizz
Apricot Mocktail
Beach Breeze
Blameless Bull
Chocolate Un-nog
Creamsicle
Egg Cream
Fuzzless Navel
Ginger Julep
Ginger-Lime Rickey
Gin-Gin
Ginless Sin
Grenada Sunset
Innocent A.J.
Jill-in-the-Box
Kickless Horse's
    Neck
Lime Rickey
Maiden Madras
Midnight Mocktail
Mild Sea Breeze
Mimosa Light
Naked Bullshot
Nogless Eggnog
Passion Perfect
Peach Cobbler
Peachy Keen
Planter's Punchless
Poco Rios
Prince's Grin
Purple Passio*nada*
Roy Rogers
Safe Sex on the Beach
San Juanita
Shirley Temple
Smart Head
Sneaky Colada
Sober Clam Digger
Soft Cider Cup

T & B
Virgin Mary

## TROPICAL DRINKS

Acapulco
Bahama Mama
Bay Breeze
Beachcomber
Biscayne
Blue Hawaiian
Bushwhacker
Caribbean Champagne
Chi-Chi
Cuban Special
Daiquiri (banana, pas-
    sion fruit)
El Presidente #2
Fog Cutter
Gauguin
Havana Cocktail
Havana Special
Hawaiian Punch
Heatwave
Honolulu Cocktail #1
Hurricane
Limbo
Mai Tai
Mexicana
Mojito
Navy Grog
Ocho Rios
Passion Daiquiri
Passion Perfect
Piña Colada
Pineapple Cooler
Pineapple Fizz
Planter's Punch
Rum Punch
San Juan
Scorpion
Tahiti Club
Waikiki Beachcomer
Yellow Bird
Zombie

# About the Authors

**Sharon Tyler Herbst,** America's foremost writer of user-friendly food and drink references, is an award-winning author of thirteen books. Her last, *Never Eat More Than You Can Lift*, was featured in *People* magazine and in an interview on *ABC World News*. Her broadly hailed *Food Lover's Companion* is the featured dictionary on the Internet sites *Epicurious* (Condé Nast) and Disney's *Family.com*.

**Ron Herbst** is the author of the renowned *Wine Lover's Companion*, praised by wine writer Jurgen Gothe as "the best new wine book in a decade or more," and by the *San Francisco Chronicle* as "a terrific book that is curiously addictive." Besides his work as a writer and industry consultant, Herbst is extensively involved in the high-tech industry as a senior manager.